God's Executioner

Oliver Cromwell and the Conquest of Ireland

MICHEÁL Ó SIOCHRÚ

faber and faber

First published in 2008
by Faber and Faber Ltd
Bloomsbury House
74–77 Great Russell Street
London WC1B 3DA
This paperback edition first published in 2009

Typeset in Minion by Palindrome
Maps by Matthew Stout
Printed and bound by CPI Group (UK) Ltd, Croydon, CRO 4YY

A CIP record for this book
is available from the British Library

ISBN 978–0–571–21846–2

4 6 8 10 9 7 5 3

This book is dedicated to the memory of
Derek O'Grady (1966–2001)
and
Teri Sternbergerova (1978–2004)

Contents

Illustrations

Maps

Preface

Research and writing are very solitary pursuits, but I received invaluable support from family, friends and colleagues in Ireland, Scotland and elsewhere during the course of this project. I am extremely grateful to them all, but there are a few who deserve a particular mention. My father Oisín and sister Mairéad volunteered (or at least I think they volunteered) to read through drafts of each chapter as I produced them. Their insightful observations and seemingly limitless enthusiasm for the book sustained me throughout this time. Similarly, Jane Ohlmeyer has (as always) been hugely supportive, both as a friend and as a colleague, and her input is evident throughout the text. Aidan Clarke, John Morrill, Ian Gentles and Pádraig Lenihan each provided an expert overview of the final draft, as well as detailed comments, and their influence on all my work is probably greater than any of them would care to acknowledge. Billy Kelly, Robert Armstrong, Tom O'Connor, Ciaran Brady, Tom Bartlett, Tadhg Ó hAnnracháin, Dave Edwards, Sean Connolly and Patrick Little all share something of my unhealthy obsession with Early Modern Ireland, while in the wider academic community, various colleagues have inspired and encouraged me in equal part. The good friendship of three in particular, Andrew Mackillop, Éamonn Ó Ciardha, and Phil Withington has proved of inestimable value to me.

Other friends have looked over particular sections, and listened patiently as I explained (usually over a few pints) yet another allegedly interesting discovery. I am particularly grateful in that regard to Andrew, Cormac, Daithí, Darren, David D, Diarmuid, Éamon, Johnny, Mick and Paul, as well as to Ana, Anastasia, Anne, Audrey, Bennet, Bríd, Carol, Cathal, Catherine, Cathy, Easter, Helen, Jacqui, Lauren, Liz, Lorna, Michal, Mick, Pauline, Peter, Siobhán and Terry for bearing with me over the past few years. Jeff and Naomi Vanderwolk provided a comfortable and fun base to work from in London for the best part of a year, and my parents allowed me to retreat to Baile na nGall once again to kick-start the writing process. Elly Rothnie and Elizabeth MacKnight both helped in locating images and securing permission to reproduce them (as did my father), while Gráinne MacLoughlin kindly sent me advance copies of translations from the Commentarius project. Matthew Stout deserves a very special mention. He produced all nine maps, which are absolutely superb, putting an impressively professional gloss on my original (very poor) hand drawings. Walter Donohue of Faber has been the epitome of patience from the outset, and I am very grateful to Paula Turner for her assistance in preparing the manuscript for publication. I would also like to thank the Leverhulme Trust for granting me a two-year research fellowship to complete my primary research.

Despite the collaborative nature of the project, any mistakes in the text are of course wholly my own responsibility. As for the dates, I have adhered to the convention of dating according to the Old Style (Julian) calendar for the days and months, and the New Style (Gregorian) calendar for the year, when dealing with Ireland, England and Scotland. Individuals writing from continental Europe used the Gregorian calendar, with dual dating evident in some cases.

Chronology of Events
1649–53*

Events taking place outside Ireland, England and Scotland appear in *italics*

1649

17 JANUARY Peace treaty signed between James Butler, marquis of Ormond, and the Catholic confederates in Kilkenny

22 JANUARY Charles, Prince of Wales, invited to Ireland by Ormond

30 JANUARY Execution of Charles I at Whitehall

[JANUARY] Arrival of Prince Rupert with seven ships at Kinsale

JANUARY–MARCH *Civil war in France as Prince of Condé blockades Paris*

5 FEBRUARY Charles Stuart proclaimed King of England, Scotland and Ireland by the Scots – Ormond makes a similar proclamation at Carrick on 16 February

13 FEBRUARY English parliament appoints executive Council of State

23 FEBRUARY Papal nuncio Giovanni Battista Rinuccini departs for France

17 MARCH Monarchy formally abolished in England

19 MARCH Abolition of the English House of Lords

30 MARCH Oliver Cromwell approved as commander-in-chief in Ireland

MARCH–MAY *Failed negotiations in Holland between Charles Stuart and representatives of the Scottish parliament*

8 MAY Truce concluded between Colonel George Monck and General Owen Roe O'Neill

* This chronology is based on the relevant sections of T. W. Moody, F. X. Martin and F. J. Byrne (eds), *A New History of Ireland*, vol. 8 (Oxford, 1982) and Jane Ohlmeyer (ed.), *Ireland from Independence to Occupation, 1641–1660* (Cambridge, 1995), supplemented by material listed in the bibliography.

14 MAY Defeat of Leveller mutineers at Burford

19 MAY England declared a 'Commonwealth'

[MAY] *Murder of Isaac Dorislaus, representative of the English parliament, in Holland*

5 JUNE Parliamentary army ordered to leave for Ireland

JULY Plague reaches Galway from the Continent

12 JULY *Charles Stuart, having left Holland, arrives at St Germain in France*

2 AUGUST Colonel Michael Jones defeats Ormond at Rathmines

15 AUGUST Cromwell lands at Ringsend near Dublin

[SEPTEMBER] Arrival of Charles Stuart on the island of Jersey

11 SEPTEMBER Fall of Drogheda to Cromwell

11 OCTOBER Fall of Wexford to Cromwell

19 OCTOBER Surrender of New Ross

20 OCTOBER Treaty of agreement between Ormond and Owen Roe O'Neill

OCTOBER–NOVEMBER Revolt of the Munster towns from royalists to the parliamentarians

[OCTOBER] Prince Rupert's royalist fleet escapes from Kinsale and takes refuge in Portugal

6 NOVEMBER Death of Owen Roe O'Neill

20 NOVEMBER Fall of Carrick-on-Suir

24 NOVEMBER–2 DECEMBER Waterford successfully withstands parliamentary siege

6 DECEMBER Defeat of Sir George Monro near Lisburn

DECEMBER Assembly of Catholic bishops at Clonmacnoise

DECEMBER Scots surrender Carrickfergus to the English Parliament

1650

[JANUARY] *Hugh Rochford arrives at Jersey from Ireland*

18 JANUARY *Arrest of Prince of Condé by Mazarin (released February 1651)*

3 FEBRUARY Fethard, County Tipperary, surrenders to Cromwell

24 FEBRUARY Surrender of Cahir Castle, County Tipperary

[MARCH] James Graham, royalist marquis of Montrose, arrives in

Orkney with 1,200 Continental mercenaries

16 MARCH *Charles Stuart arrives at Breda – negotiations with Scottish covenanters*

18 MARCH Heber MacMahon, bishop of Clogher, succeeds Owen Roe O'Neill as general of army of Ulster

27 MARCH Kilkenny, the former confederate capital, surrenders to Cromwell

27 APRIL Defeat of Montrose by the Scottish covenanters at Carbisdale (he was captured and executed shortly afterwards)

1 MAY *Treaty of Breda between Charles Stuart and the Scottish covenanters*

10 MAY Parliamentary victory at Macroom, County Cork

18 MAY Surrender of Clonmel, County Tipperary

21 MAY Arrival of Lorraine's agent, Colonel Oliver Synott, in Galway with Hugh Rochford

26 MAY Cromwell departs from Ireland, leaving his son-in-law Henry Ireton as his deputy

21 JUNE Ulster army destroyed by parliamentarians at Scariffhollis, County Donegal

23 JUNE Charles Stuart arrives in Scotland from the Netherlands – signs covenant

29 JUNE Theobald, Viscount Taaffe, departs for the Continent (arrives in Brussels for talks with Lorraine in November)

25 JULY Surrender of Carlow Town

6 AUGUST General Thomas Preston, Viscount Tara, surrenders City of Waterford

12 AUGUST Catholic bishops assembled at Jamestown repudiate Ormond's leadership

— Surrender of Duncannon Fort, County Wexford

14 AUGUST Surrender of Charlemont Fort, County Armagh

16 AUGUST Charles Stuart repudiates Ormond Peace in declaration at Dunfermline

3 SEPTEMBER Scots defeated by Cromwell at Dunbar, near Edinburgh

15 SEPTEMBER Catholic bishops excommunicate Ormond's supporters

6 NOVEMBER *Death of William II, Prince of Orange*

15 NOVEMBER Assembly of Catholic clergy and laity at Loughrea, County Galway

[DECEMBER] *Spain formally recognises the English Commonwealth*

6 DECEMBER Ormond appoints Ulick Bourke, marquis of Clanricarde, as his deputy

9 DECEMBER Ormond departs for France

1651

1 JANUARY Charles Stuart crowned at Scone in Scotland

[JANUARY] *Recognition of English Commonwealth by the Dutch*

[FEBRUARY] *Cardinal Mazarin goes into temporary exile at Brühl*

26 FEBRUARY Arrival of Abbott Stephen de Henin, ambassador of Charles, duke of Lorraine, at Galway

4 APRIL Signing of agreement between Clanricarde and de Henin

[MAY] *Parliamentary envoy, Anthony Ascham, murdered in Madrid*

14 JUNE Siege of Limerick begins

[JUNE] *Arrival of Geoffrey Browne and Nicholas Plunkett in Brussels (Nicholas French, bishop of Ferns, had arrived the previous month)*

[JULY] Invasion of Fife – parliamentary victory at Inverkeithing

22 JULY *Agreement in Brussels between the duke of Lorraine and representatives of Irish Catholics*

5 AUGUST Charles Stuart leads Scottish forces across the English border

1 SEPTEMBER Storming of Dundee by Colonel Monck

3 SEPTEMBER Defeat of Charles Stuart at Worcester

7 SEPTEMBER *Louis XIV, aged 13, is declared to have attained his majority*

9 OCTOBER English Parliament passes the first Navigation Act (included Ireland and Scotland)

16 OCTOBER *Charles lands at Fécamp in Normandy, having escaped from England*

27 OCTOBER Surrender of Limerick by Hugh Dubh O'Neill to Ireton

26 NOVEMBER Death of Ireton from fever

1652

[JANUARY] *Mazarin re-enters France at the head of 6,000 German mercenaries*

12 APRIL Surrender of Galway to Sir Charles Coote

12 MAY Surrender of Leinster forces at Kilkenny

[JUNE] *Duke of Lorraine before Paris with army – Charles Stuart helps persuade him to leave (Charles forced to flee Paris as a result)*

22 JUNE Surrender of Donough MacCarthy, Viscount Muskerry, and Munster forces at Ross, in Kerry

28 JUNE Surrender of the marquis of Clanricarde and some of the Connacht forces

8 JULY Outbreak of First Anglo–Dutch war (ends 5 April 1654)

9 JULY Charles Fleetwood appointed commander-in-chief in Ireland (arrives 10 September)

12 AUGUST Act for the Settlement of Ireland passed in the English parliament

21 SEPTEMBER Surrender of Lieutenant General Farrell and other Ulster leaders

[SEPTEMBER] *Admiral Blake destroys French squadron attempting to relieve Dunkirk – fortress surrenders to Spanish the following day*

[OCTOBER] *Barcelona surrenders to Don Juan of Austria – sporadic fighting in Catalonia until 1659*

14 OCTOBER *Condé leaves for exile in the Spanish Netherlands – Louis XIV returns to French capital shortly afterwards (with Charles Stuart)*

[NOVEMBER] *Admiral Tromp defeats English fleet commanded by Blake*

[DECEMBER] *De facto French recognition of the English republic*

1653

6 JANUARY Order to expel all Catholic priests from Ireland

4 FEBRUARY Sir Phelim O'Neill captured by parliamentarians (executed 10 March)

14 FEBRUARY Surrender of Inishbofin Island, denying royalists any access to the Continent

18–21 FEBRUARY *Blake defeats Tromp at the battle of Portland*

20 APRIL Cromwell expels 'rump' of the Long Parliament

27 APRIL Surrender of Cloughoughter, County Cavan – last formal surrender of war

[MAY] Beginnings of Glencairn rising in the Scottish Highlands (reached its height in late 1653/early 1654)

2–4 JUNE *Victory for Blake against the Dutch fleet*

20 JUNE Drawing of lots for adventurers' lands in London

22 JUNE Order authorising the 'Gross', 'Civil' and 'Down' surveys

1 JULY Order for transplantation of vagrants to American colonies

2 JULY Order for transplantation of native Irish to Connacht (by 1 May 1654)

4 JULY First meeting of the Nominated Assembly ['Barebones' parliament], including 6 MPs representing Ireland

31 JULY *English naval victory over the Dutch off Scheveningen*

SEPTEMBER Act of Satisfaction passed at Westminster

12 DECEMBER Final meeting of 'Barebones' parliament

16 DECEMBER Oliver Cromwell becomes Lord Protector

1

Introduction

Cromwell, though dead for others, survives for me.[1]
JOHN LYNCH, *Cambrensis Eversus* (1662)

In 1997, shortly after the Labour Party's victory in the British general election, the newly appointed foreign secretary, Robin Cook, received a courtesy visit from Bertie Ahern, the Irish prime minister. Mr Ahern entered Cook's office but immediately walked out again on seeing a painting of Oliver Cromwell in the room. He refused to return until the foreign secretary removed the picture 'of that murdering bastard'. Anxious to avoid a diplomatic incident, Cook made the necessary arrangements. The comedian and author Stephen Fry related this story at the launch of the Heritage Sector's 'History Matters' campaign in 2006, and commented that 'it was a bit like hanging a portrait of Eichmann before the visit of the Israeli prime minister'.[2] The idea of comparing Oliver Cromwell, voted by BBC television viewers as one of the greatest Britons of all time, to a genocidal monster appears preposterous, but at least one recent study claimed that the human misery visited on the Irish during the wars of the mid-seventeenth century 'probably equalled anything inflicted on Russia or Poland in the 1940s by Nazi Germany'.[3]

There is no doubt that Cromwell still evokes extremely strong emotions in Ireland 350 years after his death in 1658. Throughout the island people blame him for every ruined castle or tower house, while local folklore is replete with stories of terrible acts committed by his troops against the native population. Cromwell spent only nine months (August 1649 to May 1650) of his eventful life in Ireland, and yet he stands accused there of war crimes, religious persecution and ethnic cleansing on a dramatic scale. The massacre of thousands of soldiers and civilians by the New Model Army at both Drogheda and Wexford in 1649 must rank among the greatest atrocities in Anglo-Irish history, although the full extent of the slaughter is still disputed by some commentators. Irrefutable evidence, however, detailing the execution of scores of Catholic clergy, the forced transportation of thousands of women and children to work on the sugar plantations of the Caribbean, and the deliberate targeting of the civilian population during the latter stages of the war makes decidedly uncomfortable reading for those keen to focus on Cromwell's undoubted military and political achievements elsewhere.

But why does the public continue to focus so much on this one individual, rather than on a host of other equally controversial characters? The history of Anglo-Irish relations from Henry VIII's Reformation in the 1530s, through the horrors of the Tudor conquest and the wars of the seventeenth century, is a seemingly relentless tale of bloody, tragic episodes, punctuated by periods of relative peace, which did nothing more than enable both sides to regroup before resuming the struggle once again. Throughout, the Catholic Irish fought stubbornly though unsuccessfully against a militarily superior and more unified colonial power with access to far greater resources, determined to impose its will on a people perceived as barbaric and uncivilised. Atrocities abounded, but many of the serial perpetrators, such as Sir Humphrey Gilbert in the 1570s or Charles Blount, Lord Mountjoy, in the early 1600s, remain unknown to all but a handful of historians. The decisive and ultimately irreversible nature of the Irish defeat in the 1650s, however, when as much as one fifth of the population perished, created a bitter and lasting legacy. The seventeenth-century Kerry poet Seán Ó Conaill described this conflict as 'an coga do chríochnaig Éire [the war that destroyed Ireland]', and Cromwell, the greatest Englishman of his age, was un-questionably the most ruthless exponent of his country's uncompromising policy of conquest and colonisation.[4]

For almost two centuries after his death, however, the English elite reviled Cromwell for his role in the execution of the 'saintly' Charles I, while radicals condemned him for betraying the revolution he had helped to create. He ruled as a military dictator for much of the 1650s, purging and dissolving parliament on several occasions, while his army colonels enforced strict puritanical government throughout the localities. The restoration of the monarchy in 1660 put paid to the radical experiment in republican government, but during the eighteenth century, a recurring fear of excessive military interference in domestic political affairs ensured that Cromwell retained his status as the ultimate bogeyman of English history. His reputation underwent a dramatic transformation in the nineteenth century, when he emerged as the hero of the nonconforming Protestant tradition, the steadfast defender of religious and political liberties against the absolutist tendencies of the Stuart dynasty. For the brilliant but cantankerous historian, Thomas Carlyle, who published a collection of Cromwell's letters and speeches in the 1840s, he was 'the soul of the Puritan Revolt', the very embodiment of those traits that had enabled the English to build a global empire. Brave, resolute, godly, he was 'not a man of falsehoods, but a man of truths; whose words do carry a meaning with them, and above all others of that time are worth considering'. Carlyle criticised 'all the foolish lies' that circulated about him, and decided to publish his correspondence, rather than another biography, so that the reader might 'first obtain some dim glimpse of the actual Cromwell'.[5]

This rehabilitation of Cromwell by Carlyle and others not surprisingly provoked a robust response from Irish nationalists. In 1865, the eminent historian J. P. Prendergast published *The Cromwellian settlement of Ireland*, a book based on his extensive research through the state archives in Dublin, which were subsequently destroyed during the Irish civil war in 1922. Prendergast examined post-war policy in the 1650s, particularly the forced transplantation of Irish Catholic landowners and their families into Connacht, 'a scene not witnessed in Europe since the conquest of Spain by the Vandals'.[6] From this injustice, he claimed, flowed many of the miseries that subsequently inflicted Ireland. Almost twenty years later, in 1883, a Jesuit priest, Father Denis Murphy, produced the first major study to focus specifically on Cromwell's Irish campaign.[7] Writing at a time of heightened nationalist expectations, due to the Land War and

Charles Stewart Parnell's Home Rule movement, Murphy portrayed the conflict as a heroic albeit doomed struggle by the Catholic Irish in defence of their religion and culture. Critics subsequently attacked Murphy for his lurid and emotional depiction of the horrors of the Cromwellian conquest, embellished throughout with tales from local folklore of uncertain provenance. The use of such literary evidence continues to divide historians, but there is no doubt that the misdeeds of Cromwell feature prominently in Irish poetry and story telling from the mid-seventeenth century, and such material cannot be dismissed lightly. This controversy aside, and despite the use of language somewhat too strident for modern tastes, the scholarship in Murphy's book is for the most part incontrovertible.

The struggle over Cromwell's legacy came to a head in the 1890s with the plans to erect a statue on the grounds of the British parliament at Westminster. The governing Liberal Party strongly supported the proposal in the hope of consolidating the nonconforming Protestant vote, but the bitter opposition of the Irish Nationalist Party at Westminster forced the withdrawal of a motion seeking funds from the House of Commons. According to the radical MP John Morley news of the climbdown was greeted 'with anger and disgust from English Liberals; with thick-witted jibes from Unionists . . . and with wild cries of aboriginal joy from our Irish friends'.[8] The Liberal Prime Minister Lord Rosebery privately financed the project, and the statue was finally unveiled at a low-key ceremony in 1899, the 300th anniversary of Cromwell's birth. Cromwell shares this distinguished location with Richard the Lionheart, an equally ambiguous historical figure, who spent little of his life in England, and by all accounts detested the place. Neither man could be described as a democrat, and like Cromwell, King Richard famously exported his own militant brand of Christianity, not to Ireland but to the Holy Land. In fact, both statues say more about the mindset of Victorian England than the historical realities of the twelfth or seventeenth centuries.

For much of the twentieth century the topic of Cromwell and Ireland received scant attention from academics compared to the avalanche of material published on the civil wars of the 1640s.[9] The

4

authoritative nature of the works of Prendergast and Murphy, combined with the destruction of so many of the state records relating to Ireland in the 1650s, perhaps discouraged scholars from revisiting the controversies of the past. Indeed, many English historians to this day remain unsure of how best to deal with Cromwell's invasion of Ireland. Almost every biography of the man (and there have been many) analyses the 1649 campaign in a separate chapter, awkwardly appended to the main narrative. Few attempt to excuse his actions except by drawing attention to the bloody and merciless nature of warfare in the early modern period. The Thirty Years War (1618–48), which devastated large tracts of central Europe at the same period, remains a byword for wholesale death and destruction, seemingly typified by the sack of the German town of Magdeburg in 1631 by Habsburg troops under the command of General Tilly where thousands perished. The excesses at Magdeburg, however, proved the exception rather than the rule and in no way explain or justify Cromwell's shocking tactics. Moreover, there is a failure to acknowledge fully the extent to which Cromwell's views on Ireland mirrored those of the vast majority of his contemporaries in England, who applauded the crushing of all native resistance, regardless of the cold-blooded methods employed in achieving this goal. As the distinguished English historian S. R. Gardiner explained over a hundred years ago, the fact that Cromwell as an Englishman and Puritan 'should have been guilty of the slaughters of Drogheda and Wexford is a matter for regret, not for surprise'.[10]

So what can be said of Cromwell the man? The myth of the humble commoner rising to become master of England, Scotland and Ireland, although not entirely accurate, has proved very resilient. Cromwell was not of noble stock, but he did nonetheless belong to the elite of society, whose ownership of the land gave them economic wealth and social standing. In a speech to parliament, Cromwell described how he was 'by birth a gentleman, living neither in any considerable height, nor yet in obscurity'.[11] Born in 1599 in Huntingdon, Cambridgeshire, the future parliamentary constituency of Prime Minister John Major, he was the only surviving son of Robert Cromwell, a minor landowner, and Elizabeth Steward, whose father owned considerable property in the nearby cathedral city of Ely. He received a basic education, including a short stay at Sidney Sussex College in Cambridge, before returning home to manage the family lands following the death of his father. He married Elizabeth Bourchier in 1620 and together they began to raise a family, including two sons, Richard and Henry, who would subsequently play a significant role in the military and political affairs of the 1650s, and a daughter Bridget who married Henry Ireton and then Charles Fleetwood, successive Lord Deputies of Ireland. Despite his relatively humble status, Cromwell's local connections ensured his return as MP for Huntingdon in 1628. He made little impact at Westminster before Charles I dissolved the parliament and governed for the next eleven years without summoning another one. During the period of the king's personal rule, Cromwell expanded his land holdings, but the 1630s proved a tough decade economically, and he even considered emigration to the New World at one stage. Famously, he suffered some kind of nervous breakdown or spiritual awakening, and emerged from this experience a committed Puritan, one of the elect. The fervency of Cromwell's religious convictions unnerved many contemporaries and he would be considered something of a fanatic today, but there is no doubting the sincerity of his beliefs. His relationship with God was an intensely personal one, and he strongly disapproved of efforts by Charles I to impose a uniform state religion. Like many Puritans, he suspected the king and his Catholic French wife of subverting the true nature of the reformation, and moving the Church of England closer to Rome. Elected to parliament again in 1640, Cromwell's uncompromising religious views placed him firmly in the camp of those MPs seeking to restrict royal powers.

For the next two years he remained on the periphery of events at Westminster, a witness nonetheless to the deteriorating relations between king and parliament. When civil war finally broke out in England in 1642, Cromwell quickly emerged as an inspirational cavalry commander, despite lacking any formal military training or experience of warfare on the Continent. A. J. P. Taylor describes Cromwell as one of the greatest military leaders in Europe, who, like

Napoleon, understood the importance of winning decisive battles in war.[12] The rigid discipline of army life suited Cromwell's temperament, and appealed to his authoritarian instincts. First and foremost a soldier, his success on the battlefield at Marston Moor in 1644, Naseby in 1645 and Preston in 1648 provided the platform for a meteoric political career, culminating in the offer of the crown from parliament in 1657. Although he supported many of the radical initiatives of the mid-seventeenth century, Cromwell was essentially conservative in his politics. A firm advocate of the existing social order, he only agreed to the execution of Charles I in 1649 after years of failed negotiations, and spent much of the 1650s attempting to rebuild the shattered structures of government. Militant religious convictions, however, provided a genuinely revolutionary impulse in his life. Cromwell believed in a providential God, and as the Lord's servant on earth, he ascribed all his military victories to divine intervention. Repeated success on the battlefield convinced Cromwell of the righteousness of his cause, and drove him forward regardless of the consequences. As Taylor explains, 'God was for Cromwell what the general will was for Robespierre or the proletariat for Lenin: the justification for anything he wished to do.'[13] This proved particularly true of his time in Ireland, and helped create a tragedy of epic proportions.

Ireland, however, does not appear to have registered much in Cromwell's thoughts before the outbreak of the Irish rebellion in October 1641. Like many Englishmen, he may well have heard tales of the kingdom to the west, inhabited by a wild, barbarous people. Perhaps he encountered military veterans of the Tudor wars of conquest, or retired colonial officials, but good reliable information would have been hard to come by in Huntingdon or indeed at Westminster. English involvement in Ireland dates back to the late twelfth century, when Anglo-Norman invaders seized much of the fertile land in the east and south of the country, while the native Irish retained control of the more mountainous, boggy territory to the north and west. The incomplete nature of the conquest effectively partitioned the island between an English Lordship nominally loyal to the crown but dominated by increasingly autonomous Anglo-Norman

Map 1 Ireland in the Seventeenth Century

lords, and a scattering of independent native territories. The boundaries proved extremely fluid, but by the fifteenth century effective royal control was limited to the city of the Dublin and the lands within a thirty-mile radius, known as the Pale. All this began to change following Henry VIII's breach with Rome in the 1530s. He feared the great Catholic powers on the Continent would exploit Ireland as a convenient launching pad for an invasion of England. In 1541, therefore, the colonial parliament in Dublin declared Henry king of Ireland, though in reality his jurisdiction remained confined to the old lordship. Over the next sixty years, however, successive Tudor monarchs aggressively expanded their authority, brutally suppressing all native opposition, often with the active support of the original Anglo-Norman colonial community. The English victory over the native Irish of Ulster in the Nine Years War (1594–1603) gave them control of the entire island for the first time, and signalled the final collapse of the old Gaelic order. In 1603, within days of the final surrender of the Gaelic lords, James VI of Scotland succeeded Elizabeth I, becoming in the process king of Scotland, England and Ireland.

Between 1603 and the outbreak of the Irish rebellion in 1641, James and his son Charles consolidated colonial power in Ireland, through a variety of means including plantation. But what kind of kingdom had they inherited? In 1649, the Dutch physician, Gerard Boate, accompanied Cromwell to Ireland, and began writing a natural history of the country before his premature death the following year.[14] His brother, Arnold, completed the work, published towards the end of the war in order to encourage Protestant settlers to migrate over from England. Despite Ireland's seemingly remote geographic position on the periphery of Europe, Boate described how it could be reached from Holyhead in Wales in just twelve hours, 'with a reasonable good wind', while the journey across from Scotland could take as little as three hours. In reality, adverse weather conditions, and poor roads to London, meant it frequently took weeks for messages from Ireland to reach the English capital. The kingdom was divided into four provinces, with the best land situated in Leinster to the east and Munster to the south. The western province of Connacht, separated from the rest of Ireland by the river Shannon, and the northern province of Ulster were significantly less fertile and remained relatively inaccessible. Boate commented on the absence of great forests, leading to a shortage of firewood and timber for building, while he blamed the native population for allowing good land to go uncultivated. Bogs, mountains and sporadic but dense woodland created a challenging natural environment, compared to the more intensely cultivated English countryside. Moreover, the absence of an extensive network of roads made inland travel extremely difficult, especially in winter, except where possible by river.

A temperate climate meant that Ireland for the most part escaped the extremes of weather that afflicted much of Europe during the seventeenth century. Boate noted despondently, however, that it rained 'very much all the year round', which restricted the growth of crops to some degree, although the country usually provided enough corn for export. In addition to arable farming, landowners in Ireland maintained large herds of cattle and sheep, both for domestic and overseas consumption. Unusually for an island-based community, the fishing industry remained seriously underdeveloped, allowing large Spanish fleets free rein to harvest the rich seas around the Irish coast. Boate, like all colonists, believed that opportunities for economic improvement existed if the country were 'inhabited throughout by a civil nation'. Nonetheless, despite the deficiencies of climate and habitat, he noted that the people lived to a great age, 'setting aside those who through idleness and intemperance do shorten their days', with diseases such as scurvy and leprosy apparently rare. On the negative side, a particularly virulent form of dysentery, known as 'the looseness', 'the flux' or 'the country disease', caused in Boate's opinion by excessive wetness and a poor diet, proved particularly fatal to many visitors to the island, as the soldiers of the New Model Army subsequently discovered to their cost.

The majority of the population lived in small clustered rural settlements, often situated around the manorial residence of the local landlord. Many peasants drove their livestock to the highlands during the summer months seeking pasture, where they built temporary shelters for their families. English commentators frequently misinterpreted this practice and as a result described the Irish as a nomadic people. The severe dislocation caused by the wars of the 1640s did in fact lead to the emergence of 'creaghts', or highly mobile communities, constantly on the move with their cattle in an effort to avoid the worst of the conflict. While large tracts of the kingdom remained devoid of urban settlement, the fertile lands of both Leinster and Munster supported a number of well-established towns. The capital, Dublin, was by far the biggest city, with close to 20,000 inhabitants, while the next four in size, the coastal ports of Waterford, Limerick, Cork and Galway, each contained less then 5,000 people. Boate considered the port of Drogheda and the inland town of Kilkenny as 'passable and worthy of some regard', but other places, such as Belfast, Wexford and Kinsale, 'scarce worth the mentioning'. Nonetheless, Ireland's troubled past meant that even the smallest urban centres retained their original medieval walls for defensive purposes. Historical demographers estimate that the population of Ireland in the early decades of the seventeenth century probably numbered in the region of one million people divided into four distinct groups – the native Irish, the Old English, the new English and the Scots in Ulster.

The native Irish, by far the largest group, lived almost exclusively in rural communities, traditionally dominated by leading clans or families such as the O'Neills, the MacCarthys and the O'Briens. From the mid-sixteenth century these local power structures came under increasing threat from Tudor colonial expansion. Initial attempts by Henry VIII to incorporate the native aristocracy into the newly established kingdom of Ireland gradually gave way to a policy of overt military aggression. Moreover, the native Irish refused to embrace the reformed faith, creating deep religious divisions to compound the existing ethnic tensions between natives and newcomers. Following the defeat of Hugh O'Neill, earl of Tyrone, in 1603, the old Gaelic political order collapsed. O'Neill fled into exile on the Continent, to be joined by thousands of unemployed swordsmen, who found service in the armies of France and Spain. The native Irish elite who remained behind in Ireland adapted as best they could to the colonial system, but they deeply resented the power and influence of the newly arrived Protestant settlers.

A handful of the old Gaelic aristocracy, such as Donough MacCarthy, appeared to overcome the disadvantages of religious and ethnic discrimination, and integrated well into colonial society. Heir to vast estates in County Cork, MacCarthy married into the leading Old English family in the country, the Butlers, and carefully built up a network of friends and dependants across the religious divide. A consummate politician, he sat as MP for County Cork in the Irish parliaments of 1634 and 1640, and succeeded his father as Viscount Muskerry in 1641, taking a seat in the House of Lords just before the outbreak of the Irish rebellion. The subsequent polarisation of society forced Muskerry to choose sides, and in early 1642 he openly joined with the Catholic insurgents. His principal opponent in Munster for much of the 1640s was Murrough O'Brien, Lord Inchiquin, one of the few prominent native Irish leaders to forsake the Catholic religion. The O'Briens had played a key role in Munster politics for centuries, but Inchiquin, raised as a Protestant from the age of ten, adopted an extreme anti-Catholic position. The native Irish called him 'Murchadh na dótáin' or 'Murrough of the burnings' following a series of attacks on Catholic churches and monasteries around his stronghold in Cork City. Nonetheless, English Protestants remained suspicious of Inchiquin because of his native Irish lineage, and never really accepted him as an equal.

The Old English, the second largest group in Ireland, and the principal landowners in the kingdom, experienced similar mistrust as a result of their stubborn refusal to discard their Catholic faith. The descendents of the original Anglo-Norman colonists, they had for the most part supported the Tudor conquest, fighting against their traditional enemies, the native Irish. Despite this valuable military service, James VI and I described them contemptuously as 'half-subjects', politically loyal but religiously suspect. The king retained his predecessor's policy of excluding them from government posts, appointing instead more reliable though unashamedly rapacious English Protestant officials, who soon began to intrigue for control of the big landed estates. Recusancy fines, imposed for failing to attend Protestant services, proved a sporadic irritant, while the process of plantation in Ulster and elsewhere, although directed mainly against the native Irish, left many Old English feeling vulnerable about their own holdings.

In addition to their landed interests, concentrated in Munster and

Leinster, the Old English also dominated the big urban centres throughout the kingdom, with the exception of the colonial capital and the newly created plantation boroughs in the province of Ulster. A handful of merchant families monopolised civic power, growing wealthy on trade with the surrounding countryside and the Continent. They formed part of an extensive European commercial network, exporting agricultural produce, principally wool and cattle hides, and importing textiles and luxury items such as wine from Flanders, France and Spain. Each town jealously guarded its local autonomy from outside interference, and traditionally excluded the native Irish from living within the defensive walls of the settlement. Many of the big cities, however, such as Waterford, Limerick and Galway, joined the Catholic insurgency during the 1640s, and subsequently organised the most effective opposition to Oliver Cromwell and the New Model Army.

At the apex of Catholic Old English society stood Ulick Bourke, earl (and later marquis) of Clanricarde, who owned vast estates in Connacht, and enjoyed close relations with the town of Galway, one of the most important trading ports in the country. Ulick spent many years at the English court, where he enjoyed a close relationship with Charles I, and developed links across the political divide, mainly through his step-brother, Robert Devereux, the earl of Essex and future commander of the parliamentary forces. Through Essex's intercession, Clanricarde was appointed to the English Privy Council in 1641, and lieutenant of the town and county of Galway in Connacht, one of the few Irish Catholics to hold public office at this time. He returned to Ireland in September 1641, on the eve of the rebellion. Although the vast majority of the Old English aristocracy subsequently sided with the Catholic insurgents, he remained loyal to the Stuarts throughout the 1640s. Despite an impressively large physique, he suffered from very poor health, and was frequently incapacitated by either kidney stones or gallstones. These attacks compounded Clanricarde's excessively cautious nature, and seriously curtailed his effectiveness as a military commander. Another leading Catholic noble, James Tuchet, earl of Castlehaven, whose father, an English lord, owned estates in Leinster, travelled to Ireland at the same time as Clanricarde. Short in stature, the 'little earl', as he became known, experienced a traumatic childhood in a seriously dysfunctional family. In 1631, he gave evidence in court against his father, who was executed after being found guilty of gross sexual misconduct towards his wife. In order to escape the shame, Castlehaven pursued a military career on the Continent, before joining the Catholic insurgents in Ireland. Although many of his co-religionists suspected him of royalist sympathies because of his English lineage, he proved to be an energetic cavalry commander, and one of Cromwell's most implacable opponents.

The Protestant population in Ireland constituted the third and fourth groups. The new English consisted primarily of soldiers and administrators who had settled during the Tudor conquest on estates confiscated from Catholic rebels in Leinster and Munster. From 1610, a government-sponsored plantation scheme redistributed lands seized from Hugh O'Neill and his northern allies among thousands of Protestant migrants from England, alongside even greater numbers from Scotland. By the 1630s, the Protestant population of Ulster stood at around 80,000, many of whom called themselves British. Despite tensions between the new English and the Scots, for the most part the common fear of the Catholic Irish kept them united. The authorities created a whole series of new boroughs in Ulster in an effort to encourage urban development, but except for a few centres, such as Derry, Enniskillen and Carrickfergus, the vast majority of the settler population lived in relatively small fortified settlements, constantly anxious about the threat to security from bands of native outlaws sheltering in the woods, bogs and mountains of the province. The other main concentration of Protestants, apart from the colonial capital at Dublin, occurred along the southern coastline, where towns such as Cork, Kinsale, Bandon and Youghal formed the backbone of the Munster plantation. Many of the original Protestant planters from the 1580s had either been killed or driven out of the country during the Nine Years War, but the settler population soon rose in the aftermath of the rebel defeat, and by 1640 they numbered over 20,000, mainly from the southern and western counties of England.

Two of the leading planter families, the Cootes and the Boyles, enjoyed close ties through a series of marriage alliances. Sir Charles Coote fought in the Nine Years War, acquiring estates in Connacht in the process, and served in a number of important administrative positions over four decades. Violently anti-Catholic, and an aggressive advocate of further English plantations, he eagerly accepted military command on the outbreak of the rebellion in October 1641. He quickly earned a reputation for brutality, but was killed during a skirmish with enemy forces in May 1642, allegedly shot by one of his own men. His eldest son, also called Charles, proved an equally uncompromising opponent of the Catholic insurgents, commanding forces loyal to the English parliament in the west and north of the country. Richard Boyle, earl of Cork, rose from humble origins in England to become one of the largest landowners in Ireland. He ably exploited the political turmoil at the beginning of the seventeenth century to expand his estates and business interests, creating in the process an extensive network of dependants. An old man at the outbreak of the rebellion, he died in 1643, but one of his younger sons, Roger Boyle, Lord Broghill, played a key role during the wars, and fought with Cromwell during the latter stages of the conflict. He needed little encouragement to take up arms against his Catholic neighbours, and like Coote, showed no mercy to his opponents. In fact, Protestants living in Ireland, such as Broghill and Coote, committed many of the atrocities subsequently attributed to Cromwell and the New Model Army.

The leading Protestant in Ireland, however, was not a newcomer, but rather the head of the most important Old English family, the Butlers. Raised in England as a ward of court in a strict Protestant household, the young James Butler, subsequently earl of Ormond, enthusiastically embraced the new faith and resisted all entreaties from his extended family to revert to Catholicism. After succeeding to the earldom in 1633, Ormond concentrated on repairing his neglected estates, which for the most part lay in counties Kilkenny and Tipperary. On the eve of the rebellion in 1641 he enjoyed a rental income of £8,000 per annum, making him one of the wealthiest landowners in the kingdom. A man of limited abilities, he nonetheless proved to be one of the great survivors of the seventeenth century, motivated primarily by self-interest yet widely admired for his apparently steadfast devotion to the Stuarts. Despite an impressive network of clients and friends, including leading Catholics such as his brother-in-law, Viscount Muskerry, he remained a deeply controversial figure across the religious divide. Many Catholics distrusted him because of his Protestant faith, while Protestants expressed misgivings about his close familial and business links with the Catholic population. Ormond, however, enjoyed the unswerving confidence of Charles I. As a result, he retained command of the royalist armies in Ireland for much of the 1640s, and coordinated the military resistance to Oliver Cromwell at the end of the decade.

The kingdom of Ireland, therefore, was a patchwork of competing religious and ethnic groups, each vying for political and economic control of the country. Despite the traditional hostility between the Old English and native Irish elites, however, their shared adherence to the Catholic faith resulted in a slow but significant thaw in relations, facilitated by the process of intermarriage. With official discrimination limiting opportunities at home, many Catholics chose to go into exile, entering Irish religious orders based on the Continent, or seeking their fortune through military service in the armies of France or Spain. Tensions still existed in these émigré communities between the Old English and native Irish, but bonds of friendship also flourished, transcending the old divisions. Major religious houses, such as the Irish college at Louvain in Spanish Flanders, played an important role in this process. The clergy sought to preserve Irish Catholic culture through the collection and reproduction of religious, literary, historical and legal manuscripts, as well through the publication of books in the Irish language. They provided spiritual solace to their fellow exiles, but also pursued a radical religious agenda in their homeland, sending priests back to Ireland as the vanguard of Tridentine Catholicism. On the military side, men such as Owen Roe O'Neill, nephew of the earl of Tyrone, and Thomas Preston, younger son of Viscount Gormanston, commanded regiments of Irish troops in Spanish Flanders and enjoyed very successful military careers. Nonetheless, they never abandoned hope of returning home, giving active encouragement and support to disaffected elements in Ireland.

While many of the native Irish looked abroad for political leadership, the Old English elite for the most part placed their hopes in the Irish parliament, where as major landowners and representatives of the big towns they retained a powerful if no longer dominant influence. Through parliament, they sought to safeguard their land holdings, mitigate the worst excesses of religious discrimination and regain some influence in government circles. This policy achieved what appeared to be a major success in 1628, when Charles I, at war with both France and Spain, and in desperate need of money, granted a series of concessions to Irish Catholics, known as the 'Graces'. These included a crucial statute of limitations on royal claims to land, which would have protected Old English estates from possible future confiscation and plantation. In 1629, peace on the international front reduced the political pressure on the king, enabling him to renege on his promises. The failure to implement the 'Graces' caused intense resentment and bitterness in the Irish Catholic community. The following decade proved a traumatic time for the Catholic elite, both native Irish and Old English, particularly following the appointment of Thomas Wentworth as Lord Deputy in 1632. Wentworth's increasing use of arbitrary power, with the full support of the king, negated any residual influence they still enjoyed in parliament, while his plantation policies further threatened their estates. Denied the protection of the 'Graces', and unable to appeal over Wentworth's head directly to Charles, their future looked increasingly bleak.

The outbreak of conflict in Scotland in 1637, however, completely transformed the political situation throughout the three Stuart kingdoms. Scottish Presbyterians, outraged by the king's efforts to impose Anglican religious rites throughout his three kingdoms, signed a national covenant in protest. Their actions quickly escalated into a full-scale revolt, with the covenanters seizing control of Edinburgh and recruiting a large army, including many veterans who had fought for the Protestant champion King Gustavus Adolphus of

Sweden. As in the 1620s, Charles desperately needed to raise money and troops, and he looked to Wentworth in Ireland to provide both. The Lord Deputy took the radical step of recruiting Catholics into the rank and file of a new army of 10,000 men, with the intention of using them against the covenanters. Charles signed a treaty with the Scots before Wentworth could employ his force, and the Lord Deputy, raised to the title earl of Strafford, left Ireland shortly afterwards to assist the king at court. In his absence, the Old English leaders successfully colluded with Strafford's Protestant opponents in both the Irish and English parliaments to bring about the execution of the king's most ruthless and talented supporter. Despite this success, the Old English failed to convince Charles I of the need for major concessions to Irish Catholics, and they reluctantly considered a resort to arms, with the troops raised by Strafford providing a potential source of manpower for an uprising. Meanwhile, a number of native Irish landowners in Ulster, deep in debt and worried by the violently anti-Catholic rhetoric of the Scottish covenanters, initiated contacts with influential Irish exiles, such as Owen Roe O'Neill, to discuss the possibility of a rebellion supported by intervention from the Continent.

By late 1641, therefore, the kingdom of Ireland was seething with internal tensions. Taken in this context, the outbreak of the Irish rebellion in October should hardly have surprised contemporaries. Protestant and Catholic commentators, however, subsequently agreed that the uprising occurred without warning, at a time of peace and prosperity, an interpretation that continues to influence historical writing today. According to the Catholic lawyer Richard Bellings the various groups in Ireland 'setting aside their different tenets in matters of religion, were as perfectly incorporated, and as firmly knit together, as frequent marriages, daily ties of hospitality, and the mutual bond between lord and tenant, could unite any people . . . so they enjoyed at that time, more than in many ages before, the fruits of peace in a very notable increase of plenty'.[15] His bitter enemy, the Protestant lawyer Sir John Temple, a leading official in the Dublin administration, painted a similar picture of serenity and prosperity prior to the outbreak of the rebellion. Temple wrote how 'all men sat pleasantly enjoying the comfortable fruits of their own labours, without the least thoughts or apprehension of either tumults or other troubles'.[16] The Irish economy did indeed enjoy a number of good years in the mid-1630s, while technically at least the country was also at peace in 1641, with Charles I assiduously avoiding any Continental entanglements since his disastrous forays against France and Spain in the late 1620s. Ireland, however, experienced a severe economic downturn at the end of the 1630s, and the attendant hardships undoubtedly exacerbated existing frictions, creating the ideal conditions for a rebellion.

So why did so many commentators, bitter opponents in almost every way, collude in misrepresenting the situation in Ireland? Prosperity is, of course, relative, and men like Bellings and Temple may simply have been commenting on their own personal wealth and good fortune, but timing and intended audience provide the most plausible explanations. Catholics like Bellings, writing after the restoration of the monarchy in 1660, and anxious to prove their loyalty to the crown, wanted to portray the rebellion as an aberration, interrupting an otherwise peaceful coexistence between the various religious and ethnic groupings in Ireland. For Protestants, the allegedly undisturbed nature of Ireland prior to 1641 simply exacerbated the enormity of the rebels' crimes. This approach underpins the work of Temple who, domiciled in England after 1644, sought to inflame public opinion there with lurid stories of unprovoked attacks by Irish Catholics on their Protestant neighbours. His writings helped generate support for the subsequent invasion of Ireland by Oliver Cromwell. In fact, Cromwell uncritically accepted Temple's version of events, and not long after arriving in Dublin in 1649, he published a letter accusing the Catholic Irish of an unprovoked massacre of Protestant settlers 'at a time when Ireland was in perfect peace'.[17]

Quite apart from the tensions emanating from the crisis in Scotland, Ireland had actually been in a state of constant conflict for the previous hundred years. The general maintenance of law and order had become increasingly bloody from the mid-sixteenth century, owing to the potent mix of religious and ethnic tensions.

Martial law, the imposition of summary justice following the suspension of the normal legal process, emerged as an important weapon in the Tudor arsenal for dealing with the recalcitrant Irish. From the fourteenth century until the 1550s, the use of martial law had been specifically restricted to situations of war or open rebellion. This changed dramatically in 1556 when Lord Deputy Sussex introduced a new pre-emptive form of the law into Ireland, which enabled specially appointed commissioners to execute suspected offenders, even before they had committed an offence.[18] The administration in Dublin issued hundreds of commissions, and all levels of society suffered at the hands of these military administrators. From the 1570s, government-sponsored slaughter featured prominently as part of the colonial experience in Ireland.[19] The Puritan Thomas Churchyard, in his book *A General Rehearsal of Warres*, commented favourably on the brutal 'fear and terror' tactics employed by Sir Humphrey Gilbert, Lord President of Munster in the 1570s. Churchyard believed that 'severe and straight' handling of rebellious people, including non-combatants, brought them sooner to obedience, rather than 'any courteous dealing'.[20] In one six-week campaign, Gilbert reportedly captured over twenty castles, and slaughtered all the occupants, including women and children, while in 1574 raiders led by the great English naval hero, Sir Francis Drake, massacred the entire civilian population of Rathlin Island off the coast of Antrim.

The extensive use of summary justice, against both soldiers and civilians, helped the English eventually gain the upper hand in the Nine Years War. Despite the surrender of the principal native Irish leaders in 1603, the Dublin authorities continued to rely on martial law to maintain order in the localities. In 1611, the Catholic lords protested to the Irish Privy Council about the excessive abuse of summary powers, which they argued should not be used in times of peace. A similar complaint appeared in a petition to Charles I in 1625, and strict limitations on the use of martial law formed part of the subsequent 'Graces' promised by the king in 1628. In 1639, Lord Deputy Thomas Wentworth invoked martial law to prevent disturbances from the covenanting revolt in Scotland spreading to

Ulster. This action formed the basis of one of the charges at his subsequent trial at Westminster. In his defence, Wentworth emphasised that this law had 'always been practiced by the Lieutenants and Deputies of that kingdom [Ireland]', a fact confirmed by two of his political opponents, Lords Cork and Wilmot, both veterans of previous Irish administrations.[21] Long before the outbreak of the Ulster rebellion in October of that year, therefore, martial law was a well recognised, and frequently invoked, weapon of coercion, used in times of peace and war, against combatants and non-combatants alike. Heavy-handed colonial military tactics, combined with continuing Catholic resentment at the loss of lands, political exclusion and sporadic religious persecution, created an explosive atmosphere in Ireland. Revolt was by no means inevitable but it would not take much to set the kingdom ablaze.

2

Ireland Independent

Hiberni unanimes pro Deo Rege et Patria.
[Irishmen united for God, king and country.]
MOTTO OF THE CATHOLIC CONFEDERATE ASSOCIATION (1642)

On Friday, 22 October 1641, Sir Phelim O'Neill, respected Catholic landowner, justice of the peace, and member of the Irish parliament for the borough of Dungannon, paid a visit to his neighbour, Sir Toby Caulfield, governor of Charlemont Fort in County Armagh. Without warning, the men accompanying O'Neill seized control of the fortress, and imprisoned the startled Sir Toby, who later died in rebel custody. These actions triggered a war that would last over a decade and result in the death of over one-fifth of the Irish population. Although Sir Phelim belonged to the powerful O'Neill family, rulers over much of Ulster for centuries, in many ways he was not a typical rebel. His father, Turlough Oge, had fought for the English crown during the Nine Years War, and paid the ultimate price for his loyalty, killed while attempting to suppress a subsequent rebellion in 1608. In recognition of these services, Turlough's young heir, Phelim, received estates in the Ulster Plantation, as one of the 'deserving Irish'. Raised as a ward of court in the Protestant faith, Phelim attended Lincoln's Inn in London before returning to Ireland in the 1620s, where he reverted to his native Catholicism. For over a decade, he played a leading political and social role in the local community, and out-wardly at least, appeared to have assimilated well into colonial society, being knighted in 1639. Like all Catholics, however, O'Neill remained subject to sporadic religious persecution, and resentful at the power and influence of the Protestant newcomers. Moreover, Sir Phelim struggled to maintain the family estates, and by 1640 he owed the enormous sum of £12,000 to creditors in Dublin and London.

As the senior resident O'Neill in Ulster, Sir Phelim inevitably attracted the interest of similarly disgruntled Catholic landowners, such as Philip MacHugh O'Reilly and Lord Conor Maguire, anxious to obtain his support for a pre-emptive strike against a hostile colonial administration. Impressed by the success of the Scottish covenanters, they sought to gain control of the kingdom and negotiate with the king from a position of strength. Already in contact with prominent Irish exiles in Spanish Flanders, including his kinsman, Colonel Owen Roe O'Neill, Sir Phelim gradually became entangled in the complex series of plots that developed over the summer of 1641, involving not only the Ulster Irish but also the Old English grandees from the area known as the Pale around Dublin. O'Neill and his co-conspirators prepared to take action in the autumn, despite the decision of the Old English to change tactics and seek a political solution through the Irish parliament. The Ulster Irish envisaged an assault on two fronts. Sir Phelim targeted Charlemont and other key points in south Ulster, to prevent Protestant settlers in the northern province from linking up with forces from the capital. At the same time, Lord Maguire's men would storm Dublin castle, paralyse the government and gain access to the state's vast store of weaponry. Sir Phelim executed his part of the plot to perfection, successfully rallying thousands of followers to the O'Neill banner, in a dramatic demonstration of the extent to which traditional clan loyalty and structures had covertly survived the upheavals of the Ulster plantation. In Dublin, however, a companion of Lord Maguire, Owen O'Connolly, managed to slip away from his colleagues the night before the planned attack and alert the authorities. They quickly rounded up the conspirators, including Maguire, who was subsequently executed in London. This particular story, richly embellished over the centuries with tales of inebriated rebels carousing in Dublin's taverns, is an engaging mix of tragedy and farce, reinforcing in the eyes of many the crude stereotype of Irish Catholics as untrustworthy drunkards, inherently dangerous but ultimately incompetent. Whatever the truth of the matter, by failing to gain control of the country's capital, the Ulster insurgents now faced the grim prospect of retaliatory action by well-armed government troops.

Within a few days, however, the limited strike envisaged by the rebel leaders had sparked widespread unrest, with reports of attacks not only in Ulster, but in north Leinster as well. By the end of 1641, less than two months after O'Neill seized Charlemont, the violence had spread to south-west Munster, the furthest point geographically in Ireland from the source of the initial revolt. It is important from the outset to make a clear distinction between the people who initiated the rising and the forces they mobilised in the process. The conspirators, for the most part, belonged to the landed elite, motivated by a mixture of fear, resentment and financial worries. Disillusioned with the discriminatory political system, they none-theless professed their loyalty to the king, and claimed to have acted in self-defence against the unjust policies of the colonial administration. The rebel leaders vowed to continue until 'we be at better leisure to make our grievances known unto his Majesty, and he have more power to relieve us'.[1] In early November, Sir Phelim O'Neill published a proclamation, allegedly issued by Charles I, authorising Catholics to take up arms. This sensational document, although subsequently exposed as a forgery, temporarily gave the rebel actions a veneer of legitimacy. More importantly, the early successes of O'Neill and his comrades attracted a growing number of people, small tenant farmers, landless labourers and notorious out-laws among others, to the rebel cause, drawn by 'the common habit of joining the winning side'.[2] Local Catholic landowners, anxious to avoid a complete breakdown in law and order, quickly assumed command in their areas, but found it increasingly difficult to control their rank-and-file supporters. Embittered by long-standing grievances, and more recent economic hardships, the insurgents began attacking Protestant settlers, particularly in the province of Ulster. The Catholic elite subsequently criticised the excesses of the 'rude multitude' or 'landless sort', and conveniently blamed the worst outrages of the rising on 'some of the loosest of the Irish rabble'.[3]

At first, the rebels restricted their actions to theft and the destruction of property, and the surviving evidence suggests that relatively few died on either side in the early weeks of the rising. After suffering a number of setbacks against government forces, the insurgents became more inclined to murderous extremes. Initial attempts to drive a wedge between Scottish and English settlers, by attacking only the latter group, proved impossible to sustain as disorder spread throughout the localities. A number of atrocities took place, including the notorious massacre in November 1641 of as many as a hundred men, women and children at Portadown Bridge in County Armagh, an area technically under the control of Sir Phelim O'Neill, although he played no part in the killings. Terrified Protestants, exposed and vulnerable, fled their homes for the relative safety of the nearest garrison towns, before in many cases carrying on to Dublin. The rebels frequently attacked these defenceless convoys as they moved slowly towards the capital, stripping the refugees of all their possessions, including their clothing. Exposed to the harsh winter weather, without food or shelter, thousands of innocent civilians died by the roadside. Although precise figures are difficult to verify, given the chaotic nature of events, latest research suggests that up to 5,000 Protestants perished during the first few months of the rebellion, along with a similar number of Catholics, victims of retaliatory attacks by government forces. James Tuchet, earl of Castlehaven, writing during the Restoration, accepted that the war was 'very bloody on both sides' but accused the authorities in Dublin of exploiting the crisis to attack all Catholics, giving orders 'to their parties sent into the enemies [Irish] quarters, to spare neither man, woman nor child'.[4] On the other side of the political and religious divide, one of the earliest historians of the wars of the 1640s, Edmund Borlase, condemned the Catholic Irish for plunging the kingdom into a bloody conflict. Nonetheless, he felt obliged to address accusations that Protestant massacres exceeded those of Catholics, 'as well as in respect of brutishness as numerousness'. Borlase admitted frankly 'that many things (contrary to the Laws of Arms and Christianity) during the rebellion were severely committed by the English', but justified their actions because of the alleged excesses of the rebels.[5]

The ferocious reaction of the government to the revolt exacerbated an already explosive situation. On 23 October, the day after the rebellion broke out in Ulster, the Lords Justices, Sir William Parsons and Sir John Borlase (father of Edmund), issued a proclamation blaming the disorder on 'evil affected Irish papists' without distinction.[6] Following complaints by the Catholic lords of the Pale, a grudging retraction six days later identified the Ulster Irish as the chief culprits, but did little to assuage fears about the heavy-handed response of the Dublin administration to the crisis. The subsequent refusal of the Lords Justices to provide arms to the same lords to protect their estates from the Ulster rebels merely reinforced the general sense of grievance among those Catholics not yet involved in the rising. Over the next two months, brutal and indiscriminate reprisals by colonial commanders such as Sir William St Leger in Munster and Sir Charles Coote in Leinster horrified the Old English community. According to one petition to the king, a number of Catholics living peacefully near Dublin were 'murdered in their beds, and many hanged by martial law without cause by Sir Charles Coote and others here'.[7] St Leger, Lord President of Munster, launched an equally bloody offensive across the south of the country, executing large numbers of Catholics, including some landed gentry, regardless of whether or not they supported the rebellion. He explained in a letter to a sceptical colleague that 'in these days *Magna Charta* must not be wholly insisted on'.[8] According to a leading colonial administrator, Sir John Temple, St Leger killed at least 200 people, and hanged several prisoners, 'for a greater terror to all such as should adventure afterwards to follow their example', while another commentator recorded how the execution of innocent civilians 'gave the people a general apprehension that the extirpation of the Catholic religion and the nation, not the punishment of men's particular crimes, was the end he aimed at'.[9] Whatever the initial intention, the escalating conflict effectively created the pretext for confiscating lucrative Catholic estates, a policy long favoured by many officials in Dublin.

Faced with a hostile and aggressive colonial administration, seemingly determined to treat all 'papists' as rebels and traitors, and a populist rising rapidly careering out of control, the Old English elite of the Pale desperately sought to defuse the crisis. On 17 November, the Irish parliament, at the instigation of the Catholic members, appointed a delegation to approach the Ulster insurgents and discover their demands. The decision of the Lords Justices to suspend the sitting of the assembly temporarily that same day fatally undermined any attempt at reconciliation and confirmed suspicions that the authorities in Dublin actively favoured war. The success of the Ulster forces on 29 November at Julianstown, wiping out a government convoy sent to relieve the town of Drogheda, thirty miles north of the capital, finally drove the Old English leadership to initiate direct contact with the native Irish insurgents. A few days later, at a carefully choreographed meeting on the Hill of Crofty in County Meath, the two sides, habitual enemies for much of the preceding five centuries, agreed to form a defensive alliance. A second meeting a week later, on the symbolic Hill of Tara, seat of the ancient High-Kings of Ireland, cemented the union. Contrary to traditional historical interpretations, these events did not in fact represent a dramatic new departure. Since the late sixteenth century, the shared experience of religious discrimination had gradually brought the native Irish and Old English elites closer together. According to Sir John Temple, anxious to justify the confiscation of all lands held by Catholics in Ireland, regardless of their ethnic background, the original English colony, dating back to the Norman Conquest, had 'long since worn out, or for the most part become Irish'.[10] The meetings at Crofty and Tara appeared to confirm his self-serving assessment, creating a united conservative Catholic landed interest, determined to preserve, or even expand where possible, its role within the existing system. The rebel leaders clearly distinguished between the institutions of power, which they supported, and the current occupants, in this case the Lords Justices in Dublin, whom they bitterly opposed. They fought against bad governors rather than a bad system of government. As soon as they restored order locally, the insurgents hoped to negotiate a satisfactory peace settlement with the king from a position of strength.

In England, news of the rebellion caused widespread panic, aggravated by wild rumours of Irish papists landing on the west coast and rampaging through the countryside. For many MPs at

Westminster, obsessively wary of papist plots, both international and domestic, the actions of Sir Phelim O'Neill and his accomplices validated their extreme anti-Catholic paranoia. Frustrated for decades by the reluctance of the Stuarts, both James I and Charles I, to engage in a religious crusade on the Continent, alongside erstwhile Protestant heroes such as King Gustavus Adolphus of Sweden, events closer to home at last provided them with an outlet for aggressive military action. John Pym, leader of the opposition to the king in parliament, declared ominously on hearing of the Irish rebellion that 'nothing but the sword must decide the controversy'.[11] With Charles I absent in Scotland, negotiating with the covenanters, Pym and his allies eagerly grasped the opportunity to assume control of military affairs, traditionally a royal prerogative, and prepare a counteroffensive against the insurgents. In this way, events in Ireland contributed to the deteriorating relationship between king and parliament that would eventually lead to the outbreak of the civil war in England the following August. Parliament immediately began to send men and supplies to the beleaguered colonial administration, and members also agreed to finance an expedition to Ulster by an army of 10,000 Scottish covenanters. The English troops arrived in Dublin, where they soon took the offensive against the rebels in the Pale, while Scottish soldiers landed in Carrickfergus, County Antrim, from April 1642, and with the assistance of local Protestant forces, gradually established control over north-east Ulster.

Throughout the early months of the rebellion, a series of popular publications fanned hysteria among the English population at large. As the censorship apparatus collapsed, owing to the growing political tensions between king and parliament, scores of unlicensed pamphlets and news-sheets began to appear on the streets of London. Despite a relatively limited print-run, usually numbering no more than a few hundred, these cheap, weekly publications reached an impressively large audience, particularly in the capital. They ranged in style from bland, factual narratives to rabid diatribes, filled with invective, mixing fact and fiction much like the tabloid press today.[12] Within a few weeks the trickle of information/disinformation about the rebellion became a flood, and the news-sheets and pamphlets played a crucial role in whipping up anti-Irish and anti-Catholic sentiment, with a series of lurid tales (sometimes with accompanying illustrations) on the massacre of innocent Protestant settlers by bloodthirsty papist rebels. A gullible public, horrified yet titillated by the gruesome tales emanating from Ireland, accepted uncritically these wildly exaggerated stories of death and mutilation. Before long, the official estimate of Protestant deaths in Ireland rose to over 150,000, a figure far exceeding the total settler population in Ireland at that time.[13]

For the next six months increasingly frenzied reports rolled off the presses, although the attention gradually shifted from the victims of terror to the perpetrators of these heinous crimes. One infamous pamphlet by James Cranford, entitled *The Teares of Ireland*, railed against 'these bloody Papists', guilty of 'cruelties and tortures exceeding all parallel, unheard of among Pagans, Turks, or Barbarians, except you would enter into the confines of Hell itself'.[14] Another later account by Adam Meredith, whose father William served in the Dublin administration, focused more on the alleged barbaric nature of the Irish rather than their religious affiliation. He compared them to 'the savage cannibals in the Indies', and concluded that these people could not 'be ruled but with a rod of iron'.[15] Whether because of their barbarism or Catholicism, the Irish clearly could expect little understanding or sympathy from a hostile English public, outraged at the harsh treatment of their co-religionists and thirsting for revenge. There was of course a long tradition of anti-Irish prejudice in English political and historical writings, dating back to Giraldus Cambrensis and the first Anglo-Norman invasion in the late twelfth century. The production, however, of cheap news-sheets in the early 1640s made this material available to a much wider audience than had hitherto been possible.

The oral testimony of Protestants who fled from Ireland to escape the violence provided ample material for the London publishers. Moreover, in late December 1641, as refugees poured into the city of Dublin, the Lords Justices commissioned eight clergymen, including Dr Henry Jones, dean (and later bishop) of Clogher, to collect witness statements from the traumatised settlers. Over 3,000 sworn testimonies, compiled according to a set format, listed the name, address, social status and/or occupation of the deponents, along with a description of material losses, and where possible, information on those responsible. In January 1642, as the rebellion intensified, the authorities extended the scope of the commission to include allegations of murders and massacres. The bulk of the statements were taken in 1642–3, but the Commission for Despoiled Protestants continued its work until September 1647. Initially intended as a straightforward inventory of losses, Irish Protestant leaders quickly recognised the propaganda value of these testimonies. Henry Jones and his colleagues skilfully exploited the harrowing accounts of death and destruction to construct a seemingly irrefutable case for the re-conquest of Ireland by an English army.

In March 1642, Jones travelled to Westminster to present the commission's findings, along with a selection of the depositions, to parliament. This report, subsequently published under the title *A Remonstrance of Divers Remarkable Passages Concerning the Church and Kingdom of Ireland*, described a general massacre of innocent English and Scottish Protestant settlers by savage and cruel Irish Papists. Jones's account, combined with alarmist letters from the administration in Dublin, and the sensationalist outpourings of the London popular press, convinced MPs of the need for further intervention in Ireland. That same month, parliament passed the Adventurers' Act to raise money for a military campaign using 2,500,000 acres of forfeited Irish land as collateral. Under pressure to crush the rebellion as quickly as possible, Charles agreed to sign the act, which was based on the assumption of the unconditional defeat of the rebels. The king's acquiescence in this matter, therefore, condemned Irish Catholic landowners to economic, political and social ruin in the event of an English victory. Almost unnoticed, one of those charged with organising the relief effort was a relatively obscure MP called Oliver Cromwell. Although lacking any experience in Irish affairs, Cromwell sat on a number of key parliamentary committees dealing with the rebellion throughout 1642, as well as investing £600 of his own money, an enormous sum for a man of modest means, under the terms of the Adventurers'

Act.[16] The growing crisis in England increasingly diverted Cromwell's attention towards domestic matters, but these initial contacts, forged during the highly emotive early months of the insurrection, proved formative, and heavily influenced his subsequent thinking on Irish affairs.

After some initial successes in late 1641, the rebels in Ireland found themselves on the defensive by early 1642. Sir Phelim O'Neill's efforts to capture the town of Drogheda, on the road south to Dublin, failed disastrously, exposing his limitations as a military commander. The irregular rebel forces, poorly armed and lacking rudimentary military training in most cases, suffered a number of reverses on the battlefield. The Lords Justices, buoyed by reinforcements from England and the promise of a major intervention from Scotland, adopted an increasingly aggressive strategy, confident they could crush the insurgents in a matter of months. In a serious escalation of the conflict, they declared that any commander could 'execute to death or otherwise by martial law any pillager, or any rebel or traitor', practically inviting attacks on civilians.[17] The contemporary diarist, Father Turlough O'Mellan, listed a series of atrocities subsequently committed by Lord Moore in the vicinity of Dublin, including the murder of over 140 men, women and children in one particularly gruesome incident.[18] Contrary to early modern conventions, the Lords Justices believed that women should be specifically targeted, 'being manifestly very deep in the guilt of this rebellion, and as we are informed, very forward to stir up their husbands, friends and kindred'.[19] A handful of Protestant refugees fleeing Ulster did indeed accuse individual women of inciting violence, but these depositions provided little more than a veneer of justification for indiscriminate attacks on non-combatants. Similarly, government forces routinely executed captured Catholic clergy, and one officer later observed that 'whatever priests, friars or Jesuits [e]scape the sword, the gallows claims and has them'.[20] Few believed the protestations of the Lords Justices when they insisted indignantly that they did not intend the total extirpation of the Irish nation, 'though some to render us the more odious report so of us'.[21] In the face of this savage onslaught, the rebellion appeared likely to collapse. The deaths of St Leger and

Coote, however, removed two of the most energetic colonial commanders from the field, while diseases such as the Irish 'flux' ravaged those troops sent over from England. The outbreak of civil war between king and parliament in August 1642 after months of growing tension also prevented further supplies of men and equipment reaching Ireland. All these factors combined to halt the government offensive by late summer. This provided Irish Catholics with a temporary breathing space, and an opportunity to organise both militarily and politically.

Caught unawares by the ferocity of the rising, the Catholic elite, both native Irish and Old English, gradually sought to regain the initiative through the creation of the confederate association. They desperately needed to restore law and order, to enable the collection of financial subsidies and those supplies vital for maintaining their military forces. The support of the Catholic Church proved crucial in consolidating the authority of the fledgling confederate regime. The bishops eagerly embraced the concept of aligning religious affiliation with national consciousness, and in May 1642 an Ecclesiastical Congregation declared the war, fought to defend the Catholic religion and the liberties of the kingdom, to be both 'lawful and just'.[22] Over the next six months, throughout rebel-controlled areas, priests administered an oath of association to the civilian population, who pledged their loyalty to Charles I, the kingdom of Ireland and the Roman Catholic Church. The confederate motto, 'Hiberni unanimes pro Deo Rege et Patria', meaning 'Irishmen united for God, king and country', neatly encapsulated this multilayered allegiance. In October, following a number of lengthy meetings, the confederates created elaborate power structures, based in Kilkenny, the heartland of rebel-controlled territory. A legislative General Assembly, similar in function to the Dublin parliament, would debate the big issues of war and peace, while an executive Supreme Council assumed responsibility for the daily functions of government. Provincial and county councils extended confederate authority throughout the localities, while standing provincial armies replaced those irregular levies badly mauled by government forces. In effect, the confederates established a parallel government to the colonial administration in Dublin, raising taxes and maintaining armies, as well as minting coins and sending envoys to foreign courts, activities usually reserved to the crown.

Traditional accounts focus on the existence of two distinct groups within the confederate association, based primarily on ethnic grounds. Internal confederate tensions throughout the 1640s are usually ascribed to the antipathy between the Old English and the native Irish, and like all generalisations this interpretation contains a kernel of truth. Despite recent shared experiences, they had indeed been rivals for centuries, and many on both sides felt uncomfortable with the new alliance. Nonetheless, the confederates made strenuous efforts to preserve ethnic harmony within their ranks, and from the outset the General Assembly ordered that no distinction or comparison be made between 'old Irish, and old and new English, or between septs [clans] or families, or between citizens and townsmen and countrymen, joining in union, upon pain of the highest punishment'.[23] As Catholics they had grouped together for mutual protection, but the confederate leadership actively espoused an inclusive form of national identity, and insisted that in future the king treat all his Irish subjects equally before the law. Place of birth, rather than ancestral blood, now provided the essential criterion for membership of the Irish nation, potentially enabling Protestant newcomers to share a sense of community with their Catholic neighbours. As a confederate delegation explained during subsequent peace talks with the royalists in 1644, 'for he that is born in Ireland, though his parents and all his ancestors were aliens [foreigners], nay if his parents are Indians or Turks, if converted to Christianity, is an Irishman as fully as if his ancestors were born here for thousands of years'.[24] This remarkable statement of inclusiveness, although motivated largely by self-interest, in an effort to preserve and extend the privileges of the Catholic elite, contrasts starkly with the bigoted outpourings of the London news-sheets.

Is it possible, therefore, to describe the confederates as proto-nationalists? Nineteenth-century accounts, in portraying Irish history as a relentless march towards self-determination, oversimplified and thus discredited a complex phenomenon, while modern historians, in rejecting this idealised version of events, deny the possibility of any genuinely nationalist tendencies in Ireland or indeed elsewhere prior to the French Revolution. From the mid-sixteenth century, however, a sense of corporate or national constitutionalism emerged as the preserve of the social elite in a number of European societies, with a series of rights and liberties enshrined in a written constitution or a body of law. Not surprisingly, lawyers played a key role in developing the concept that each nation had a distinct historical or constitutional identity.[25] The increasing use of the Latin word 'patria' (fatherland) at this time also suggests the formation of national communities of interest, and in an Irish context the term quickly became associated with the Counter-Reformation movement. This confessional nationalism originated in the Catholic colonial community of the Pale during the second half of the sixteenth century. Hugh O'Neill, earl of Tyrone, adopted similar rhetoric in his struggle against Tudor expansionism, but the traditional hostility of the Old English towards the Ulster Irish prevented the creation of a broad alliance under his leadership. These ideas did not disappear with O'Neill's defeat but continued to prosper, particularly among those clergy and soldiers who left Ireland for the Continent. Over the next four decades, the shared experience of exile forged a strong sense of common identity, one inextricably linked with the Catholic religion.

In Ireland itself, the political crisis of 1640–1 saw Catholic and Protestant MPs working together at the Dublin parliament, jealously defending their constitutional privileges and opposing the earl of Strafford's authoritarian rule, until the outbreak of the Ulster rebellion once again split the country along crude religious lines. The national constitutionalism of the Catholic elite, combined with the widespread resentment of the discriminatory religious policies of the state, produced a shared sense of patriotism between those living in Ireland and the exiles on the Continent. Richard Bellings, secretary of the confederate Supreme Council throughout the 1640s, described how those attending the historic meeting on the Hill of Crofty in December 1641 greeted with wild applause the statement that the native inhabitants of Ulster and the Catholic colonial community of the Pale belonged to 'the same religion and the same nation'.[26] Even among the lower social orders evidence exists of the emergence of a distinctive national identity. The French traveller, François le Gouz, wrote in 1644 how the people he met on his journey throughout the kingdom invariably described themselves as *Éireannach*, meaning Irish.[27] Local and especially provincial sentiment continued to exercise an important influence, but even here traditional barriers began to break down. General Owen Roe O'Neill, for example, who commanded the provincial army of Ulster, reminded those troops who followed him back from the Continent that 'they were no mercenary soldiers but natives of the kingdom'. Another returnee, General Thomas Preston, commander of the provincial army of Leinster, appealed to a Catholic nobleman from the province of Connacht, as 'an Irishman', to join the confederate ranks.[28] The leadership in Kilkenny saw no contradiction between their national identity and loyalty to the Stuart monarchy. Reluctant rebels at the best of times, continuing hostilities between king and parliament in England enabled them to seek common ground with Charles I. From the outset, they favoured a negotiated settlement with the royalists, offering military assistance against Westminster in return for significant political and religious concessions.

Initially, the administration in Dublin, staffed for the most part by English parliamentary sympathisers, rejected all peace overtures from Kilkenny. Unable to sustain a military offensive against the Catholic rebels, the Lords Justices instead consolidated control of enclaves around Dublin in the east, Cork in the south and Derry in the north, launching occasional raids in support of isolated outposts. In February 1643, Captain William Tucker described in glowing terms one such foray by Sir Richard Grenville, 'killing and destroying by fire and sword all that came in his way'.[29] Before long, however, startling news reached Dublin of the king's willingness to receive peace proposals from the confederates in the hope of obtaining supplies and manpower for use against the English parliament. The Lords Justices argued against any peace 'before the sword or famine should have so abated them [the Catholic Irish] in numbers as that in reasonable time English colonies might overlap them'.[30] Despite

Map 2 Confederate Wars, 1641–9

these protestations, talks began shortly afterwards, while the commander of the colonial forces, the staunchly royalist James Butler, earl (and subsequently marquis) of Ormond, gradually tempered the military conduct of his troops. As a result, Ormond's parliamentary opponents suspected him, quite without justification, of secretly sympathising with the confederates. One critic later accused the earl of 'a slack and unfaithful prosecution of the war', and reported incredulously how he refused to retaliate for an alleged breach of quarter by the Catholic Irish.[31] With the support of Charles I, Ormond gradually seized control of Dublin for the royalist cause, removing the Lords Justices and their supporters from office, and establishing tentative lines of communication with Kilkenny. The king's need for reinforcements from Ireland clearly helped moderate his attitude towards the Catholic confederates and curbed the worst excesses of individual royalist commanders.

In addition to these important political developments, the impact of Continental veterans helped change the nature of the war in Ireland. With the outbreak of hostilities in the three Stuart kingdoms, thousands of Irish and Scottish veterans returned from the Continent to fight at home. After prolonged exposure to the horrors of unrestrained warfare, they appreciated the advantages of military discipline, which had become increasingly evident in the latter stages of the Thirty Years War. The sacking of Magdeburg had typified for many the brutality of that conflict. According to a member of the town council, in the space of just a few hours 'many thousand innocent men, women and children were abominably murdered or wretchedly executed in all kinds of ways', although the fires that killed as many as 10,000 of the inhabitants may not have been started deliberately.[32] Whatever the truth of the matter, the vast number of civilian deaths horrified contemporaries, and increasingly military commanders saw the need to moderate the behaviour of their troops both on and off the battlefield. The most famous Irish Continental veteran, Owen Roe O'Neill, was shocked on his return to Ulster to witness on both sides a degree of cruelty he considered inexcusable among Christian peoples. He complained bitterly about the lack of obedience among the soldiers of his new command, 'if one can call men soldiers who behave nothing better than animals'.[33] O'Neill immediately set about enforcing his authority, and within a short time, according to an officer in the opposing Scottish covenanting army, he 'reduced many of the natives to a more civil deportment and to a pretty good understanding of military discipline'.[34]

Among the Scots in Ulster, led by Major General Robert Monro, a veteran of the Danish and Swedish armies and author of a work on the art of warfare, a reciprocal professionalism slowly began to emerge.[35] On first arriving in Ireland in April 1642, the covenanter forces under his command embarked on an orgy of revenge for the killing of Protestant planters, while a number of Campbell regiments persecuted local MacDonnells, traditional clan rivals from Scotland who had settled in northeast Ulster during the sixteenth century. Following the capture of Newry, the covenanters summarily executed sixty townsmen, and drowned a number of women in a nearby river. Raiding parties in the surrounding countryside massacred men, women and children indiscriminately, and put to death captured Irish troops, although at least one of Monro's officers conveniently, though probably with some justification, blamed local Irish Protestants for the worst of the excesses.[36] As their initial ardour began to cool, those Scots with experience of Continental warfare began to re-appraise the situation. The murder of civilians and prisoners had simply enraged their enemies, and with no immediate end to the war in sight, the possibility arose that covenanting troops might well fall into confederate hands at some stage. Sir James Turner, who had served in Germany, witnessed the execution of some Irish prisoners after a skirmish in 1642, and wrote that for the Scots 'revenge overmastered their discretion, which should have taught them to save the lives of those they took, that the rebels might do the like to their prisoners'. The realities of the conflict in Ulster gradually tempered the conduct of the covenanting forces, and by late 1642/early 1643, Turner recorded how the covenanters either released Irish prisoners, or 'made them work at our fortifications'.[37]

This principle of reciprocity (as outlined by Turner) increasingly formed the basis of the 'rules' of war in Ireland. From late 1642, the increased professionalism of the various armies, along with the threat of retaliation, acted as a moderating influence, as all sides acknowledged that the introduction of some general rules of engagement would be of mutual benefit. The conflict continued to rage across the four provinces, with frequent raids and skirmishes, as well as sieges and the occasional set-piece battle. Yet, at least until

1647, no major massacres took place, terms of surrender were honoured, and prisoners exchanged on a regular basis. The publication of strict codes of conduct also signalled efforts to regulate the behaviour of troops during large-scale military campaigns. This is not to suggest that atrocities did not take place, even though the majority of commanders tried for the most part to act honourably towards their enemies. Unfortunately, the demand for victory did not always allow for overly courteous behaviour on the battlefield. As the seventeenth-century diarist John Evelyn commented sadly, 'it is impossible to avoid doing very unhandsome things in war'.[38] The reality in Ireland during much of the 1640s, however, was far removed from the indiscriminate butchery of the early months of the conflict, as conventional armies on all sides operated largely according to accepted military standards.

Increasing moderation on the battlefield gradually created the space for political dialogue, and in September 1643 the confederates and royalists finally agreed a truce, which enabled Ormond to ship thousands of troops back to assist the king in England. For the next three years, both sides engaged in tortuous peace negotiations, seeking a settlement that would allow them to unite their forces against the English parliament and the Scottish covenanters, who had signed their own treaty of alliance, the Solemn League and Covenant, also in September 1643. Confederate politics during this period was not divided along ethnic grounds but rather over the terms of a settlement with the king. Two main power blocs dominated the political landscape at Kilkenny, namely the peace and clerical factions. The peace faction, which consisted primarily of existing landowners, favoured a limited settlement that would guarantee religious toleration, allowing Catholics to worship in private without hindrance, while preserving their estates and granting them access to public office. This conservative elite provided an element of continuity in Irish political life, and a significant number had sat in the Dublin parliament of 1640–1. The leadership included both native Irish and Old English, men such as Richard Butler, Viscount Mountgarret, chairman of the Supreme Council, Richard Bellings, secretary of the Supreme Council, and

Donough MacCarthy, Viscount Muskerry, influential Munster politician and another member of the Supreme Council. The close relationship of many in this group with the marquis of Ormond, primarily through marriage, led confederate rivals to refer to them contemptuously as 'Ormondists', a term subsequently adopted by historians. The label is misleading, as the dominant position of the Butler family in Irish politics for over a century had created a network of connections that few of the elite could possibly avoid. Motivated mainly by the desire to preserve their personal estates and social status, Mountgarret, Muskerry and their allies controlled proceedings in Kilkenny through the Supreme Council, at least until 1646.

On the opposite political wing, the clerical faction emerged as an increasingly vocal opposition in Kilkenny after 1644, particularly when peace talks with the royalists looked like reaching a conclusion. Convinced, with some justification, that the confederate leadership would not insist on major religious or political concessions, this group favoured a more radical settlement. They argued, not illogically, that only the full restoration of the Roman Catholic Church, recognised by the state, could guarantee permanent religious security. They viewed with suspicion, if not outright hostility, the more moderate impulses of the Kilkenny leadership, which threatened to dilute the specifically Catholic elements of the confederate association. The clerics received crucial support from returning exiles such as General Owen Roe O'Neill. Living for decades in Spanish territories, men like O'Neill never had to compromise on religious matters in the same manner as those who remained in Ireland. The returnees, the majority of whom came from a native Irish background, also demanded a more comprehensive land settlement, in the hope of recovering confiscated estates. The internal tensions within the confederate association increased dramatically with the arrival of a papal nuncio, Giovanni Battista Rinuccini, in late 1645. Appointed by Pope Innocent X to uphold the dignity of the Catholic Church in Ireland, he reacted in horror to the fact that Protestant services continued to be held in confederate towns and cities throughout the 1640s. He did everything in his power to stop the practice, and not surprisingly, refused to countenance any treaty with the royalists that did not contain significant religious concessions.

The demands of the clergy created enormous difficulties for the king, anxious to exploit the financial resources and manpower of Ireland, yet acutely conscious of the deep hostility felt by his English subjects towards the Catholic Irish. His royalist supporters in Ireland, including the marquis of Ormond, appointed as lord lieutenant in early 1644, felt equally compromised. After the initial shock of the insurrection, Irish Protestants eagerly joined the forces mobilised by the colonial administration and advocated a purely military solution to the crisis. This made their loyalty to the king highly conditional. Many of them deeply resented Ormond's truce with the confederates in 1643, and the following year local Protestants in Munster declared their resolve to 'die a thousand deaths rather than to condescend to any peace with those perfidious rebels'.[39] When the confederates sent a delegation to the royal court at Oxford to begin formal peace negotiations in early 1644, representatives from the rump parliament still sitting in Dublin also travelled to put the Protestant case. They demanded 'the establishment of the true Protestant religion in Ireland', the strict imposition of penal laws against Catholics, and an extension of the policy of plantation throughout the kingdom. After a short period of consultation, the king's advisers rejected these terms as too extreme.[40]

Charles I urgently required a settlement with the confederates before organised Protestant opposition completely undermined his Irish strategy. Typically, rather than take any tough decisions himself during the Oxford talks, the king instructed Ormond to negotiate with the Kilkenny regime on his behalf. Unfortunately for Charles, the marquis, fearful that any possible deal would result in Irish Protestant royalists switching their allegiance to the English parliament, proved unequal to the task. The extent of the problems faced by Ormond became clear when, in July 1644, the royalist commander in Cork, Lord Inchiquin, declared for parliament in protest at the continuing peace talks with the confederates. Similarly in Ulster, army officers loyal to the king watched helplessly as their subordinates eagerly embraced the Solemn League and Covenant.

With his authority now restricted to Dublin and its environs, Ormond diverted his energies to negotiations with Kilkenny. Despite holding few cards, he remained determined not to concede on key religious issues such as the redistribution of church property and revenue, urging the confederate peace faction to agree terms and ignore the protestations of the clergy. Ormond's intransigence failed to produce any significant military aid for the king in England, undermined the peace faction within the confederate association, and ultimately enabled the English parliament to re-enter the Irish war.

Frustrated for the moment in their Irish ambitions, parliamentarians targeted instead Irish troops fighting for the king in England. Traditional racial and religious hostility, reinforced by graphic propaganda about the massacre of Protestant settlers in 1641, legitimised for many the violent treatment of Catholic Irish prisoners. One pamphleteer in the early stages of the war provided helpful advice for distinguishing the Irish from the Scots by making them 'pronounce any word which has the letter H in it, as Smith, Faith etc., which they cannot do', or to say their prayers in English. Failing that, the inquisitor merely had to uncover the bosoms of the accused, as all Irish Catholics, 'especially the women', apparently wore crucifixes.[41] Following the truce between the confederates and the royalists in September 1643, Ormond had transferred as many as 8,000 soldiers back to England.[42] No confederate troops accompanied this force, which consisted primarily of Englishmen returning home along with some Irish Protestants. Parliamentary propaganda, however, exploited widespread fears in England of a Catholic Irish invasion, and individual commanders dealt harshly with any captured soldiers. In July 1644, for example, a parliamentary squadron intercepted a royalist troop ship coming from Ireland. The commander, Captain Richard Swanley, threw fifty men overboard, 'to swim to their own country'.[43] In October, Westminster issued an ordinance of no quarter for any Irish Catholics 'taken in hostility against the Parliament'. MPs instructed military commanders to specifically exclude the Irish from surrender agreements, and 'forthwith put every such person to death'. Anybody who refused to implement these orders would be 'reputed a favourer of that bloody rebellion of Ireland' and be liable to punishment.[44] Significantly, the ordinance applied to the war in England, Wales and on the High Seas, but not in Ireland. Surrounded by confederate Catholic forces, Lord Inchiquin, commander of the newly declared parliamentary enclave in Cork, realised that any attempt to apply the 'no quarter' ordinance risked provoking immediate retaliation from his enemies.

The Irish in England, however, enjoyed little protection, despite the best efforts of some individual officers. In February 1645 Colonel Thomas Mytton captured the royalist town of Shrewsbury and hanged a number of Irish soldiers, according to Parliament's instructions. In retaliation, the king's German-born nephew, Prince Rupert, executed the same number of parliamentarian prisoners and threatened a similar response in future cases. Outraged, the House of Commons ordered the earl of Essex to explain to Rupert the difference between Catholic Irishmen and Protestant Englishmen. Essex wrote to Rupert expressing dismay at the prince's actions, claiming that the Irish had already killed thousands of 'harmless British Protestants, men, women and children', and been declared traitors by the king. Moreover, he continued, in Ireland 'they neither did give nor receive quarter'. In light of all this, parliament could not consent to the Catholic Irish being 'made equal in exchange with the English nation, and Protestants'. Rupert, the consummate professional soldier, dismissed Essex's arguments out of hand. He described the Irishmen executed at Shrewsbury as 'His Majesty's good subjects taken prisoner in the act of their duty'. They had served the king faithfully in Ireland and therefore the circumstances of the 1641 rebellion did not apply in their case. Rupert condemned the killing of prisoners after granting them quarter as 'a proceeding contrary to the laws of nature and nations, contrary to the rules and customs of war in any part of the Christian world'. He concluded that any further incidents of this nature would elicit a similar response from him.[45] Rupert never carried out his threat, departing for the Continent shortly afterwards, and executions of the Irish by the parliamentarians continued unchecked. Throughout the 1640s, a significant proportion of the documented massacres in the English Civil War have an Irish connection, either directly or indirectly. The execution of seventy-five Irish prisoners at Conway Castle, for example, is a pretty straightforward case, while the royalist camp followers at the battle of Naseby in 1645, exclusively Welsh women and children, appear to have been butchered in the mistaken belief that they were Irish.[46]

By 1644 the Scottish covenanting regime had entered the war in England on the side of parliament, sending an army of 20,000 men south of the border. The covenanters displayed a similar antipathy towards native Irish Catholics, though their failure in many cases to distinguish between Irish and Scottish Gaels further complicated matters. A confederate/royalist expeditionary force, comprising Irish and Highland Scots, conducted a lightning campaign across Scotland in 1644–5, winning a series of stunning victories against the covenanters. The MacDonald/MacDonnell element in this army, led by Alasdair MacColla, seized the opportunity to settle old scores with their clan rivals, the Campbells, while further east, city residents blamed the Irish contingent for the worst excesses during the sack of Aberdeen. The covenanters finally defeated this small force, in MacColla's absence, at Philiphaugh in September 1645, and massacred around one hundred Irish soldiers, despite a promise to spare their lives. Even though they fought on the same side, the royalist Patrick Gordon of Ruthven did not hold this Irish contingent in high regard, describing how they allegedly butchered men 'with the same careless neglect that they kill a hen or capone for their supper'. Nonetheless, he condemned the slaughter of the Irish camp followers at Philiphaugh, 'cut in pieces with such savage and inhumane cruelty, as neither Turk not Scithean was ever heard to have done the like'.[47] According to local tradition, those killings were in revenge for the massacre of Protestant settlers by the native Irish, at Portadown Bridge in County Armagh, at the beginning of the rebellion, though in reality, the covenanters felt little need to justify their harsh treatment of the Catholic Irish.[48] In December, the Scottish parliament ordered that Irish prisoners be 'executed without any further assise or process', as granting them quarter was contrary to the covenant and therefore a sin.[49] Throughout 1646, the covenanters ruthlessly hunted down and massacred the remnants of this expeditionary force, as well as those Highland Scots, particularly among the MacDonalds and their allies, suspected of royalist sympathies.

Defeated in Scotland, the royalist cause suffered similar misfortune in England, when in June 1645 a parliamentary army commanded by Sir Thomas Fairfax and Oliver Cromwell crushed the king's forces at Naseby in the final decisive battle of the first English civil war. In just three years since the outbreak of the conflict, Cromwell had risen rapidly through the ranks of the parliamentary army. He proved a highly innovative and effective cavalry officer, prepared to share all the dangers of war with his troops, who worshipped him as a result. Cromwell's cavalry units played a major role in the crushing victory over the royalists at Marston Moor in July 1644, re-entering the battle after the initial charge to help turn the tide in favour of parliament. The battle of Naseby, less than twelve months later, witnessed the first major triumph of the New Model Army, created by Fairfax and Cromwell the previous winter. Frustrated by the limitations of the parliamentary forces in the early years of the civil war, both men wanted an army unrestricted by local ties, staffed by highly disciplined, well-trained, and suitably God-fearing men. The New Model Army gradually developed into one the most formidable and effective fighting machines in English history, emerging victorious in the English Civil Wars and leading the subsequent invasions of both Ireland and Scotland. The phenomenal success of this army was due in no small part to the inspirational leadership provided by Oliver Cromwell, whose assiduous attention to detail in matters of supply and pay proved equally important as any battlefield innovations.

Unable to assemble another field army after Naseby, Charles I surrendered to the Scottish covenanting army at Newark in Nottinghamshire in May 1646, effectively bringing the war in England to an end. The king spent the next two years negotiating a possible settlement with parliament, while at the same time attempting to form a new royalist alliance, incorporating supporters in England, Scotland and Ireland. Relations between the Scots and the English parliament gradually soured, owing primarily to the latter's reluctance to implement a Presbyterian religious settlement as originally envisaged in 1643 under the terms of the Solemn League and Covenant. The Scots eventually handed the king over to their English allies in early 1647 and withdrew their army north of the border in return for a cash payment. In Ireland, however, the war continued unabated, with confederates, royalists, parliamentarians and covenanters engaged in a complex series of interlocking conflicts. In late July 1646, after three years of talks, the marquis of Ormond, on behalf of the king, finally proclaimed a peace with the Catholic confederates. Although too late to intervene in the English Civil War, Ormond still hoped to force concessions from parliament by threatening a royalist/confederate invasion from Ireland. The peace treaty granted many of the political and economic concessions sought by the confederates, including guarantees for their estates, but fudged the controversial issue of religion, postponing any decisions until the king regained his liberty. This compromise satisfied the conservative landowning leadership in Kilkenny, but outraged the Catholic clergy, led by Rinuccini. The nuncio condemned the treaty as contrary to the confederate oath of association, and excommunicated all those who favoured peace with the royalists. With the support of General Owen Roe O'Neill, fresh from his overwhelming victory over the covenanters at Benburb, County Tyrone, in June 1646, Rinuccini staged a coup d'état and seized power in Kilkenny. He ordered O'Neill, along with General Thomas Preston, to march against Ormond in Dublin, but the potentially decisive offensive failed because of confederate infighting and the onset of winter.

The setback before Dublin weakened the authority of the nuncio and his faction, allowing a group of moderates, led by Nicholas Plunkett, to dictate confederate policy. A trained lawyer and major landowner from one of the most important Old English families of the Pale, Plunkett initially attempted to steer a middle course at the outbreak of the rebellion and only committed himself to the confederate association in October 1642. Plunkett's popularity can be gauged from the fact that despite his initial reluctance to take sides, the first general assembly elected him as chairman, a position he held for the remainder of the 1640s. Plunkett also sat continuously on the supreme council between 1642 and 1649, and played a key role in peace negotiations with Ormond. Few, if any, confederates matched his record of active involvement and political influence during this period. Plunkett's enduring ability to appeal to all sides enabled him to exploit dissatisfaction with the excesses of the two principal factions, and move the confederate association towards the political middle ground. In August 1646, sent by the ruling junta in Kilkenny as an envoy to assuage clerical opposition to the Ormond treaty, he dramatically switched sides in a move that facilitated the nuncio's seizure of power. He soon developed his own agenda, ably assisted by Nicholas French, the bishop of Ferns. Initially an enthusiastic member of the clerical faction, French adopted a hard line against Protestants in his hometown of Wexford during the early years of the war. The failure of the Dublin offensive convinced the bishop to adopt a more pragmatic approach. The moderates advocated a new deal with the royalists, albeit with significantly enhanced conditions, particularly on matters of religion, but Ormond proved intractable. The marquis felt betrayed by the confederate rejection of the peace treaty, while the assault on Dublin convinced him of the futility of the king's cause in Ireland, despite the growing prominence of the moderates at Kilkenny.

With Ormond isolated in Dublin, and the Scottish covenanters seriously weakened following their disastrous defeat at Benburb, the English parliament sensed an opportunity to seize the military initiative in Ireland. The end of the war in England allowed them to consider diverting resources to Ireland for the first time since early 1642. In February 1647, a parliamentary expedition landed in Munster, ostensibly to support the local Protestant commander, Lord Inchiquin. Tensions between Inchiquin and the expedition's leader, Philip Sidney, Lord Lisle, undermined the mission, which achieved nothing of consequence, apart from providing some desperately needed military supplies to local Protestant forces. A second foray into Ireland that summer proved far more successful, when in June commissioners from Westminster convinced Ormond to surrender the city of Dublin to the English parliament. Ormond's actions directly contravened orders from Queen Henrietta Maria at the exiled royal court in France, who favoured an accommodation with the confederates as the basis for a renewed alliance against parliament. Ormond, failing to recognise the significance of the shift of power in Kilkenny, refused to hand Dublin over to 'the tyranny of those that then ruled amongst the Irish'.[50] In a conspicuous display of his own prejudices, the marquis preferred English Protestants of whatever political persuasion to Irish Catholics, a decision that subsequently proved disastrous for both royalists and confederates. Ormond left for England shortly afterwards, where he visited the king, imprisoned by parliament at Hampton Court, before joining the other royalist exiles on the Continent.

The new parliamentary governor of Dublin, Colonel Michael Jones, brother of Bishop Henry Jones, commanded an army comprising local Protestants and troops recently arrived from England. On 8 August 1647, he defeated a confederate force at Dungan's Hill near Dublin, and the largest single massacre of the entire war ensued, with somewhere between three and five thousand killed. A battlefield rout often resulted in the slaughter of the fleeing enemy, but at Dungan's Hill the surrounded confederates retreated into a bog before surrendering. The diarist, Turlough O'Mellan, who saw the rotting bodies when passing through the battlefield area with Owen Roe O'Neill's army shortly afterwards, describes the killing of the rank and file soldiers 'agus iad ceangailte, iar ceathramha [do ghealladh] dóibh' (manacled after quarter had been granted to them).[51] Not surprisingly, English sources make no mention of granting terms to the confederate troops, and the official parliamentary report of the battle, approved by Jones and published by order of the House of Commons, insisted that only those 'not admitted to quarter' were executed.[52] According to Sir Thomas Fairfax, if troops surrendered upon mercy rather than quarter, the victorious commander was 'free to put some immediately to the sword, if he s[aw] cause'.[53] An anonymous pamphlet, however, published during the Restoration, insisted that the parliamentarians had killed many wounded officers the day after the battle.[54] At Dungan's Hill, therefore, Jones apparently ignored accepted military conventions, and acted instead according to the harsh dictates of

Westminster. Similarly in Munster, the rabidly anti-Catholic Lord Inchiquin, reinforced with fresh supplies of arms and men from Lisle's abortive expedition, launched a bloody offensive deep into confederate territory. He massacred the handful of surviving defenders at the siege of Cashel in September, and executed the Scottish Highland/Irish contingent after the battle of Knocknanuss two months later, including their feared commander, Alasdair MacColla.

Practical considerations may well have sealed the fate of the confederate troops at Dungan's Hill. The resounding nature of the parliamentary victory resulted in far too many prisoners to guard, feed or ransom. Moreover, unlike the war in England between king and parliament, religious and racial antipathies prevented any recruitment from among the defeated forces.[55] Similar considerations applied throughout much of the 1640s, and yet massacres only began to occur in the summer of 1647. Bolstered by reinforcements and confident of total victory, both Jones and Inchiquin displayed the arrogance and self-assurance born of recent parliamentary successes in England. They unleashed a brief period of unrestrained warfare, which presaged in many ways the brutal tactics adopted by Cromwell and his commanders in the Irish wars two years later. When dealing with the Catholic Irish, on the battlefield at least, parliamentary commanders, both Irish and English, did not feel in any way constrained by rules of war, particularly when they enjoyed the upper hand. As Sir John Byron, an English royalist and Continental veteran, commented bitterly, the parliamentarians 'when they have an advantage, think it a dishonour to use those civilities practised by soldiers in foreign parts'.[56]

Nonetheless, despite the increased intensity of the fighting from 1647, the surviving evidence indicates that neither Jones nor Inchiquin deliberately targeted civilians in their campaigns against the confederates. With supplies from England still unreliable, they required a cooperative local population to provide basic provisions. All sides in the conflict pillaged enemy quarters, but the parliamentarians proved no more thorough or brutal than their confederate opponents in this regard. In fact, within days of his arrival in Dublin in June 1647, Jones issued a series of ordinances to regulate the conduct of his army, which were read to the troops each week, 'that none may be ignorant of the laws and duties required'. The vast majority of the rules dealt with discipline within the army itself, but a number related to the civilian population. The death penalty applied to certain crimes, such as murder, rape and theft, along with unlicensed destruction of goods and property, 'be it of friend or foe'.[57] The outbreak of the second English Civil War in 1648 prevented further military supplies reaching Ireland that year, and stalled the parliamentary offensive, but the respite for the Catholic Irish proved temporary.

In England, the king, although in close confinement, had managed to create a new royalist alliance. His Scottish supporters, known as 'Engagers', mobilised a large army and invaded England, where local royalists staged a series of small uprisings. In August, the New Model Army, commanded by Cromwell, inflicted a crushing defeat on the 'Engagers' at Preston, while north of the border a regime more sympathetic towards the English parliament seized control in Edinburgh. In addition to enhancing Cromwell's formidable reputation as a military commander, the second civil war also radicalised political opinion in England, with many in parliamentary and army circles insisting that Charles I, that 'man of blood', pay for his crimes. A final attempt at a negotiated settlement failed, and following a purge of moderate MPs by the army in early December, parliament took the momentous decision to put the king on trial. Throughout the three Stuart kingdoms the military and political situation remained extremely fluid and unpredictable. In April 1648, Lord Inchiquin declared for the king and agreed a controversial truce with Kilkenny, while the return of Ormond to Ireland in September raised the possibility of a renewed formal alliance between the royalists and confederates. Rinuccini, supported by Owen Roe O'Neill, opposed these moves, plunging the confederate association into open civil war. Starved of supplies, Jones could do little to take advantage of the situation, and instead waited anxiously for the outcome of the king's trial. A triumphant parliament, shorn of all moderate members, and without the restraining influence of the king, was likely to commit significant resources to the 'pacification' of the Catholic Irish. Moreover, opinion in England made no distinction between active rebels and those living peacefully at home, as the time to avenge the massacre of Protestant settlers in 1641, and reassert English dominance in Ireland, moved ever closer to hand.

3

Prelude to Invasion

The proverb's true, though very stale/Those that will England win
Must if they mean to conquer it all/ With Ireland first begin.[1]
MERCURIUS ELENCTICUS (1649)

On Wednesday, 17 January 1649, at a lavish ceremony in Kilkenny
Castle, the Catholic confederates signed a peace deal with the lord
lieutenant, James Butler, marquis of Ormond. In an emotional speech,
Richard Blake, chairman of the confederate General Assembly,
anticipated that the agreement would 'restore this nation in its former
lustre'. Ormond responded generously, with a promise of further
concessions from the king. In an uncharacteristically emotional
outburst, the marquis concluded dramatically: 'There are no bounds
to your hopes.'[2] The mutually congratulatory nature of the
proceedings belied the six years of torturous and often rancorous
negotiations that preceded the agreement, but with King Charles I
now on trial for his life, Ormond and the Catholic Irish finally agreed
terms. Although too late to intervene on behalf of the beleaguered
monarch, by a stroke of a pen the marquis assumed control of most of
the kingdom of Ireland at the head of a powerful royalist/confederate
alliance. Following the execution of Charles I at the end of the month,
Ormond quickly declared the dead monarch's son, Charles Stuart,
Prince of Wales, king not only of Ireland, but of England and Scotland
as well, a move reciprocated by the Scottish covenanters in Edinburgh.
Whereas the new parliamentary regime in London was prepared to
tolerate a hostile Protestant regime to the north, as long as the
covenanters remained militarily inactive, they did not respond to
developments in Ireland, seen by many as a dependent kingdom of
England, in a similarly detached fashion. In addition to the strategic

threat posed by the royalists in Ireland, the parliamentarians were also motivated by a traditional hatred of the Catholic Irish and a desire to avenge the massacre of Protestant settlers in 1641–2. As a result, they immediately began to prepare for an invasion.

In early 1649, the political and military landscape of the Irish kingdom remained difficult to interpret. Ormond commanded an uneasy coalition, consisting primarily of Irish Catholics and Protestants, who had spent much of the previous decade on opposing sides in a bitter and bloody conflict. In addition, hundreds of English cavaliers flocked to Ormond's banner, in the hope not only of restoring the Stuart dynasty through force of arms, but also of obtaining lucrative appointments. Their arrival in Ireland, and rapid advancement through the military ranks, often at the expense of native candidates, added yet another combustible element to an already volatile mix. The poet John Milton, in a typical rhetorical flourish, described the new allies as 'a mixed rabble, part Papists, part fugitives, and part savages'.[3] Temporarily united against the regicidal parliamentary regime, they nonetheless viewed each other with suspicion, or in some cases outright hatred and contempt. The southern ports of Munster, such as Youghal, Cork and Kinsale, contained a significant concentration of Protestant settlers. Their commander, Lord Inchiquin, sided with the English parliament for much of the 1640s, but he had switched allegiance to the king in April 1648, in protest at the increasingly radical demands of his former colleagues. The following month he concluded a cessation with the confederates, alienating many of his Irish Protestant supporters in the process, whose principal goal remained the complete destruction of Catholic military, political and economic power. Inchiquin removed potential troublemakers from positions of influence and, through sheer force of personality, managed to retain the loyalty of the majority of Munster Protestants. Nonetheless, they remained deeply suspicious of any contacts with their Catholic neighbours, and when Ormond returned to Ireland as lord lieutenant in September 1648, he sought to reassure his co-religionists about the forthcoming negotiations with Kilkenny. On receiving reports from Inchiquin of unrest among the troops under his command, the marquis travelled to Cork and addressed the Protestant garrison directly. The lord lieutenant declared his determination to defend the Protestant religion in Ireland, but neglected to explain how exactly this would be achieved in a peace treaty with Catholic confederates. Outrage over the fate of the king temporarily quelled disquiet in the ranks, but it would not take much for trouble to flare once again.The loyalty of the Protestant settlers in Ulster appeared to be equally ambiguous. In late 1648, following the defeat of the Scottish 'Engagers' by Cromwell at Preston, the parliamentary commander Colonel George Monck had seized all garrisons in East Ulster held by the covenanters, including Belfast and Carrickfergus. Around the same time, in the western part of the province, the Protestant planter Charles Coote, whose father had been killed in action in 1642, arrested army officers suspected of royalist sympathies and replaced them with committed parliamentarians. Many Protestants, bewildered by the constantly changing political landscape, simply returned home to defend their families. News of the trial and execution of the king deeply shocked the settler community, and the vast majority instinctively rallied to the royalist cause. On 15 February, the Belfast Presbytery, following the lead of the covenanting regime in Edinburgh, condemned the actions of the English parliament. Even though there was little support in Ulster for Ormond's peace treaty with the confederates, the parliamentary position there quickly collapsed during the first half of 1649. Forces loyal to the king, and nominally at least to Ormond as well, took possession of garrisons across the province. They forced Monck to retreat to the small port of Dundalk, less than 50 miles north of Dublin, and from late March besieged Charles Coote in the fortified town of Derry. Without major reinforcements, neither enclave could expect to survive through the summer.

The final major concentration of Protestants in Ireland centred on Dublin and the neighbouring town of Drogheda. Colonel Michael Jones, the parliamentary commander at Dublin since Ormond surrendered the city to him in June 1647, initially took the offensive against the confederates, culminating in his major victory at the battle of Dungan's Hill in August 1647. Starved of supplies from England, however, the area under his control gradually constricted, forcing him to adopt an increasingly defensive strategy. Although not immediately under threat in early 1649, Dublin and its environs remained vulnerable to a determined assault by the resurgent royalist forces. Apart from parliamentary soldiers, the Protestant population in this enclave contained a large number of refugees from Ulster, driven out of their homes during the early stages of the rebellion in late 1641–2. Anxious to avenge family and friends, as well as recover their property, they opposed any compromise with Irish Catholics. Nonetheless, the trial and execution of Charles I prompted a significant number of desertions to the royalist side throughout 1649. For the moment, the parliamentary commander managed to hold the line, but as with Coote and Monck to the north, he desperately needed reinforcements from England.

Many Catholics viewed the new arrangements in Kilkenny with distaste and unease. The truce with Lord Inchiquin in May 1648 had split the confederate association and provoked a full-blown civil war. The papal nuncio, Rinuccini, led the opposition to an alliance with Protestant royalists, excommunicating those who advocated a renewed peace treaty, with the backing of Owen Roe O'Neill. The clerical faction fared badly in the civil war, but still refused to be party to the Kilkenny treaty, due to the absence of sufficient guarantees for the Catholic religion. Not long after the signing ceremony, however, Ormond received some welcome news from his old ally, Richard Bellings, former secretary to the confederate Supreme Council. Bellings reported from Galway, a perceived stronghold of the papal nuncio, how the city celebrated news of the settlement in Kilkenny 'with extra-ordinary magnificence', including the shooting of artillery, the ringing of bells and 'great, great drinking'.[4] Although the nuncio ordered the church bells to be silenced, he nonetheless started to make preparations to leave the country and return to Rome. His impending departure removed the main obstacle to reconciliation between Owen Roe O'Neill and Ormond, who before the end of the month initiated negotiations, to encourage, according to one acerbic observer, 'the bringing of our

Tartars into obedience'.[5] Not everybody in the royalist/confederate alliance welcomed these developments. Former confederates criticised the depredations allegedly committed by the Ulster forces and the large civilian hordes attached to them. Bishop Nicholas French warned that O'Neill's troops, in poor condition and hungry, would 'destroy and starve all the people in their way', and even though Ormond admired their martial abilities, he too compared them to 'devouring caterpillars'.[6] The subsequent talks stalled over the proposed size of O'Neill's army in the reorganised royalist forces, which his opponents in Kilkenny wanted to restrict as much as possible. Residual bitterness over the Inchiquin truce and its aftermath undoubtedly made any reconciliation difficult, but O'Neill controlled the most formidable army in Ireland, and obtaining his support should have been Ormond's priority. Instead, he allowed the prejudices of his confederate allies to undermine the negotiations, and in the process lost whatever slim opportunity existed for gaining complete control of the island before the arrival of the expected invasion force from England.

Beset with difficulties on all sides, Ormond focused his energies on consolidating his authority within the new royalist/confederate alliance. This involved a major restructuring of the military, civil and judicial authorities. According to the terms of the peace settlement he would hold a parliament in Ireland within six months, or call a general assembly if that proved impossible, and remove all impediments to Catholics voting in elections. The confederates urgently required legal confirmation of the treaty, to counter Westminster's claims of jurisdiction over Ireland, and the threat of a large-scale confiscation of Catholic lands by the terms of the 1642 Adventurers Act. A legally constituted Irish parliament, particularly one dominated by Catholics, would be in a position to block any such predatory moves. In the meantime, the peace treaty established a simplified structure of government compared to the elaborate, multilayered model favoured by the confederates. In place of the supreme council, general assembly, provincial and county councils, Ormond now governed the entire kingdom, apart from the cities of Dublin and Derry, with the assistance of twelve commissioners of treaty chosen by the confederates, three from each province. Based for the moment in the city of Kilkenny, the old confederate capital and ancestral home of the marquis, the commission, an exclusively Catholic body, included leading political figures such as Nicholas Plunkett and Donough MacCarthy, Viscount Muskerry.[7] The commissioners also consulted with Bishop Nicholas French and Thomas Fleming, archbishop of Dublin, although in an effort to placate the concerns of Protestant royalists, neither cleric used his ecclesiastical title in any official documentation.

Despite this careful political balancing act, the appearance of genuine representation was illusory. The Ulster commissioners belonged to the small clique of Catholic landowners in that province opposed to Owen Roe O'Neill and his supporters. They enjoyed little influence, either political or military, outside of Kilkenny. With the notable exception of Nicholas Plunkett and the two clerics, all the commissioners of treaty belonged to the peace party, which had strongly supported a settlement with Ormond throughout the 1640s. Many enjoyed close personal ties to the lord lieutenant and had bitterly opposed the papal nuncio and the clerical faction. Finally, the involvement of the two bishops represented an uneasy compromise on a number of different levels. While the public support of leading members of the Catholic Church guaranteed widespread acceptance of the new regime, many leading confederates remained deeply concerned that any overt exercise of political influence by Catholic clerics would almost certainly alienate Irish Protestants, thus destroying the fragile anti-parliamentary alliance. Moreover, an exclusively Catholic Irish army would have little hope of recovering Protestant England or Protestant Scotland for the young Charles Stuart.

In reality, the powers of the Catholic commissioners, which included overseeing the supply of the armed forces, regulating customs duties, and appointing justices of the peace to maintain law and order in the localities, proved very limited. They performed no direct military functions, although Ormond technically required their consent before appointing governors to towns and garrisons under Catholic control. Ormond, as commander-in-chief of the combined royalist/confederate forces, wielded supreme authority and his clerical opponents criticised him for acting 'more like a tyrant monarchy, than any way a subject'.[8] The peace settlement stipulated that the lord lieutenant confer key positions in the army and administration on Catholics, and that thereafter no distinction be made on religious grounds. Ormond did indeed nominate a few leading Catholics, such as the marquis of Clanricarde and earl of Castlehaven, to top military posts, but almost exclusively from among his small circle of close friends. This shortsighted policy also extended to the administration of justice, vital for maintaining harmony not only between the major factions in the new alliance, but also between the regime and the population at large. Without widespread support among the people, the royalists could not hope to raise sufficient cash or supplies for the war effort. Ormond, however, never established the judicature envisaged in the treaty, operating a system based purely on petitions instead. The surviving records show that until his authority began to collapse in the summer of 1650, the marquis dealt personally with hundreds of supplications, ranging from requests for employment to complaints about abuses committed by royalist troops. In the military, political and judicial fields, Ormond's policy of consolidating power in a single figure exposed his deficiencies as a national leader, distracted him from the major task of managing the war effort, and left many potential allies disappointed and disaffected. As long as the royalist cause in Ireland continued to thrive, these tensions could be ignored, but any setback would threaten the entire edifice of government.

Ormond, fully aware of the exhausted state of the kingdom after over seven years of continuous warfare, believed foreign inter-vention, in the form of both military supplies and cash, was necessary to sustain the royalist cause in Ireland. In a series of letters to English exiles on the Continent, the lord lieutenant presented a positive picture of Irish affairs, to encourage fund-raising efforts. The marquis explained how, after years of dissension and dis-agreement, news of the king's impending trial 'put a speedy end to our contentions about the conditions of peace, for it gave me and all others such a horror that we judged it a very unseasonable thrift to spend time in disputing about circumstances of government, while the whole frame of it was so near subversion'.[9] He assured royalist supporters that even with only 'moderate' assistance from abroad, Ireland would 'very speedily be in absolute subjection to the king's authority'.[10] At the same time, however, Lord Inchiquin received intelligence reports that the parliamentarians intended sending major reinforcements to their enclave in Dublin, while stirrings of discontent had once again started to appear within the ranks of Munster Protestants. Suspicious of their erstwhile allies, the Catholic Commissioners of Treaty requested that Inchiquin's own forces be reduced in the interests of equality among the religious groups.

Not surprisingly, Ormond continued to play down internal divisions, and investigated instead the possibility of drawing the parliamentary commanders in Ireland into the royalist camp. On receiving confirmation of the execution of Charles I, the marquis wrote directly to Henry Jones, Anglican bishop of Clogher and brother of Colonel Michael Jones, pleading with him to join forces against the regicides in England. He accused Oliver Cromwell of attempting to establish 'a perfect Turkish tyranny', supported by the 'dregs and scum of the House of Commons, picked and awed by the army'.[11] The following month, presumably after receiving no satisfactory answer from the bishop, he sent a similar letter directly to Colonel Jones in Dublin, and another to Charles Coote in Derry. As for the peace settlement with the confederates, the marquis assured both men that 'the advantages which the Romish professors are supposed to have in point of religion or authority are no other but pledges for his majesty's confirmation'.[12] Although strictly correct in his interpretation of the treaty terms, Ormond's assessment directly contradicted the generous gloss on the agreement he presented at the signing ceremony in January, and exposed the difficulties he faced in trying to maintain a united royalist front among such a diverse group of potential supporters. Nonetheless, Colonel Jones rejected these overtures, arguing that only the English parliament could 'give and assure pardon to those bloody rebels'. He was confident that Westminster would 'never assent to such a peace', particularly as it contained no provisions for Protestants, and he did not deem recent occurrences in England as justification for an alliance with Catholic rebels. He concluded by reminding Ormond how in 1647 he surrendered Dublin to parliament rather than the confederates, believing 'that the English interest in Ireland must be preserved by the English and not by the Irish'.[13] The marquis responded to this rebuff in equally robust terms, accusing Jones of hypocrisy for condemning the native Irish, and yet allegedly entering into talks with a clerical agent working on behalf of Owen Roe O'Neill. Ormond dismissed simplistic assumptions on the nature of the conflict, by pointing out that royalist ranks in Ireland consisted of more than Catholic troops. As for protecting the English interest in Ireland, he knew 'of no English interest separate from or independent of the king and crown of England'.[14] Not surprisingly, Jones viewed any further correspondence as a waste of time, and he threatened to punish any further messengers from the royalist leader, 'this being a dispute to be decided by the sword, not by the pen'.[15] Consequently Ormond set about preparing for a campaign against Dublin, to give him complete control of the kingdom and deny a parliamentary invasion force access to a major port.

The contacts between the Ulster Irish and Colonel Michael Jones, alluded to by Ormond, are not as anomalous as they first appear. Many native Irish, hostile to the Kilkenny peace treaty, believed they could make a deal with Westminster, based on religious toleration, a grant of indemnity for all acts committed during the rebellion and assurances about land holdings. In return they offered military support against Ormond and the royalists. The key figure in developing this strategy was Randal MacDonnell, marquis of Antrim, a descendant of the Scottish MacDonalds, who had settled in north-east Ulster during the fifteenth and sixteenth centuries. Antrim, the ultimate political opportunist, had alternated between the royalist and confederate camps during the 1640s, but following the defeat of the king in England, he began to explore the possibility of an alliance with parliament. In late 1648, Antrim despatched Patrick Crelly, Cistercian abbot of Newry, to London, where he engaged in secret talks over the next six months with key figures in the parliamentary regime, such as Edmund Ludlow. Around the same time, royalist exiles in France wrote to Ormond, warning him that leading English Catholics had initiated similar contacts. It is likely, however, that Ludlow and others simply used these negotiations to plant the seed of division among their opponents, while they prepared their expeditionary force for Ireland, encouraging Crelly 'to heighten the demands of the Catholics, and especially to keep Owen Roe from joining on the other side'.[16]

In Ireland, General Owen Roe O'Neill sent a priest, Edmund Reilly (later archbishop of Armagh), to Dublin in the spring of 1649. His mission was supposedly to negotiate prisoner releases, although one hostile source described Reilly as Colonel Jones's 'inseparable confidant and intelligencer'.[17] Desperately short of supplies, O'Neill needed allies to resist the resurgent royalist forces. More isolated than Jones in Dublin, both Monck in Dundalk and Coote in Derry agreed to temporary ceasefires with the Ulster Irish in order to exchange goods and information. They also forwarded O'Neill's demands for religious and political concessions on to London, where the authorities at Westminster not surprisingly rejected them. Nonetheless, the parliamentarians in Ireland benefited greatly from this alliance with the Ulster army throughout the summer of 1649, particularly as it delayed any reconciliation between O'Neill and Ormond until after the arrival of Cromwell. Moreover, the Ulster general scattered the royalist forces besieging Derry, thus enabling Charles Coote to preserve a parliamentary presence in the Northern Province. For his part, O'Neill obtained little practical assistance from this temporary arrangement. Ensnared, according to one source, 'in a false expectation of agreement', events across the Irish Sea cruelly exposed his political naivety.[18]

In England the parliamentary Council of State was specifically directed to oppose the pretensions of Charles Stuart to the throne and to reduce Ireland to submission. Milton believed that no 'true born Englishman' could read the terms of the Ormond peace 'without indignation and disdain'.[19] In early March, following a petition from the army, the Council of State appointed a committee headed by Cromwell to examine the military situation in Ireland, which recommended that 12,000 troops be sent over as soon as possible. Events now moved quickly, and on 10 March John Bradshaw replaced Cromwell as president of the Council of State, which five days later offered the general the position of commander-in-chief of the proposed expedition. Cromwell had little direct experience of Irish affairs prior to this, apart from helping to organise and finance the troops sent over by parliament during the first six months of the rebellion. In late 1645, following the decisive battle of Naseby, Sir Hardress Waller, Munster planter and MP at Westminster, had engaged in 'many free and serious discourses' with Cromwell about the possibility of an Irish expedition, but nothing came of their discussions.[20] Now in 1649, Cromwell delayed accepting the command, not because of any scruples over the campaign, but in order to secure the best possible terms both for himself and for the army. Finally, on 23 March, at a meeting of the General Council of the army at Whitehall, he publicly announced his willingness to go, declaring that 'if God be amongst us, and His presence be with us, it matters not who is our Commander in Chief'.[21]

Deeply unpopular in England as a result of the king's execution, war in Ireland would enable the parliamentary government to assume the role of defender of the English nation and Protestantism against the dual threats of native Irish barbarism and aggressive international popery. As Virgilio Malvezzi, confidant of the Spanish chief minister Olivares, explained, 'It is an old and true saying that fear of an external enemy is the greatest remedy for internal dissensions.'[22] Indeed, Cromwell justified the proposed expedition on the grounds that Catholics and royalists intended 'to root out the English interest in Ireland' and to invade England shortly afterwards, making it 'the most miserable place on earth'. He neatly prioritised the preferences of the new regime stating that he would rather 'be overrun with a Cavalierish [English royalist] interest than a Scotch interest; I had rather be overrun with a Scotch interest than an Irish interest; and I think this is the most dangerous'. Cromwell believed that the mere possibility of Irish troops landing in England would 'awaken all Englishmen who perhaps are willing enough he [Charles Stuart] should have come in upon an accommodation, but not [that] he must come from Ireland and Scotland'.[23]

Cromwell's speech to the army council struck a chord not only among his fellow officers but also with a wider English audience. MPs at Westminster, fed on a diet of horror stories from Ireland throughout the 1640s, were genuinely concerned about the fate of their Protestant co-religionists, and feared an invasion led by Ormond. Whether the royalist forces in Ireland posed an immediate threat to the new regime in England is highly debatable, but in the paranoid environment following the execution of the king, anything seemed possible. Victory over English and Scottish opponents in 1648 freed troops and resources for a renewed intervention in Ireland, which, unlike Scotland, Cromwell and his supporters viewed as a dependency of England, directly subject to the dictates of parliament. As Henry Ireton later explained, 'Ireland being a conquered country, the English Nation might with justice assert their right and conquest.'[24] They hoped to use Irish land to repay massive debts to those who had advanced loans to parliament, secured by the promise of confiscated rebel estates. Finally, and in some ways most importantly from the point of view of recruitment and public support, Cromwell intended to avenge the widely reported massacre of Protestant settlers in 1641–2. Populist publications in London bolstered this crude appeal to nationalist and religious sentiment with renewed attacks against the Catholic Irish. The authorities at Westminster authorised Thomas Waring to revisit in print the massacre of the Protestant settlers at the outbreak of the rebellion, which 'would much tend to the vindication of the Protestant cause and perpetuating infamy upon the Irish Papists'.[25] In a pamphlet published the following year Waring dismissed Irish Catholics as 'merely a kind of reptilia ... creeping on their bellies, and feeding on the dust of the earth'. He argued that there could be 'no safety in cohabitation with them', and concluded that parliament could 'warrantably and righteously endeavour the extirpation of them'.[26] Milton launched a similarly scathing attack, denouncing 'those Irish barbarians' as 'mortal enemies' of the English, responsible for the 'merciless' massacre of over 200,000 Protestant settlers, while William Hickman, a friend of Cromwell, later wrote that 'God hath marked out that people for destruction'.[27] With the ideological ground for the resumption of brutal military tactics in Ireland so clearly stated, the handful of dissenting voices in England proved all too easy to ignore.

Discontent in the ranks of the New Model Army, much of it associated with the radical Leveller movement, appeared almost from the moment the first regiments were selected by lot to serve in Ireland. As these units marched westwards towards their ports of embarkation, they committed violent disorders against the civilian population, while more wide-scale mutinies threatened to derail the expedition even before it left England. In April, Cromwell and Fairfax intervened directly to arrest and execute a number of mutineers, including one Robert Lockyer. The large turnout at his funeral in London demonstrated a growing dissatisfaction with the parliamentary regime, and by mid-May hundreds of deserters had gathered near Oxford, before once again Cromwell and Fairfax acted decisively to restore order. Organised opposition dissolved, although local communities continued to complain about excesses committed by marauding bands of soldiers on their way to Ireland. But was any of this unrest triggered by sympathy for the Irish, and opposition to English military intervention overseas? Much of the surviving evidence consists of attacks by supporters of the government on the alleged motives of the Levellers and other radicals. One of the most effective ways to discredit an opponent in seventeenth-century England was to associate them with Irish Papists. Parliamentarians successfully employed this tactic against Charles I throughout the 1640s, and adopted a similar strategy in 1649, accusing the Levellers of attempting to undermine the Irish expedition. In fact, more detailed research suggests that the Leveller leadership proved extremely reluctant to take a stance on Ireland. A few anonymous pamphlets seemed to question the legitimacy of an invasion, but the vast majority of opinion in England enthusiastically supported the enterprise. The soldiers' discontent stemmed primarily, and understandably, from a reluctance to engage in a venture widely perceived as hazardous, with the climate and disease likely to claim more victims than warfare. Moreover, some troops openly displayed royalist sympathies. Many of the rank and file in Colonel Tothill's regiment, for example, one of the first to be transported to Dublin in late April, claimed to have previously served the king, and would 'do so again when there shall be occasion'.[28] The Council of State ordered Tothill to administer an oath of loyalty to everybody under his command, and to dismiss those who refused the test. Guarantees about the prompt payment of wages finally helped silence the few remaining opposing voices, allowing Cromwell to continue his preparations without further interruption.

Cromwell made it abundantly clear from the outset that he would only agree to take command of the invasion on certain conditions, including the provision of adequate resources. Although heavily in debt from the two English Civil Wars, the parliamentary regime raised large loans for the expedition from London financiers and assigned monies to the army from the sale of church lands, as well as further income from customs and excise. Significantly, Cromwell demanded £100,000 in cash, enabling him to provide for the army in Ireland for three months, without additional supplies from England. Despite the best efforts of the navy, the sporadic nature of communications with England during winter necessitated a degree of self-sufficiency on Cromwell's part, at least during the initial stages of the invasion. Campaigning so late in the season, food would have to be coaxed from a potentially hostile population, and access to coinage, in a land starved of cash, would enable Cromwell to buy support, particularly among Ireland's Protestants. The provision of adequate financing for the expedition proved a major factor in Cromwell's subsequent success.

Meanwhile, Ormond, working with far more limited resources, prepared to attack Dublin, gathering all available supplies. Although insignificant compared with the large sums made available to Cromwell, Ormond exulted in the £7,000 in cash and grain provided by the city of Waterford, Ireland's second city, hoping that this example would encourage other urban centres to make similarly generous contributions.[29] With much of the country ravaged by war, and money in short supply, the royalist forces resorted to foraging for provisions, providing little more than promissory notes to a disgruntled peasantry. Petitions flowed in to Ormond, complaining about the rapacious behaviour of the royalists, which made the collection of taxes through the monthly assessment all the more difficult. The lord lieutenant recognised the serious nature of the problem, but could do little apart from writing to his allies abroad, pleading for aid.

At this stage, the prospect of assistance from overseas depended on the intentions of the exiled prince, Charles Stuart, who monitored developments in the three Stuart kingdoms from his base in The Hague. Practically bankrupt, and bereft of allies among the major powers of Europe, despite plentiful expressions of sympathy, Charles could provide no material assistance. His arrival in Ireland, however, would unquestionably have united Irish Catholics behind the royalist cause, increased the desertion rates from parliamentary forces in the country, and eased the concerns felt by many Irish Protestants over their alliance with the Catholic confederates. On 22 January, shortly before the execution of the king, Ormond had written to Prince Charles, giving a very optimistic assessment of the military situation in Ireland, and urging him to come over from the Netherlands, particularly if furnished with money and supplies.[30] All early indications suggested that the young prince favoured Ireland as a destination rather than England or Scotland. He trusted Ormond implicitly, and Ireland was the only kingdom with a strong royalist army in the field. The declaration of the Scottish covenanters in favour of Prince Charles, on condition he took the covenanting oath, complicated matters by providing a viable alternative. Charles' exiled counsellors split on the issue, with the influential Edward Hyde arguing passionately for the Irish option as early as mid-January. The arrival of Prince Rupert at Kinsale at the end of the month, with a fleet of ships that had mutinied from the parliamentary navy, greatly strengthened Hyde's hand. Lord Byron journeyed from Ireland in late February, and presented a full report of recent developments to the exiled Stuart court. Shortly afterwards, Prince Charles wrote to Ormond, expressing his resolve 'to confirm and ratify fully and entirely, all the articles of the treaty with our Roman Catholic subjects of the kingdom of Ireland', while Secretary Robert Long assured the lord lieutenant that only a lack of money prevented Charles from joining the marquis.[31]

With the political situation in the three kingdoms changing on a daily basis, Hyde explained to another influential exile, Lord Jermyn, that Ireland represented 'the nearest way' back to England, although he admitted to the existence of 'close combinations [at court] against it'. Hyde did not want to alienate the covenanters, particularly as they appeared keen to support the royalist cause, and so he stressed that 'great care should be taken to satisfy the Scots with the king's [Charles II] going into Ireland'.[32] In April, commissioners from Scotland increased the pressure on Charles to subscribe to the covenant, but Lord Byron described their conditions as 'insolent'.[33] Disagreements among the prince's advisers led to growing inertia at the exiled Stuart court, and Hyde wrote despondently that some avowed 'sitting still here [the Hague] to be much better than going into Scotland or Ireland'.[34] Finally, in early May, after months of indecision, Charles delivered a paper to the States General of the Dutch Republic, outlining a plan for recovering his patrimony. He described the deplorable conditions prevalent in England, and dismissed the possibility of accepting the terms demanded by the Scottish covenanters because of the 'limitations and restrictions against his exercise of his regal power, that in truth they have only given him the name, and denied him the authority'. Ireland, therefore, was his preferred destination, and he sought assistance from the Dutch, in the form of transport ships and a loan of £20,000.[35] At the same time, Charles decided to dispatch two of his must trusted advisers, and strong supporters of the Irish option, to seek aid from Philip IV of Spain. The secret instructions, carried by Hyde and Lord Cottington to Madrid, included assurances about protecting Catholics in the Stuart dominions from the severity of penal legislation, and raised the possibility of actually repealing such laws. In May, the murder by royalists of Dr Isaac Dorislaus, an emissary from the English parliament to The Hague, precipitated Charles' departure from the Netherlands before he had obtained any significant aid. In late June he travelled through Paris, on route to the island of Jersey, the most convenient point of embarkation for Ireland. For the next six months, the exiled Stuart court anxiously awaited news of Ormond's summer campaign.

Before beginning to move against Dublin, Ormond realised the importance of disrupting parliamentary control of the seas, not only to prevent supplies reaching Colonel Michael Jones, but also to harass any expeditionary force sailing from England. Privateers based in the southern port of Wexford preyed on isolated English ships, taking many prizes, but the royalists needed Prince Rupert's small fleet in Kinsale to become fully operational. At the end of March, Ormond wrote to the prince, requesting that his warships be 'employed to interrupt the coming in of relief to Dublin'.[36] Unrest at the fleet's base in Kinsale thwarted any hopes of immediate action, while the arrival of Rupert, who cared little for confessional differences, appears to have upset the delicate balance in the region between the Catholic and Protestant communities. A report from Cork at the end of the month alluded to increasing antagonism between natives and settlers, including a number of assaults. The public celebration of Catholic services further increased the tension, and Inchiquin pleaded with Ormond 'to let the prince have some little hint of the discontent of the people about the Irish and saying mass in our garrisons'.[37] Ormond received further complaints from Charles' Secretary of State, Sir Edward Nicholas, in Caen about Irish vessels at sea using 'great cruelty towards all English', and making no distinction between royalists and parliamentarians.[38] Continuing shortages of supplies, particularly manpower, severely curtailed Rupert's scope for action. Already experiencing difficulties equipping his own army for the forthcoming campaign, the lord lieutenant had little or no surplus to share with the nascent royalist navy. In April, rumours surfaced that Rupert was scheming with the marquis of Antrim, who owned a number of privateers operating out of Wexford. In return for providing the prince with some desperately needed sailors, Antrim, who still refused to accept the January peace treaty, would receive a commission in the royal navy. Antrim's plans came to nothing, but Ormond nonetheless advised that Colonel Vangary, the agent employed to negotiate with Rupert on behalf of the Ulster Irish, be 'kept to his work if any he have' rather than meddle in affairs of state.[39] At the end of the month, the lord lieutenant wrote again to the prince, pleading for shipping to blockade Dublin, without which the proposed assault on the capital would be 'a desperate undertaking and I shall be forced to a defensive war'.[40] Prompted no doubt by an unsubstantiated report of the seizure of large amounts of coinage, including silver 'judged to amount to near fourscore thousand pounds', he also requested that a percentage of the money from prizes taken at sea be placed in the central coffers.[41]

The Council of State in London received news of Rupert's arrival at Kinsale with some concern. Fully aware of the threat he posed to English ships, they appointed three colonels, Edward Popham, Robert Blake and Richard Deane, as commanders of the navy, with orders to get the fleet out to sea as soon as possible, as the enemy was 'like to be very strong and active'.[42] Indeed, the following day, 6 March, the council received news of a daring raid by an Irish frigate on the Welsh coast, and the capture of a number of prisoners. The English navy's principal responsibilities, apart from countering the actions of the Wexford privateers and of Rupert's fleet, consisted of keeping the shipping lanes between England and Ireland open, providing transport for troops and supplies to the parliamentary enclaves in Dublin and Derry, and preventing communications between Ireland and the Continent. Popham, Blake and Deane vigorously set about these tasks, and by early April they had begun to intercept traffic from Ireland, including a ship carrying Colonel Oliver French and 170 officers and men, who claimed the Spanish Netherlands as their destination, 'but tis more like for Holland for the service of Charles Stuart'.[43] Capturing enemy vessels created difficulties for the navy, as the Council of State explained to Colonel Popham 'that by some ordinances of parliament, those Irish prisoners and their adherents cannot be exchanged or released'.[44] In 1644, parliament had ordered that no quarter be given to any Irish taken in the service of the king either in England or on the High Seas. Realising the dangers of retaliatory action by the Irish, the Council of State, after consultation with parliament, ordered the speedy exchange of 'persons of quality', notwithstanding the earlier ordinances. As for the 'common men', the council rather ambiguously left it to the discretion of naval officers 'to set them on shore somewhere in the enemy's quarters to avoid further charge and trouble with them or otherwise to dispose them as you shall see cause'.[45] Over the next few months, the parliamentary navy enjoyed increasing success against the Wexford privateers, and managed to transport both troops and supplies to Derry and Dublin. On 22 May, William Legg reported the arrival of ten parliamentary ships off Kinsale, instigating a blockade of the port that lasted until October, when Rupert eventually broke out with a number of vessels and escaped to Lisbon.[46] By the early summer, therefore, the English could legitimately claim control of the seas around the eastern and southern coasts of Ireland, an essential prerequisite to any invasion.

Increasingly on the defensive at sea, Ormond tried instead to force the issue on land. The royalists spent much of April and May mopping up garrisons in the Midlands held by the Ulster forces of Owen Roe O'Neill, such as Tecroghan in Meath and Athy in Kildare. The earl of Castlehaven boasted after taking the fort at Maryborough that the combined effort of the various provinces would be 'enough to make Owen O'Neill's people eat one another'.[47] Internal divisions, however, continued to blight Ormond's efforts at securing control of the entire kingdom. A royalist force of 1,500 men sent against O'Neill's supporters in the Wicklow Mountains south of Dublin suffered heavy losses, while Clanricarde complained of growing disorder across Connacht. Patrick Darcy reported an attack on the mayor's daughter in Galway city by 'rude people', and 'though her body escaped defiling yet it escaped not blows'.[48] Meanwhile, Ormond attempted to prevent a meeting of clergy at Kilconnell in County Galway, believing it would be openly hostile to the government. The Protestant bishop of Cloyne urged the marquis to exercise greater discipline over the native Irish, but the continued focus on internal affairs exasperated Inchiquin, who argued in favour of a quick and decisive move against Dublin, before major reinforcements arrived from England. For the moment, the lord lieutenant's more cautious counsel prevailed.

Increasingly overwhelmed by his administrative and judicial duties, Ormond nonetheless remained 'hopeful' for a successful summer campaign, although he conceded that the presence of

Charles Stuart in Ireland would 'infallibly remove the contentions that remain amongst any pretending for him'.[49] The marquis continued to experience great difficulty in keeping his troops 'in any kind of discipline', and he complained that tensions between English and Irish soldiers made his life 'a perpetual vexation'.[50] He feared that in Charles' absence the Catholic clergy would insist on major religious concessions, 'the true and original ground of the Irish rebellion', while such demands, he speculated, would unquestionably alienate Protestant support 'without whom your majesty's work here much less in England and Scotland is not to be done'.[51] The fractious nature of the royalist alliance was not Ormond's only concern, as the lack of supplies and cash, due to 'the great and universal poverty' throughout the kingdom, continued to hamper his preparations for a summer campaign. Finally, in late May, after months of preparation, he began to move against the parliamentary enclave in Dublin. In a letter to Secretary Nicholas, he estimated the royalist army at 10,000 infantry and 3,000 cavalry, a wildly exaggerated figure, but no doubt meant to encourage Charles to come to Ireland. In reality, he commanded less than 10,000 troops in total, an insufficient number to encircle Dublin fully. Moreover, he lacked the big guns required to breach the city's defences. The plan of campaign, therefore, did not envisage a siege or an assault, but rather involved restricting Jones' forces within the city walls, where they could not continue to subsist 'if he be not powerfully and presently supplied' from England.[52]

In fact, Ormond's march towards Dublin in June marked the high point of royalist fortunes. In Ulster, an army of Protestant settlers, loyal to the crown, kept Charles Coote closely confined within the walls of Derry, at least until the arrival of Owen Roe's relief force, while further east Sir George Monro had driven the parliamentarians out of Belfast and Carrickfergus. The marquis received further good news in early July when Clanricarde informed him of the surrender of Sligo, the lone parliamentary outpost in the western province of Connacht. Not long afterwards, Inchiquin, operating north of Dublin in characteristically aggressive fashion, seized Drogheda before driving Colonel Monck out of Dundalk, thus allowing Ormond to concentrate on a loose blockade of the capital with somewhere between 6,000 and 8,000 infantry and cavalry. Without the ships to impose a naval blockade, however, the royalists could do little to prevent Jones from receiving reinforcements from England. The question must be asked, therefore, why did Ormond bring his army before Dublin at all, wasting valuable supplies and money in the process? Perhaps the lord lieutenant feared that without some sort of action, internal tensions might tear the royalist/confederate alliance apart. Moreover, he hoped that the presence of a royalist army outside the city would encourage desertions from the parliamentary garrison. The lack of strategic alternatives created serious difficulties for Ormond, but he compounded his inertia with a major tactical error. In a move designed to deny grazing to cavalry units based in Dublin, he divided his forces on either side of the river Liffey, thereby making joint action almost impossible.

. The arrival of reinforcements from England finally forced Ormond's hand. A council of war at Rathmines on 27 July made the fateful decision to split the royalist army still further by sending Inchiquin south to Munster, while at the same time increasing the pressure on Dublin by advancing the besieging forces closer to the city walls. These moves only appear reckless with the benefit of hindsight. As Cromwell gathered his army at Milford Haven in south Wales, a typical point of departure for Munster, reports from England suggested that he intended to land in the southern province, exploiting the unrest among Protestant settlers fostered by agents dispatched by parliament earlier in the year. All too aware of the doubtful loyalty of many Irish Protestants, Ormond hoped that Inchiquin's presence would forestall any such schemes. When Cromwell's invasion flotilla eventually set sail in mid-August, a significant proportion, under the command of Henry Ireton, did indeed head south, but none of the ports would admit his troops so he diverted back to Dublin. Ireton's mission, however, was largely diversionary, as Cromwell had already dispatched his artillery train to Dublin in early July. To gain control of the kingdom in a quick and decisive campaign, Cromwell needed to defeat royalist forces in the field, and Ormond's army outside Dublin was the obvious target.

Similarly, Ormond's decision to tighten the blockade of Dublin also made good tactical sense, but should have been attempted weeks earlier with his full army, and before the arrival of reinforcements from England. One contemporary critic blamed this fatal delay on Ormond's obsession with capturing minor garrisons on route to the capital, but in his defence, the royalist commander needed time to gather supplies and manpower.[53] Whatever the truth of the matter, by early August the two armies at Dublin were roughly of equal size, but the royalist forces, divided by the Liffey and lacking sufficient cavalry support, had become dangerously exposed. Regardless of this threat, Ormond pushed ahead, seizing the important fortress at Rathfarnham on the outskirts of the city. He then attempted to strengthen defensive works at Baggotrath, near Rathmines, in order to prevent parliamentary cavalry from grazing outside the walls. An experienced confederate officer, Lieutenant General Purcell, led about 1,000 men forward under cover of darkness, but somehow they got lost, and a march of less than a mile took most of the night. Consequently, at daybreak they had only just begun to fortify their new position. Jones quickly seized the initiative, taking advantage of the enemy's temporary vulnerability by launching an immediate attack with his entire army. Despite some spirited resistance, Purcell's men broke and fled back towards the royalist camp, with the parliamentarians in hot pursuit. Ormond, despite displaying great personal courage, failed to rally any significant forces around him, which he hoped 'might have given encouragement to some horse and foot that were untouched on the other side of the river', while the royalist cavalry commander, Sir William Vaughan, died fighting at the head of his troops.[54] The parliamentarians completely routed the royalist army and seized valuable supplies from 'the richest camp that had been won in any [of] these three kingdoms', including large sums of money.[55] This unmitigated disaster enabled Cromwell to land unopposed almost two weeks later, and radically altered the nature of the subsequent campaign. With no major field army to confront the invaders, the royalists adopted an entirely defensive strategy, fortifying key strongholds throughout the kingdom. Cromwell's nine months in Ireland, therefore, would be spent besieging towns and cities in the provinces of Munster and Leinster, with no opportunity for him to land a decisive knockout blow as he had done at Naseby in 1645 and Preston in 1648.

A number of contemporaries accused Purcell or his guides of treachery, but the Irish commonly ascribed every military setback to the actions of traitors. On this occasion, however, there may well be some justification for these allegations. In the aftermath of the war in 1653, the High Court of Justice, established to try Catholic rebels, condemned an Irishman named O'Toole, 'yet for his service in betraying the royal camp at Rathmines [he] suffered no further punishment'.[56] The Commissioners of Trust saw the Hand of Providence in the defeat, but hoped it might be 'the last of those just punishments for the sins of the people'.[57] Others blamed Ormond, and his close cohort of friends, who, they claimed, drank and gambled in the camp, rather than attending to their military duties. While some of the officers may well have caroused in their tents until late, Ormond supervised operations to the best of his very limited abilities. In reality, major strategic and tactical errors in the lead up to the battle exposed the royalists to the possibility of the type of counter-attack so deftly executed by Jones. As soon as the parliamentarians received reinforcements towards the end of July, Ormond should have lifted the blockade, and withdrawn to prepare for battle on more favourable terms. Cromwell's subsequent campaign provided ample opportunities for the royalists to seize the initiative, but lack of supplies and manpower, exacerbated by the debacle at Rathmines, invariably thwarted their plans. The attempt to fortify Baggotrath carried a high degree of risk, as it was almost guaranteed to provoke some sort of response from Jones. Greater care should have been taken to ensure Purcell had sufficient manpower and time to complete the task. Despite the incompetence of his opponents, credit must also be given to Jones for identifying the weakness of Purcell's position and acting so decisively and quickly to take advantage of the situation.

In the days and weeks after the battle, Ormond and his supporters desperately tried to diminish the importance of the encounter. Although the Commissioners of Treaty in Kilkenny described the rout as a 'disaster', they nonetheless reported that all of the cavalry and most of the infantry had escaped. The commissioners claimed that Ormond was already in the process of rallying the dispersed forces, and would soon be 'in a good condition to perform what remains of the service of the kingdom unfinished'.[58] Similarly, the lord lieutenant could not deny that the defeat 'was full and general', although he accused Jones of exaggerating both the size of the royalist army, and the extent of the losses. Instead of the thousands of casualties listed by the parliamentarians, Ormond informed Charles Stuart that the enemy 'killed not above six hundred officers and soldiers in all'.[59] With Inchiquin absent in Munster, and a significant proportion of the forces across the Liffey, this assessment is almost certainly more accurate than Jones's inflated figures. In addition to the physical losses, however, including his artillery and other vital military supplies, Ormond understood the possible psychological repercussions, particularly given the fragile nature of the royalist alliance in Ireland. While the war progressed favourably during the summer the lord lieutenant could afford to ignore the rumblings of discontent in his own ranks. Defeat, as he admitted in a letter to the marquis of Clanricarde, gave the advantage to others 'to work upon the fears of the people'.[60] The first major cracks appeared in the immediate aftermath of the battle, when the Protestant Irish troops in the royalist army, who by all accounts had acquitted themselves well, deserted en masse to the parliamentarians. This decision not only exposed the depth of hostility felt by the settler community towards the Catholic Irish, but also rendered suspect all those Protestants who remained loyal to the king. On the Catholic side, Ormond's many detractors, silent for the previous few months, suddenly found new voice, replaying the grievances of the previous eight years. Although the lord lieutenant continued in office for over a year, his prestige and authority never fully recovered from the disaster at Rathmines.

For the moment, Ormond did what he could to recover the initiative, although the lack of manpower restricted his options. The release of the prisoners could be obtained from Jones at a rate of 18 shillings each for common soldiers, increasing thereafter according to rank. With no money available from central funds, many of these royalist troops remained in captivity unless freed following the intervention of relatives and friends. Bizarrely, Ormond did enjoy one small success at this time. While fleeing south after the battle, he convinced the important parliamentary outpost at Ballyshannon in County Kildare, bypassed on the march to Dublin, to surrender by informing the commander that the royalists had in fact triumphed at Rathmines. On arriving in Kilkenny the marquis set about rallying dispersed forces around the country, and marched northwards to assist those towns he identified as vulnerable to parliamentary attack. Colonel Jones, anxious to exploit his victory, moved quickly against Drogheda, which Inchiquin had recaptured for the royalists only a few weeks earlier. On 11 August, he brought 3,000 infantry and 800 cavalry before the town, along with four cannon transported up the coast by ship. Two days later, however, the parliamentarians raised the siege 'in some confusion and haste' on receiving news of Ormond's approach. His confidence temporarily restored, the lord lieutenant resolved 'once again to attempt the reduction of Dublin', which he believed, despite all the evidence to the contrary, to be 'more feasible than ever'.[61] Not surprisingly, the royalist advance on the capital never materialised, as word arrived shortly afterwards of the appearance of English ships off Dublin. Oliver Cromwell had finally arrived.

4

Cromwell at Drogheda and Wexford

Many of their fellow subjects have they slaine
Cryinge for quarter, though too much in vaine.[1]
THOMAS COBBE, '*A poeme uppon Cromwell*' (1650)

On Wednesday, 11 July 1649, around five in the evening, after months of careful preparation, Oliver Cromwell finally left London to join the vast expeditionary army assembling to the west. Parliamentary news-sheets described his almost regal departure, in a coach drawn by six gallant Flanders mares, accompanied by a large entourage, including 'very many great officers of the army'. Curious onlookers watched him leave the capital, with 'trumpets sounding almost to the shaking of Charing Cross had it been now standing'.[2] Cromwell travelled first to the port of Bristol, which declared a public holiday in his honour, and spent the next month organising for the forthcoming campaign. Westminster successfully raised £100,000 in cash, an enormous sum at the time, mainly in the form of loans from London merchants. The English parliament's ability to finance the New Model Army gave it a decisive advantage over the royalists, and the marquis of Ormond later described this war chest as 'more formidable' than any military strength at Cromwell's disposal.[3] Access to cash enabled Cromwell to purchase food and other commodities in England, independently of the slow-moving central bureaucracy, and to quell discontent among the army rank and file, by providing pay in advance of their departure for Ireland.

Cromwell's meticulous preparations, however, delayed the expedition, creating serious logistical problems in England and Wales. Local communities complained of growing disorders as troops passed through the countryside and deserters scavenged for food. In late July, already well into the traditional campaigning season, Cromwell finally issued a general order to assemble at Milford Haven, despite increasingly bleak news from Ireland. Reports suggested that royalist forces, led by Ormond, continued to sweep all before them, threatening the few surviving parliamentary enclaves, including Dublin. In early August, Colonel George Monck unexpectedly arrived back in England, bearing news about the fall of Dundalk to Lord Inchiquin. Cromwell and the Council of State had known for months about Monck's temporary alliance of convenience with the native Irish general, Owen Roe O'Neill, but kept it secret. The loss of Dundalk, along with the desertion of hundreds of Monck's men to the royalist side, threatened to expose this damaging information to the public. In an attempt to forestall any backlash, particularly among the troops assembling for Ireland, the Council decided to take pre-emptive measures, with Monck acting as a willing scapegoat for the regime. Parliament publicly criticised his cooperation with the Catholic Irish but took no further action against the colonel. Nonetheless, the entire episode cast a shadow over the impending invasion.

A week later, however, Cromwell received word of Ormond's defeat at Rathmines, which he described as 'an astonishing mercy'.[4] In addition to routing the largest royalist field army in Ireland, and clearing the way for an unopposed landing at Dublin, Jones's victory provided clear evidence to the parliamentarians that God looked favourably on their endeavours. Indeed, the earl of Leicester believed that many of Cromwell's men would simply have refused to go to Ireland 'if they had not been encouraged by this extraordinary victory'.[5] Although the earl exaggerated the level of discontent in army ranks, news of Rathmines undoubtedly invigorated the parliamentary campaign at a crucial moment. Shortly afterwards, on 13 August, the invasion fleet set sail, with Cromwell and thirty-five ships heading directly for Dublin. Henry Ireton and seventy-seven ships departed from Milford Haven that same day, destined for the southern coast, to discover whether any of the Munster ports held by Irish Protestants would declare for parliament. For the moment they remained loyal to the king, so Ireton changed course for Dublin, joined by a third squadron of eighteen ships, commanded by Colonel Thomas Horton. Cromwell, travelling abroad for the first time in his life, suffered greatly while crossing the Irish Sea. The army chaplain, Hugh Peters, described him as looking 'as sea-sick as ever I saw any man in my life'.[6] After two stormy days, the flotilla arrived off Dublin, and the troops landed at Ringsend, just outside the city. Large crowds and celebratory shots of artillery greeted Cromwell's arrival. The general made a short speech, praising God for the safe passage of the invasion force. He promised rewards for all those carrying on 'that great work against the barbarous and bloodthirsty Irish', including 'the propagating of the Gospel of Christ', and talked of 'restoring that bleeding nation to its former happiness and tranquillity'.[7] Cromwell's inflammatory words received rapturous applause from an audience of Irish Protestants eager to take the offensive, avenge the settlers killed in 1641–2, and regain control of the country.

As his forces gradually assembled in Dublin, Cromwell planned for the forthcoming campaign against the town of Drogheda, 30 miles to the north of the capital. Control of Drogheda would open the gateway into Ulster as well as protecting his rear while the New Model Army marched south against the former confederate heartland in Leinster and Munster. Anxious to ensure order in Dublin after his departure, Cromwell issued a public proclamation on 24 August, prohibiting soldiers from harming civilians. Furthermore, he encouraged farmers and merchants to bring their goods to market, promising them 'ready money'. As long as civilians paid all contributions, and did not disturb the peace, they would have 'free leave and liberty to live at home with their families and goods', at least until the issuance of fresh protections the following January.[8] This declaration, along with the subsequent execution of a handful of soldiers for unlicensed pillaging, has been used to suggest that Cromwell did not harbour any hostility towards the ordinary Catholic inhabitants of Ireland. In fact, his actions represented nothing more than prudent military practice, motivated by genuine necessity. Starting a campaign so late in the season, with a large army and a limited supply base, he desperately required a cooperative local community to provide vital commodities, especially fresh food. Moreover, the New Model Army maintained strict internal discipline at all times, crucial for preventing the spread of disorder among the ranks.

Cromwell's conciliatory policy towards the civilian population unsettled the Catholic leadership. Sir Edmond Butler, governor of County Wexford, wrote to Ormond complaining that he had experienced great difficulty in preventing the country people from making terms with the parliamentarians, as 'the rogues allure them by speaking that they are for the liberty of the commoners'. The earl of Castlehaven concurred, as he noted incredulously how Cromwell paid a local inhabitant £5 for a night's lodging.[9] In contrast, each day fresh petitions reached Ormond, detailing abuses committed by royalist troops against the inhabitants. In the absence of regular pay, royalists simply seized whatever they needed, sometimes in exchange for worthless credit notes. The lord lieutenant published a declaration for the punishment of serious offences, but to no avail. The parliamentarians, for their part, as the royalist Sir Lewis Dyve noted wearily, 'had money to pay for what they took'.[10] Throughout the next four years of the Cromwellian conquest, elements of the local population played a key role in sustaining English armies, both in garrisons and on campaign. Cromwell's first military action in Ireland, however, soon exposed the true nature of the parliamentary mission.

The marquis of Ormond was already in Drogheda when news arrived of Cromwell's landing at Ringsend. Following the defeat at Rathmines, the marquis had issued a defiant declaration, forbidding royalists to capitulate to the enemy 'upon any terms save in the language of the sword, but upon all occasions to fight it out to the last man'. Now, in the face of a dramatic new threat, he summoned a council of war to discuss military strategy.[11] Ormond, vigorously supported by the earl of Castlehaven, wanted to fortify Drogheda and draw the parliamentarians into a protracted siege, depleting their resources, and allowing the royalists time to re-assemble a significant field army. Colonels Warren, Wall and Byrne, the three regimental commanders charged with holding the town, disagreed, and argued unsuccessfully in favour of a tactical withdrawal.[12] Before departing south, Ormond appointed Sir Arthur Aston as garrison commander. Aston had served in Russia, Poland and Germany during the Thirty Years War, before returning to England to fight for King Charles I against parliament. He lost a leg in a riding accident, but as governor of Oxford, the royalist capital during the English civil war, he acquired a fearsome reputation as a strict disciplinarian. The royalist Edward Hyde mischievously described him as 'having the good fortune to be much esteemed when he is not known and very much detested where he was'.[13] An English Catholic, experienced in foreign warfare, Aston must have felt very much at home among the eclectic mix of Irish and English soldiers, both Protestant and Catholic, who comprised the royalist garrison of Drogheda.

According to folklore, Aston claimed that 'the man who could take Drogheda could take Hell', an unlikely statement from such a seasoned veteran given the precarious situation faced by the defenders, although they did enjoy some advantages. The river Boyne divided the town in two, and if Cromwell attacked from the south, Aston would be able to withdraw across the river, using a drawbridge that could be pulled up behind his retreating troops. Moreover, as Ormond's forces slowly regrouped following the debacle at Rathmines they posed a growing threat to any besieging army. The impressively high medieval town walls, however, had not been designed to withstand cannon fire, and Cromwell possessed the largest artillery train yet seen in Ireland. Aston ordered the construction of obstacles behind the walls, but could do little else to prevent the inevitable breach in Drogheda's defences. A lack of cavalry limited attempts to gather supplies before the siege began, and made sorties almost impossible once Cromwell's vanguard reached the outskirts of the town. Finally, the defenders suffered from severe shortages of key military supplies, such as gunpowder, match and shot. Ormond, supervising developments from a vantage point some 20 miles away, frequently promised to send the necessary materials, but despite Aston's desperate pleas, he provided little apart from encouraging words and some additional manpower.

Cromwell, his arrangements complete, departed from Dublin in great style, with trumpets sounding, drums beating and colours flying. He arrived before Drogheda on 3 September, followed shortly afterwards by his siege guns, transported by ship from Dublin. The parliamentarians spent a week preparing to assault the town, and on 10 September Cromwell issued a summons to surrender, warning Aston that 'if this be refused you will have no cause to blame me'.[14] On receiving a defiant rejection from the royalist commander, Cromwell ordered the white flag over the camp replaced by a red ensign, and the bombardment began in earnest. The night before the summons, Sir Edmund Verney, an English Protestant gentleman, had written to the lord lieutenant from inside Drogheda. Verney had served under Ormond earlier in the decade against the Catholic Irish, but now stood side by side with his previous opponents against a new enemy. Although fully aware of the impending parliamentary assault, Verney exuded confidence in his letter, 'being in great hopes and expectation that the service I am at present engaged in will receive a happy issue'. He warmly complimented the royalist officers, especially Colonels Warren and Wall, describing them as his 'most intimate comrades', and insisted that the ordinary soldiers were equally 'all in heart and courage'. Verney concluded a review of the defences by stating that he little feared 'what the enemy can do forcibly against us', but nonetheless he urged Ormond to move towards Drogheda, in order to distract Cromwell and break up the siege.[15] The marquis received this letter the following day, as the parliamentary artillery began to shatter the town walls, but he remained a mere spectator to the unfolding tragedy. Within forty-eight hours, Verney, Warren, Wall and Aston were all dead, along with approximately 2,500 officers and men of the garrison, and an indeterminate number of civilians.

The storming of Drogheda on 11 September shocked contemporary opinion and established Cromwell's reputation for cruelty and savagery, which has persisted in Ireland until the present day. And yet, despite all the subsequent condemnation and outrage, as well as some crude attempts at justification, doubts persist over what exactly happened on that day. Not surprisingly, few eyewitness accounts survive from the royalist side, although hundreds of the garrison did manage to slip away over the north wall in the confusion of battle. Many of these men made their way to Ormond or Inchiquin, and reported what they had seen. Unfortunately, apart from the reflections of the Anglican clergyman, Dean Nicholas Bernard, the town's inhabitants left no diaries or letters describing the tragic events. Petitions presented to Ormond over the next twelve months, in addition to those dating from the Restoration in 1660, contain some information on individual fatalities but little else. As a result, we must rely heavily on parliamentary statements, with all the attendant problems of bias (deliberate or otherwise) and a lack of corroborating evidence. The following reconstruction is based almost entirely on the reports of those actually present at Drogheda, in an attempt to separate fact from fiction, and reality from propaganda, be it parliamentarian or royalist.

The key evidence consists of the letters composed shortly after the event by Oliver Cromwell, who led his troops through the breach of the town's southern walls. Cromwell's correspondence provides a first-hand account of that dramatic day, much of which is verified by another key parliamentary participant, Colonel John Hewson.[16] Cromwell's first letter, to the president of the Council of State John Bradshaw, was written five days after the storming of Drogheda. In it Cromwell speaks of 'stout resistance' provided by the enemy. The defenders repelled the initial assault, but a second attack drove them back from their entrenchments within the walls. Cromwell then explains how the parliamentarians refused to grant quarter, 'having the day before summoned the town'. He believed the entire garrison was subsequently killed, including 'almost all their prime soldiers'. Cromwell heard of only one officer escaping, and he believed the enemy was 'filled upon this with much terror'. In typical fashion, he ascribed 'the glory of this to God alone', before concluding that 'this bitterness will save much effusion of blood'.[17]

The second letter, written the following day to William Lenthall, speaker of the parliament at Westminster, was clearly intended for public consumption. It describes in vivid detail the artillery barrage and the opening of a breach in the walls. Cromwell conceded that the enemy had provided stiff opposition, inflicting 'considerable' losses, before they began to retreat in some disorder, with the parliamentarians in hot pursuit. In the confusion, the garrison failed to pull up the drawbridge over the Boyne in time, allowing the New

Model Army to cross over to the north side of the town. Meanwhile, Sir Arthur Aston had occupied a fort called Millmount on top of a steep hill, not far from the breach in the walls, 'a place very strong and of difficult access, being exceedingly high, having a good graft, and strongly palisadoed'. Cromwell simply stated that 'our men getting up to them, were ordered by me to put them all to the sword'. How exactly the parliamentary troops managed to take Millmount is not recorded, and Hewson sheds no additional light on this issue. The slaughter continued elsewhere and according to Cromwell 'being in the heat of the action, I forbade them to spare any that were in arms in the town'. He remarked ironically how on the Sunday before the assault, the inhabitants celebrated mass in St Peter's church, having expelled the local Protestants from the building. Two days later 'in this very place near one thousand of them were put to the sword, fleeing thither for safety'. Clerical robes provided no protection, and Cromwell witnessed the summary execution of a number of 'friars', including two killed the following day in cold blood.[18]

After describing the action in graphic detail, Cromwell then proceeded to justify his actions. In a reference to the massacre of Protestant settlers in 1641–2, he claimed that the killings at Drogheda constituted 'the righteous judgement of God upon these barbarous wretches, who have imbrued their hands in so much innocent blood'. The Catholic Irish, however, never controlled Drogheda during the 1640s, as the town remained in either parliamentary or royalist hands until Cromwell's arrival. It appeared, therefore, to be a highly unsuitable target for the purposes of revenge. Moreover, in addition to Catholic troops, the garrison contained English and Irish Protestants, who could not possibly have taken part in the events of 1641–2. Cromwell, fully briefed by Michael Jones and other Irish parliamentary supporters after landing in Dublin, knew this, but parliament had predicated the invasion of Ireland on the need to punish Catholic rebels for the massacre of Protestant settlers, and the new regime desperately needed military success to bolster flagging popularity on the domestic front. Like Charles I before them, the defenders of Drogheda, both Irish and English, Catholic and

Protestant, were adjudged guilty of prolonging the conflict un-necessarily, and they suffered accordingly. In a purely military sense, Cromwell's severity set a marker for the campaign of conquest, and once again he expressed the hope that the harsh tactics at Drogheda might discourage further resistance and 'prevent the effusion of blood for the future'.[19]

Despite all the self-congratulatory and self-justifying rhetoric, Cromwell implicitly conceded that something terrible had happened at Drogheda. He wrote that without 'the satisfactory grounds to such actions', outlined in his letters to Bradshaw and Lenthall, the scale of the slaughter could not 'but work remorse and regret'.[20] This sentence, largely ignored by historians, strongly suggests a man ill at ease with his conscience. As always, Cromwell found solace and comfort in his religious convictions, the unshakeable belief that he was doing God's will. Moreover, although this savage act sent shock waves throughout Ireland and abroad, in refusing quarter to enemy troops Cromwell had acted entirely within the accepted conventions of warfare at the time. The commander of Drogheda, Sir Arthur Aston, had refused a summons to surrender, thereby technically at least forfeiting the lives of the garrison in the event of a successful assault. Indeed, centuries later the duke of Wellington remarked, 'that it has always been understood that the defenders of a fortress stormed have no claim to quarter'.[21] So why did the events at Drogheda in September 1649 prove so controversial at the time and continue to be contested even today? It is important to stress that in the context of an Irish siege during the 1640s, or indeed one in England or Scotland, the sheer scale of the killing was simply unprecedented. Even after the fall of the town, Cromwell did not bother to preserve any prisoners for ransom or future exchanges with the enemy. The message seemed to be that his opponents could expect little mercy in what amounted to a war of extermination.

Cromwell's account raises a number of questions, principally relating to the nature and extent of enemy casualties. The two letters above are filled with internal contradictions, perhaps understandable given the confusion of battle. When writing to Bradshaw, Cromwell estimated the garrison of the town to number around 3,000, a figure based on a captured royalist muster roll compiled shortly before the town fell, and on his belief that the parliamentarians 'put to the sword the whole number of defendants'.[22] He speculated that no more than thirty soldiers, subsequently shipped to Barbados, escaped with their lives. In his account to Lenthall, however, he lists the casualties as somewhere in the region of 2,000, along with the officers seized when the last strongholds surrendered. Later in the same report, he speculates that up to 1,000 perished in the vicinity of St Peter's, having fled there for safety.[23] Did this 1,000 consist entirely of garrison troops, or in the chaos of the assault did civilians also perish? Uncertainty also surrounds events at Millmount. This imposing fortress would have proved difficult to storm, and yet it appears as if Aston and the other defenders threw down their weapons after no more than a cursory show of resistance. Cromwell specifies in the letter to Lenthall that he alone ordered the execution of all the prisoners, but why did Aston surrender before obtaining sufficient guarantees that his life and those of his men would be spared? Perhaps, given his experience of warfare on the Continent and in England, he simply presumed they would be taken prisoner, to be ransomed or exchanged. The alternative explanation is that somebody offered the defenders of Millmount quarter, which Cromwell subsequently overturned, as he had expressly forbidden his men 'to spare any that were in arms in the town'.[24]

A parliamentary broadsheet, published in London in early October, provides some insight into Aston's fate. According to *A Perfect Diurnall of Some Passages in Parliament*, Lieutenant Colonel Daniel Axtell went with twelve men to the top of the mount to confer with the garrison commander. They tried to convince him to surrender, but Aston 'was very stubborn speaking very big words'. Axtell persevered, eventually persuading the defenders to hand over their arms, at which time they were 'all slain'.[25] A royalist eyewitness account agrees with this version of events, but adds another vital piece of information. Garrett Dungan, one of the 'many men and some officers' who escaped from Drogheda, managed to reach Lord Inchiquin's camp, nearly forty miles away at Castlejordan. Inchiquin recorded Dungan's story in a letter to the marquis of Ormond.

According to Dungan, Aston was killed 'after quarter given by the officer that came first there', presumably Axtell.[26] This same Axtell subsequently gained a fearsome reputation in Ireland for brutality, and was temporarily suspended from active service in 1651, after executing eighteen civilians in retaliation for the deaths of some soldiers under his command. It may well be that Axtell simply broke his promise and slaughtered the helpless prisoners. More likely, and as Cromwell made clear in his letter, the decision to kill these men rested solely with the commander-in-chief. Such a calculated act of cold-blooded murder, not taken in the heat of action, was not only highly dishonourable but also a clear breach of the contemporary military code. Two years later, in 1651, Henry Ireton, Cromwell's son-in-law and replacement as commander-in-chief, dealt with a similar case in a very different matter. Ireton summoned a council of war to examine charges against Colonel Tothill, accused of executing troops who had surrendered on terms to a junior officer. The colonel argued that he possessed the authority to override a subordinate officer's actions, but the council disagreed and stripped Tothill of his command. Ireton worried that the punishment 'fell short of the justice of God required therein to the acquitting of the army from the guilt of so foul a sin'. He notified the royalists of the court martial, and released other prisoners without exchange or ransom, but he blamed a subsequent military setback on Tothill's earlier 'violation of faith'.[27] This case received extensive coverage in parliamentary news-sheets in London, and the parallels with his actions at Drogheda must have troubled Cromwell.

Dungan's tempered account of the storming of Drogheda provides a fascinating counter-balance to parliamentary reports. He confirmed Cromwell's responsibility for the massacre of the garrison, but related that 'many were privately saved by officers and soldiers'. This suggests that, like Ireton two years later, not everybody in the New Model Army shared their commander's views on how best to deal with the enemy. Intriguingly, Dungan insisted that a number of the leading royalist officers, such as Sir Edmund Verney and Colonel John Warren, were still alive twenty-four hours after the assault, although he could shed no light on their subsequent fate.[28]

This corresponds with later reports of the execution of these men in the days following the fall of Drogheda, another highly dishonourable act, as according to the Continental veteran, Sir James Turner, 'in such cases mercy is the more Christian, the more honourable, and the more ordinary way in our wars in Europe'.[29] It appears, however, as if the accepted military conventions did not apply in the case of the Catholic Irish and their royalist allies. In addition to Dungan, a number of other officers, such as Lieutenant Colonel Daniel Kavanagh, managed to escape the carnage. Captain Arthur Dillon also fled the doomed town and reported to Ormond on the 'putting to the sword of all the garrison', while Captain Tadhg Connor, left for dead, 'the rest of his men being all killed', slipped away under cover of darkness.[30]

If, as the evidence suggests, some of the garrison fled over the north wall of the town, and the parliamentarians spared other defenders, then the casualty figures presented by Cromwell and others, based on the captured muster rolls, are clearly inaccurate. The real controversy, however, revolves around the issue of civilian deaths. It seems highly unlikely that while storming a town in the face of stiff resistance, 10,000 parliamentary troops would at all times have distinguished, or been able to distinguish, between enemy soldiers and non-combatants. The account of Dean Bernard, an ardent royalist and Protestant cleric, who had resided in the town throughout the 1640s, appears to confirm this. Although no friend of the parliamentarians, Bernard was a keen advocate of Protestant unity in Ireland, to counter the influence of 'popery, heresies, blasphemies and such like errors that strike at the foundation of religion'. In a series of sermons composed in the months after the storming of the town, he tried to persuade Drogheda's Protestants not to quarrel among themselves, by reflecting on the events of early September. The dean reminded them of the threat to their lives and goods, spared 'by a special providence of God', and similarly how divine intervention saved hundreds of Protestants a few months later when a gallery packed with people collapsed during a service at a meeting house, but nobody suffered serious injuries.[31] Historians have seized on Bernard's comments as proof that no wholesale massacre of civilians took place at Drogheda, as the population apparently survived the initial assault and continued to thrive months later. In support of this case, the extant minutes of the corporation assembly, which begin on 6 April 1649, and continue through the 1650s, make no mention of the siege. These minutes, however, were not actually written up until after Cromwell's departure from Drogheda, and the fact they ignore the parliamentary assault, the biggest event in the town's history, is like records from London in 1666 not mentioning the Great Fire. After all the 'troubles' and upheaval of the summer, parliamentary sympathisers may simply have been trying to present an appearance to the world of business as usual.[32] As for Bernard, he only referred to the town's Protestant inhabitants and made no comment on the fate of the Catholics.

In many ways, a subsequent passage in Bernard's sermons is far more illuminating about the realities of warfare and the horrors of the storming of Drogheda. He describes how, 'in the heat of prosecution' immediately following the assault, parliamentary troops shot through the windows of his house, where over thirty Protestants had gathered seeking sanctuary, killing one person and seriously wounding another. The soldiers broke into the building, discharging their weapons, before the timely intervention of an officer known to the dean restored order.[33] This account raises a number of key issues. According to Bernard, the soldiers fired on civilians sheltering indoors, which belies claims that the parliamentarians only targeted those in arms. Moreover, the group was only saved from further harm when an officer recognised Bernard and identified his companions as Protestants. The implications of this sequence of events for the town's Catholics do not require any further explanation. A more detailed relation of Bernard's experiences, apparently penned after the Restoration, alleged that the parliamentarians attacked the dean's house because of his well-known loyalty to the king and Ormond.[34] This second document, written to demonstrate Bernard's royalist credentials, nonetheless confirms the basic thrust of the earlier narrative. Therefore, according to the one surviving civilian account of the storming of Drogheda, troops of the New Model Army deliberately attacked non-combatants in their homes.

During the 1660s, petitions to the court of claims, established to resolve land disputes following the restoration of Charles II, listed a number of people, including Captain Thomas Archer and Robert Hartlepoole, as 'slain at Drogheda in his majesty's service'. Alongside these military personnel, however, others, such as James Fleming, are described as 'murdered', while Henry Mortimer, an alderman of the town, was killed 'being then about seventy years of age'.[35] Cromwell similarly distinguished between soldiers and non-combatants in his reports to England. On 27 September 1649, he sent Lenthall an update of developments in Ireland, along with specific details of enemy losses at Drogheda. In addition to the 3,000 military casualties, the list included the phrase 'and many inhabitants'. Unfortunately, the original letter does not appear to have survived, but parliament ordered a copy to be published on 2 October.[36] Writing in the mid-nineteenth century, Thomas Carlyle claimed, without any evidence whatsoever, that the offending phrase must have been added in a later printed compilation, while C. H. Firth suggested that the printers in 1649 may have tagged the casualty list on to Cromwell's letter, perhaps on parliament's command.[37] Carlyle's supposition is easy to dismiss, as the original pamphlet from October 1649, complete with the incriminating phrase, still exists. As for Firth's theory, the parliamentary regime in England took a close interest in the world of publishing, and passed an act in late September to control output. John Field and Edward Husband, official printers to parliament, risked losing their positions if they tampered with official documents in any way. Moreover, Firth never explained why parliament might have added something so important to one of Cromwell's letters, without his approval. Oftentimes, the most straightforward answer is the correct one. In his report, Cromwell, who had witnessed the assault on Drogheda at close quarters, simply acknowledged that the casualties included many civilians.

In deciding to publish Cromwell's dispatches from Ireland, parliament publicly signalled the support of members for his conduct in the field. The general received a letter of thanks, taking notice 'that the House doth approve of the execution done at

Drogheda as an act both of justice to them and mercy to others who may be warned by it'.[38] The parliamentarians fully understood the importance of this victory in bolstering support for the Commonwealth regime in England. The Council of State ordered that Captain Samuel Porter be paid £100 'for his pains and charges in his journey bringing the news of taking Drogheda', which was officially proclaimed in churches across London.[39] In Ireland, Cromwell proved eager to exploit the psychological advantage the massacre gave him over his opponents. On 12 September, the day after taking the town, he wrote to the commander of Dundalk, the nearest royalist garrison, demanding that the town capitulate without delay in order to avoid a similar fate. The defenders, however, had already fled, while Carlingford and Newry subsequently surrendered without a fight. As word of Cromwell's severity at Drogheda spread throughout Ireland, it appeared as if his harsh policy might indeed pay immediate military dividends.

Outside Ireland, news of the massacre travelled fast, as letters flooded back to England, a number of which were subsequently published. Bulstrode Whitelocke, a leading figure in the parliamentary regime, acknowledged that the various accounts provided different perspectives on events at Drogheda, but 'they all agreed in the not giving of quarter'.[40] In some instances, parliamentary soldiers returning home from service in Ireland provided eyewitness testimony. Thomas Wood, for example, fought at Drogheda, and regaled his family in England the following year with colourful and lurid stories about the killing of civilians, which his brother later published.[41] In early October 1649, reports reached the Continent of Cromwell's bloody victory in Ireland. The Venetian ambassador in Paris received a letter from England (dated late September 1649), which told of 'a sanguinary encounter' at Drogheda, which according to the exiled royalist John Evelyn, 'makes us very sad, forerunning the loss of all Ireland'.[42] Shortly afterwards, Charles Stuart's secretary, Sir Edward Nicholas, also in Paris, wrote to Ormond about Drogheda, 'and the cruelty used by those inhumane rebels that took it, which had made a great impression of grief in his Majesty'.[43] By November royalists circulated detailed accounts of the killing of officers in breach of quarter. James Buck, for example, wrote to Sir Ralph Verney describing the cold-blooded murder of his brother Edmund as he walked alongside Cromwell three days after the town fell, and the execution of Colonel Boyle around the same time, allegedly summoned away to his death while dining with Lady Moore.[44]

Despite the best efforts of the parliamentarian regime, underground royalist news-sheets continued to appear regularly in London throughout 1649, publishing bitter diatribes against the new political order. The English press had become increasingly preoccupied with the affairs of Ireland during the course of the year, and eagerly awaited news of Cromwell's progress. On 22 September, a vessel from Ireland brought information that Drogheda had fallen, with the loss of 3,000 defenders. *The Moderate Messenger*, a pro-parliamentary publication, wanted to believe the news, 'but reports are commonly accompanied with such incredible stories, that it diminisheth that credit which otherwise would be given thereto'.[45] The royalist press also responded cautiously, with the editor of *Mercurius Elencticus* declaring that he would not render himself 'so ridiculous as others have done, in reporting falsities improbable, nay impossible things, to please the credulous readers'.[46] Other news-sheets simply denied the veracity of recent stories from Ireland, claiming as late as the first week in October that Drogheda still held out against Cromwell. The parliamentarian press mocked the unwillingness of royalists to accept the growing body of evidence about the storming of the town, particularly following the publication of letters from Hugh Peters and Cromwell on 2 October. Peters, however, did not witness events at Drogheda, as he only arrived in Dublin from Milford Haven on 11 September with the final detachments of the expeditionary force, and one critic poked fun at his precise figure of 3,552 enemy losses, 'not a man more or less'.[47] Casualty lists were notoriously inaccurate in the early modern period, and frequently manipulated by the victors. Following the rout of Ormond's army at Rathmines in early August, *Mercurius Elencticus* claimed that the parliamentarians had tampered with a letter from Dublin giving details of the battle, doubling the number of royalist casualties 'with an ink of a blacker temper than the letter was written in'.[48] Similarly, *The Man in the Moon* questioned the figures from Drogheda, and declared that the besiegers themselves had lost 3,000 men.[49] In an effort to convince a sceptical public, the parliamentary press published Cromwell's report, including his full casualty list, although a handful of news-sheets, perhaps uncomfortable with the large-scale slaughter of civilians, did not include the incriminating phrase 'and many inhabitants'.[50]

All pro-parliamentary accounts, however, accepted Cromwell's justification that events at Drogheda would hasten the end of the conflict in Ireland. An official government publication insisted that the sacking of the town had so terrified the enemy, 'that they scarce can make a defensive war against us, but leave us everywhere masters of the field'.[51] According to another report, 'though some are of opinion, that the enemy's rage will be the greater, by the slaughter at Tredagh, yet we find the terror great that is upon them'.[52] Unable to refute the evidence any longer, the royalist press instead focused on the 'inhuman cruelty' of the parliamentary forces, and for the first time stories about a wholesale massacre of civilians began to emerge. In early October, *Mercurius Elencticus*, until then the most moderate of the royalist news-sheets (at least in its Irish coverage), made a number of specific and shocking allegations. The dead at Drogheda included women and children, while many officers died after quarter had been promised them, 'in the most cruel manner they could invent, cutting off their members, and pieces of their flesh, which they wore in their hats triumphantly two days after'.[53] *The Man in the Moon* picked up on the allegations of civilian deaths the following week, claiming that the figure of 3,000 dead included 2,000 women and children. Drawing a direct comparison between Cromwell and the Catholic rebels in 1641–2, the editorial condemned the 'barbarous cruelty in that abhorrid act [at Drogheda] not to be paralleled by any of the former massacres of the Irish'.[54] Whether based on first-hand accounts from Ireland or rumours circulating around London, these stories added to Cromwell's growing reputation for cruelty.

Back in Ireland, the marquis of Ormond admitted in a letter to Charles Stuart that it was 'not to be imagined how great the terror is that those successes and the power of the rebels have struck into this

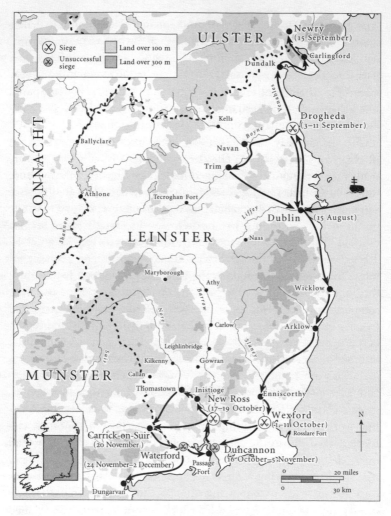

Map 3 Cromwell's Campaign, August–December 1649

people', while another contemporary believed that the royalists lost 'both courage and resolution' as a result of the defeat.[55] Basing his account of developments on the reports of survivors, Ormond quickly put his pen to work, denouncing the actions of Cromwell and the New Model Army. On 18 September, he informed Prince Rupert of the fall of the town, with the 'bloody execution of almost all that were within it'.[56] The following week, in a letter to Charles, Ormond accused Cromwell of 'much more than anything I ever heard of in breach of faith and bloody inhumanity'.[57] He compared the behaviour of the parliamentarians to that of the royalists, giving as an example the storming of a small fortification outside Dublin the previous July. The royalists took the entire garrison at Rathfarnham prisoner on that occasion, 'and though 500 soldiers had entered the castle before any officers of note yet not one creature was killed, which I here tell you by the way to observe the difference between ours and the rebels making use of a victory'.[58] While unreserved in condemning the massacre at Drogheda to royalist leaders abroad, Ormond proved uncertain on how best to exploit the affair in Ireland itself. Cromwell's severe tactics had clearly unnerved his opponents in the field. Dundalk, Newry and Carlingford all surrendered without a fight, and when units of the parliamentary army approached Trim on the march back to Dublin, the panicked garrison fled, failing to burn the town and castle as ordered. Surviving evidence suggests that Ormond might well have played down the horrors of Drogheda on the domestic front, so as not to unduly alarm his supporters. Nonetheless, the story of an atrocity committed at Cromwell's express order was in circulation not only in Ireland, but also in England and on the Continent within weeks of the fall of the town. By the 1660s, following the restoration of Charles II, Irish clerical sources confidently asserted that 4,000 civilians had died in Drogheda, the result of 'an unparalleled savagery and treachery beyond that of any slaughterhouse'.[59] The issue remains contentious to the present day but the surviving evidence clearly shows that a significant number of non-combatants were killed during the storming of the town.

Despite the widespread and long-lasting repercussions of events at Drogheda, it merely represented the opening salvo in a long war of conquest. After a week replenishing supplies in Dublin, Cromwell departed from the capital again on 23 September, leaving sick and wounded soldiers behind, and headed south though County

Wicklow, on route for Wexford. Described by a parliamentary news-sheet as 'the Dunkirk of Ireland, and a place only famous for being infamous', the port of Wexford provided a base for a large privateering fleet, consisting primarily of Irish and Flemish vessels, which successfully targeted English shipping throughout the 1640s.[60] This unofficial confederate navy maintained valuable trade and communication links between Ireland and the Continent, as well as posing a major threat to Cromwell's vital supply lines with England. As they marched southwards, the parliamentarians captured a number of smaller garrisons, but they also proved vulnerable to ambush in the mountainous terrain of south Wicklow and north Wexford. In one such encounter, a contingent of O'Byrnes seized some horses, including Cromwell's own charger, and other supplies. Nonetheless, a force of around 9,000 troops reached the outskirts of Wexford town on 1 October relatively unscathed. The royalists had garrisoned the town only a few days earlier with 1,500 troops commanded by Colonel David Sinnott, who warned Ormond of the inhabitants' inclination to make terms, 'such impression they have of Drogheda'.[61] The chances of a successful defence, already undermined by low morale and internal divisions over whether or not to surrender, further diminished when, on the approach of a parliamentary detachment, royalist troops inexplicably abandoned the fort of Rosslare, which guarded the entrance to the harbour. The fort occupied a strong position but was possibly undermanned. Whatever the reason, capturing Rosslare allowed the English navy, commanded by Admiral Deane, to discharge vital military supplies, including the siege artillery.

Confident of success, Cromwell summoned the town to surrender on 3 October, but as the weather turned wet and stormy, Sinnott played for time, entering into protracted negotiations during the following week. His initial demands included a complete cessation of hostilities while the talks took place, and more controversially the continued free exercise of the Catholic religion. Irritated by Sinnott's tactics, Cromwell angrily refused to halt preparations for storming the town, as 'our tents are not so good a covering as your houses'.[62] While the parliamentary troops suffered in the exposed conditions, the defenders continued to receive supplies, including 500 additional troops, by ferry from the north of the harbour, suggesting that, as at Drogheda, Cromwell had not carried out the basic requirement of surrounding and cutting off the besieged town. Finally, on 10 October, the siege artillery opened fire, creating two breaches in the medieval walls the following day, and forcing Sinnott to reopen negotiations. The two sides argued over surrender terms, including a guarantee for the life and liberty of the garrison, and protection for the townspeople from violence and plunder. At the same time, however, Captain Stafford, governor of Wexford Castle, a stronghold overlooking the town, initiated his own contacts with the parliamentarians. Stafford, 'a vain, idle young man . . . nothing practised in the art military', agreed to open the gates to the besiegers, who immediately turned the castle guns on the town.[63] Panicked, the defenders fled, allowing parliamentary soldiers to scale the walls unopposed. The garrison rallied near the market place, but their spirited resistance proved futile. Cromwell wrote that over 2,000 Irish soldiers and civilians, including Sinnott, died as the English 'put all to the sword that came in their way'.[64] According to a petition of the surviving inhabitants, all the men, women and children of the town 'to a very few' were killed during the assault, while a clerical account described how 'the blood lust of soldiers flooded the streets and houses'.[65] Many perished when overcrowded boats overturned in the harbour, but at least one eyewitness claimed that the parliamentarians spared more soldiers at Wexford than at Drogheda, to use them as forced labour during the campaign.[66] Others apparently escaped the carnage, as by the end of the week, the Commissioners of Treaty in Kilkenny complained to Ormond about large numbers of troops, many of them wounded, streaming into the city, 'that pretend all of them to come off from Wexford'.[67] Cromwell seized over seventy pieces of artillery, and tons of supplies, along with a number of warships, but widespread pillaging by his troops upset Cromwell's plans for using the town as a winter base. Nonetheless, the fall of Wexford permanently crippled the royalist/confederate navy. Not long afterwards, Prince Rupert broke through the English blockade at Kinsale and fled with a small fleet of seven ships to Portugal. By the end of the year, therefore, Irish naval activity was reduced to a handful of privateers working out of Continental ports such as Dunkirk and Ostend.

Unlike Drogheda, Cromwell did not participate directly in the storming of Wexford, and there are no reports of breach of quarter, such as happened at Millmount. Nonetheless, the deaths of large numbers of civilians at the hands of soldiers under his command further tarnished Cromwell's reputation with the Catholic Irish. Worryingly for the parliamentarians, there was growing evidence that their tactics had begun to generate a military backlash. When Cromwell's forces approached the strategic fort of Duncannon in late October, the commander, Thomas Roche, rejected a summons to surrender, as 'I and those under my command are sensible of your cruel and tyrannical quarter'. Shortly afterwards, when the royalists attempted to retake the town of Carrick, recently seized by the parliamentarians, the attackers cried out to the besieged 'that they would soon give them Tredagh [Drogheda] Quarters'.[68] Rather than bring an end to the conflict, the massacre at Drogheda, and to a lesser extent events at Wexford, may have actually stiffened the resolve of the Catholic Irish to fight on against an indiscriminate and merciless enemy. With no end to the war in sight, and unable to use Wexford as a winter base, Cromwell faced a difficult choice. He could retreat to Dublin, through hostile territory, and risk losing many of the gains of the previous months, or attempt to break into Munster, by crossing the river Barrow at the town of Ross. Despite continuing losses through disease, reducing his effective combat force to as little as 3,000 men, and Ormond's presence nearby with a numerically superior army, Cromwell characteristically chose to march on Ross.

After this second crushing defeat at Wexford, the royalist alliance received a timely boost with the news of Owen Roe O'Neill's decision to join forces with Ormond. The arrival of Cromwell had convinced Ormond of the need for a speedy reconciliation with the Ulster Irish, which the marquis of Clanricarde believed 'would unquestionably unite the whole kingdom'.[69] After months of violent confrontations and fruitless negotiations, the lord lieutenant sent emissaries north in late August, including the Ulster general's Protestant nephew,

Daniel O'Neill, to agree terms as a matter of urgency. Owen Roe responded positively, though he honourably waited for his temporary truce with Charles Coote in Derry to expire before giving the order for his army, estimated at about 5,000 strong, to march south. Ormond hoped that news of these manoeuvres might have relieved the pressure on royalist forces elsewhere, but 'an unexpected fit of sickness' delayed the Ulster general's departure.[70] In fact, O'Neill, almost seventy years of age and seriously ill with gout, which made any movement almost unbearably painful, had only a few weeks to live. Progress proved tortuously slow, so in mid-October he sent 2,000 troops on ahead, who according to one report were 'ill-armed, but very useful men if but fed'.[71] A few days later, on 20 October, O'Neill finally agreed to serve under Ormond at the head of an army of 6,000 infantry and 800 cavalry, terms almost identical to those rejected by the royalists at the start of the year. Bitterness engendered by confederate infighting in the late 1640s, along with a general mistrust of the Ulster Irish, had prevented an earlier rapprochement, thus enabling Cromwell to gain a vital foothold in the kingdom. Moreover, O'Neill's decision to intervene in Leinster now allowed a parliamentary force of 5,000 men, commanded by Colonel Robert Venables, to advance north from Drogheda into Ulster practically unopposed. Many of the Scots in Ulster, equally hostile to Irish Catholics and English parliamentarians, observed a position of strict neutrality, while an attempt by George Monro and Lord Clandeboye to rally royalist forces resulted in a catastrophic defeat at Lisburn near Belfast in early December. By the end of the year, Colonel John Reynolds, supported by Charles Coote in Derry, controlled much of the northern province, including all seaports apart from Castle Doe in County Donegal.

In the south, despite the arrival of the Ulster Irish vanguard, Ormond proved incapable of stemming the parliamentary offensive. Just over a week after the fall of Wexford, the strategically crucial town of Ross surrendered to the parliamentarians after a brief siege, opening the gateway into Munster. According to an official account of the proceedings of the English army in Ireland, the parliamentarians feared that taking the town might have cost 'much blood, it being of a considerable strength'.[72] Cromwell attempted to undermine royalist morale by allowing two captured officers from Wexford, Majors Dillon and Byrne, to travel to Ross in advance of his army. They undoubtedly related stories of the horrors suffered by the inhabitants of Wexford, and the garrison commander, Lucas Taaffe, suspected the townsmen of seeking to avoid a similar fate by agreeing terms with the parliamentarians. On arriving outside the walls of Ross, Cromwell summoned Taaffe to surrender, claiming, despite recent events at Drogheda and Wexford, that he had always 'endeavoured to avoid effusion of blood'. According to Cromwell, both towns, by refusing terms, had suffered 'through their own wilfulness'.[73] Taaffe urgently requested assistance, and Ormond assured the Commissioners of Treaty in Kilkenny that he would send reinforcements, as Cromwell's failure to take Ross would prove 'a great dishonour and loss to the [English] rebels'.[74]

On the morning of 19 October, however, the parliamentary artillery created a breach in the town walls. Before the inevitable infantry assault began, Taaffe surrendered, with Cromwell permitting the garrison to march away with arms and baggage, and guaranteeing the civilian population protection from 'injury and violence'. The reward for non-resistance did not extend to religious freedom, despite Cromwell's assurances that he did not 'meddle' with any man's conscience. In an exchange of correspondence with Taaffe, he explained in typically blunt terms that 'if by liberty of conscience you mean a liberty to exercise the mass, I judge it best to plain dealing, and to let you know, where the Parliament of England have power, that will not be allowed of'.[75] Cromwell's position was entirely consistent with his Independent religious convictions. Nobody would coerce the Catholic Irish to attend Protestant services, but at the same time the Catholic Church would not be tolerated. The loss of Ross dealt yet another blow to the royalist war effort and to Ormond's rapidly diminishing authority, particularly as Taaffe insisted that the lord lieutenant had authorised his actions. Discontent with Ormond was not restricted to the ranks of the Catholic clergy, and 500 Protestant royalist troops at Ross defected to the New Model Army.

Successive defeats, starting with the rout at Rathmines, had strained the uneasy alliance between confederates and Irish Protestants to breaking point. For Protestants in the ports of Youghal, Cork and Kinsale, under the control of Lord Inchiquin for much of the 1640s, Irish Catholics, not English parliamentarians, remained the principal enemy. The success of royalist forces during the first half of 1649 kept them in check, but the arrival of the New Model Army provided Protestants with a viable alternative to fighting alongside their hated Catholic neighbours, and the number of desertions from royalist forces increased dramatically, despite the introduction of the death penalty for offenders. Even before the fall of Wexford, officers sympathetic to the parliamentary regime had attempted unsuccessfully to seize Youghal, but the relentless advance of Cromwell's forces finally convinced many Munster towns to renounce Ormond's authority and declare 'for the Protestant religion and interest of the English nation'.[76] This switch of allegiance by Youghal, Cork and Kinsale probably prevented the premature end of Cromwell's expedition, by providing winter quarters for his depleted forces, as well as suitable ports to receive supplies from England. The local Protestant population also enthusiastically volunteered to join Cromwell's army, each one of whom, according to a contemporary correspondent, was worth six soldiers from England.[77] These new recruits possessed an intense determination to pursue total victory by force of arms.

Before Cromwell could fully take advantage of local Protestant support, however, he needed to secure a passage into Munster by crossing the river Barrow, already swollen with winter rains, using a specially constructed boat bridge. This provided an ideal opportunity for a royalist counter-attack against weakened forces engaged in a difficult manoeuvre. Unfortunately for the royalists, Ormond proved unequal to the task. An apocryphal story tells how Cromwell, when staying in the house of Francis Dormer in Ross, came across a portrait of Ormond, and announced that his opponent, whom he had never met, looked 'more like a huntsman than any way a soldier'.[78] In Ormond's defence, following a series of catastrophic setbacks, the royalists faced enormous obstacles in trying to reorganise their shattered forces. In addition to low morale, intensified by the seemingly unstoppable momentum of the parliamentary offensive, the royalist lord lieutenant also had to contend with military supply problems and a severe lack of cash. All gunpowder, for example, had to be imported from the Continent, a more difficult task after the fall of Wexford, while the city of Limerick would only offer £100 towards the war effort, 'so inconsiderable a sum' that the royalist leadership refused to accept it.[79] Moreover, the slow progress south of the Ulster Irish, due to O'Neill's illness, delayed the arrival of significant reinforcements. In these circumstances, the Ulster general cautioned Ormond not to fight Cromwell except on 'great advantages'. He believed that the weather would almost certainly defeat the parliamentarians before any army the royalists could possibly muster. On 1 November, O'Neill again warned that any precipitous engagement with Cromwell would be 'of a most dangerous consequence', resulting in the loss of the kingdom.[80] Ormond needed no lessons in prevarication and delay, but this correspondence suggests that the great Ulster general would have adopted a similarly wary approach.

A few days later, Owen Roe O'Neill, his body ravaged by decades of campaigning on the Continent and in Ireland, died at Cloughoughter Castle in County Cavan, the home of Sir Philip MacHugh O'Reilly, a staunch ally, and one of the original conspirators in the 1641 rebellion. His death deprived the Catholic Irish of their most successful military commander, and perhaps the only general with the necessary skills and experience to challenge the parliamentarians on the field of battle. One source lamented how the enemy now no longer feared the name General O'Neill, 'which not long before did sound like a thunderbolt in his ears'.[81] Nonetheless, despite this serious setback all was by no means lost. By making a stand on the Barrow, Ormond would have created serious difficulties for the parliamentarians, denying them access to the Munster ports and precipitating a retreat to Dublin. A royalist officer, Major Benson, compiled a detailed report on the possibility of preventing a crossing 'without the hazard of our whole fortune upon a battle'. He argued that the royalists should avoid a set piece encounter 'until their courage be a little [recovered] by some small successes against the enemy, either by surprisal, ambush or other advantage'. Both Benson and Lord Inchiquin strongly recommended the destruction of any bridge thrown across the Barrow before the entire parliamentary army had crossed, thus restoring royalist morale.[82] On 6 November, however, John Walsh, Ormond's lawyer, reported the presence of English troops on the west side of the river. Their sudden appearance caused panic in the local population, who fled with their cattle and portable goods. With the parliamentary forces now spilt while they completed work on the pontoon bridge, the earl of Castlehaven urged Ormond to take immediate action, stressing the vulnerability of Cromwell's position. According to the earl's scouts, the parliamentary bridgehead contained no defensive works and few troops to ward off any assault. Ormond, naturally cautious and crippled by indecision, failed to take advantage of the situation, hoping instead that 'Colonel Hunger and Major Sickness' would further diminish enemy forces. Within a week the entire parliamentary army had crossed the river unopposed. Deeply disappointed, Castlehaven informed the marquis of the growing discontent of the Catholic population with his poor military performance.[83]

Ormond desperately needed some success to bolster his waning authority, and after months of disastrous defeats and missed opportunities, he finally received good news from Duncannon. Situated on the mouth of the Suir, the fort of Duncannon, one of the most modern in the country, guarded the entrance to Waterford Harbour. A heroic defence of the fort in early November severely dented the New Model Army's myth of invincibility, and gave hope to other royalist towns and garrisons. Undaunted by this setback, the parliamentarians maintained their offensive, with one column, commanded by Michael Jones and Henry Ireton, pushing north towards Kilkenny. Despite enjoying a significant numerical advantage, Ormond declined an engagement, and Jones eventually withdrew to rejoin the main army moving south against Waterford. Cromwell, after recovering from a serious fever, which had already killed or debilitated hundreds of his own troops, hoped to exploit internal tensions within the city and avoid a lengthy siege in difficult conditions. Castlehaven blamed Catholic clerics for attempting to undermine royalist authority there, but he acknowledged that four out of five of Waterford's citizens would have gladly sold the city for private gain.[84] Many former confederates never forgave Ormond for his unwillingness during the 1640s to grant major concessions to Irish Catholics, despite authorisation from Charles I, while dissatisfaction with his military performance simply exacerbated a growing sense of grievance. On 21 November, John Lyvett, mayor of Waterford, informed Ormond that Cromwell had arrived at the city walls but that reinforcements could still get through. Lyvett identified certain unnamed troops, almost certainly those under Ormond's command, as unacceptable.[85] Instead, the municipal authorities granted access to a detachment of Ulster Irish, proven fighters and committed Catholics, led by Lieutenant General Richard Farrell. Faced with determined resistance and appallingly wet weather, which made moving siege artillery almost impossible and facilitated the spread of disease through his exposed forces, Cromwell lifted the siege in early December and retired to the southern ports of Munster.

Secure at last in his winter quarters, Cromwell could reflect on a relatively successful autumn campaign. In the space of just four months, he had inflicted a series of spectacular defeats on the royalists, and seized control of the entire eastern, northern and southern coastlines, with the exception of Waterford and Duncannon. The royalists appeared incapable of opposing him in the field, and the tenuous alliance between Catholics and Protestants had all but collapsed. Nonetheless, Cromwell failed to land a decisive military blow, and large tracts of the country remained in hostile hands. Naval supply lines had proved crucial so far, but this advantage would no longer be available to him as soon as his forces marched inland. The English army, ravaged by disease, continued to suffer grievous losses, including the death of Colonel Michael Jones in early December, 'whose finger', according to Cromwell, 'to our knowledge never ached in all these expeditions'.[86] Moreover, his opponents, initially demoralised by successive defeats, appeared re-energised at the end of the year by the intervention of the Ulster Irish, despite the death of Owen Roe O'Neill. Questions remained, however, over whether Ormond and his lieutenants possessed the necessary military skills and popular support to counter the parliamentary offensive. Fully aware of the difficult task ahead, Ormond remarked pessimistically that 'the breathing time which probably the enemy will give us this winter is like to be but a short reprieve'.[87] Cromwell remained characteristically busy during the winter months, planning his next move. On the last day of the year, he wrote to John Sadler, town clerk of London, blaming Catholic landlords and 'great men' for the 'injustice, tyranny and oppression' suffered by the ordinary people of Ireland. He argued that the free and impartial administration of justice, no doubt meaning English justice, would make the country 'look so much the more glorious and beautiful'.[88] After the atrocities at Drogheda and Wexford, it is doubtful if any Irish Catholics shared his vision of a bright future under parliamentary rule.

5

Cromwell's Advance

The truth is I am already condemned amongst them,
and I believe your Excellency has but a short reprieve,
for . . . they cannot trust you, except you go to Mass.[1]
LORD INCHIQUIN TO THE MARQUIS OF ORMOND (1649)

In early November 1649, Ormond's vice-treasurer, James Dillon, the earl of Roscommon, spent an evening out carousing in the city of Limerick, in the company of his Protestant compatriots, the bishops of Derry and Clonfert. On the way home, 'after his accustomed over much civility' in leading the way in the dark, and no doubt somewhat the worse for wear, he fell down a flight of steps and cracked his head. Although everybody expected the earl to recover, the mayor of Limerick immediately ruled out any suspicion of foul play, primarily 'to prevent busy and evil tongues'. Indeed, according to one sarcastic commentator, such an accident might well have happened coming out of church, 'if the church had been above stairs'.[2] Unfortunately, Roscommon's condition deteriorated and after a few days he died, but not before a major row had erupted between the Protestant and Catholic clergy in the city. Apart from the earl, the extended Dillon family was entirely Catholic, and Bishop Bramhall of Derry, Roscommon's companion on the night of the accident, reported to Ormond how Catholic clerics had entered the noble's bedchamber while their servants kept everybody else outside. Although he was lifeless as a corpse, the priests somehow reconciled the fatally injured earl to the Catholic Church, and intended to bury him according to their rites. Outraged, Ormond described the alleged deathbed conversion as 'amongst the saddest of my apprehensions'.[3] Religious tensions threatened to boil over, with people afraid to visit 'a Protestant but in the night lest it should give distaste to others of the town'.[4] Shortly afterwards, in an effort to defuse the situation, the Catholic bishop of Limerick, while insisting that the earl had died in the bosom of the Church of Rome, agreed that he could be laid to rest in the family tomb of the Protestant earls of Thomond without public solemnities. After consulting with his priests, however, the bishop added that any attempt to remove the body from the city would be resisted.[5] This extraordinary battle for the body and soul of the earl of Roscommon presaged the complete breakdown in relations between the Catholic Irish and Protestant royalists, including Ormond.

The rapid advance of parliamentary forces temporarily pacified this damaging internal dispute and focused attention instead on military affairs. In early December, less than a month after Roscommon's death, the Catholic bishops assembled at the historic monastic site of Clonmacnoise in an unprecedented show of clerical unity. Although bitterly divided among themselves since the furore over the confederate truce with the Protestant Lord Inchiquin in 1648, the prelates nonetheless recognised the far greater threat posed to their interests by Oliver Cromwell and the New Model Army. Shocked by events at Drogheda and Wexford, including the deliberate targeting of Catholic clergy, the bishops issued a public proclamation in a desperate effort to rally support for the royalist cause.[6] They claimed that the parliamentarians intended 'to extirpate the Catholic religion out of all his Majesties dominions', which could not be effected 'without the massacring or banishment of the Catholic inhabitants'. Once the conquest was complete, everybody would be uprooted to make room for a new wave of colonists. Crude parliamentary attempts to appeal to the 'common sort of people' were 'to no other end but for their private advantage, and for the better support of their army'. The bishops expressly condemned any attempts to sow divisions 'between either Provinces or families, or between old English and old Irish, or any English or Scots adhering to his Majesty'. In a direct echo of the confederate oath, they declared themselves, 'by the blessing of God', to be united in the interests of the Catholic Church, as well as 'the advancement of his Majesties rights, and the good of this Nation in general'. Conscious of growing clerical hostility to his authority, Ormond expressed pleasant surprise that the Ecclesiastical Congregation had not issued a protest against him, but the clear lack of enthusiasm for his continuing leadership was an ominous sign. In fact, the meeting at Clonmacnoise represented the opening gambit by the clergy to resurrect the confederate association and regain a central role in Irish political affairs. Sidelined to a large degree by the Kilkenny peace treaty, the bishops deeply resented the loss of the power and influence they had enjoyed for much of the 1640s. Although prepared for the moment to present a united front against the parliamentary invaders, any further military setbacks would provide them with the motivation and opportunity to challenge Ormond directly.

Despite the belated efforts of the Catholic bishops at Clonmacnoise, the confederate/royalist alliance had already begun to unravel, as increasing numbers of people blamed Ormond for the litany of military disasters since the debacle at Rathmines. One of the first public criticisms appeared as early as mid-October, when an English royalist news-sheet *Mercurius Elencticus* drew attention to the marquis's failure to attempt a relief of Drogheda, 'to the wonder and amazement of all the king's friends'.[7] A few weeks later, Donough MacCarthy, Viscount Muskerry, Ormond's brother-in-law, voiced concern in a letter to the lord lieutenant that the resentment and bitterness of the past decade had begun to bubble to the surface once again. Expressing a personal as well as a public grievance, the viscount identified Ormond's policy of favouring Englishmen over 'Catholic natives' as causing particular offence. He accepted the need to encourage recruits from across the Irish Sea, but with Cromwell's arrival and 'your fortune changed from being successful, it is not to be expected that they will be so faithful to the declining side against their prevailing countrymen'. Given the alarming rate of desertions to parliamentary forces since August, Muskerry argued that Ormond should rely exclusively on an army of native Irishmen.[8] Around the same time, the ardent royalist John Barry reported on the growing chaos in east Cork, 'hitherto held the securest of this kingdom'. Barry no longer knew 'whom to destroy or what to preserve and yet it is necessary I do both'. He concluded with a portentous warning that if

Cromwell's advance was not halted soon 'you will not only find the English, but also the Irish will desert you'.[9] Developments elsewhere in Munster appeared to confirm Barry's worst fears. On 16 November John Walsh described an encounter near Waterford with the marquis of Antrim, a long-time adversary of the lord lieutenant. According to Antrim, 'it was the opinion of many a considerable man though not of the common sort' that their leaders had betrayed them.[10] The following day, the earl of Castlehaven, also writing from Waterford, confirmed the existence of widespread unrest in former confederate circles.[11] Neither man proposed a solution to the growing crisis, but in Muskerry's opinion, the Catholic Church held the key to future royalist success, as nothing could prejudice Ormond 'or his majesty's service more than this apprehension in them who have so great an influence upon the consciences of the people'.[12] The marquis of Clanricarde agreed, and advised Ormond in late December on the importance of maintaining good relations with the Catholic bishops, or else nothing could be expected in the future 'but rebellion, factions and all manner of confusions'.[13]

Although some of these criticisms related specifically to the conduct of the ongoing military campaign, many of them arose from a personal dislike of Ormond and of his policies during the 1640s. Irish Protestants distrusted the marquis because of his alleged leniency towards Catholics, who in turn accused him of withholding vital religious concessions granted by King Charles I. In many ways, Ormond faced an impossible task, as any attempt to unite Irish Protestants and Catholics would invariably attract hostile comment from both camps. The initial success of the royalists in early 1649 silenced most internal opposition, but only the physical presence of Charles Stuart could realistically have kept such diverse factions together. His decision not to travel to Ireland seriously weakened the new alliance, while Cromwell's spectacular victories re-opened old wounds, and led many to question Ormond's abilities or even his loyalty to the crown. Ormond's surrender of Dublin in 1647 to the parliamentarians rather than the confederates clearly still rankled, but accusations of treachery made by Antrim and others relating to his conduct after Cromwell's arrival in Ireland are completely without foundation. His failure, however, to prevent the New Model Army from crossing the river Barrow at Ross, and gaining access to the former confederate heartland of south Leinster and Munster, appeared at best grossly negligent. As commander-in-chief of the armed forces, Ormond ultimately had to accept responsibility for the catastrophic defeats at Rathmines, Drogheda and Wexford, while his lacklustre military performance in the latter months of 1649 undoubtedly contributed to the haemorrhaging of royalist support. Facing an enemy superior in terms of equipment, supplies and finances, the marquis appeared totally bereft of ideas or even a coherent strategy.

Charges of favouritism towards Protestants and the English are also not easily dismissed. As a leader of a mainly Catholic Irish alliance, Ormond needed to display great sensitivity in maintaining a strict religious and ethnic balance where possible. Instead, he consistently favoured his own family, friends and clients, as well as new arrivals from England, in making appointments to key military and administrative posts. In addition, he displayed poor political judgement when dealing with disputes of a religious nature. In late January 1649, just two weeks after the ceremonial signing of the peace treaty in Kilkenny, the marquis of Clanricarde, the leading Catholic nobleman in the kingdom, voluntarily resigned as second in command of the army in favour of the Protestant Lord Inchiquin, who allegedly would only answer directly to Ormond. Clanricarde's typically selfless act, intended to placate the volatile Inchiquin, made good sense in purely military terms, replacing an indifferent performer with an energetic commander of proven ability, but politically it created enormous problems. Not only did Protestants now occupy the top two positions in the army, but also most Irish Catholics detested Inchiquin for perpetrating a number of atrocities during the 1640s, including the massacre of civilians and clergy at Cashel. Increased religious tensions might well have been avoided if Ormond had simply refused to accept Clanricarde's resignation, or failing that, replaced him with another Catholic general, preferably from outside his own intimate circle.

The lord lieutenant proved similarly ineffectual at the end of 1649 when Cromwell, after the fall of Wexford, sent a detachment of troops to besiege Duncannon. The commander of the fort, a prominent local Catholic, Thomas Roche, complained about the shortage of men and provisions. The marquis responded by sending his own Protestant lifeguards as reinforcements, and replacing Roche with the flamboyant Colonel Edward Wogan, a deserter from the New Model Army. Ormond freely acknowledged that the arrival of the Protestant Wogan had upset the Catholic garrison at Duncannon, but he did not intend to pander to religious sensibilities 'whilst I think I do my duty'.[14] As in the case of Inchiquin, this prioritisation of military needs above all else proved damagingly naïve, and convinced many people that in a crisis the marquis only trusted his Protestant soldiers. Under huge pressure, Ormond finally consented to Roche's return, but he insisted that Wogan remain in command for the duration of the siege. This compromise did little to ease religious tensions, which flared up again shortly afterwards when the local bishop, Nicholas French, sent a chaplain into the fort, and according to one report, the Protestant minister was not permitted to preach openly to his flock 'until he had spoken with the priest'. Despite all evidence to the contrary, the earl of Castlehaven received assurances when he visited Duncannon in early November that the garrison remained 'entirely united'.[15] Within a few days, however, 120 Ulster troops under Sir Phelim O'Neill, and a similar number under a Colonel Walter Butler, replaced most of the Protestant soldiers. Shortly afterwards, faced with increasingly determined resistance, the parliamentarians lifted the siege. Despite this rare military success, Ormond's insensitivity had once again damaged the fragile royalist alliance.

The lord lieutenant claimed to be unperturbed by all the allegations directed against him, and informed Viscount Muskerry that 'want of [military] success is always accompanied with the dislike of the people and that with calumny'. In a stoical mood, he reflected how 'when things go well every body approves the conduct how improper soever to attain so good an end, and when things fall out cross, the conduct is blamed though never so good'.[16] Despite these tempered philosophical musings on human inconstancy,

Ormond busily attempted to deflect any of the blame for successive military failures from himself, both in Ireland and abroad. As early as 29 September, in a letter to the exiled Lord Byron, the marquis, anticipating condemnation of his inaction during the siege of Drogheda, promised to pen a detailed rebuttal at a later stage. Not long afterwards, he assured Charles Stuart that he had provided supplies and ammunition to the town 'for a much longer time than it held out'.[17] Criticism of his subordinates, implied in the case of Drogheda, became more overt following the storming of Wexford. Two days after the fall of the town, Ormond informed Owen Roe O'Neill that Cromwell's success was due to the 'cowardice of the soldiery and treachery of the townsmen and inhabitants, and not for the want of any manner of things necessary for the defence thereof for a much longer time'.[18] At the end of November, Ormond admitted that the military defeats occasioned 'a jealousy in the Irish of the English [royalists]', but he still refused to accept that his own shortcomings had in any way contributed to this disastrous state of affairs.[19] He complained bitterly about the lies spread by his opponents, particularly 'the ever disloyal party of the Irish [Catholic] clergy'.[20] The lord lieutenant's close associates on the Continent similarly went to great pains to defend his reputation, blaming incompetent officers, cowardly soldiers or duplicitous Catholic clergy for every setback. Shortly after arriving in Holland from Ireland, Sir Robert Stewart explained to the exiled Stuart court that Sir Arthur Aston's over-confidence caused the disaster at Drogheda, which otherwise would have been relieved by Ormond.[21] A few months later, another close colleague, Sir Lewis Dyve, published a pamphlet in The Hague, in which he roundly criticised the Catholic bishops, and accused them of encouraging internal dissent within royalist ranks. In Dyve's opinion, these fractious clerics had effectively undermined Ormond's leadership, as well as his ability to wage war against the parliamentarians.[22] This version of events played well with the exiled Stuarts, and has dominated subsequent historiography of the Cromwellian Wars, but it failed to impress the bulk of Catholics in Ireland, or prevent the spread of rumours and gossip throughout the kingdom.

The growing tensions within the royalist/confederate alliance manifested themselves most noticeably in the major urban centres. During the 1640s, cities such as Waterford, Limerick and Galway, along with towns like Wexford and Clonmel, enjoyed a large degree of political and commercial autonomy. They regularly contributed to the confederate coffers, albeit reluctantly at times, but far from the contested military zones the traditional civic authorities retained control of their own affairs, even in matters of defence. The relentless stress of war, however, increasingly unsettled the existing social order, and in many cases the lower classes started to challenge the ruling oligarchies. Confederate factionalism further radicalised Irish urban life, as the clergy urged townspeople to take a more proactive role in supporting an overtly religious agenda, particularly after the arrival of Rinuccini as papal nuncio in 1645. The following year, as a result of clerical and popular pressure, including on occasion violent unrest, Waterford, Limerick and Galway all backed Rinuccini in rejecting the first Ormond peace. The new clerical regime in Kilkenny did not survive for long, and internal divisions over the next two years allowed the major cities to re-assert their independence from central authority, while remaining nominally loyal to the confederate government. Following the signing of the peace treaty in Kilkenny and the execution of Charles I, most towns moved firmly into the royalist camp. Even the supposed clerical stronghold of Galway publicly celebrated the formation of Ormond's new alliance, and willingly financed the marquis's war against the English parliament. Successive military defeats, starting with the rout at Rathmines, generated a more cautious approach, as in the absence of a royalist field army the urban centres of Munster and south Leinster soon emerged as the principal targets of Cromwell's campaign.

In the latter part of the year, Ormond increasingly found himself in conflict with the major cities. A policy of installing royalist garrisons, answerable directly to him, guaranteed greater central control of the war effort, but posed a serious threat to urban autonomy. Not surprisingly, the fate of Drogheda and Wexford weighed heavily on the minds of the ruling oligarchies. An outbreak of plague in Galway, during the summer of 1649, further complicated matters, causing a demographic and economic crisis, while at the same time making all towns reluctant to admit any strangers, let alone hundreds of potentially disease-ridden soldiers. Limerick proved particularly refractory over the next twelve months, rejecting numerous pleas from the lord lieutenant to accept royalist troops. The marquis of Clanricarde believed that the city had 'many discreet and well-affected men in it,' but he feared they might be 'overswayed by an unruly multitude'.[23] The citizens of Clonmel feared drawing Cromwell's attention by accepting a royalist garrison, particularly in view of what happened to other towns, lost 'as they speak it by the cowardice of soldiers'.[24] The earl of Castlehaven reported from Waterford, the city most immediately in the firing line in late 1649, of serious unrest apparently instigated by two clerics, John Farrell and Patrick Strong, who spread rumours that both Inchiquin and Ormond had already betrayed the kingdom to the parliamentarians. Castlehaven identified the lawyers Geoffrey Barron and Hugh Rochford, along with Bishop Nicholas French, all close associates of the marquis of Antrim, as the principal ringleaders of the internal opposition.[25] For much of 1649 Antrim had explored the possibility of an accommodation between Irish Catholics and the Independent faction in England, based on religious toleration. Allegedly, he played an important role in persuading the defenders of Ross to surrender to Cromwell, and in early December Ormond hauled him before a commission of examination in Clonmel, on suspicion of colluding with the English invaders. Antrim apparently confessed responsibility for a series of forgeries defaming Inchiquin, but no punitive action ensued, probably for fear of further alienating his supporters.[26] Instead, the disgraced nobleman headed north to his native Ulster, and within a few months he openly joined forces with the parliamentarians.

Many of Antrim's supporters and clients remained behind to coordinate resistance to Ormond. Rochford, a former MP for the Wexford borough of Fethard, had played a leading role in the confederate association during the 1640s, both as a judge and a member of the Supreme Council. In 1648, he opposed attempts by the ruling faction in Kilkenny to reach an accommodation with the

Protestant royalist leadership, and sided instead with the Catholic clergy and Owen Roe O'Neill. Arrested for a short time in October 1648, following an abortive rising against the confederate authorities, he returned to his native county in 1649. Rochford angrily denied accusations by Castlehaven that he intended betraying Wexford town to the parliamentarians, but he remained under a cloud of suspicion nonetheless.[27] Barron, former MP for Clonmel and nephew of Luke Wadding, an influential Irish cleric based in Rome, was another leading figure in the confederate government, serving as its official representative to the French Court and as a member of the ruling Supreme Council. Although described by Richard Bellings as one 'noted for his particular zeal for the nuncio', Barron's role during the 1640s in fact placed him firmly in the moderate camp, concerned above all else with preserving confederate unity.[28] His views on the Kilkenny peace treaty are unrecorded but by November, with Waterford under threat, he had clearly lost confidence in Ormond. Bishop French, another important moderate during the 1640s, served on a key confederate mission to Rome, and played a crucial role in promoting peace with the royalists in January 1649. Like Barron, he grew increasingly disillusioned with Ormond's conduct of the war, particularly following the fall of his native town, Wexford.

The loss of influential moderate support, represented by Barron and French, was indicative of the major internal crisis now facing Ormond, even as he tried to stem the tide of Cromwell's military offensive. In late November, the mayor of Waterford, John Lyvett, informed the lord lieutenant that despite the imminent threat of a parliamentary siege, the city authorities would not accept royalist troops, 'least any aversion between the citizens and soldiers or officers may breed a distraction to his Majesty's service and defence of the city'.[29] Ormond wrote gloomily to an exiled royalist in Paris that the Catholics were only 'with much ado withheld from sending commissioners to entreat Cromwell to make stables and hospitals of their Churches'.[30] Eventually, Waterford admitted a contingent of Ulster soldiers, commanded by Lieutenant General Richard Farrell, sent south by Owen Roe shortly before his death. Less than fifty years earlier, such men would have been regarded as deadly enemies, but now the townspeople welcomed them into their city as fellow Catholics and respected fighters, only nominally under Ormond's control. The lord lieutenant felt the snub keenly, fully aware that his authority had been very publicly undermined. Although appallingly bad weather forced Cromwell to lift the siege of Waterford in early December, the marquis gained little solace from this welcome news. In a deeply pessimistic mood, he declined an invitation from Clanricarde to celebrate Christmas at the latter's home in Portumna near Galway city, and not even the offer of 'venison and good wine' could tempt him west of the Shannon.[31]

In just five months, practically the entire eastern, northern and southern coasts had been lost to the parliamentarians, and the grumbling of internal dissent threatened to grow even louder. In a detailed review of the military and political situation in Ireland at the end of the year, Ormond ascribed the difficulties in getting towns to accept garrisons to the 'natural distrust of the people', and the machinations of the marquis of Antrim and hostile Catholic clerics. He suspected that the catastrophic military defeats of the past few months, coupled with the desertions of Protestant troops and the failure of royalists in either Scotland and England to create any significant diversions had begun 'to breed in them [the Irish] such aversion to your Majesty's authority and to me to whom all their misfortunes, the negligences, cowardice and treachery of others are attributed'.[32] As always with Ormond, the blame lay anywhere other than with himself, although on this occasion his assessment did contain an element of truth. Only a significant improvement in the fortunes of war could possibly restore his prestige, but a continued lack of military success fatally compromised his position over the next twelve months.

In January 1650 Cromwell began to re-assemble his forces, barely four weeks after withdrawing from Waterford, but the general fired the opening shots of the new campaign with his pen after reading a copy of the bishops' declaration at Clonmacnoise. His reply, a remarkable document entitled 'for the undeceiving of deluded and seduced people', exposed the depth of his hostility towards the Catholic leadership in Ireland.[33] Cromwell began by denouncing the very concept of a hierarchical church, and condemned what he described as the Catholic bishops' covenant with 'death and hell'. He accused the prelates of hypocrisy, misleading the 'poor laity' to destruction, poisoning them 'with your false, abominable and antichristian doctrine and practices'. The clergy might claim to be fighting for king and country, but in reality they sought instead to preserve their authority and power over the people on behalf of the Antichrist, 'whose Kingdom the Scripture so expressly speaks should be laid in blood'. Cromwell justified the military invasion of Ireland on the grounds that England received God's blessing 'in persecuting just and righteous causes, whatever the cost and hazard be', and the parliamentarians now came 'to hold forth and maintain the lustre and glory of English liberty in a nation where we have an undoubted right to do it'. According to Cromwell, in 1641 the Catholic Irish had broken the peaceful union between the two kingdoms, and 'unprovoked, put the English to the most unheard-of and most barbarous massacre (without respect of sex or age) that ever the sun beheld'. The innocent blood of these Protestant settlers needed to be avenged, and 'lawless rebels' subdued. Despite having committed such terrible outrages, the common people could yet enjoy all the benefits of liberty equally with Englishmen, as long as they laid down their arms, and abandoned the Catholic Church. If they refused to comply with these demands, Cromwell would 'rejoice to exercise utmost severity against them'. As for his conduct of the war, he defied anybody 'to give us an instance of one man since my coming into Ireland, not in arms, massacred, destroyed or banished', and concluded that justice had always 'been done *or endeavoured to be done* [my emphasis]'.[34] This crucial caveat not only justified the atrocities committed by his troops since August, but also exposed an unexpected degree of sensitivity to criticism. These comments reflect the self-doubt already apparent in his earlier letters to Lenthall, where he spoke of the need for tough tactics, which otherwise would 'but work remorse and regret'.[35] Cromwell, unlike some of his subsequent apologists, was clearly troubled by some of what he had seen at Drogheda and Wexford.

After unleashing this literary salvo, Cromwell wasted no time in

Map 4 Cromwell's Campaign, January–May 1650

resuming his military campaign, anxious to achieve as much as possible before returning to England. In early January the English parliament ordered the Council of State to recall the general from Ireland, and rumours to this effect reached Cork by the middle of the month. Negotiations on the Continent between the exiled Prince Charles and the Scottish covenanters resurrected the prospect of a war between England and Scotland, and with General Thomas Fairfax still equivocal in his support for the new regime, Cromwell was the ideal candidate to lead a pre-emptive strike against parliament's former allies. Over the next three months, however, he ignored a series of pleas from Westminster and ruthlessly pursued his objectives in Ireland. His strategy consisted of dividing the southern-based forces into three columns to mop up outlying garrisons in Munster and Leinster, systematically isolating the two key targets, Clonmel and the old confederate capital at Kilkenny. Once these had been captured, the parliamentary forces would be free to focus on the more formidable obstacles of Waterford and Limerick. The unseasonably mild winter weather, along with a steady supply of manpower, materials and money from England, facilitated an early start to the campaign, which caught the royalists totally unprepared. The arrival of two fresh regiments, commanded by his son, Henry, and Sir Hardress Waller, bolstered Cromwell's forces, while surviving accounts show that in the space of just twelve months Westminster had disbursed over £430,000 in cash and supplies for use of the army in Ireland.[36] Ormond could only dream of such resources, and this money alone gave Cromwell a potentially decisive advantage over his royalist opponent. Cromwell spent the weeks after the siege of Waterford visiting each garrison under his command, raising morale, attending to the needs of his troops and preparing for the forthcoming campaign. This assiduous attention to detail endeared him to his men, and played an important role in ensuring his subsequent success.

Cromwell seized the strategic initiative from the outset, departing from Youghal on 29 January with a highly mobile column of cavalry and infantry, unencumbered by large siege guns. His rapid advance unnerved the royalists and spread panic through the garrisons of central Munster. Cromwell arrived at the walled town of Fethard in south Tipperary four days later. Lacking any artillery or ladders, and anxious not to be delayed by a prolonged siege, he agreed generous surrender terms with the royalist commander, Lieutenant Colonel Pierce Butler. On hearing the news, the nearby garrison at Cashel fled before receiving a summons. Meanwhile, a second parliamentary column commanded by Colonel John Reynolds and Henry Ireton, which included a train of siege artillery, enjoyed similar success, capturing Callan just 10 miles south of Kilkenny on 3 February, while a third column under Lord Broghill protected the western flank, ready to engage with any enemy forces that appeared in the field. Ormond struggled to respond to this three-pronged offensive, unsure of parliamentary objectives or how best to utilise his own forces. Most royalist troops remained scattered in winter quarters, and desperate for men, the marquis ordered the release of all soldiers in custody, except those charged with capital offences. He wrote increasingly frantic letters to royalists on the Continent seeking aid, but to no avail, while the marquis of Clanricarde and Daniel O'Neill warned him to expect little assistance from either Connacht or Ulster. Even as reports of Cromwell's offensive flooded into Kilkenny, Ormond and the Commissioners of Treaty quarrelled over the appointment of commanders to key garrisons. The marquis reflected on how the entire kingdom was 'terrified beyond imagination, and no means left to me to persuade them into any settled way of resistance'.[37] Events at Cahir Castle in late February appeared to confirm his pessimistic assessment. The castle, an important symbol of Irish resistance during the Elizabethan conquest, and a secure crossing point over the river Suir, fell to the parliamentarians, cutting the lines of communications between Clonmel and Limerick. The impressive-looking medieval walls proved vulnerable to artillery fire, and despite spirited resistance by a single company of Ulster Irish troops, the commander, Ormond's half-brother, Captain George Matthew, quickly agreed to surrender on terms. The marquis, furious at the loss of this strategic stronghold, ordered Matthew to appear before him to explain his conduct, but the captain, supported by their mother, Elizabeth Poyntz, Lady Thurles, refused to comply. Facing open dissent, even among his most intimate circle of advisers, family and friends, Ormond's carefully crafted coalition had begun to fall apart.

Cromwell, exploiting the evident disarray in enemy ranks, now directed his attention towards Kilkenny, defended by Sir Walter Butler with only 300 troops, all that remained of a garrison decimated by disease. Ormond and the Commissioners of Treaty had already fled the city to a more secure location west of the Shannon, leaving the earl of Castlehaven and around 3,000 men to face the parliamentary onslaught in south Leinster. Castlehaven camped in the vicinity of Kilkenny, hoping to strengthen his army with reinforcements from the north of the province promised by Viscount

Dillon. A controversial Catholic convert and former close associate of the papal nuncio, Dillon proved an unreliable ally, more interested in preserving the family estates than assisting the royalist cause. Even before the start of Cromwell's spring campaign, Daniel O'Neill reported on tensions between Dillon and his provincial colleagues over issues of precedence. In February Clanricarde accused Dillon of financial corruption, collecting over £2,000 each month for 'men in the air and not visible', while according to another source, the viscount destroyed the country 'in the maintenance of imaginary forces'.[38] Earlier in the month, Ormond had issued an order against false musters, which he claimed seriously weakened the army by 'eating up the revenue into officers' purses'.[39] When presented with evidence of Dillon's abuses, however, he proved unable or unwilling to act, fatally compromising the defence of Kilkenny in the process. Despite desperate pleas from Castlehaven, Dillon refused to send reinforcements south on the dubious pretext that he needed every available man to prevent Ulster Catholic troops passing through north Leinster from 'doing more prejudice to it than any enemy'.[40] Castlehaven described the news, the result of 'treachery or neglect', as 'a great blow'.[41] On 10 March the earl had launched a rare counter-attack against the New Model Army, and recaptured the town of Athy, less than 30 miles north of Kilkenny, taking hundreds of parliamentary prisoners. Without Dillon's reinforcements, however, he could not exploit this victory or challenge Cromwell in the field. Unable to keep his own forces together, Castlehaven released the prisoners and not surprisingly 'showed no forwardness to engage' the main enemy army, in what must rank as yet another missed opportunity.[42]

As the royalist position in south Leinster disintegrated, Cromwell rendezvoused at Gowran with Colonel Hewson, who brought additional soldiers from Dublin. At the head of a combined force of nearly 4,000 infantry and cavalry, Cromwell summoned Kilkenny to surrender on 22 March. Butler refused the offer of terms, and for the next five days the garrison and townsmen repelled a series of attacks, inflicting heavy casualties on the parliamentarians. Indeed, according to one account, Cromwell lost more troops at Kilkenny than at

Drogheda, where as many as 150 had died.[43] On 25 March the parliamentary artillery breached the southern wall of the city, but the defenders twice beat off an infantry assault 'with amazing courage'. Cromwell attempted to rally his demoralised troops but 'the third time he could not get on his men'.[44] Meantime, Colonel Ewer seized Irishtown to the north, but the inhabitants prevented him from crossing over into the main city. The parliamentarians resumed the attack the following day without success, although they did manage to create a second breach in the walls. Vastly outnumbered, and with no relief force in sight, Butler could not be expected to hold out indefinitely. The arrival of Ireton with over 1,500 reinforcements convinced him to seek terms rather than 'expose the townsmen to be massacred'.[45] He surrendered on 27 March on receiving a free pass for the garrison to march away with their weapons, baggage and horses. Later accounts accused the inhabitants of treachery, but contemporary descriptions of the siege, including Butler's report, suggest they acquitted themselves well. Cromwell exulted in the capture of the former confederate capital, as it seriously weakened the enemy's strategic position, the city being 'so much in their bowels'.[46] Despite the heavy losses incurred during the siege, Cromwell immediately turned his attention to Clonmel, the final objective of his spring campaign.

The town of Clonmel, situated about 10 miles east of Cahir on the road between Waterford and Limerick, was defended by Hugh Dubh O'Neill, a veteran of Spanish service, and 1,500 Ulster troops from the detachment sent south by his uncle Owen Roe O'Neill at the end of 1649. A wily, experienced officer, Hugh Dubh returned to Ireland in 1642, not long after the outbreak of the rebellion. Captured the following year during a skirmish near Clones in County Monaghan, he spent three years in captivity, before being released as part of a hostage exchange after Owen Roe's victory over the Scottish covenanters at Benburb in 1646. An unlikely-looking soldier, short of stature and rotund, he nonetheless proved himself an innovative and dangerous adversary. Clonmel was his first major independent command, and Ormond believed the place to be 'stronger of itself than either Drogheda, Wexford or Ross', but like all Irish towns, vulnerable to a sustained artillery bombardment.[47] Surrounded by twenty-five-foot-high walls and a deep ditch, with extensive swampland to the east and west, and the river Suir to the south, Clonmel could only be approached from the north. Shortly after the surrender of Cahir, Ormond assured O'Neill that to prevent Clonmel from falling he would 'draw all the forces of the kingdom into a body for its relief' within ten days. As with so many of Ormond's promises, the reinforcements never materialised, so when Cromwell approached the town towards the end of April, O'Neill and the mayor wrote to the lord lieutenant, urgently requesting assistance 'to prevent any bloody tragedy to be acted here as in other places for want of timely relief'.[48] Ormond, seemingly paralysed in the face of the relentless parliamentary advance, failed to respond, even though the southern approaches to Clonmel remained open throughout the subsequent siege. A determined, decisive commander might well have re-supplied or reinforced the garrison, but instead Ormond prioritised the defence of Limerick, a place not immediately under threat. Castlehaven in Leinster lacked infantry, while Clanricarde, not for the first time, refused to leave Connacht and cross the Shannon. David Roche did mobilise a force of 2,000 men in Kerry, and marched east into Cork in early May. Any hope that this diversion would draw some of the besieging forces away from Clonmel disappeared when on 10 May Broghill, guarding Cromwell's flank against just such a threat, routed Roche near Macroom, killing over 600 Irish, including the bishop of Ross, whom he executed the day after the battle. Once again, Ormond's leadership inspired little confidence, and his opponents predictably accused the marquis of treachery for abandoning O'Neill and his Ulster Irish troops to their fate. In fairness to the lord lieutenant, Cromwell's strategy of dividing parliamentary forces, and advancing quickly on a number of different fronts, had effectively isolated Clonmel, making any relief very difficult. Whether as a result of Ormond's incompetence or Cromwell's genius, O'Neill now faced the might of the New Model Army, fresh from its victory at Kilkenny, without any outside assistance.

English forces had been in the vicinity of Clonmel since February, maintaining a loose blockade of the town, which created serious supply problems for the garrison and inhabitants, already dealing with the devastating effects of plague. Cromwell arrived in person on 27 April, with a force of almost 9,000 infantry and cavalry, and immediately issued a summons to surrender. Hugh Dubh refused, and for the first few weeks of the siege he launched numerous sallies against the parliamentary forces, successfully disrupting their preparations for an assault. Cromwell finally began the artillery bombardment on 8 May, but his twelve field guns made little impression on walls reinforced with an escarpment of earth on the inside and a counter-escarpment on the outside. By 16 May, additional heavy guns succeeded in blasting an 80-foot breach in Clonmel's defences. The slow progress, however, had enabled O'Neill to lay a trap for the parliamentary forces. He constructed a channel behind the widening breach, designed to herd the enemy vanguard into a long cul-de-sac, where they could be shot at from behind a 5-foot-high barricade of rubble. At 8 a.m. on 17 May the infantry assault finally began. The first wave poured through the breach, while Cromwell and the cavalry waited outside the town's main gate to be admitted, but after sustaining heavy casualties, the parliamentarians retreated in some disarray. An attempt to rally the soldiers for a second attack failed, and instead dismounted cavalry stormed the gap that afternoon. They encountered little resistance at first, before being exposed to murderous artillery and musket fire from defenders shielded behind barricades. The fighting lasted for hours, and hundreds perished in O'Neill's carefully prepared 'killing zone' before the survivors eventually fled over the bodies of their comrades. Estimates of the total number of parliamentary dead range from 1,500 to 2,500, and even the lowest figure represents the single biggest loss ever suffered by the New Model Army on any of its campaigns in Ireland, Scotland or England.

Despite the appallingly high casualties, Cromwell was determined to renew the assault the following day. Unknown to the parliamentarians, O'Neill, his troops exhausted and running out of ammunition, had decided to abandon the town that night under the cover of darkness, rather than passively await his fate. The garrison escaped across the bridge over the river Suir and fled south to Waterford, while John White, mayor of Clonmel, negotiated surrender terms. When Cromwell entered the town the following morning and discovered the garrison had already left, he allegedly swore 'by God above, he would follow that Hugh Duff O'Neill wheresoever he went'.[49] Despite his anger, Cromwell behaved with comparative restraint, as any further atrocities would have complicated future negotiations with cities such as Waterford, Limerick and Galway. Outside Clonmel he proved less magnanimous. His cavalry pursued O'Neill's column, and ruthlessly cut down 200 stragglers, including camp followers and those wounded in the fighting the previous day.[50] Arriving at Waterford, the Ulster contingent found the city gates closed to all but the leading officers, apparently for fear of the plague. Although temporarily without a base, O'Neill and his troops would still play a leading role in halting the parliamentary offensive later that summer.

More than any other military encounter during the Cromwellian Wars, events at Clonmel severely dented the New Model Army's myth of invincibility. Experienced and highly motivated native Irish troops, ably and energetically led, proved more than a match for elite English forces. One parliamentary eyewitness described O'Neill's soldiers as 'the stoutest enemy that ever was found by our Army in Ireland, and it is in my opinion, and very many more, that there was never seen so hot a storm of so long a continuance, and so gallantly defended, neither in England nor Ireland'.[51] Another source wrote of Cromwell being 'as much vcxcd as cvcr hc was sincc hc first put on a helmet against the king, for such a repulse he did not usually meet with'.[52] Although the siege dramatically exposed Cromwell's military limitations, his subsequent abrupt departure was not directly related to this bloody setback. Having achieved all his immediate objectives, and unable any longer to ignore the increasingly shrill appeals from Westminster to return, he sailed for England just over a week later, leaving his son-in-law Henry Ireton to command in his absence. After a stormy crossing, taking three days, Cromwell arrived home to a hero's welcome. The port of Bristol fired its guns in his honour, while at Hounslow Heath in London, MPs and army officers turned out in large numbers to greet him, with expressions of 'much joy for the safe return of his Excellency and of those with him after so many dangerous enterprises'. Shortly afterwards, Cromwell visited Westminster, where he received 'the hearty thanks of the House for his great and faithful services to the Parliament and Commonwealth'.[53] A liberal use of poetic licence, and complete ignorance of the facts, enabled both Andrew Marvell and John Milton to heap praise on their idol. Marvell, in his *An Horatian Ode upon Cromwell's return from Ireland*, wrote 'And now the Irish are ashamed/To see themselves in one year tamed', while in his Latin polemic, *Pro Populo Anglicano Defensio Secunda*, published a few years later, Milton described how 'Ireland save for one city, was wholly lost, when you transporting an army, in one battle broke the power of the Irish'.[54]

Despite the lavish plaudits, Cromwell typically did not rest on his laurels for long. Charles Stuart and the covenanting envoys had finally reached an agreement in early May, and the young prince landed in Scotland on 23 June, a few weeks after Cromwell's own return to England. In July English forces crossed the border into Scotland, and for the next twelve months, until the defeat of the prince at Worcester on 3 September 1651, Cromwell directed all his energies northwards. Although stretched militarily and financially with the opening of this second front, the parliamentary regime worked hard to ensure that Ireton remained supplied with sufficient men, equipment and cash to pursue the war in Ireland. Between March and May an additional seven regiments arrived over from England, while the flow of supplies continued unabated for the rest of the year. More than any other factor, this unprecedented logistical effort enabled the Commonwealth to sustain the offensive against the Catholic Irish. The royalist/confederate alliance struggled to compete against such a determined and well-resourced foe. Moreover, each military setback further diminished the chances of a recovery, as loss of territory meant that the potential tax base contracted yet further.

While the New Model Army continued its remorseless, though at times costly, march though Munster, Ormond remained largely preoccupied with internal affairs. The first issue to be resolved concerned the fate of those Irish and English Protestants still serving in the royalist armies. Seriously depleted in numbers as a result of the defeats at Rathmines and Drogheda, Cromwell's string of stunning military victories had encouraged a steady stream of desertions thereafter. The Catholic Irish resented the influence wielded by those who remained, not trusting them to fight against parliamentary forces. By early 1650, Lord Inchiquin commanded less than 2,000 men, quartered for the most part in the vicinity of Kilmallock in County Limerick. The defeat of this force by Broghill in March gave Inchiquin's many opponents an opportunity at last to move against him. The Commissioners of Treaty wanted to disband the remnants of his units, while Ormond, anxious to avoid 'a national distinction or quarrel' and risk losing further Catholic support, agreed that Protestant troops should treat for conditions with the enemy. In the meantime, he sought guarantees for their safety from the Commissioners of Treaty, who protested that they had 'never harboured a thought of general exception' against English or Protestant royalists. While suspicion of disloyalty had indeed fallen on some of Inchiquin's forces in particular, the commissioners argued that financial reasons alone dictated the need to reduce troop numbers, Catholics as well as Protestants, Irish as well as English.[55] Cromwell welcomed the subsequent overtures from Protestant royalists and on 26 April, the day before he marched to Clonmel, he signed an agreement in Cashel with their representatives, Dean Michael Boyle, Colonel Robert Starling and Colonel John Daniel. After taking an oath not to prejudice the English Commonwealth in any way, the Protestant royalists were free to settle anywhere in Ireland controlled by parliament, or go into exile on the Continent. Cromwell specifically excluded Ormond and Inchiquin from the settlement, but Dean Boyle accepted unsolicited passes for the two royalist noblemen to leave the kingdom. Shortly afterwards, using this information, Lieutenant Colonel Daniel Axtell urged Thomas Preston, governor of Waterford, to surrender on similar terms. Ormond, conscious that the Irish already harboured suspicions of him, quickly returned the passes to Cromwell, and with his tongue firmly in his cheek, assured the parliamentary general 'that when you shall desire a pass from me and I think fit to grant it, I shall not make use of it to corrupt any that commands under you'.[56] In Ulster, Sir George Monro, royalist commander of Enniskillen, independently announced his intention to treat with the enemy 'for securing the remnant of the Protestant party' in the northern province, and they too gained the benefits of the Cashel treaty.[57]

Despite the relatively small numbers involved, the surrender of these Protestant units effectively signalled the end of the confederate/royalist coalition, proclaimed with such optimism in Kilkenny just fifteen months earlier. Inchiquin described the hostility of the citizens of Limerick towards their former Protestant allies, admitting candidly that 'if we were in their power, we should not [e]scape them with our lives'.[58] Catholics and Protestants never made easy bedfellows, and the appearance of an English Puritan army in Ireland complicated matters still further. Cromwell's success and the seeming hopelessness of the royalist cause fatally undermined the relationship, while the increasingly vocal criticisms of Ormond, encouraged by radical Catholic clerics, left many Protestants feeling isolated and threatened. Shorn of his English and Protestant followers, Ormond found himself totally reliant on Irish Catholics, many of whom actively sought his removal from office. The marquis devoted much of his remaining time in Ireland to negotiations with Catholic leaders functioning in the manner of a confederate General Assembly. During the 1640s, the assembly had exercised supreme authority in the association, and now Ormond required the sanction of this body to maintain even the semblance of royal authority in Ireland. His military strategy essentially revolved around the city of Limerick, whose formidable defences had been modernised, providing a potentially secure base 'from whence to make a hopeful war'.[59] Most of 1650, however, would be spent trying to convince the city to accept troops under Ormond's command, and to make a significant financial contribution to royalist coffers. Success would provide the marquis with a platform to counter the parliamentary offensive, but failure would signal the end of any centralised royalist war effort.

Before focusing exclusively on military affairs, however, the lord lieutenant needed to resolve political tensions with his Catholic allies. Once again the marquis of Clanricarde took the lead in trying to smooth relations between the two sides. He urged the Catholic bishops to observe the terms of the Kilkenny treaty and to air any grievances publicly, 'so that nothing may remain in the dark to the disturbance of the government'. Unity was absolutely essential, and the clergy should suppress and punish all those spreading scandalous reports, and those who blamed recent setbacks on having 'a Protestant governor'.[60] Clanricarde forwarded a copy of the letter to Ormond, primarily to assure the marquis of his loyalty because of widespread rumours that the clergy wanted him to replace the lord lieutenant. Clanricarde explained that his understanding of the Catholic faith bore no relation to those 'rebellious principles' espoused by the bishops.[61]

The opening salvo in this struggle for power came from a meeting of the bishops and Commissioners of Treaty in Limerick on 8 March. The assembly presented a list of demands to Ormond, which in addition to the usual complaints about the lack of Catholic appointments to the army, argued for a major re-structuring of civil and military government, with the bishops taking a decision-making rather than a consultative role.[62] Under this new arrangement, Ormond would govern alongside a privy council consisting of Catholic peers 'and other natives of the kingdom, as well spiritual as temporal', whose remit would not be restricted to the terms of the peace treaty. Anticipating Ormond's objection that he did not possess sufficient authority to appoint councillors, they insisted he could still select people who would act as such until confirmed by Charles Stuart. Another major grievance centred on the administration of justice. Despite provisions in the Kilkenny treaty for the establishment of a judicature, Ormond continued to deal exclusively with legal matters through a system of petitions addressed directly to him. The bishops and commissioners demanded the immediate creation of a judicature, to be staffed exclusively by Catholics. Finally, the meeting accused the Receiver General of failing to clear his accounts, and called on the Commissioners of Treaty to examine all financial matters. An

Ormond loyalist, Viscount Muskerry, had raised the issue of financial misappropriation as far back as October, and without question the royalist administration, like the confederate model during the 1640s, was overly bureaucratic and wasteful. In the absence of detailed financial records from this period, claims of systematic and widespread corruption are difficult to substantiate. Regardless of the facts, many people believed the allegations to be true, particularly as, despite high levels of taxation, the lord lieutenant struggled to pay for supplies and to keep armies in the field.

Ormond stalled for time, seeking clarification on a number of points, and questioning the need for a privy council. Inchiquin warned him that the bishops planned to model a new form of government and 'you will be desired to be gone'.[63] As if to directly counter such accusations, the bishops, meeting subsequently in Loughrea, publicly declared their loyalty to the crown, and requested instructions from the lord lieutenant on how to remedy all grievances. The marquis, however, criticised the 'double dealing' of the prelates, and the glaring contradiction between their public statements and private messages.[64] Ormond ascribed continuing difficulties in getting Limerick to accept a garrison to clerical opposition, and he dispatched two trusted advisers, Gerald Fennell and John Walsh, to negotiate directly with the municipal authorities. Fennell advised Ormond to compromise where possible, as a deal would prove 'a prevalent introduction for you to order all at your pleasure within a little time'.[65] Walsh explained that the townsmen insisted on Ulster troops, 'principally for that they hold a more valorous opinion of them than of others'. He described the city's proposals as 'unbefitting' of good subjects, but nonetheless, like Fennell, considered it 'better to give them this will at present'.[66] Ormond was unimpressed, interpreting the demand for Ulstermen, strong supporters of the clerical faction throughout the 1640s, as nothing more than a ploy by the bishops to obtain 'absolute power to dispose of the kingdom as shall best like them'.[67] He remarked gloomily how the clergy, who totally dominated the city, professed to avoid national or religious distinctions, 'yet foment a provincial distinction'.[68] Unless the authorities in Limerick moderated their position, the lord lieutenant threatened to deal with them as enemies or leave the kingdom altogether. It was hard to determine, he continued, 'whether to prevail by such hands be any better than to be destroyed by Cromwell'.[69]

The clergy may well have wielded significant influence within the walls of Limerick, but the city authorities, conscious of the fate of Drogheda and Wexford, also wished to retain as much autonomy as possible, including the freedom to negotiate independently with Cromwell if necessary. Ormond's agents reported on a meeting of the city council summoned by the mayor after receiving the lord lieutenant's ultimatum. The council affirmed that their proposal for a garrison of Ulstermen was 'assented unto and concluded by an Assembly of all citizens . . . and that they had no power to change or recede from any particular of them without the concurrence of another Assembly'.[70] These protestations about the integrity of their democratic mandate simply masked the determination of the councillors not to be cowed by Ormond. Ultimately, the lord lieutenant's threats amounted to little more than empty rhetoric, as he needed Limerick more than the city needed him. Only by leaving the country, and taking the king's commission with him, could Ormond potentially damage the Catholic interest in Ireland. Abandoned by the royalists, Irish Catholics would be required to obtain a foreign protector, or come to terms with the parliamentarians. A handful of clerics, backed by the marquis of Antrim, had already been exploring these possibilities, but for most they represented a step too far. The clear majority wanted to bring Ormond more firmly under control, or failing that to replace him with a Catholic deputy. Catholic leaders representing all four provinces gathered at Loughrea towards the end of April in the nature of a general assembly. Bishops constituted almost half of the notables present, while apart from Ormond the only Protestant in attendance was Inchiquin. The lord lieutenant expressed his hopes for a satisfactory outcome, but Daniel O'Neill warned him to expect a degree of hostility, with radical clerics already spreading rumours that the marquis would shortly leave the country anyway 'to perfect an old engagement to the parliament'.[71]

The assembly at Loughrea began by issuing a declaration of loyalty to the crown, and attributed the atmosphere of animosity and suspicion to 'the want of success in services'. More specifically, members claimed that Ormond had failed to address previous grievances, including allegations of corruption and inefficiency. The assembly concluded with the urgent demand that commanders be appointed to each of the four provinces to coordinate the war effort. Ormond replied the following day with a blistering attack against the disobedience of the major cities, which he argued should 'immediately be put under a military government for military matters'. He denied any knowledge of misappropriation of money, and warned members of the 'slavery they will be subject unto' should the parliamentarians prevail. He expressed surprise that the assembly raised the issue of military appointments, as each province already had a Catholic commander, Castlehaven for Leinster and Munster, Clanricarde for Connacht and Bishop Heber MacMahon, recently appointed by an assembly in Ulster. The meeting at Loughrea, however, wanted a new, more dynamic military leadership to provide 'some visible opposition to the growing power of the enemy'.[72] The lord lieutenant stood his ground, but not without difficulty. Despite the mutual recriminations, the correspondence concluded on a more positive note. Assembly members insisted that they in no way supported the behaviour of Limerick in refusing a royalist garrison, and appointed a mission to the city, led by the archbishop of Tuam and Sir Lucas Dillon, to resolve the dispute. After some negotiations John Creagh, mayor of Limerick, informed Ormond that the city council and general meeting of the citizens had agreed that his nominee, Colonel Piers Walsh, should command the garrison.[73]

Assured, for the moment at least, of continuing Catholic support, Ormond prepared to face his new parliamentary adversary, Henry Ireton, and the inevitable assault on the Shannon defensive line. Cromwell's departure, after nine bloody months, generated surprisingly little comment in royalist or confederate circles. Lord Inchiquin, for example, in a letter to Ormond on 1 June, simply noted a report from Colonel John Barry that the English general had sailed from Youghal a few days earlier, before moving on to discuss other matters. Despite Cromwell's fearsome reputation, and the military success he enjoyed in Ireland, this reticence is perhaps not so difficult to explain. Nobody knew at the time that the Lord General would never return, while the expeditionary force, regularly supplied from England and commanded by talented subordinates, remained in place to complete the conquest. Cromwell's opponents simply could not afford the luxury of reflecting on the implications of his departure, being too preoccupied with the immediate struggle for survival. Nonetheless, his absence must have encouraged the Catholic Irish to some degree, and even after all the military setbacks since August their position remained far from hopeless. The alliance between the Scottish covenanters and Charles Stuart had opened a second front against the parliamentarians, prompting Cromwell's precipitous return to England. In Ireland, Ormond and his allies could still call on large numbers of troops, although supplying them became increasingly difficult due to the diminishing area under royalist control. Waterford, Ireland's second city, along with other key strongholds in Leinster such as Carlow and Tecroghan, continued to hold out, while further west, Limerick, Athlone and Sligo guarded the entrances into the province of Connacht, untouched so far by the ravages of the Cromwellian invasion. To the north, the Ulster army, the most successful confederate force during the 1640s, prepared to launch a major new offensive under the command of Bishop Heber MacMahon. Whether or not Cromwell's departure provided an opportunity for a major royalist recovery would be determined over the summer months.

6

Royalist Collapse

Death's darts hold this great heart,
unbeatable in battle, laid to rest in the earth.[1]
EPITAPH FOR OWEN ROE O'NEILL (1649)

Cromwell's departure from Ireland at the end of May 1650 made little immediate impact on the war. The royalist/confederate coalition remained on the defensive throughout the country, except in Ulster, where the Catholic forces seized the initiative. In mid-March, at Belturbet in County Cavan, after months of delay due to the ongoing conflict and bad weather, the aged Bishop Sweeney of Kilmore chaired a provincial assembly of clergy, gentry and army officers. The Ulster forces, many of them returning from Munster, had spent the winter quartered in the Longford/Cavan area, and now as the summer campaigning season approached they needed to elect a new leader to replace their inspirational general, Owen Roe O'Neill. His experienced officer corps provided numerous potential candidates, and a handful had already acquitted themselves well in battle against Oliver Cromwell and the parliamentarians. Lieutenant General Richard Farrell, for example, sent south by the Ulster general in October, played a key role in the defence of Waterford, while Major General Hugh Dubh O'Neill, generally recognised as the most capable soldier in the army, would shortly distinguish himself during the siege of Clonmel. Other contenders included Owen Roe's only son Henry, along with two of the original conspirators from 1641, Philip MacHugh O'Reilly and Sir Phelim O'Neill. While all these officers enjoyed large personal followings, none commanded widespread support across the province, and delegates at Belturbet feared an outbreak of factional or familial strife in the event of a disputed election. The assembly wanted somebody with sufficient authority, both politically and militarily, to unite the Irish of Ulster in the difficult times ahead. Daniel O'Neill, a nephew of Owen Roe, appeared to possess the requisite qualities, but his Protestant faith and close relationship to the lord lieutenant counted against him. The marquis of Antrim, a Catholic nobleman of national standing, had organised a number of successful military ventures during the 1640s, including Alasdair MacColla's expedition to Scotland in 1644. A self-serving schemer, the marquis had spent the previous two years nurturing contacts with the English parliamentarians, and could not be trusted. In the absence of an acceptable alternative, the assembly turned to Heber MacMahon, bishop of Clogher, and elected him unanimously, 'to cut of[f] all motives of both jealousy and emulation'.[2]

A leading figure in the confederate association, Bishop MacMahon represented Ulster on the Supreme Council throughout the 1640s and had enjoyed good relations both with Owen Roe O'Neill and the papal nuncio, Rinuccini. A consummate politician, he had no military experience whatsoever. According to one contemporary commentator, the bishop 'was no more a soldier fit to be a general than one of Rome's cardinals', while the anonymous author of the 'Aphorismical Discovery' described him as a 'brave prelate, but alas, ignorant general'.[3] Although undoubtedly ambitious, the bishop probably accepted the post more out of a sense of duty, to keep the army united, rather than for any reasons of self-advancement. Ormond initially regarded MacMahon with suspicion, but Owen Roe's reconciliation with the royalist regime had brought about a thaw in their relationship. By early 1650, Ormond enthusiastically supported the bishop's candidature, primarily to thwart Antrim's plans 'to betray his king and country'.[4] MacMahon's election at Belturbet, however, did not meet with universal approval, and the Protestant minister Humphrey Galbraith, who attended the assembly as representative of the royalist garrison at Enniskillen, recorded the objections of Sir Phelim O'Neill and other officers to undue clerical interference in military matters. The majority soon made their peace with the bishop, but a few refused to serve under the new commander. Antrim, frustrated in his military ambitions, openly sided with the English shortly afterwards, prohibiting his men 'to fight a stroke against the Parliament', while Daniel O'Neill left Ireland to join Charles Stuart's expedition to Scotland, and never again returned to his native land.[5] MacMahon's appointment also accelerated the final collapse of the royalist/confederate alliance in Ulster. Following his defeat near Lisnagarvey in early December, the royalist Sir George Monro had retreated to Enniskillen in County Fermanagh 'with the remains of his broken forces'.[6] Willing to accept Daniel O'Neill or even Antrim as his superior, Monro simply could not countenance taking orders from a Catholic bishop, and when Galbraith confirmed the news from Belturbet, he decided to seek terms from the parliamentary commanders in Ulster, Colonel Robert Venables and Charles Coote, on behalf of those Protestant royalists still remaining in the province.

Undeterred, Bishop MacMahon, after consulting with Ormond at the general assembly of nobility and laity at Loughrea in April, prepared to take the offensive. Using his administrative experience to good effect, he successfully mobilised the Ulster army despite serious shortages of key military supplies such as lead for musket balls. In early May, MacMahon marched north through County Tyrone with 4,000 infantry and 500 cavalry, seeking to engage the enemy on the battlefield. All went well at first, and on 14 May the marquis of Clanricarde reported the bishop's success in taking a strategic bridge over the river Bann at Toome, where the enemy casualties included 'one Colonel Gye, Robin Ormsby and some other officers'.[7] This victory forced Coote and Venables to divide their forces, with the latter sent to recover the vital crossing point on the Bann. At the end of the month, MacMahon summoned the garrison at Dungiven in County Derry to surrender, and warned the commander, Colonel Michael Beresford, that if he 'shed one drop of my soldiers' blood, I will not spare to put man, woman and child to the sword'. Beresford rejected the summons, and so when the town fell after a brief fight, the Irish executed all sixty defenders. According to Clogher, Beresford managed to save himself by hiding 'amongst ladies and other gentlewomen'.[8] The Ulster army then moved west to gather badly needed supplies of food and to engage Coote, before Venables rejoined him. The bishop also possibly expected some support from the local Scottish settlers because of their hostility to the English parliamentary regime.

On 2 June, the two armies clashed at Lifford on the river Foyle. Despite a clear superiority in numbers, MacMahon failed to press home his advantage, enabling Coote to withdraw relatively unscathed. Although a shortage of munitions may have been partly to blame, the bishop's performance in his first major battlefield encounter did not augur well for the rest of the campaign. Almost three weeks later, on 21 June, both sides faced each other again at Scariffhollis, on the river Swilly near Letterkenny. On this occasion the numbers favoured the parliamentarians, as Venables sent reinforcements to rendezvous with his colleague. For his part, MacMahon received no assistance from Clanricarde in Connacht, while the Scots in Ulster, although technically on the royalist side, refused to fight under a Catholic bishop. Moreover, Clogher had also despatched Miles Sweeney's regiment to gather desperately needed supplies, reducing his army to about 3,000 men in the process. The bishop enjoyed a good defensive position, but perhaps conscious of the missed opportunity at Lifford, he decided to engage the enemy against the advice of his senior officers, including Henry O'Neill. The Irish fought bravely, inflicting heavy casualties, before a parliamentary flank attack broke their ranks. Coote's cavalry wreaked havoc in the ensuing rout, and over 2,000 of the Ulster Army, the most experienced Catholic soldiers in the kingdom, were killed as they desperately tried to escape, particularly as the local Scots, their erstwhile allies, now 'fell upon them that fled'.[9]

The Ulster campaign of 1650 exposed the folly of appointing a politician to lead an army. Owen Roe O'Neill would never have abandoned a strong defensive position and risked battle against a numerically superior enemy. O'Neill's victory at Benburb in 1646, the only major battlefield victory of the Irish during this period, vindicated his cautious methods, and it had established the Ulster army as the most formidable fighting force in the country. The disaster at Scariffhollis undid all of his work. The loss of so many veterans, including most of the officers, in the space of just a few

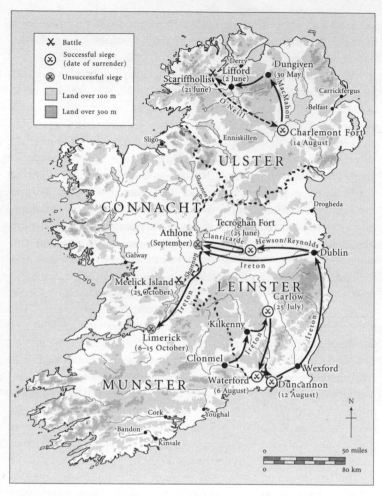

Map 5 Summer Campaigns, 1650

hours, proved catastrophic. The high-profile casualties included Colonel Hugh Maguire, Colonel Hugh MacMahon and Henry O'Neill, executed after the battle, along with many other colonels, majors and captains, by that 'cruel butcher and human blood sucker', Charles Coote.[10] Deprived of experienced leaders to train and command new recruits, the Ulster Irish would never again be in a position to challenge the parliamentarians in the field. Bishop MacMahon escaped the disaster with most of the cavalry, but was eventually hanged following his capture in a skirmish a few days later. Lieutenant General Farrell fled into Connacht, where he attempted to reorganise the scattered remnants of the Ulster forces, while Sir Phelim O'Neill made his way to Charlemont, the last Catholic stronghold in the northern province. Behind the impressively modern fortifications, controlled by the Irish since the first days of the rebellion in October 1641, O'Neill prepared as best he could for the inevitable siege. Coote and Venables wasted little time, arriving before Charlemont towards the end of July. On 6 August, after blasting a breach in the defences, Coote's infantry launched a full-scale assault, while their commander watched the action from a distance, smoking tobacco. Three times that day O'Neill's men repelled the enemy, inflicting over 800 casualties, as once again in a siege situation Ulster Irish troops proved more than a match for the parliamentarians. A week later, running low on supplies and 'having lost the most of his chief officers and soldiers to a very few', Sir Phelim sought terms. On 14 August the garrison surrendered, and marched west with their baggage towards the Shannon.[11] Although leaders of the calibre of Farrell and O'Neill lived to fight another day, for many the hopes of Catholic Ireland died on the battlefield at Scariffhollis.

While responsibility for this disastrous defeat lies primarily with Bishop MacMahon, the royalist leadership must share at least some of the blame. Ormond had fully endorsed the bishop's appointment as military commander, but despite allegedly promising military support he made no effort to coordinate MacMahon's campaign with Clanricarde's manoeuvres in Connacht, thus failing in a basic responsibility of a supreme commander.[12] A joint attack by Clanricarde and MacMahon might well have overwhelmed Coote and allowed the combined royalist force to move against Venables, isolated and vulnerable in east Ulster. Throughout the month of June, however, Clanricarde directed his attention across the Shannon into Leinster towards Tecroghan, an important fortress adjacent to the road between Dublin and Athlone, besieged by Colonel Hewson and Colonel Reynolds. While the parliamentarians built elaborate siege works around the fort, leading royalist officers in Leinster argued among themselves. The earl of Castlehaven and the bishop of Dromore both commanded more than enough troops to attempt a relief effort, but the lord lieutenant proved unwilling to risk alienating either man by appointing one over the other. Instead he committed a major strategic error, ordering Clanricarde to march to Tecroghan, thereby drawing forces out of Connacht rather than prioritising the Ulster Irish offensive. Ormond maintained that failure to capture the fort would leave the parliamentarians 'every way much disappointed and their prosperity notably checked', and yet he did not lead the campaign himself.[13] Clanricarde, always reluctant to leave Connacht, showed little enthusiasm for the mission, and invited Ormond to replace him, 'if there appear a party so considerable as to invite your Excellency to be in the head of them'.[14] The lord lieutenant declined the offer, explaining that he had to remain in the vicinity of Limerick, 'where there is not so much as a proposed form of government or defence', an unconvincing excuse given the lack of any serious parliamentary threat in that area in early June.[15] Not for the first time, Ormond delegated a crucial task to incompetent and feuding subordinates, and then washed his hands of the ruinous consequences.

Clanricarde crossed the Shannon in mid-June, and rendezvoused with Castlehaven at Tyrrellspass in County Westmeath, just over 10 miles from Tecroghan. The combined army consisted of 1,800 infantry and about 800 cavalry, although Castlehaven expected more to arrive. Clanricarde complained that the bishop of Dromore, despite all his promises, 'brought no other assistance but a dexterous story of his great useless endeavours', and that the Leinster forces, the officers excepted, contributed little apart from stealing valuable supplies.[16] Plagued by ill health, Clanricarde also appears to have suffered from chronic depression from the moment Cromwell landed in Ireland. Not surprisingly, therefore, he tended to exaggerate campaign difficulties, while many in Leinster did not take kindly to the imposition of a commander from outside the province.

On 19 June, Castlehaven volunteered to lead 1,400 infantry towards Tecroghan, through the boggy ground that surrounded much of the fort. Although the terrain protected the Irish at first from the English cavalry, infantry units from both sides eventually clashed towards nightfall. Several hundred Irish troops successfully broke through to the fort, destroying some of the enemy's siege works on the way, but Castlehaven eventually retreated with the main force, blaming the ill discipline of his men for the setback. Unwilling to risk another encounter with the parliamentarians, Clanricarde, his money and supplies apparently exhausted, favoured a tactical withdrawal. He reported to Ormond that 'all conclude but Castlehaven that my stay here can nothing advantage the besieged'. Without waiting for a reply, the marquis marched towards the Shannon, still complaining about how 'barbarously' the Leinster Irish had treated him.[17] Castlehaven remained behind to disrupt the besieging forces, but on 25 June, Sir Robert Talbot surrendered on terms, and the garrison followed Clanricarde west. In an attempt to put a gloss on his failure, Clanricarde described the relief effort as 'courageous and gallant', adding that the fort had surrendered on 'very honourable and advantageous conditions'.[18] Ormond concurred, stating that the terms were such as he 'should have been very well satisfied with if they had been accepted a month since'.[19] Despite the self-congratulatory tone of this correspondence, the loss of Tecroghan, while not a disaster on the scale of Scariffhollis, exposed all of north Leinster to parliamentary attack, as well as opening up the route from Dublin to the Shannon. Castlehaven, the only royalist commander to emerge from this fiasco with any sort of credit, bemoaned the fall of this almost impregnable fortress, one of the strongest in the country. He did not attribute any blame, although clearly Clanricarde's incompetence and Ormond's neglect had contributed to yet another significant setback.

After the misfortunes in Ulster and Leinster, the royalist cause suffered the final blow of the summer in Munster. Obsessed with defending the Shannon, Ormond paid little attention to the plight of Waterford, the second largest city in the kingdom, reduced to an isolated outpost behind enemy lines. Royalist possession of the city prevented the enemy from gaining undisputed control of the southern coastline, and tied up parliamentary resources that might otherwise have been directed westwards towards Limerick. Overstretched militarily on a number of different fronts, the English did not possess sufficient manpower to besiege Waterford properly, so they established a loose cordon of garrisons in the vicinity instead. This blockade, in conjunction with Cromwell's gains during the spring campaign, effectively cut the city off from its hinterland, and only Carlow, over 40 miles to the north, still held out for the royalists in south Leinster. By early summer, Waterford experienced severe food shortages, while the plague claimed as many as 400 victims each week. Nonetheless, the city defences remained intact, overseen since February by General Thomas Preston, a distinguished Continental veteran and expert in siege warfare. The general won considerable renown across Europe for his spirited defence of Louvain in Spanish Flanders against the French in 1635, while ten years later, fighting under the confederate banner, he captured Duncannon, one of the most modern fortifications in Ireland, after a textbook siege. The catastrophic defeat to Colonel Michael Jones, however, at Dungan's Hill in 1647 exposed Preston's limitations as a battlefield commander, and this may have contributed to his chronic drink problem. Moreover, the continued success of Cromwell's offensive during the spring of 1650 gradually drained the morale of Waterford's citizens and defenders. In early April, following the fall of Kilkenny, Preston warned Ormond that without relief 'this place will not I fear be kept from making its conditions'. By the end of the month the general reported that leading civic figures wanted to surrender, which he could hardly prevent with a garrison reduced by sickness to only 600 men. He desperately needed more troops and supplies.[20] The mayor, John Lyvett, wrote to the lord lieutenant with details of proceedings against a prominent citizen, John Leonard, for attempting to correspond with Cromwell. Leonard claimed to have attended meetings of the council and clergy, where a majority voted to treat with the parliamentarians. The mayor and council, anxious to assure Ormond of their continuing loyalty, vigorously denied this, although they did admit to discussing and subsequently rejecting the idea of an accommodation with the enemy. They ordered Leonard to be committed to solitary confinement and copies of his letter to be burnt the following Saturday by the common hangman at the market cross, but clearly deep divisions existed within the city on how best to respond to the parliamentary offensive.[21]

In early May, Ormond promised Preston 'a convenient party' of reinforcements from Leinster, but the troops never arrived.[22] Castlehaven, the royalist commander for that province, had already retreated northwards towards Tecroghan with his few remaining units after the parliamentarians captured Kilkenny, while the besieged garrison at Carlow could not provide any assistance. News of the fall of Clonmel at the end of the month cast a further gloom over Waterford, despite confirmation of Cromwell's abrupt departure to England. On 5 June, the mayor, council and citizens sent an address to Preston, claiming 'no moral or human possibility left us to resist the power of that great enemy' surrounding the city. With ammunition for only three days, food in short supply and the plague still raging within the walls, they pleaded with the general to open negotiations with the parliamentarians.[23] Preston sympathised with their plight, and even the arrival of Hugh Dubh O'Neill with the Clonmel garrison only temporarily stiffened the resolve of the defenders. The aged commander sought clarification from Ormond on 'whether [to] leave my bones in the place as a sacrifice to my country', or to seek the best terms possible. He feared the city already lost without 'speedy miracles', but the lord lieutenant could provide none.[24] In any event, the marquis claimed that Preston possessed sufficient resources to hold out over the summer. If the enemy took a city such as Waterford, Ormond knew not 'what to look for from places of less strength, commanded by less knowing soldiers'.[25] Preston continued to press for reinforcements, arguing that a relatively small number of troops would prove sufficient for the task, 'considering the inconsiderable forces that block us up'. Increasingly frustrated at the lack of support from the lord lieutenant, the general contrasted his current plight with his experiences in Spanish service, where he received 'all the necessaries' during a siege.[26] Coincidentally, that very same day, in a move reminiscent of Hitler's action in bestowing the title of field marshal on the doomed General Von Paulus in Stalingrad, Ormond issued a royal decree confirming Preston as Viscount Tara. Unfortunately for the inhabitants of Waterford, the ennoblement of Preston had no discernible impact on the siege.

Responding to Preston's criticisms, the marquis dismissed accusations of neglect, blaming the obstinacy of the inhabitants, and their reluctance to accept a royalist garrison in late 1649, for 'the distress they are reduced to'. He also reminded Preston that Charles Stuart, exiled from England and only recently returned to Scotland, could hardly be compared to the king of Spain in terms of resources. With little hope of being able to provide any relief, Ormond gave the general permission 'to do what in your judgement you conceive fit'.[27] Similarly neglected, Carlow finally surrendered on 25 July, allowing the enemy to concentrate all their forces in the region against the beleaguered port. As soon as Ireton appeared before Waterford in person with a considerable train of artillery, the citizens, clergy and officers all favoured treating for terms, believing it better to 'live for some day's service to come than be massacred upon a desperate holding out'.[28] Ormond wrote one last letter on 8 August, full of wildly optimistic rumours from England and Scotland of major gains by Charles Stuart. Unknown to the marquis, however, Waterford had surrendered two days earlier, followed within a week by the fort at Duncannon. As the initial promise of a royalist resurgence turned to defeat and retreat in Ulster, Leinster and Munster, Ormond as commander-in-chief did nothing to retrieve the situation. He seems to have suffered a psychological block, and unable to deal with urgent strategic demands on a number of different fronts, he effectively ignored them. Like a chess player in what he believes to be an irretrievably lost position, he made no more moves and simply let his time run out.

In fact, Ormond subordinated consideration of all military issues to that of imposing his personal authority over the city of Limerick. As early as 14 May, long before the defeats at Scariffhollis, Tecroghan and Waterford, the mayor and council of the city agreed to accept the lord lieutenant's nominee, Colonel Piers Walsh, as commander, but the troops of the garrison had to live in huts and cabins outside the walls, to prevent the spread of plague. Not content with this, the marquis insisted on open access for all royalist soldiers, including himself and his lifeguards. Using Limerick as a secure base, and exploiting the city's resources, Ormond planned to recruit new royalist regiments. He claimed to have already assembled about 1,700 infantry, and 350 cavalry, 'which if this city would but listen to what tends to their safety would soon [grow] to an army'.[29] Ormond's demands, however, generated fierce opposition and not only because of the potential threat to Limerick's autonomy. In 1646 a violent mob in the city had rejected the first peace treaty between Ormond and the confederates, and residual distrust of the lord lieutenant threatened to derail his plans once again. On Friday, 24 May, the more militant young 'blades', led by a former mayor, Dominic Fanning, seized two of Ormond's trunks off a Dutch ship in the harbour, on hearing rumours that the lord lieutenant intended to sail to the Continent with tax money raised to finance the war effort. The assailants found no cash and subsequently apologised for their actions, but the situation in the city remained tense.[30] Shortly after his arrival in early June, Colonel Walsh reported to Ormond on the poor state of Limerick's defences. Many of the garrison lacked weapons, while Walsh suspected leading citizens of 'endeavouring to be independent of any authority', leaving them free to choose their own course of action. The colonel warned Ormond not to approach the place unless he brought enough troops with him to subdue all opposition.[31]

With his nominee already commanding the city garrison, the lord lieutenant might have been better advised to defuse the situation by withdrawing from the area and personally directing relief efforts at Tecroghan. Military success would have silenced his critics, at least temporarily, encouraged volunteers to join the royalist forces, and perhaps inclined the authorities in Limerick to be more conciliatory. 'If we prosper', as the marquis of Clanricarde commented shrewdly, 'we may be numerous.'[32] Ormond, however, in the grip of denial of any crisis other than the refusal of Limerick to fully accept his authority, would not be diverted by issues elsewhere. He seemed intent on provoking controversy with his Catholic allies regardless of the consequences. As the king's representative in Ireland, Ormond demanded immediate access to the city, along with a body of troops necessary 'for the dignity of the place we hold and to prevent any popular tumult that might be raised by desperate . . . persons against us'. In a conciliatory move, the lord lieutenant sought to assure the citizens and clergy that his guard would be restricted to 150 cavalry, all Catholics 'constantly of your confederacy'.[33] In response, a Dominican friar, Father James Wolfe, raised 'a multitude of loose people', and shut the gates to keep him out.[34] Colonel Walsh informed the lord lieutenant of plans for another public meeting to discuss the issue of a garrison, which he feared would produce 'no other birth but a monster'. The colonel reported that even he dared not walk the streets at night.[35] The bishop of Limerick, seen by many as a moderate, finally intervened in the dispute, conveniently blaming the disorders on an 'unruly unquestionable [and un-identified] multitude'.[36] He proposed that all sides forgive and forget the recent upheavals, and admit a garrison of Ulster troops, commanded by Major General O'Neill, the hero of Clonmel. A sceptical Ormond reluctantly agreed, though as O'Neill would not arrive from Waterford for some weeks, he argued that Limerick should in the meantime open its gates, and hand over hostages to ensure future good behaviour. In this atmosphere of mutual distrust, the negotiations not surprisingly stalled once again, leaving Ormond no closer to gaining admission into the city.

At the end of June, the lord lieutenant sent reports on the military situation in Ireland to a number of royalists abroad, including Prince Charles, who by now had landed in Scotland. He described Limerick as 'in a neutrality nearer rebellion than obedience', with the city still refusing to accept a garrison or provide maintenance for the regular army. The war, he continued, had disintegrated into a number of disjointed conflicts, fought on the royalist side at least by small bodies of troops, and disbanded soldiers 'by way of freebooting'. Although anxious to cooperate with the Catholic bishops in Ireland where possible, Ormond nonetheless blamed his difficulties on clergy 'to whom I knew lying was as natural as rebellion'. Despite facing increasingly strident internal opposition, he argued that his departure from Ireland would in fact worsen the situation, forcing those who supported the Kilkenny peace treaty to immediately make terms with the parliamentarians rather than live under clerical rule.[37] Perversely, Ormond practically welcomed news of the catastrophic defeat of the Ulster Irish at Scariffhollis, and he was 'far from entertaining thoughts of despair upon the blow given the Northern Army'. He hoped in adversity to awaken the 'courage and industry' of the native Irish, as well as bring an end to dissensions within royalist ranks.[38] Nonetheless, Ormond desperately needed significant contributions from the major cities, and he speculated morosely that his critics would soon discover that 'their own ruin will follow mine close at the heels'.[39] The mayor and council in Limerick, however, refused to compromise any further.

On 10 July, with few cards left to play other than the threat to quit the kingdom entirely, Ormond finally accepted the appointment of Hugh Dubh O'Neill as governor of Limerick without preconditions. He promised to put his resentment aside, forgive all previous acts, and depend upon O'Neill's 'faith and honour that in case of necessity I shall not be refused a retreat thither nor be given up there'.[40] Moreover, as soon as the Ulster forces reorganised following the rout at Scariffhollis, he would send north for 1,000 troops to reinforce the garrison. Despite this agreement, tensions remained, and the lord lieutenant complained to John Walsh about the letter he received from the mayor, 'giving such slender thanks as you mention for my concessions'.[41] Increasingly prone to bouts of self-pity and melancholy, the lord lieutenant displayed little understanding or appreciation of the growing crisis enveloping the royalist war effort, a symptom of the psychological paralysis that had by now overwhelmed him. Instead of utilising the obvious talents of Ulster officers, such as Major General Hugh Dubh O'Neill, to spearhead resistance to the parliamentary offensive, he allowed the dispute with Limerick to drag on unnecessarily, fatally neglecting military developments elsewhere in the process and undermining any hope of raising significant field forces. Galway now followed Limerick's example, refusing to accept any royalist troops until directly threatened by the enemy. Even then the garrison would have to be commanded by one 'of their own naming', preferably the ubiquitous Hugh Dubh O'Neill, rather than somebody nominated by Ormond. Outraged, Clanricarde suggested a blockade of the town by his Connacht forces to enforce greater obedience. Although 'weary and ashamed of going so often like a dog in a chain', the lord lieutenant urged one last effort at compromise before attempting 'the sharper remedies'.[42]

Potentially damaging reports also began to reach Ireland at this time that Charles Stuart's recent treaty with the Scottish covenanters included a denunciation of the 1649 peace deal between Ormond and the Catholic confederates. The lord lieutenant desperately stalled for time, claiming that he had not yet seen any agreement and would await more certain news from the Continent.[43] Privately, he expressed concern over the rumours and the implications if true for his efforts to retain Catholic Irish support. Ormond wrote to Charles' secretary on the Continent, seeking a declaration from the prince in favour of his loyal subjects in Ireland, without which 'his Majesty cannot with honour acquit himself towards this people'.[44] In agreeing to travel to Scotland, however, Prince Charles had effectively become a prisoner of the covenanting regime and its anti-Catholic agenda. Shortly after landing there, the covenanters forced him to sit through an interminably long sermon criticising his father for various sins, and denouncing his mother, Queen Henrietta Maria, as a papist whore. On 16 August at Dunfermline Charles publicly subscribed to the covenanter programme and repudiated the Kilkenny treaty 'made with the bloody Irish rebels'.[45] Although he later claimed to have acted under duress, this declaration represented a gross betrayal of his Catholic Irish subjects, and particularly of those confederates who had argued in favour of a royalist alliance. Ormond, another victim of the capricious Stuarts, remained steadfastly loyal, in public at least, hoping that Charles' alliance with the Scots might at least divert the attention of the English parliamentarians away from Ireland. Many Irish Catholics, however, had already decided to seize control of their own affairs.

The fall of Waterford on 6 August, almost exactly one year after

Cromwell first landed at Dublin, finally forced the bishops to act before the military position of the Catholic Irish collapsed entirely. With the parliamentarians marching towards the Shannon, and the royalist forces in total disarray, it appeared possible that the war might be over before the end of the year. Flushed with success, Ireton divided his army, moving simultaneously against Limerick and Athlone. Sir Hardress Waller commanded the Limerick campaign, while Ireton marched on Athlone, 'which place it is thought the Lord Dillon will deliver up, there being some divisions amongst the Irish'.[46] Even if the rumours about Viscount Dillon, garrison commander at Athlone, had been correct, by failing to concentrate his forces against Limerick, Ireton granted the royalists a temporary reprieve and gave Ormond's internal opponents an opportunity to launch an effective coup d'état. Although a personal dislike of Ormond and a distrust of his religious affiliations motivated many clergy, the lord lieutenant's miserable military record provided ample ammunition for those determined to see him removed from office. As for a successor, the majority of the dissidents favoured resurrecting the old confederate power structures, with the Catholic clergy playing a prominent role. The immediate military crisis, however, required a unifying figurehead, preferably from among the ranks of the nobility. Despite his widely acknowledged military talents, Hugh Dubh O'Neill simply did not possess sufficient political authority to hold together the disparate Catholic alliance, while the fate of Heber MacMahon tragically illustrated the dangers of appointing a bishop to the role of commander-in-chief. Among the leading nobles, Viscount Mountgarret, former president of the confederate Supreme Council, suffered from increasing bouts of senility, while the marquis of Antrim, former favourite of clerical hardliners, had by now deserted to the parliamentary side. Although militarily active in their respective provinces, neither Viscount Muskerry in Munster nor the earl of Castlehaven in Leinster could count on significant support elsewhere.

By this process of elimination, Clanricarde, the most senior Catholic nobleman in Ireland and commander of the royalist/confederate forces in Connacht, emerged as the most viable alternative. The marquis, however, suffered from serious health problems, both physical and mental, which periodically incapacitated him, and led to prolonged bouts of melancholy, ominously like those that afflicted his good friend the lord lieutenant. As with Ormond, Clanricarde's abysmal military record did not inspire confidence, and he appeared increasingly reluctant to leave the relative security of his native province. Moreover, he remained a deeply divisive figure in his own right. Throughout the 1640s, Clanricarde consistently rebuffed overtures from Kilkenny to take the oath of association, before eventually siding with the peace faction during the confederate civil war in 1648–9, during which he displayed uncharacteristic energy in pursuing the Ulster forces of Owen Roe O'Neill. Clanricarde's close personal relationship with Ormond rendered him suspect in the eyes of many clerics, and his opponents dismissed him as 'a counterfeit or seeming Catholic'[47]. Others would happily tolerate an objectionable Catholic over a hated Protestant, though Clanricarde for his part refused to countenance such a suggestion, insisting that he would depart from the kingdom at the same time as Ormond.

Determined to effect a change of leadership, with or without Clanricarde's support, the clergy convened a meeting of bishops at Jamestown in County Leitrim on 6 August, to do whatever possible 'for the amendment of all errors and the recovery of this afflicted people'. They invited Ormond to send a representative, but the intent on this occasion, unlike the similar gathering at Clonmacnoise in December of the previous year, was clearly hostile towards the lord lieutenant. In correspondence with Ormond, the bishops explained that, despite their best efforts, they found the jealousies and fears of the Irish as 'thorns hard to take out'. Throughout the kingdom, many Catholics now openly contributed towards the enemy occupation, while few supplies materialised to maintain royalist armies. They believed that Ormond's continuing presence in Ireland hindered efforts at uniting all those opposed to the English parliamentary forces.[48] The lord lieutenant vigorously defended his record, seeking to exploit dissension within clerical ranks, evident from the fact that a number of leading Munster prelates, such as the archbishop of

Cashel and the bishops of Limerick and Emly, refused to travel to Jamestown. In addition to the defiance of the cities of Limerick and Galway, Ormond blamed supply problems on the failure of the clergy to condemn those natives colluding with the enemy. Developing this theme, he observed that 'the spring of the disobedience arises from the forgeries invented, the calumnies spread abroad against government and the incitements of the people to rebellion by very many of the clergy'. He called on the bishops to urgently address these problems, in which case he might be willing to discuss possible solutions to the leadership issue.[49] The lord lieutenant's reply constituted a direct challenge to clerical autonomy, seeking to bring an end to internal dissension, or failing that, to flush out his enemies by provoking a major crisis.

Refusing to be intimidated, those clerics who successfully managed the difficult journey to Jamestown duly responded. On 12 August, after months of prevarication, they issued an unequivocal statement against the continuance of Ormond's government. They called on all Irish Catholics to serve against the parliamentarians, and freed people from their obligation to obey the lord lieutenant, threatening to employ the spiritual weapon of excommunication against anybody who opposed the declaration. The list of charges against Ormond included the appointment of Protestant army commanders who subsequently betrayed the royalist cause and deserted. The bishops described the defeat at Rathmines, two weeks before Cromwell's arrival, as 'shameful', with the royalist camp before the battle given over to 'drinking and pleasure'. Over the next twelve months, Ormond had repeatedly failed to relieve besieged towns such as Drogheda, or to engage the enemy in the field, in contrast to his vigorous pursuit of Catholics during the early years of the rebellion. The bishops pointed out that despite raising concerns about a series of corrupt and abusive practices as far back in February, little had changed in the interim. As a result of Ormond's repeated failures the clergy now sought to resurrect the confederate government and the original oath of association.[50] The following day, the bishop of Dromore and Dr Charles Kelly, acting on behalf of the Jamestown assembly, wrote to Ormond requesting that he depart immediately from the kingdom, and leave his authority in Ireland 'in the hands of some person or persons faithful to his Majesty and trusty to the nation'.[51]

The lord lieutenant, as always, stalled for time, promising to send an answer when the bishops reassembled at the end of the month.[52] A detailed response does survive in draft form among copies of his papers in the Royal Irish Academy in Dublin, and this must have formed the basis of his subsequent reply. Ormond accused the bishops of attempting to undermine his authority, and in the process seizing 'an unwarranted power'. Regarding charges of misgovernment in civil and military affairs, the lord lieutenant acknowledged 'no earthly competent judges of us but his Majesty and the established laws', but he felt obliged to justify his actions nonetheless. The marquis defended the record of his Protestant supporters, most of whom he dismissed from service earlier in the year, and 'cast our self wholly upon the assurances those bishops and others had so often and so solemnly made to us'. Ormond angrily refuted the charge of dereliction of duty before the battle of Rathmines, claiming that he ran a 'well ordered camp', while during the fighting he had personally attempted to rally the fleeing forces though without success. Despite his authoritarian leanings, the lord lieutenant insisted that all officers present at Rathmines should share responsibility for the disaster, including leading Catholics such as Preston. As for his military tactics after Cromwell's arrival, Ormond argued that 'it was then plain we were to be on the defensive part of the war'. At Drogheda, he could not possibly have relieved the town with only 700 cavalry and 1,500 infantry, 'and of those, some not to be trusted, others newly raised, [and] all discouraged'. Similarly, a lack of supplies and the revolt of the Munster towns frustrated his efforts to thwart Cromwell's advance into the southern province. He concluded by blaming the ruin of the kingdom on the 'sedition, disloyalty, pride, covetousness and ambition' of the clergy, who aimed to control 'the supreme temporal power' of the kingdom, contrary to orthodox doctrine in Catholic states on the Continent. Ironically, given the disdain with which he treated confederate assemblies during the 1640s, Ormond now sought a meeting of the leading Catholic nobility and gentry in the kingdom, which would constitute 'a more authentic representative of the nation, than those Archbishops [and] Bishops'.[53] Confident of their ability to manipulate any such assembly, the prelates willingly agreed to his demand, but the ongoing parliamentary offensive delayed these plans.

A few days after the bishops' declaration, a provincial assembly of the nobility, gentry and clergy of Ulster unanimously elected the marquis of Clanricarde to be general of their army, in a move clearly designed to prepare the way for the unification of all Catholic forces under his leadership. The lord lieutenant insisted he would not stay in the country to satisfy some new agenda of the clergy, 'in a ridiculous, dishonourable condition with the name and not the power of a governor'.[54] Shortly afterwards, news of the fall of Charlemont, the last major Catholic stronghold in Ulster, convinced Clanricarde that Ormond should leave the kingdom immediately, or else gather all available forces and attack the parliamentarians before they had an opportunity to join into a large body. Ormond characteristically chose neither course, focusing instead on defending his personal and professional reputation. At the end of August, he announced his decision to stay in Ireland until ordered to leave by Charles, arguing unconvincingly that the internal dissensions would be 'greater upon our removal'.[55] He fully expected further condemnations from the bishops, and bemoaned the lack of communication from the royal court in Scotland, which gave a major advantage to his clerical opponents. In a letter to royalist exiles in Paris, he warned of another Catholic revolt against royal authority in Ireland, incited by the clergy, 'who notwithstanding the treason in their hearts yet profess loyalty with their tongues and pens'. In typical fashion, he blamed everybody other than himself for the recent military disasters, and although an 'impassable river' [the Shannon] defended the province of Connacht, Ormond argued that without supplies and military distractions in Scotland, it too would be lost. He concluded by requesting permission to leave Ireland, either removing Charles' authority completely, or transferring it 'to some other more acceptable to the people'.[56]

By now, even Ormond accepted the necessity for a change in

leadership, though typically he could not be decisive even about his own departure. The sudden re-appearance of the enemy in the field, following the fall of Waterford and Tecroghan, brought a temporary halt to the internal feuding in royalist ranks. In early September, Sir Hardress Waller, at the head of a column of parliamentary troops, arrived before the walls of Limerick. He immediately wrote to Hugh Dubh O'Neill, offering safe passage to whomsoever the city authorised to negotiate on their behalf. In a sinister addendum, Waller reminded the garrison commander that 'those places that have neglected to lay hold on the first summons have dearly paid for it afterwards'.[57] At the same time, Ireton moved towards the town of Athlone, hoping to gain admittance by offering very generous personal terms to the garrison commander, Viscount Dillon. On 16 September, Ireton rendezvoused with Coote's forces from Ulster outside Athlone, but contrary to his expectations, Dillon, having informed Ormond of the attempted bribery, burnt the suburbs on the eastern side of the Shannon, before withdrawing across the drawbridge.

The gravity of the situation was now such that it penetrated the paralysis of indecision enveloping Ormond since his catastrophic defeat at Rathmines. For the first time in twelve months he roused himself to action. He reinforced river crossings near Limerick, and marched with the remainder of his troops towards Athlone. Meanwhile, the Catholic bishops assembled in Galway, on receiving reports of the enemy advance through Leinster, tried to delay publication of the excommunications, and urged all Catholics to serve under the marquis of Clanricarde in defence of Athlone.[58] The order arrived too late in some instances, as priests in a number of towns proclaimed the censures after mass on the Sunday. Ormond moved immediately to crush his most vocal clerical opponents, ordering Colonel Wogan, commander of his lifeguard, to arrest John Mollony, bishop of Killaloe and other clergy assembled at Quin in County Clare, not far from Limerick. Outraged, the bishops of Ferns, Killala and Raphoe wrote to army commanders fulminating against the arrest of their colleague, and describing Ireland as 'an accursed country that hath so many rotten members'.[59] Intoxicated by his unexpected success after months of humiliation, the lord lieutenant declared the excommunications to be of 'some advantage to us', finally exposing the disloyal elements in the royalist alliance.[60]

The recorder of Limerick, Bartholomew Stackpole, reported that although the bishops there did not publish 'that hellish declaration', the townspeople were divided and confused, with some taking the opportunity to make overtures to Waller, 'to which I perceive most are inclined'.[61] Ormond once again seized the initiative. He refused to apologise for arresting the bishop of Killaloe, and instead informed the mayor of Limerick of his intention to enter the city along with a royalist garrison. The clerical faction retaliated by issuing the excommunication in Limerick, despite the best efforts of the mayor and council. Clerical censures had brought about the collapse of the first Ormond peace treaty in 1646, but frequent use by Rinuccini in subsequent years diminished their impact among the Catholic elite. Nonetheless, the censures remained a powerful weapon in the clerical armoury, particularly when directed against the population at large. Inchiquin found the country 'generally inclined to obey the excommunication', and he urged the lord lieutenant to flee abroad as soon as possible. Hugh Dubh O'Neill, although prepared to accept orders from Ormond, would not openly disobey the clergy, so he sought to resign all public duties until the conflict had been resolved.[62] Ireton's continuing presence in the vicinity of Athlone temporarily refocused royalist attention on military matters, as each faction understood that if the parliamentarians succeeded in crossing the Shannon at that point, the war would be all but lost. Facing a determined defence, however, the parliamentarians lacked sufficient boats or appropriate engineering equipment to launch a full-scale attack. With winter fast approaching, Ireton belatedly decided to concentrate his forces against Limerick.

Despite this rare military success for the royalists in holding Athlone and the Shannon line, Ormond's position had become completely untenable. Without the support of the Catholic Church he simply could not hope to lead a Catholic alliance. On 30 September, as the internal revolt intensified, he informed Viscount Dillon at Athlone of his decision to leave Ireland. The lord lieutenant had threatened to quit the kingdom before, confident in the knowledge that no suitable alternative could be found. On this occasion, all the surviving evidence suggests that Ormond fully intended to go, although he remained undecided on whether to appoint a deputy. With no official royal representative in the country, the lord lieutenant feared that the Catholic Irish would immediately make terms with the parliamentarians, leaving Charles Stuart dangerously exposed in Scotland. On 3 September, Cromwell had crushed the Scottish covenanters at the battle of Dunbar, 30 miles outside Edinburgh, forcing the royalists to try and raise another army, all of which would take time. Ormond received news of the defeat in early October, and this may well have helped convince him to leave his commission with the marquis of Clanricarde, apparently with the wholehearted support of the Commissioners of Treaty and the bishops. Viscount Muskerry described Clanricarde as 'the fittest man' for the job, but the marquis distrusted the bishops and their ambitions, and stated on a number of occasions his desire to go into exile with his close friend, Ormond.[63] Intensely loyal to the Stuarts, and with a deep sense of public duty, Clanricarde ultimately proved susceptible to pleas from supporters to maintain some semblance of royal authority in Ireland. He signed a declaration, however, along with a number of leading lay Catholics, condemning the bishops' recent actions as 'an unwarranted and unexampled usurpation of his Majesty's royal power and authority'. The signatories promised to obey Ormond in political and military affairs, while at the same time recognising the 'just rights and jurisdictions and privileges in spiritual matters' of the clergy.[64]

Not surprisingly, the parliamentarians sought to exploit these internal tensions, and on 6 October Ireton, having joined forces with Waller outside Limerick, demanded the immediate submission of the city. The defenders divided into three distinct factions – those who wanted to surrender on terms, supporters of the clergy, and royalists loyal to Ormond. The new mayor, Thomas Stritch, elected on the same day as Ireton's summons, pledged that the city would not yield during his term of office. Ignoring past disputes, he wrote to Ormond requesting that the lord lieutenant move with all available forces towards the city, to draw off the besiegers.[65] On 15 October, the parliamentarians, informed that the dominant faction within Limerick, commanded by the formidable Hugh Dubh O'Neill, intended to conduct a spirited defence, decided against a prolonged siege so late in the campaign season, and withdrew to nearby garrisons for the winter. Around this same time, Clanricarde launched his second major offensive of the year across the Shannon, with 3,000 infantry but little cavalry support. His uncharacteristically swift counter-attack caught the parliamentarians completely off guard, and threatened to break communications between their forces at Athlone and Limerick. Clanricarde seized a number of garrisons in the vicinity of Birr, and shortly afterwards received further reinforcements from James Preston, son of General Thomas Preston. Within a few days, however, Colonel Axtell, veteran of the siege of Drogheda, had assembled sufficient forces to confront the Connacht Irish. Rather than risk open battle, Clanricarde retreated to a strong defensive position on Meelick Island in the river Shannon. At this crucial moment, Ormond, still obsessed with Limerick, ordered Clanricarde to return to Connacht to supervise the transfer of forces to assist in the defence of that city, despite Ireton's withdrawal. On 25 October, the parliamentarians attacked Meelick Island. Taken by surprise, the Irish fell back across the river in total disarray, losing as many as 1,000 men and all their military equipment in the process. Once again, Clanricarde and Ormond had somehow contrived to undermine the most promising Irish offensive of the autumn. Clanricarde, confined to bed shortly afterwards with various illnesses, described the disaster as 'so unhandsome that I am not willing to have any written records of it'.[66] Despite the setback, the Shannon defensive line held, but only because of Ireton's strategic error earlier in the summer, dividing his forces rather than directing them immediately against either Limerick or Athlone. The return of spring, however, would enable the parliamentarians to renew their offensive against Connacht.

The defeat at Meelick Island increased the pressure on Ormond to relinquish command immediately and depart from the kingdom. The bishop of Limerick, previously a supporter of the lord lieutenant, advocated a change of leadership. He explained to John Walsh how he had used all means to get Ormond's authority accepted until he saw 'the general opinion of all men commonly being against his continuance in the same'. He urged Walsh to ensure that the lord lieutenant left Ireland at the earliest possible opportunity.[67] Ormond made one final bid to retain power, informing the Commissioners of Treaty residing in Ennis of a report from Dean John King, recently returned from the Continent, in which Charles Stuart attempted to justify his agreement with the covenanters, including the disavowal of Ormond's peace treaty. Charles maintained that on first arriving in Scotland he had refused to countenance such a move, but 'at length finding that not only his liberty but his life lay at stake . . . his Majesty with unspeakable dissatisfaction and regret signed the [Dunfermline] declaration'.[68] On the basis of this report, Ormond insisted that the Kilkenny treaty remained valid, including his leadership of the confederate/royalist alliance. The marquis listed his conditions for continuing to serve as lord lieutenant, principal among them the revocation of clerical censures and the admittance of garrisons into Limerick and Galway. The commissioners departed for Galway to consult with the bishops in residence there, promising Ormond that they would attempt to have the excommunications revoked, and 'a more perfect union' established for the future. They urged the marquis to call 'an assembly of the nation' as soon as possible, in the belief that a large meeting of Catholic laity would condemn clerical attempts to establish an alternative government.[69] The lord lieutenant agreed, and immediately summoned prominent individuals to meet on 15 November in Loughrea, County Galway.

Meanwhile, the Commissioners of Treaty and bishops engaged in lengthy negotiations at Galway in an effort to reach a compromise. The commissioners stressed the importance of maintaining royal authority in Ireland to discourage people from making conditions with the enemy, and pleaded for the revocation of clerical censures. The bishops replied that Charles Stuart at Dunfermline had effectively removed Ormond's commission as lord lieutenant, necessitating the establishment of an alternative government. The commissioners dismissed this argument, as Charles had signed the declaration under duress, but the bishops sought a return to the confederacy of the 1640s, 'as was intended by the Nation, in case of a breach of the peace on his Majesty's part'. The clergy interpreted the scale of the military setbacks and the virulence of plague as signs of God's displeasure with them for accepting a Protestant governor in place of the Catholic association, though as the commissioners pointed out, they had happily proclaimed their loyalty to a Protestant king when agreeing to the peace treaty in January 1649. Clerical leaders, however, would clearly only remain loyal to the royalist cause if the government of the kingdom remained in the hands of Catholics. Their experience of Ormond, whether during the prolonged negotiations of the 1640s, or since the signing of the 1649 treaty, merely confirmed the impracticality of a Protestant leading a Catholic alliance. The bishops sought the appointment of Clanricarde in place of Ormond, at least until the sitting of 'a free and lawful Assembly'. Having learnt from harsh experience in 1646–7 the pitfalls associated with a clerical coup d'état they insisted that the forthcoming assembly ratify any decision on the structure of a future government. Confident of the support of the majority of Catholics, the clergy declared their willingness to abide by the rulings of this meeting, even if it decided to make an agreement with the parliamentarians.[70]

Much now depended on the attitude of Clanricarde. Following the fiasco at Meelick Island, the potential saviour of Catholic Ireland appeared in no physical or mental shape to assume a leadership role. Ormond, taking the war for lost, began to provision ships in Galway, although, conscious as ever of his historical legacy, the marquis delayed sailing in order to defend his conduct before the assembly. Aware that most exiled royalists faced increasing financial hardship, the lord lieutenant also wanted to collect some money promised him by Clanricarde.[71] The first meeting of the assembly on 15 November issued a declaration of loyalty to the crown, and denied that the bishops proposed any usurpation of royal powers in Ireland. The members beseeched Ormond to leave his commission with somebody agreeable to the nation, who would be given all due obedience. Ormond responded positively, agreeing to discuss the matter in greater detail, but bad weather delayed the appointment of a select committee until 26 November. The committee consisted of nineteen members, including many supporters of the lord lieutenant, such as Clanricarde and Richard Bellings, while others, such as Bishop French and Hugh Rochford, were openly hostile. The following day, the full assembly heard readings of all the correspondence between Ormond, the Commissioners of Treaty and the Catholic hierarchy, before the committee retired to debate the matter in private. After due consideration, committee members reported back to the assembly, whose chairman, Sir Richard Blake, wrote to the lord lieutenant, repeating the request that royal authority be left in 'acceptable' hands.[72] Ormond still could not commit himself to depart, and he engaged instead in further debate, ostensibly designed to secure guarantees against undue clerical interference in government. The assembly was prepared to provide such a statement, but Ormond, fearing that a parliamentary blockade of Galway harbour might prevent any escape to the Continent, suddenly decided to quit the kingdom. Before leaving on 9 December, he sent Clanricarde the king's commission 'either to make use of or not', while warning his successor to seek clarification from the assembly whether the clergy or anybody else claimed the power 'to set free or discharge the people upon any ground or pretence whatsoever from yielding obedience to any such governor'.[73] Once again, Ormond went out of his way to court controversy on an insolubly divisive issue, creating untold difficulties for his successor. Having fulfilled his official duties, the lord lieutenant finally left Ireland and sailed for France, to join the exiled Stuart court in Paris.

Ormond's leadership of the royalist/confederate coalition had proved disastrous in both military and political terms. While military fortunes favoured the royalists in early 1649, internal opponents remained silent, but as the tables turned during the summer old resentments burst forth. Irish Protestants, uncomfortable with the confederate alliance from the outset, suspected Ormond of pro-Catholic sympathies, while former confederates never forgave him for surrendering Dublin to the English parliament in 1647. Outmanoeuvred and out-classed by Jones at Rathmines, the marquis never recovered his military nerve to tackle Oliver Cromwell on the battlefield. His strategy of fortifying key towns to resist the parliamentary invaders failed spectacularly at Drogheda and Wexford, undermining royalist morale and exacerbating existing religious tensions in the royalist/confederate alliance. With the surrender of Protestant units to Cromwell in April 1650, this coalition effectively came to an end, leaving Ormond totally reliant on the Catholic population to maintain the war effort. Unable to command clerical support, his position quickly became untenable, and he should have left the country around the time of Cromwell's departure. This might well have prevented the worst disasters of the summer campaign, and avoided much of the subsequent internecine strife. Continuing setbacks during the course of 1650 effectively sealed his fate, but it was the unwillingness of Galway or Limerick to accept a royalist garrison that eventually forced the marquis to admit defeat. By the time Ormond set sail for France in December 1650, the military situation seemed increasingly hopeless, with royalist forces restricted to Connacht. According to one parliamentarian commentator, Ireton would endeavour to make the province 'their prison until such time as God make way for us to get over amongst them'.[74] Limerick, Galway, Athlone and Sligo provided a potential platform for a renewed offensive, but without foreign assistance in the form of trained officers, military supplies and most importantly of all, cash, Ireton would almost certainly complete the conquest of the kingdom the following year. All eyes now turned to the Continent, in the hope of major intervention from abroad.

7

Foreign Intervention

*I dare promise you so much in the word of my master that all
officers and commanders as shall be seen in relieving this place [Galway]
shall be respectively remunerated, and their names shall be registered
in the catalogue of chivalry.*[1]

JO. WANDERMASTER, AGENT FROM THE DUKE OF LORRAINE (1652)

In early 1654, troops in the service of Charles IV, duke of Lorraine,
devastated the district around Liège in the Spanish Netherlands,
provoking a fierce armed response from local peasants, and a storm
of protest at the court of Archduke Leopold in Brussels. The
archduke, already concerned by rumours that Lorraine, an
experienced general and long-time ally of the Habsburgs, intended
to betray certain towns to the French, decided to take immediate
action. He arrested Lorraine, who consequently spent a number of
years in comfortable confinement in Spain. Many of the duke's
marauding soldiers were recruited from among the thousands driven
from Ireland during the parliamentary conquest. In fact, between
1650 and 1652, the duke of Lorraine played a key role in Irish affairs,
as the only significant foreign ally of the beleaguered Catholics in
their struggle against Oliver Cromwell and the New Model Army.
Whereas France, Spain and the papacy, traditional supporters of the
Catholic Irish, provided little beyond expressions of sympathy,
Lorraine sent vital military supplies and helped raise morale at a
crucial stage of the war. Despite all this, the duke has been relegated
to a mere footnote in Irish history, as Cromwell's victories seemingly
rendered all contacts with continental Europe obsolete.

Traditional accounts of the 1640s tend to play down links between
Ireland and the Continent, focusing almost exclusively on Anglo-
Irish relations. Without significant foreign intervention, however, in
terms of financial and military supplies, the Catholic rebels stood

little chance of success. For this reason, the idea of a Continental protector had been discussed from the early stages of the rebellion, and influenced confederate policy at key moments over the following decade. At first, unofficial representatives, such as the clerics Hugh Bourke in Spanish Flanders and Luke Wadding at Rome, did what they could for the war effort at home. Exploiting traditional sympathy for the plight of the Catholic Irish, and equal antipathy towards Protestant England, their initial supplications proved moderately successful, but as the Thirty Years War raged on in central Europe, it became increasingly difficult to keep Irish affairs on the agenda of Continental rulers. From late 1642, therefore, the General Assembly of the confederate association, while reluctant to usurp traditional crown prerogatives, nonetheless decided to appoint permanent envoys to the major Catholic courts on the Continent. Churchmen proved ideal for the role, as they could converse and correspond in Latin, the international language of diplomacy, and rely on their extensive clerical connections to provide introductions to the European elite. Moreover, their use as envoys reinforced the image of the war in Ireland as a religious conflict, which the government in Kilkenny hoped would elicit generous contributions from Catholic states.

Unfortunately for the confederates, religion alone no longer determined the political stance of the great Continental powers, a fact demonstrated by the alliance between Catholic France and Protestant Sweden in the 1630s to counter Habsburg aggression. Despite a shared religious affiliation with the confederates, the two major Catholic monarchs of Europe, Louis XIII of France and Philip IV of Spain, proved unwilling to offend Charles I, or the powerful English parliament, by officially recognising envoys from Kilkenny. In addition to heavy military and financial commitments in Germany, both kingdoms remained locked in a titanic struggle against each other on at least four different fronts – Flanders, the Pyrenees, northern Italy and the Rhine valley. Spain also faced major revolts in Portugal and Catalonia from 1640, while the death of Louis XIII in 1643 heralded a period of internal instability in the French kingdom, culminating in the civil wars of the Fronde. Quite simply, even had they so wished, neither Paris nor Madrid possessed sufficient resources to intervene decisively in Ireland. Nonetheless, the affairs of that country could not be completely ignored. Both France and Spain sent agents to Kilkenny during the 1640s, rather than fully accredited ambassadors, primarily to prevent the other from gaining a foothold on the island, but also to raise recruits for their armies. Ireland, although relatively poor and on the periphery of Europe, did possess an abundance of manpower, an increasingly rare commodity on the war-torn Continent. Irish troops enjoyed a reputation for toughness, and as Catholics, were deemed acceptable by both the Habsburgs and the Bourbons. Despite incessant intriguing in confederate politics, however, a succession of junior French and Spanish diplomats enjoyed relatively little success in encouraging Irishmen to serve abroad.

In contrast to France and Spain, the papacy initially appeared more receptive to the pleas of Irish Catholics for assistance. The emergence of the confederate association not only struck a blow against the Protestant Reformation, but also created a launching pad for the possible re-conversion of England. Publicly at least, Pope Urban VIII adopted a cautious policy on Ireland, as he still hoped to entice Charles I back to the Church of Rome. Privately, the pope encouraged the confederates, but despite sending an agent, Pietro Francesco Scarampi, to Kilkenny in 1643, he provided little in terms of practical assistance. In fact, Rome's parsimonious attitude towards Ireland throughout the war effectively undermined confederate chances of a decisive military victory. In 1644, the succession of Innocent X heralded the only notable confederate diplomatic success of that turbulent decade, with the appointment of Rinuccini as papal nuncio to Ireland. The nuncio's arrival in 1645, however, proved something of a mixed blessing. While his presence undoubtedly bestowed international status on the regime in Kilkenny, it also exacerbated tensions within confederate ranks. On the military front, an injection of papal cash enabled the confederates to enjoy their most successful campaign to date in the summer of 1646, although it did not significantly alter the course of the war. Politically, many Old English landowners, who had benefited from the dissolution of the monasteries during the reign of Henry VIII a hundred years earlier, now feared the nuncio would attempt to claim this land back for the Catholic Church. More importantly, Rinuccini's inflexible views on religious matters generated huge resentment among the confederate leadership at what they saw as unwarranted foreign interference in their internal affairs. The confederate truce with the Protestant Lord Inchiquin in May 1648 precipitated a complete breach with Rinuccini, and shortly after the signing of the Ormond peace treaty in January 1649 the nuncio sailed for the Continent, where the recriminations over his mission would rumble on for decades. Realistically, any hope of further assistance from Rome disappeared with him.

With the traditional channels all but closed to the confederates, they needed to look elsewhere for support, and Charles IV, duke of Lorraine, quickly emerged as the most likely candidate. A cousin of Maximilian I, elector of Bavaria, Charles succeeded to the duchy in 1624. His inheritance stretched south from Luxembourg towards the Alps, and from the river Meuse to the Rhine. More importantly it straddled the strategically vital 'Spanish Road', linking Habsburg lands in Italy with those in Flanders, and was also France's gateway into Germany. Louis XIII claimed parts of Lorraine for France, while the Holy Roman Emperor, Ferdinand II of Austria, insisted that the duchy was an imperial fief. The French took advantage of Habsburg commitments during the Thirty Years War to launch three separate invasions of Lorraine from 1631, before finally driving the duke into exile in 1634. Apart from one brief interlude in 1641, he did not return home until 1661. For almost twenty years, using Brussels as his headquarters, the Catholic Lorraine served the Spanish Habsburgs as a mercenary commander and military contractor, in the manner of his famous contemporary Albrecht of Wallenstein, duke of Friedland. By the early 1650s, Lorraine had amassed a great fortune, estimated at £500,000 in bullion, and £75,000 in ready money or bills of change, much of it deposited in Switzerland.[2] To put this in some sort of context, the cash figure alone exceeded the entire amount the confederates received from Continental sources during the 1640s.

An experienced military entrepreneur, rich in cash, capable in command, but free from territorial ties, the duke could provide

Map 6 Western Europe about 1650, showing the location of Lorraine

military muscle and financial assistance to any prospective employer. Lorraine's association with the House of Stuart dated back to the 1620s, when Venetian sources spoke of the 'good understanding' between the duke and the English.[3] During the 1630s, Charles I supported the restoration of Lorraine to his patrimony, and also gave permission to the duke to recruit troops in Stuart territories. In 1644–5 Queen Henrietta Maria, exiled in Paris as a result of the English Civil War, contacted Lorraine, seeking aid for her husband in his struggle against parliament. Cardinal Mazarin, anxious to detach the duke from Habsburg service, offered to pay for the transport of his troops to England. The failure to obtain suitable shipping thwarted the scheme, but Lorraine had at least been alerted to the possibility of profitable employment and investment in the wars of the three Stuart kingdoms.

The duke took a particular interest in Irish affairs following the outbreak of the 1641 rebellion. Lorraine's family enjoyed a reputation for militant Catholicism, and the duke's predecessor, Charles III, had played host to leading exiles from Ireland, such as Hugh O'Neill, earl of Tyrone, in the early decades of the seventeenth century, despite protests from English diplomats. One hostile source wondered of Charles IV, 'Where can a more desperate and Jesuited Prince, or a more declared enemy to Protestants be found out?'[4] In 1645, the duke responded favourably to a request from the papal nuncio, Rinuccini, for munitions and supplies to bring on his mission to Ireland. This was not a case of pure altruism, as Ireland represented a potentially lucrative source of manpower, and throughout the duke's long career, self-advancement, rather than religious zeal, provided his primary motivation. Shortly after this engagement with Rinuccini, Lorraine attempted to obtain permission from the confederate association to recruit soldiers for service in Flanders but without success.

In 1647, as the peace negotiations in Westphalia reached a conclusion, it became clear that Emperor Ferdinand III, in the face of determined French opposition, would not insist on the duke's restoration. In response, Lorraine once again offered to assist the exiled Queen Henrietta Maria, Louis XIV's aunt, in return for her intercession at the French court. Following the signing of a peace treaty between Spain and the Netherlands in January 1648, Lorraine joined with the Protestant William II, prince of Orange, an avowed enemy of the Catholic Habsburgs, in planning an expedition to assist a Scottish invasion of England, on behalf of Charles I, William's father-in-law. Lorraine and William began to assemble their forces on the island of Borkum off the Dutch coast to await shipping, but news of Oliver Cromwell's victory over the Scots at Preston in mid-August destroyed any immediate hope of a royalist revival in England. The troops at Borkum disbanded and Lorraine returned to campaign in the service of Archduke Leopold. With the Thirty Years War now drawing to a close, and prospects for future employment diminishing as a result, the duke established direct contact with Mazarin, to explore once again the possibility of a rapprochement with the French.

The execution of Charles I in January 1649 shocked the rulers of Europe, and energised royalist supporters in Ireland and Scotland, who proclaimed the Prince of Wales as Charles II. Based temporarily in the Netherlands, the young monarch dispatched ambassadors across Europe, seeking foreign assistance. In May, Charles instructed two envoys, Edward Hyde (later earl of Clarendon) and Lord Cottington, to meet the duke of Lorraine in Brussels, who readily agreed to finance their onward journey to Madrid. On his way to Paris shortly afterwards, Charles also visited Brussels, and while both Lorraine and Archduke Leopold, whose chamberlain, Patrick O'Muledius, was 'an Irishman by nationality', listened sympathetically to his plight, they failed to offer more concrete assistance.[5] Charles experienced similar difficulties with the French and Spanish, who despite the Peace of Westphalia, remained at war with one another. Financially crippled and facing serious internal dissent, neither state wished to oppose, openly at least, the new parliamentary regime in England. Of the major European powers, only Sweden responded to the plea for military aid, providing arms and ammunition for the royalist cause, some of which Charles directed towards Ireland. Although anxious to secure foreign support, Ormond expressed deep concern over reports of possible military assistance from Catholic Spain. The marquis favoured Protestant Sweden, and warned Charles against alienating Irish Protestants, 'without whom your majesty's work here much less in England and Scotland is not to be done'.[6] This hostility towards intervention by a Catholic power resurfaced later during Ormond's dealings with the duke of Lorraine. There is no evidence that Lorraine had any designs on Ireland at this time, but in August 1649, the same month as Cromwell and 12,000 soldiers landed at Dublin, popular publications in London spread rumours of the duke's imminent departure there with up to 4,000 men.[7] The stories proved groundless, but in the eyes of the English public at least, Lorraine now emerged as a potential ally for the Irish rebels in their struggle against parliament.

In early 1650, with Cromwell seemingly sweeping all before him, the lawyer and former MP, Hugh Rochford, 'a man of impeccable astuteness and worthy of trust', initiated direct negotiations between the duke of Lorraine and the Catholic Irish.[8] Rochford, a leading figure in the confederate association, enjoyed close relations with the clerical faction, and supported demands for greater concessions on religious and land issues. As early as April 1648, Rochford's benefactor, Randal MacDonnell, marquis of Antrim, who controlled a small fleet of privateers operating out of Wexford, had instructed Abbot Crelly of Newry to approach the Venetian ambassador in France. The marquis proposed 'to hand over to the republic as a security the most important fortresses and ports in the kingdom', in return for financial assistance. The ambassador politely declined the offer.[9] Following this rebuff, Antrim explored instead the possibility of an accommodation with the English parliament. Once again, Crelly acted as intermediary. He negotiated with parliamentary representatives during the early months of 1649, but Cromwell's invasion of Ireland in August put paid for the moment to any idea of an alliance.

Antrim's accomplices now returned to the idea of a Continental protector. In January 1650 Rochford arrived unannounced at Jersey in the Channel Islands, the temporary residence of Charles Stuart and his exiled courtiers. Suspicious of his motives, the royal advisers speculated wildly as to the exact nature of this mission. Charles confirmed that the former MP did not possess authority from Ormond, although he had brought a letter from Lieutenant General Richard Farrell of the Ulster army. Secretary Robert Long subsequently read this letter and claimed that it did not contain any credentials, 'but only civilities and professions of loyalty to the king'.[10] Another royal official at Jersey, Sir Edward Nicholas, feared that Rochford had come over 'with a malicious design', particularly as he sought 'to make larger demands of the king in point of religion, and for those of the Old Irish', than Ormond had recently agreed with

Owen Roe O'Neill, in the treaty signed shortly before the latter's death.[11] The contents of Rochford's petition to Charles, as outlined by Nicholas, strongly suggest a link between this mission and the earlier scheme of the marquis of Antrim involving Venice. Rochford, however, only revealed his true objective, and the means by which it might be achieved, after Charles left Jersey.

Charles had originally planned to join Ormond in Ireland, but reports of the spectacular success of Cromwell's campaign convinced him to pursue a different strategy. A number of royal advisers, unhappy at the prospect of an alliance with the Catholic Irish, advocated instead an agreement with the Scottish covenanters. The Presbyterian covenanters had fought alongside the parliamentarians in the first English civil war, but outraged by the execution of Charles I, they now supported the restoration of his son. In return for military assistance they demanded a Presbyterian religious settlement throughout the three Stuart kingdoms. Although not yet prepared to abandon his Catholic subjects in Ireland, Charles nonetheless travelled to the Netherlands in March 1650, hoping to negotiate a treaty with the Scots. Rochford followed him to Breda, and unveiled a plan to introduce a new and potentially decisive force into Ireland on the royalist side. According to Secretary Long, Rochford proposed that Charles offer the Fort of Duncannon as security for a loan, 'and saith he hath found persons that will furnish a considerable sum upon it'.[12] Situated at the mouth of the river Suir, the fortress controlled access to Waterford, the only major port on the eastern or southern coasts still in royalist hands. Both Waterford and Duncannon had successfully withstood parliamentary sieges in late 1649, although they remained under threat. Rochford's scheme would have provided additional security for Duncannon, as well as much needed cash for the war effort. More importantly, Rochford's scheme also offered an opportunity for Lorraine to become directly involved in the struggle against the English parliament.

Charles Stuart appears to have maintained contact with Lorraine after their initial meeting in May 1649, in the hope of exploiting the duke's military and financial potential sometime in the future. Despite some misgivings, he now decided to sanction negotiations between Rochford and Lorraine, offering the fort of Duncannon 'or some other place to raise money for the supply of our army in Ireland'. Charles instructed Sir Henry de Vic, his representative in Brussels, to assist Rochford, and authorised Ormond to cooperate with the project, but only if the lord lieutenant approved of the agreement.[13] Conscious of growing opposition in Ireland to the lacklustre royalist leadership, Secretary Long explained to Ormond that by rejecting the proposal out of hand, 'occasion would have been taken to lay all envy upon us here, of any loss, or misfortune that should happen in Ireland, by reason of want of money'. Nonetheless, the lord lieutenant criticised the decision to deal with Rochford, and pleaded that in future Charles would only receive properly accredited agents from Ireland.[14]

The negotiations commenced in Brussels and in early April Lorraine agreed to provide a loan as soon as he received possession of Duncannon. Contact with Ireland, however, proved difficult and Rochford could not confirm that the fort still remained in royalist hands, although it did not in fact surrender to the parliamentarians until the following August. In the absence of any assurances about the fate of Duncannon, Sir Henry de Vic observed that the duke 'appeared less forward to engage upon those suggestions'. Instead, Lorraine proposed sending a representative to Ireland, to compile a first-hand report on the state of affairs in that beleaguered kingdom.[15] The duke appointed Colonel Oliver Synott, an Irish officer serving in his army, to accompany Rochford back to Ireland and negotiate directly with the lord lieutenant. The two agents arrived in Galway on 21 May 1650, after a difficult journey. Fearing capture during a pursuit by English parliamentary frigates, the envoys apparently threw all their papers overboard, including letters from Charles Stuart and the duke of Lorraine.[16] The loss of the letters certainly allowed Rochford and Synott a comparatively free hand in the subsequent negotiations. Royalists in Ireland, like many of their exiled counterparts, viewed Rochford with suspicion, primarily because of his links with the treacherous marquis of Antrim, now openly allied with the English parliamentarians. The marquis of Clanricarde, governor of Galway, ordered Rochford's immediate arrest, before Ormond intervened and, anxious to learn of developments on the Continent, agreed to a meeting. The conference took place in Ballinasloe, County Galway, but the lord lieutenant, deeply embroiled in the dispute with Limerick over the admittance of a royalist garrison, refused to commit himself to any deal 'without express order from the king'.[17]

For the next few weeks, Rochford and Synott explored the possibility of using the western port of Galway as security for the loan, instead of Duncannon. Despite a severe outbreak of the plague in the summer of 1649, Galway provided a potentially more attractive base for Lorraine's operations in Ireland, particularly as the province of Connacht for the moment at least remained free of enemy troops. Theobald, Viscount Taaffe, informed Ormond of Synott's interest in the city, as well as his offer to provide £10,000 worth of credit through Captain Antonio. Highly sceptical of the whole affair, the lord lieutenant dismissed the idea that Galway would admit any garrison, 'much less [one] of strangers'. He suspected that Colonel Synott claimed 'more authority than he hath to engage his Majesty', and Captain Antonio 'to more credit than he can give'.[18] Nonetheless, conscious of the urgent need for foreign aid, Ormond authorised Viscount Taaffe, Lord Athenry, and Geoffrey Browne to treat for the £10,000, but only on condition that Taaffe subsequently sought approval from Charles Stuart for any deal.[19]

Ormond's commissioners travelled to Galway in the last week in June to begin talks, but just prior to their arrival, Captain Antonio suddenly set sail for the Continent. A flustered Viscount Taaffe, who had no other means of reaching the exiled royal court, hurriedly packed his bags and boarded the frigate further along the coast. The abrupt departure of Captain Antonio suggests that Ormond's doubts about the existence of the £10,000 may well have been justified. More importantly, it also meant that Taaffe left Ireland without an approved deal on the transfer of Galway to Lorraine. According to Geoffrey Browne, the city authorities displayed little enthusiasm for the plan in any case, and he decided 'not to put it to a public trial till the money were present'.[20] Synott, however, alleged that Taaffe had misled him over the willingness of Galway to engage with Lorraine,

1 Oliver Cromwell (1599–1658). Portrait by Robert Walker from
c.1649, the year of Cromwell's invasion of Ireland.

Sʳ.ᵗPhillom O Cheife Traytor · neale of all Ireland

2 Sir Phelim O'Neill (1603–53). Leader of the rebellion in 1641, his execution in 1653 signalled the end of the war.

3 Owen Roe O'Neill (c.1583–1649). Inspirational commander of the Ulster Irish, he died before meeting Cromwell in battle.

4 King Charles I (1600–49). His trial and
execution in January 1649 helped forge the
confederate–royalist alliance in Ireland.

5 Prince Rupert
(1619–82). He
commanded the small
royalist navy based at
Kinsale for much of 1649.

6 Roger Boyle, Lord Broghill (1621–79).
He convinced the principal ports of
Munster to declare for Cromwell
in late 1649.

7 Colonel Michael Jones
(c.1606–49). Victories at
Dungan's Hill (1647) and
Rathmines (1649) prepared the
way for Cromwell.

8 John Hewson (*fl.* 1630–60). Took part in the storming of Drogheda in 1649 and subsequently served as governor of Dublin.

9 George Monck (1608–70). Parliamentary commander of Dundalk, he agreed a temporary truce with the Ulster Irish in 1649.

10 Henry Ireton (*c.*1611–51). Cromwell's replacement as commander-in-chief, he died shortly after the fall of Limerick.

11 Ulick Bourke, Marquis of Clanricarde (1604–58). Lord Deputy of Ireland after Ormond's departure in late 1650.

12 King Charles II (1630–85). This portrait
(1648) is by Adriaen Hanneman, famous for
his paintings of the exiled Stuart court.

13 Charles IV, Duke of Lorraine
(1604–75). Adventurer and military
entrepreneur, he took a keen
interest in Irish affairs.

14 James Butler, 1st Duke of Ormond (1610–88). The great survivor of seventeenth-century Irish politics.

and announced his intention to return to Brussels for further instructions. Clanricarde fumed over the dishonesty of Captain Antonio 'and those that accompanied him over [Rochford and Synott]', and once again suggested arresting them until Charles Stuart resolved the matter.[21] Ormond, however, may not have been too upset at this dramatic turn of events. Hostile to the idea of a Spanish alliance a year earlier, he appeared deeply uncomfortable with the prospect of the Catholic duke of Lorraine gaining a foothold in Ireland. As his clerical opponents grew more vocal and militant, the lord lieutenant feared for the safety of the Protestant Irish. He denounced Rochford and his associates as 'knaves', and complained about the disloyalty of the Catholic clergy. In Ormond's opinion, only a Protestant army could provide security for Protestants in Ireland, though he gave no indication of how he expected such a force to materialise anytime in the near future.[22] While Ormond dreamed of Protestant intervention, the royalist military position continued to deteriorate throughout the summer of 1650, with defeats in Ulster, Leinster and Munster.

This initial attempt to secure assistance from the duke of Lorraine faltered in part owing to existing tensions within the royalist/confederate alliance, which severely hampered the decision-making process. Ormond's obvious reluctance to deal with Rochford and Synott further complicated matters, although by sending Viscount Taaffe to the exiled Stuart court the lord lieutenant at least kept the project alive. Taaffe arrived in Jersey in July 1650, only to discover that Charles had already departed for Scotland, following his agreement with the covenanters. After receiving letters of commendation from the duke of York and Queen Henrietta Maria in Paris, Taaffe finally reached Brussels in November, where Lorraine immediately supplied the viscount with £5,000 worth of arms and ammunition. Although the proposal to use certain ports as security for loans lacked official approval, Taaffe assured Lorraine that Charles Stuart would certainly agree to the measures. The viscount also cautioned against any delay, which might have sounded more convincing if his own journey from Jersey to Brussels had not taken a leisurely four months.[23] In fact, the timing of Taaffe's arrival proved opportune, as the duke's prospects on the Continent appeared particularly bleak. Taking advantage of the upheavals caused by the civil wars of the Fronde in France, the duke had launched an invasion of Lorraine earlier that year. Despite some initial successes, capturing 'most places of strength into his hands', the French eventually routed the duke's forces.[24] With hopes of recovering his patrimony temporarily thwarted, the proposal to intervene in Ireland must have provided a welcome distraction.

At the end of December, with no word yet from Charles Stuart in Scotland, the duke decided to send a member of his inner-council, Abbot Stephen de Henin, to Ireland, with full powers to negotiate an agreement on his behalf. Unsure of Ormond's whereabouts, Lorraine addressed a letter to the nobility of Ireland, assuring them that nothing concerned him more than 'the necessity itself of supporting, and restoring religion [Catholicism] to its liberty'. However, the duke's terms of engagement had changed dramatically from the original offer of a secured loan in early 1650. Lorraine now coveted the prestigious title of 'protector', and promised that if invited to Ireland, and 'the command of that kingdom be put into his hands', he would employ 'his men, treasure, shipping and person in the reducing thereof'.[25] Apart from an irrepressible sense of adventure, there are a number of possible explanations for Lorraine's redirected priorities. The duke was an increasingly anomalous presence in post-Westphalia Europe and the military setbacks against France urgently increased his need for fresh recruits. With Germany exhausted after thirty years of continuous conflict, Ireland represented a potentially rich source of manpower, which the position of Protector would enable him to exploit. Moreover, by taking the offensive against heretics in Ireland, Lorraine hoped to persuade Pope Innocent X to legitimise his marriage to Beatrix de Cusance, even though his first wife, Nicole, was still alive. The birth of a son to Charles and Beatrix in 1649 provided even greater incentive to resolve his marital affairs. Lorraine wrote to Innocent X in February 1651, seeking a papal blessing and military supplies, but he assured Taaffe of his determination to send assistance to Ireland regardless of the outcome of all other negotiations.[26]

The lack of options, apart from Lorraine, appears to have convinced the staunchly royalist Taaffe of the need for drastic measures to revive Stuart fortunes. He wrote to Ormond, assuring him that the duke should not be 'suspected to have any sinister ends', and argued that all other prospects for foreign intervention in Ireland appeared poor. Starting with Scotland, Taaffe believed that they could expect 'nothing but destruction' from the covenanters, in view of their well-documented hostility towards Irish Catholics. The possibility of assistance from the French court, in the midst of civil conflict, seemed equally forlorn, while according to the latest reports the Spanish had 'already concluded a League, which some say is defensive and offensive with the parliament', after Philip IV instructed his ambassador in London to recognise the English Commonwealth.[27] As for the papacy, the bitter recriminations following Rinuccini's departure from Ireland in early 1649 precluded the likelihood of any further help from that quarter. In a second letter, Taaffe assured the lord lieutenant that if Lorraine did in fact attempt to make himself master of the Irish, 'it's in ourselves to prevent it', as he would be reliant for the most part on Irish troops. Taaffe insisted that Henrietta Maria supported this initiative, but it seems highly unlikely that the queen would have consented to such a radical plan in the absence of her eldest son. The viscount explained to Ormond that while he had written to Charles Stuart, informing him of Lorraine's proposal, as long as he remained in Scotland, 'his connivance is all I expect or desire'.[28]

Unknown to Taaffe, the lord lieutenant had already left Ireland to join the exiled royalist court in Paris. Following Ormond's departure in December 1650, his reluctant deputy, the marquis of Clanricarde, faced the unenviable task of trying to unite the increasingly divided royal supporters, and reverse the seemingly inexorable tide of parliamentary victories. Initially at least, Clanricarde received strong support from the general assembly at Loughrea, despite an attempt by Bishop Nicholas French, 'and some few other violent clergy', to drive out royal authority altogether and 'renew their confederacy' of the 1640s.[29] A few months earlier, the clerical congregation at Jamestown had authorised Bishop French, along with Hugh

Rochford, to treat with any Catholic state or person willing to offer assistance. Temporarily thwarted on the domestic front by Clanricarde, the bishop made preparations early in 1651 to travel to the Continent in the company of a leading clerical supporter and friend of the marquis of Antrim, Dr Walter Enos. In addition to his clerical commission, French obtained further letters of credence from representatives of Limerick and Galway. The bishop made one final appeal to Clanricarde prior to his departure, but the Lord Deputy refused to cooperate. Clanricarde did not trust French or Enos, and he warned Ormond to keep 'a watchful eye over their proceedings' on the Continent.[30] After arriving safely in France, Enos travelled on to Rome hoping to secure papal backing for the idea of a Catholic protector, while Bishop French headed for Brussels. According to the royalist George Lane, who met the bishop in Nantes, French proposed offering Limerick and Galway to any foreign prince who would preserve the clerical interest in Ireland.[31]

Less than two weeks after the departure of Bishop French from Ireland, Taaffe's uncle, Father George Dillon, and Abbot Stephen de Henin arrived in Galway, with supplies of arms and ammunition, as well as some money. Some reports suggest that the abbot may have brought as much as £20,000 in cash, although this figure probably included the value of the military supplies. The envoys sought recognition of the duke of Lorraine as protector of Ireland, and control of the ports of Limerick and Galway as security for any loans. Clanricarde rejected the terms as 'totally inconsistent with the king's authority', and summoned an emergency meeting of clergy and laity in Galway to advise him on the matter.[32] Over the next three weeks the Lord Deputy engaged in an increasingly bitter debate with this assembly, 'having to deal', according to Richard Bellings, 'with a clergy violently bent to be under the protection of a Catholic prince'.[33] To further complicate matters, a Father Anthony MacGeoghegan arrived in Ireland at this time, with a commission from Dionysius Massari, secretary of the Sacred Congregation *de Propaganda Fide* in Rome, the agency that nurtured the Catholic cause abroad. Antrim's agent, Abbot Crelly, had recommended MacGeoghegan to Massari, who served as Rinuccini's secretary during his mission to Ireland. Massari now enthusiastically promoted the idea of a renewed confederation, under the protection of a leading Continental Catholic. The Catholic bishops present at Galway, however, proved unwilling to complicate their own negotiations with Lorraine, and wished to steer clear of any plan associated with the discredited marquis of Antrim. Despite this setback, MacGeoghegan remained in Ireland and continued to lobby among those clerics dissatisfied with Clanricarde's government.

At the assembly, Clanricarde, adamant that Lorraine should have no other role or title in Ireland, argued strongly in favour of the original terms agreed with the duke's representatives back in 1650. Anxious to avoid a complete rupture with the Lord Deputy, assembly members eventually backed down. The articles of treaty, signed by Clanricarde and Abbot de Henin on 4 April 1651, guaranteed £20,000 for the royalist war effort, with provisions for Lorraine to garrison Limerick and Galway as security for the loan.[34] This represented no real advance on the proposals of the previous year, although the royalist military position had deteriorated significantly in the interim. The eagerness of many Catholics to conclude a deal with Lorraine at almost any cost had shocked Clanricarde, who condemned a plan put forward by the archbishop of Tuam as representing 'no better than a total transferring of the Crown from his Majesty to a foreign Prince'. The staunchly royalist earl of Castlehaven concurred, denouncing any agreement which gave 'footing or the least pretence or title to any foreign prince'.[35] Clanricarde believed that Abbot de Henin had been poorly advised 'by seditious and ill-affected persons', one of whom, Hugh Rochford, left Ireland shortly afterwards, almost certainly to report directly to Bishop French.[36] The Lord Deputy, anxious lest his clerical opponents try to subvert negotiations on the Continent, instructed Geoffrey Browne and Nicholas Plunkett, two experienced confederate diplomats, to travel to Brussels, visiting the Stuart court in St Germain on the way. The marquis expressly ordered the two men not to proceed further than giving security for Lorraine's money and supplies, 'until you are enabled to go on in the rest, as his Majesty's Ministers shall direct you'.[37] Despite persistent internal divisions, the royalists entered the 1651 campaign season with renewed optimism, encouraged by improved prospects of military assistance from the Continent.

The English commonwealth regime, painfully aware of its diplomatic isolation in 1649–50, genuinely feared foreign intervention on behalf of the Stuarts, and the authorities in London and Dublin monitored the duke of Lorraine's involvement in Irish affairs with growing concern. The arrival in Galway of Lorraine's envoy, Abbot de Henin, aroused great interest, and an extensive intelligence network kept the parliamentarians well informed about the subsequent negotiations. Not everybody was convinced of the threat posed by the duke, and one correspondent in Kilkenny described talk of his intervention as 'to be only an old Bug-beare'.[38] In March 1651, however, William Basil, parliament's attorney general in Ireland, wrote to Henry Ireton with details of the talks, presumably obtained from spies, prisoners or intercepted correspondence. Ireton passed this information on to the Council of State, which began to pay particular attention to the shipping of troops from Ireland for service overseas. Since Philip IV's recognition of the Commonwealth in late 1650, English authorities in Ireland had actively encouraged Spanish recruitment there, in order to clear the country of enemy soldiers. Suspicion fell upon certain officers, however, working 'under pretence for the king of Spain, yet have been contracted for by an agreement with Fortescue, an agent for the duke of Lorraine in London'. The Council of State ordered Ireton to discontinue the transports, in an effort to prevent the duke from filling his regiments with raw Irish recruits, thus freeing more experienced troops for service in Ireland.[39] In March 1651, the English parliament sent ambassadors to Holland and to Spanish Flanders to deny Lorraine access to ports in either jurisdiction. They also seized the Scilly Isles off Cornwall from the royalists in May, while Admiral Popham led a strong squadron into the English Channel to disrupt communications between Ireland and the Continent throughout the summer, and 'keep in the duke of Lorraine's fleet'.[40] The Council of State tried as best it could to keep news of Lorraine out of the public domain, but parliamentary reports nonetheless spoke of the Catholic

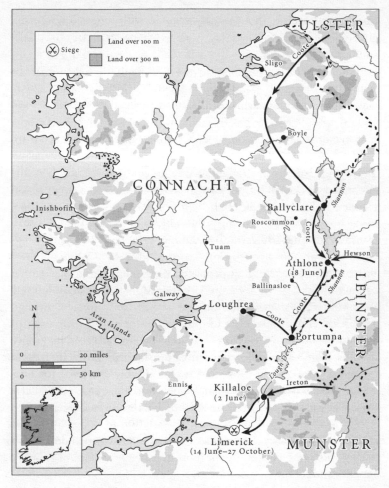

Map 7 English Assault on Connacht, June 1651

Irish confidently expecting 'large and speedy supplies, both of men and money' from abroad.[41]

In addition to these precautionary measures on the Continent and the high seas, Ireton prepared to launch an offensive against the Shannon defensive line, targeting the key garrisons of Athlone and

Limerick. According to one parliamentary report, the rendezvous of parliamentary troops in May was 'pretty full, lively, and well appointed, and (which we hope to) be too quick for the duke of Lorraine, and make his landing more difficult than he expects'.[42] Ireton envisaged a multi-pronged attack, with Charles Coote penetrating into Connacht from Ulster with 5,000 men, while Ireton crossed the Shannon further south, near Limerick. As Coote marched on Athlone, Colonel Hewson would threaten the town from the Leinster side of the river, with other commanders ordered to 'prevent the landing of strangers' along the coastline, in case Lorraine attempted to despatch troops to Ireland.[43] At the same time, Ireton planned to lead the bulk of the army, numbering over 8,000 men, towards Limerick, encircling the city, while the English navy transported 'our artillery, ammunition, provisions, and all things necessary for the siege'.[44] Units commanded by Colonel Robert Venables and Lord Broghill protected the flanks from any potential counter-attack by Irish forces in Ulster or Munster respectively. Only Westminster's sustained commitment to the Irish campaign, through a logistical effort unparalleled in English history until then, enabled Ireton to plan his offensive on such an impressive scale. In the twelve months after Cromwell's departure, the English army in Ireland increased from 25,000 to almost 35,000, despite the need for over 20,000 troops to subdue Scotland. High attrition rates, particularly from disease, put a huge strain on English resources of manpower, and in April 1651, parliament passed legislation to conscript 10,000 men for Irish service. Ireton also received almost £200,000 in cash during this same period, in addition to a steady stream of military supplies and food.[45]

Faced with such a well-resourced enemy, the Catholic Irish struggled to prepare for the inevitable onslaught, as the area under royalist control in Ireland itself continued to contract, reducing the tax yield and access to crucial supplies. Nominally, Clanricarde commanded 30,000 men, but many of these remained scattered in small units throughout Ulster, Leinster and Munster. Apart from the garrisons at Limerick and Galway, royalist forces appeared disorganised and demoralised, lacking basic equipment, and many quickly disintegrated with the onset of the parliamentary offensive. In early June, Coote advanced through County Sligo on his way to Athlone, while further south Ireton successfully crossed the Shannon near Killaloe, and established a bridgehead on the west bank, scattering the earl of Castlehaven's forces in the process. With parliamentary armies converging from the north and south, Viscount Dillon surrendered Athlone on 18 June without a shot being fired. Predictably, though understandably in the case of Dillon, Irish sources suspected treason, but Clanricarde's failure to present any sort of threat in the field proved equally damaging. On 14 June, Ireton, having encircled the city and set up his artillery, issued a formal summons to Limerick, which the garrison commander, Hugh Dubh O'Neill, defiantly rejected. Towards the end of the month, Lord Broghill defeated a relief column from Kerry, led by Viscount Muskerry, and with royalist forces throughout the country in total disarray, the parliamentarians appeared poised to take Connacht in a matter of weeks. One source lamented how 'the said Shannon, the Irish bulwark and loyal spouse of the nation, was now become a prostitute, rendering free passage unto all comers, and denied any favor unto its former possessors'.[46]

Clanricarde, predictably ineffectual in military matters, desperately needed outside intervention to drive back the parliamentary offensive. In the first six months of the year, Taaffe, unaware of the controversy in Ireland over Lorraine's proposal to become protector of the kingdom, made good progress in convincing the duke to dispatch troops to Limerick and Galway. Although the duke's agents had been busy since the spring in several ports, raising contribution 'for the relief of the rebels' in Ireland, the inability to secure a suitable point of embarkation caused serious problems.[47] According to Taaffe, plans for sending the force through Germany required 'much time, expense and danger', so he asked Ormond to enquire about the possibility of using French ports.[48] The marquis suspected that transport through France would prove as costly and time-consuming as going through Germany. When Taaffe persisted, Ormond urged Lord Digby to raise the matter at the French court, though he considered the proposal 'very unlikely' to succeed given the unsettled nature of affairs in France. Digby confirmed Ormond's negative assessment, reporting on 4 June that the French had vetoed the suggestion in order to avoid an open breach with the English parliament.[49] In fact, from early 1651 the French had begun to explore the possibility of reaching an agreement with the English Commonwealth. Meanwhile, Parliament's continuing naval dominance frustrated any hope of transporting significant numbers of troops or supplies to Ireland. Ormond, although he had expended little energy in assisting Taaffe, commented smugly that the duke of Lorraine was 'doubtless too great a lover of his money which is all his fortune to lay it out upon a remote and hazardous adventure'.[50]

Despite the lack of progress on the military front, Brussels bristled with activity and intrigue. In early May 1651 Taaffe reported the arrival of Bishop French, who quickly gained an audience with the duke. Nicholas Plunkett and Geoffrey Browne reached Brussels in mid-June, without first visiting Paris, contrary to their orders from the marquis of Clanricarde. Instead, they dispatched Taaffe to the French capital, where Queen Henrietta Maria gave her guarded approval to this new mission. Plunkett and Browne shrewdly used the presence of Bishop French in Brussels to encourage royalists in Paris to look more favourably on a treaty with Lorraine. Browne informed Ormond that if he and Plunkett failed to make a deal, 'we find that others are authorized in the behalf of the clergy and people to proceed, which in good faith I never knew of till I came hither'. He warned of the dangers of Lorraine establishing a foothold in Ireland without the consent of royalist ministers, but Ormond continued to express serious concern about the clerical agenda.[51] He complained bitterly to Edward Hyde that the clergy had 'long endeavoured to bring that nation to a necessity of calling for a Roman Catholic Protector from which office to absolute sovereignty the way is short and easy'. He hoped that the future success of Charles Stuart and the Scots would render any treaty with Lorraine meaningless. 'If the king recover England', he explained to Secretary Nicholas, 'Ireland will soon follow'.[52] Ormond could not deny that Queen Henrietta Maria had given Viscount Taaffe a letter for the Irish commissioners in Brussels, approving of Clanricarde's treaty with Lorraine, although she had insisted that her son be consulted if the duke sought exorbitant terms. On 21 July Hyde reported that on his return to Brussels, Taaffe claimed to have found 'great approbation' at court, which pleased all the parties in the negotiations.[53]

The apparent success of Taaffe's mission to Paris greatly relieved both Plunkett and Browne, who had come under enormous pressure from Bishop French not to conclude a deal with Lorraine on behalf of Clanricarde, but to do so instead in the name of the Irish people, announcing in effect the reconstitution of the confederate association. French argued that Clanricarde and his supporters had been 'for several causes excommunicated' following the breach with Rinuccini over the Inchiquin truce in 1648. By acquiescing in Clanricarde's leadership, Catholic forces in Ireland had suffered repeated setbacks on the battlefield, and only by seeking forgiveness from the pope could they hope to turn the tide of the war.[54] Around this same time in Ireland, the archbishop of Armagh convened a meeting of Ulster clergy at Cloughoughter in County Cavan. The clerics ordered that no bishops or members of the nobility should appear at any general assembly of the kingdom until all excommunicates, including Clanricarde, had begged for papal absolution.[55] They also dispatched Anthony MacGeoghegan, the agent from *de Propaganda Fide* in Rome, to Leinster, where an ecclesiastical congregation of the province fully supported the archbishop of Armagh's initiative. The Leinster clergy went one step further, however, and called for 'the renovation and framing of a Catholic confederacy', as advocated by MacGeoghegan and by Bishop French in Brussels.[56] The stage was now set for an open confrontation between Clanricarde and his increasingly vocal opponents, both in Ireland and on the Continent.

On 22 July 1651, back in Brussels, Browne, Plunkett and Taaffe, styling themselves 'deputies authorized on the behalf of the kingdom and people of Ireland', signed an agreement with the duke of Lorraine. The deliberate use of this provocative title, and the fact that the treaty closely resembled those terms proposed by clerical supporters, suggests that Plunkett and Browne not only listened to French's advice, but may well have arrived in Brussels with a different agenda to the one outlined by Clanricarde. The treaty stipulated that Lorraine (and his heirs) would become 'the true and royal Protector of Ireland', with complete control of the affairs of the kingdom. The signatories pleaded for papal support, and confirmed that they would 'most constantly preserve in the perpetual obedience and faith of the see apostolic and his Holiness'. A Catholic deputy would be appointed in Lorraine's absence, with Galway, Limerick, Sligo and Athlone providing security for a £20,000 loan. In an effort, however, to placate royalist concerns, the second article stated that, 'having restored religion and kingdom to their right state', Lorraine would resign all his authority to Charles Stuart, 'being first reimbursed of all his charges expended in that business'.[57] Nonetheless, the prominence of religious concessions confirms the extent of Bishop French's input into the final draft of the settlement. Taaffe immediately travelled to Paris and assured Ormond that the commissioners in Brussels had 'as yet perfected no articles' with the duke.[58] It seems highly unlikely that Taaffe would have deliberately misled the lord lieutenant, and his comments probably reflected the commissioners' view that the treaty remained invalid without Clanricarde's approval. Whatever the truth of the matter, not long after Taaffe's return to Brussels, the commissioners and Bishop French quarrelled over the latter's continuing questioning of Clanricarde's authority. The timing of this argument, whether due to a hostile response to the treaty in Paris, or to the commissioners' own concerns at having far exceeded their authority in signing such a comprehensive agreement with Lorraine, foreshadowed the bitter dispute that erupted in Ireland shortly afterwards.

In a letter to Clanricarde, Lorraine described the treaty, in language strongly reminiscent of the Catholic confederate motto, as 'for the good of the catholic religion, the service of the king, and re-establishment of the kingdom'.[59] The duke began at once to organise supplies for Ireland, and offered to transport 2,000 troops from either France or Holland. The arrival of thousands of well-supplied Continental veterans would have greatly boosted Catholic morale, and provided an experienced, professional core for a rejuvenated Catholic Irish army. Developments in Ireland, Scotland and England gave further cause for optimism. Ireton's forces suffered heavy losses at the siege of Limerick, due primarily to disease, and throughout June and July, Hugh Dubh O'Neill's Ulster troops, many of them veterans of Clonmel, inflicted significant casualties in a number of encounters with the enemy. In late summer, news reached Ireland that Charles Stuart had invaded England at the head of a large Scottish army. Although opposed by vastly superior parliamentary forces, royalists hoped that Charles' physical presence would rally support throughout the country. Nonetheless, with royalist and Catholic Irish prospects seemingly better than at any time in the past twelve months, the tide of war began to turn once again.

Without immediate outside intervention, or a spectacular and decisive victory for the royalists in England, O'Neill could not be expected to hold out in Limerick indefinitely, but finding a suitable port of embarkation for Lorraine's troops proved difficult. Admiral Popham's naval force lay before Ostend and Dunkirk, while 'a tumult raised at the suggestion of the Parliamentary English' frustrated attempts to muster at Middleburg and Flushing in the Netherlands.[60] Unable to breach the defences of 'the strongest fortress in Ireland', Ireton had resolved to starve the inhabitants of Limerick into submission.[61] With as many as 28,000 people crammed inside the city walls, including soldiers and refugees, the besieged experienced increasing hardships, with basic foodstuffs in short supply, while the plague continued to claim large numbers of victims. O'Neill attempted to ease the pressure by evicting the sick and elderly, but the parliamentarians summarily hanged some of the refugees to effectively stem the flow. On 6 October, the citizens elected a new mayor, Piers Creagh FitzPiers, who did not share the previous incumbent's determination to resist. At this very moment, Colonel Synott, despatched by Lorraine to deliver the treaty to Clanricarde, reached Galway, unaccompanied by any troops, supplies or cash. Plunkett and Browne did not travel with him, but instead forwarded correspondence from Queen Henrietta Maria and Ormond in an attempt to justify their actions. Clanricarde desperately needed the military supplies promised by Lorraine, yet he could barely contain his anger at what had taken place in Brussels. In a letter to Plunkett and Browne, he complained that the terms bore 'no relation to my commission or instructions'. Charles Stuart had not authorised the agreement, and the people of Ireland, in whose name the agents had signed the treaty, did not possess 'such powers to treat at all with any foreign prince, they professing obedience, and being under the governance of the king's authority'. He considered the actions of Plunkett and Browne a 'breach of friendship', and refused to believe that Taaffe could have had 'a hand in such a dark design'. On the same day, Clanricarde wrote to Lorraine declaring the agreement 'null and void', and denouncing all those involved on the Irish side, particularly Bishop French, 'a person that has been ever violent against and malicious to his Majesty's government and authority'.[62] Despite the desperate straits of the defenders in Limerick, the Lord Deputy refused to compromise his strict royalist principles.

Not everyone shared Clanricarde's sense of outrage. Colonel John Jones, a parliamentary commissioner in Dublin, explained to a colleague that Lorraine remained 'high in the hopes and expectations' of many in Ireland, while the mayor and council of Galway openly supported the agreement, sending a letter to the duke, addressed to the 'Protector Royal of Ireland'.[63] They dispatched Nicholas Lynch to Flanders to speed up the transport of supplies, and pleaded with Clanricarde that if anything was missing from the treaty, 'to wink at it, for fear of giving any occasion of breach'. Implacable as always, Clanricarde condemned Galway's use of the title 'Protector Royal' as 'an absolute transferring of the kingdom from his Majesty'.[64] While the marquis fulminated over alleged breaches of etiquette, Hugh Dubh came under increasing pressure in Limerick to open negotiations with the parliamentarians, particularly when news of the royalists' disastrous defeat at Worcester in early September reached the city. Ireton ensured that the besieged saw copies of all the news-sheets 'that related and confirmed' the full extent of Oliver Cromwell's victory over the Scottish invasion force.[65] With all hope of assistance from abroad cruelly dashed, the defenders began to turn on one another, and on 27 October O'Neill finally agreed to surrender, though on less advantageous terms than those offered back in June. One parliamentarian commented smugly that 'you may see how far God suffered them to be hardened then, to their own loss in the issue'.[66] The garrison, reduced to only 1,300 men, marched away to Galway, but without their weapons, while the inhabitants retained possession of their personal property, although they could be removed at short notice for security reasons. Ireton drew up a list of prominent individuals exempted from pardon, which included the former mayors Thomas Stritch and Dominic Fanning, along with leading clergy, such as the Bishop of Emly, hoping that 'the terror and sad example of it may so work upon other places remaining'.[67] Among those executed was the former MP Geoffrey Barron, advocate of continued resistance in both Waterford and Limerick, who claimed no other crime than fighting for 'the liberty and religion of his country'.[68] The name of the garrison commander, Hugh Dubh O'Neill, also appeared on the condemned list. According to Edmund Ludlow's memoirs, extensively edited and rewritten in the 1690s after his death, Ireton demanded O'Neill's immediate execution, probably in revenge for the slaughter at Clonmel, but Ludlow and other officers successfully interceded on his behalf. No other records substantiate Ludlow's claims, and the anonymous author of the 'Aphorismical Discovery' claimed that Ireton treated O'Neill as 'an honourable and brave warrior'. Whatever the truth of the matter, O'Neill survived, and when Ireton died a few weeks later of a fever, the Ulsterman accompanied the body back to London as a prisoner.[69]

With Limerick finally in parliamentary hands, only Galway, loosely blockaded by Coote, remained under royalist control, although the death of Ireton, and the onset of winter, granted the city a temporary reprieve. Unless supplies and reinforcements arrived from Lorraine over the next few months, all organised resistance to the parliamentarians would cease in the spring. The fall of Limerick, however, alongside Clanricarde's rejection of the Brussels treaty, effectively destroyed all hope of significant intervention from the Continent. Half-hearted attempts to breathe new life into the project continued for a while, but achieved little. When he received news of the disaster at Worcester, Taaffe could see little point in continuing his negotiations with Lorraine. According to the viscount, Lorraine also felt the situation in Ireland to be hopeless, 'considering how undisturbed and absolute the parliament have rendered themselves in England and Scotland'.[70] Charles Stuart's dramatic escape from England to France in October temporarily re-energised the project, and in early November, Taaffe returned to Paris from Brussels, with fresh proposals from Lorraine, including, according to one account, an offer of £100,000. In Ireland, as the military situation continued to deteriorate, even one of Clanricarde's closest allies, Viscount Muskerry, decided to approach Lorraine directly. He instructed an agent to request that the duke divert supplies to Muskerry's own area of operations in south Kerry, or failing that, to enquire about possible employment for the viscount on the Continent.[71] In the meantime, Lorraine continued to send food and military hardware to Ireland, along with another agent, Joseph Wandermaster, but little else happened over the winter months. Deteriorating relations between England and the Dutch republic, which would lead to war the following summer, encouraged exiled royalists further, until Clanricarde's letters denouncing the treaty with Lorraine finally reached Paris early in 1652.

Both Charles Stuart and Ormond denied any knowledge of the treaty until informed of it by the Lord Deputy. This seems highly unlikely, particularly as one of the signatories, Geoffrey Browne, wrote regularly to Ormond, and kept him fully informed of the negotiations. Moreover, Viscount Taaffe had visited the French capital immediately after signing the agreement. Charles and the marquis of Ormond, both Protestants and guests of the French king, had probably decided not to inquire too closely into the dealings of the Irish agents at Brussels with the Catholic duke of Lorraine, an ally of the Spanish Habsburgs. Now exposed to the public glare, Ormond launched an unequivocal attack on the treaty, the terms of which, he argued, amounted to an abdication of regal power, however temporary, and would result in the banishment of Protestants from the kingdom. Charles could not possibly consent to conditions, Ormond continued, 'contrary to his duty as a king, and to his religion as a Protestant'.[72] Charles, for his part, did try to repair relations between Plunkett, Browne and Clanricarde, excusing the agents' actions as the result of dire necessity. His willingness to write on behalf of the two emissaries, who according to Clanricarde had blatantly ignored his instructions, suggests that Charles, although not party to the negotiations during his time in Scotland, did not entirely disapprove of their conduct.[73] Although furious with Clanricarde over his repudiation of the treaty, Lorraine did not abandon Ireland altogether. A small flotilla, commanded by a Colonel Vicourte, arrived at the fortified island of Inishbofin sometime in the late summer of 1652, but by then Galway had already surrendered.

Earlier, in January, Clanricarde had tried unsuccessfully to muster an army for a new campaign, but only General Preston with a garrison of 2,000 men in Galway, and Lieutenant General Farrell with 3,000 men in north Connacht, still commanded significant units. The Lord Deputy's relations with Galway's citizens had deteriorated significantly over the winter as a result of his rejection of the Lorraine treaty, and a number now favoured making terms with the English. Clanricarde warned them that their lives and liberty would be subject to 'arbitrary martial law' under parliamentary rule, but he failed to obtain a signed declaration of their obedience to royal authority.[74] Anthony MacGeoghegan and Hugh Rochford, the latter recently returned from the Continent, were also active in the city, arguing for a renewal of the confederate association, and in favour of the Lorraine treaty. In early February, however, with foreign aid uncertain, an assembly of Catholic laity in Galway, 'much impoverished and exhausted by an inhuman ten years war', implored Clanricarde to open negotiations with the parliamentarians.[75] The marquis corresponded with Edmund Ludlow, who had taken command of the army following Ireton's death. He replied that upon submission of the Catholic leadership 'such moderate terms will yet be consented unto, as men in their position can rationally expect'.[76] Richard Blake, chairman of the assembly in Galway, reminded Ludlow that the Catholic Irish remained 'numerous in arms and capable of foreign succours', but the parliamentary commander refused to be intimidated by threats of Continental intervention.[77] With the negotiations apparently stalled, Coote, anxious to avoid a prolonged siege, offered very generous terms on his own initiative, guaranteeing the citizens of Galway the full privileges of the city charter. Clanricarde opposed the surrender on the grounds that he alone should negotiate general conditions for the entire nation, but on 12 April the city 'basely and perfidiously yielded'.[78] Clanricarde vowed to fight on, but the earl of Castlehaven, the most active of the Catholic lords, sailed for France shortly afterwards, ostensibly to seek military assistance but in reality acknowledging the hopelessness of the royalist cause.

On the Continent, Viscount Taaffe continued to act as an intermediary between the exiled Stuarts and Lorraine, and in October 1652 he travelled from Brussels to Paris with fresh offers of assistance from the duke. The royalists, however, had given up on Ireland, and nothing more was heard of this initiative. Hyde, a holder of high office and a key supporter of the notoriously disingenuous Stuarts, noted without a hint of irony that although Lorraine made many promises, 'what he says is not always to be depended upon'.[79] As late as January 1653, rumours still circulated on the Continent that Lorraine intended sending soldiers to Connacht, while that same month the parliamentary commissioners in Dublin reported that the Irish were not yet 'out of hopes of succour from Lorraine and other foreign princes'.[80] The surrender the following month of the island of Inishbofin off the coast of Galway signalled the end of the duke's involvement in the war in Ireland, as the Catholic Irish no longer possessed a suitable base to receive supplies. The governor of the island, Colonel George Cusack, took 1,000 troops with him to Flanders to serve under Lorraine. For the remainder of the year, increasing numbers of Irishmen entered the duke's army. Around this time, a garrison of Lorraine's troops in Spanish service surrendered to a French regiment commanded by the duke of York, younger brother of Charles Stuart. Many of the defenders voluntarily joined York's forces, much to the irritation of Lorraine. According to Hyde, Lorraine expressed 'great dissatisfaction with more passion than you can imagine', and according to another source, allegedly threatened to arrest the exiled monarch on sight.[81] Whatever the truth of these reports, it is clear that any lingering possibility of cooperation with the Stuarts had finally disappeared.

The failure to obtain significant military assistance from abroad contributed greatly to the final defeat of the Catholic Irish. The interests of France and Spain did not extend beyond the recruitment of Irish manpower, while the spectacular falling out between Rinuccini and the confederates, along with the general parsimony of successive popes, negated the possibility of decisive intervention from Rome. The duke of Lorraine did engage in a serious manner with the affairs of Ireland for the best part of three years, from early 1650 until 1652. The repeated successes of the parliamentary forces in Ireland, however, along with their precautionary measures at sea and on the Continent, thwarted him at every turn. In addition, the inability of his erstwhile allies, the royalists and Irish Catholics, to reach an agreed position, ultimately dealt a fatal blow to the project. By 1650, many in Ireland had lost faith in the marquis of Ormond. The more radical clerical leaders sought to renew the confederate association, and would have happily negotiated a deal independently of the royalist leadership. Lorraine, however, insisted throughout on royal approval for any plan. Charles Stuart deferred to Ormond in these matters, and the lord lieutenant's negativity, together with the inflexibility of Clanricarde, proved insurmountable obstacles to the procurement of foreign aid. Ormond simply could not accept a Catholic Protector, believing that only Protestant forces could truly safeguard Protestant interests in Ireland. For Clanricarde, the treaty signed in Brussels, directed by Bishop French, confirmed his fears of the inherent dangers of dealing with a foreign prince. As Lorraine noted angrily in 1652, his plans for assisting Ireland had been destroyed 'by the jealousy of those who desired the loss of it, than they should be obliged for its recovery to the protection of his said Highness'.[82] With centralised royalist resistance at an end, and no hope of foreign intervention, the Catholic Irish now resorted to guerrilla warfare, as the conflict entered its final and most tragic phase.

8

The Guerrilla War

*These fastnesses are of better use to them [the Irish]
in point of strength than walled towns.*[1]
PARLIAMENTARY REPORT ON THE STATE OF IRELAND (*c.* 1652)

On Saturday, 29 September 1651, less than a month before the surrender of Limerick, a large force of Catholic Irish troops, commanded by Sir Walter Dongan and Thomas Scurlock, stormed the town of Ross in County Wexford. Operating behind enemy lines, 75 miles from the main theatre of conflict along the river Shannon, the assailants surprised the parliamentary defenders by striking at 2 a.m., using ladders to scale the town walls. They killed at least twenty English soldiers, and 'only the church and a house being fortified stood out'.[2] The garrison commander, Colonel Markham, received quarter for his life, but the inhabitants had to pay £700 compensation to prevent the town being burnt to the ground. The Irish withdrew the following day on hearing reports of an approaching relief force. The fall of Ross to Dongan and Scurlock, albeit temporarily, dramatically illustrated the tenuous nature of parliamentary control over much of the country. This strategically important garrison on the river Barrow, situated between Waterford, Kilkenny and Wexford, had surrendered to Cromwell almost exactly two years earlier. With the bulk of parliamentary forces now engaged in the siege of Limerick, irregular bands of Catholic Irish soldiers acted with apparent impunity throughout much of Leinster, Munster and Ulster. The parliamentary commissioners in the capital reported to Ireton the 'unpleasing story' of widespread attacks up to the very gates of Dublin, and expressed concern that little could be done 'till Limerick be reduced, which some fear may be a winter's work'.[3]

It is clear from such testimony that the rapid conquest envisaged by Oliver Cromwell had in fact degenerated into an increasingly bitter and protracted conflict. Indeed, following Cromwell's departure from Ireland in May 1650, the Irish war entered what one historian has described as 'the bloodiest and most prolonged aspect of the struggle'.[4] Native resistance, rather than crumbling in the face of devastating and demoralising losses, intensified the longer the fighting lasted. Ironically, Cromwell's initial success created the ideal conditions for widespread partisan activity. The New Model Army, although numbering over 35,000 men by 1652, simply did not have enough troops to pacify large swathes of the country, in addition to all the towns and cities captured since 1649. Moreover, as royalist field armies disintegrated in the face of Cromwell's relentless advance, those commanders cut off from headquarters began to adopt guerrilla tactics, utilising local knowledge and support, to harass enemy supply lines, and ambush isolated units. The leadership on both sides used the pejorative term 'Tory', derived from the Irish word *tóraigh*, meaning to hunt or pursue, or 'Idle Boys', to describe those Catholic troops not under some degree of central control. Throughout the 1640s, the confused nature of the war in Ireland facilitated the proliferation of armed bandits, who preyed on the local population, stealing cattle and goods, or extorting contributions from already hard-pressed communities. Loyal to no group, they adored 'liberty, spoil and rapine', and the confederates, royalists, parliamentarians and covenanters all failed to bring them under control.[5] The collapse of the centralised royalist war effort in 1649–50 across much of the kingdom dramatically altered the composition of these irregular units. Thousands of well-trained, well-armed soldiers, led by experienced confederate officers, began to operate as Tories, targeting parliamentary forces rather than the civilian population.

Viewed with suspicion by royalist grandees, the parliamentarians treated them with contempt, at least initially, while subsequent historical accounts largely ignored their exploits, focusing instead on set-piece battles and sieges. Yet between 1650 and 1652, as many as 30,000 Catholic Irish troops, acting independently of Ormond and Clanricarde, posed a major threat to the New Model Army, exploiting over-extended parliamentary military resources to strike against vulnerable garrisons and convoys. In June 1650, only weeks after Cromwell's departure from Ireland, local Tory units took advantage of Colonel Hewson's absence at the siege of Tecroghan to launch a series of raids in the vicinity of Dublin. Shortly afterwards, parliamentary news-sheets reported that a group of officers serving in Colonel Axtell's regiment had been ambushed and killed while travelling on the road between Kilkenny and Ross. This incident occurred just three months after the surrender of Kilkenny city to Cromwell and the subsequent withdrawal of recognised royalist forces from the area. As the summer progressed, further attacks took place in the wake of the parliamentary offensive across Ulster, Leinster and Munster. In at least one crucial instance, the activities of these irregular troops impacted significantly on the course of the war. Following the fall of Waterford in early August, Ireton directed his army towards Connacht, hoping to crush all royalist resistance before the end of the year. Conscious of the growing military pressure on Dublin, however, he first marched northwards to counter the Tory threat in the mountainous Wicklow region next to the capital city. Although he managed to seize cattle and other supplies, the guerrilla units, led by Hugh MacPhelim O'Byrne, eluded his forces. The resultant delay in besieging both Athlone and Limerick prevented the parliamentarians from crossing the Shannon before the onset of winter, thus prolonging the field war by at least another twelve months.

As Ireton retired to winter quarters in late 1650, the parliamentary attorney general in Ireland, William Basil, reflected on a largely successful summer campaign, with one important caveat. He commented that the three provinces were 'now wholly in our possession, only much infected with Tories'.[6] Much as Napoleon and Hitler discovered to their cost during their respective invasions of Russia, the rapid advance of field armies, and the occupation of key towns and garrisons, did not guarantee control of the surrounding countryside, and left forces in the rear vulnerable to attack. Partisan activity intensified during the winter months, even as the regular royalist forces retreated into Connacht. Letters from Kinsale in

County Cork, for example, recorded that in early 1651 the Tories remained 'very active and busy' in the area.[7] One particularly audacious attack took place in March on a convoy of eleven boats laden with merchant goods, sailing down the river Barrow from Ross to Waterford. Irregular forces successfully captured nine of the vessels, killing 'most of the men and passengers' in the process.[8] Throughout the year, Irish privateers, operating for the most part out of Continental ports or the Isle of Man, raided the eastern seaboard of Ireland, seizing shipping between Wexford and Carrickfergus, including a number of packet boats from Holyhead, which seriously disrupted communications with England. The parliamentary commissioners complained to London about the lack of naval support, 'so as the enemy at sea hath done much mischief', but the large English warships struggled to contain the small, speedy Irish frigates, and the year finished with a Captain Wilmot, 'the great pirate', taking prizes in Dublin Bay.[9]

Back on land, in May 1651 Ireton prepared to resume the offensive against Connacht, fully conscious of the threat to supply lines as soon as his main army crossed the Shannon. As a result, he assigned a number of cavalry units, which specialised in guerrilla warfare, to protect his rear against mounted irregular troops, like Dongan's men, who exploited their mobility rather than inaccessibility. According to one account, the parliamentarians also began to master the skill of 'tripping after' the enemy as they escaped into the bogs, yet if the Tories had enough time to slip off their breeches and 'wade up to the middle, as oft they do, they thereby avoid us'.[10] Despite Ireton's precautionary measures, enemy raids rendered much of the country 'very uncomfortable' for the English throughout the summer months.[11] The parliamentary commissioners in Dublin reported to the Council of State in London that while successive victories had driven royalists to seek refuge in woods and bogs, 'that dispersed enemy is (according to their old manner) within a few days gathered together again'.[12] These irregular bands of soldiers then engaged the New Model Army on advantageous terms before quickly retreating into 'inaccessible quarters'. According to the commissioners, no one could travel safely 2 miles from a town without a convoy, and even

Map 8 The Tory War, 1651–2

'some of the garrisons they have surprised'.[13] In response, they ordered a three-pronged attack on County Wicklow, 'a nest and harbour of rebels and Tories in all times', with Colonels Pretty and Cooke advancing from the south, while Colonel Hewson attacked with the main force from Dublin.[14] Hewson carried special instructions to destroy all corn and other supplies, in an effort to starve the enemy into submission, but once again Hugh MacPhelim O'Byrne, who commanded as many as 3,000 men, not only evaded capture but continued to disrupt communications between the capital and the south of the country.

The cavalry units commanded by Scurlock and Dongan regularly engaged with the enemy during the summer months prior to the capture of Ross. In one major raid Scurlock brought over 2,000 infantry and 400 cavalry to within 6 miles of the capital. He inflicted heavy casualties on a force sent to pursue him, and took prisoner 'several persons belonging to Dublin'. In anticipation of ransom demands, the parliamentary commissioners ordered the arrest of Lady Dongan, Sir Walter's wife, for the purposes of exchange, and pleaded with Colonel Hewson to send reinforcements to the city, warning of the dangers to the parliamentary cause should it fall to the enemy.[15] In the meantime, they called on all persons capable of bearing arms to help defend the place against a possible attack. Scurlock, however, lacked sufficient manpower or artillery for a siege, and subsequently withdrew, demonstrating in the process the military limitations of these guerrilla forces. The Tories might cause widespread damage to property, seize supplies, ambush convoys and surprise isolated garrisons, but they could not hold towns or territory. The approach of a sizeable parliamentary army inevitably resulted in a retreat. Nonetheless, one London news-sheet grudgingly described these irregular soldiers as the enemy's 'only party both for number, policy and valour'.[16] Throughout the country, in places as diverse as Kilkenny, Louth and Tyrone, guerrilla units targeted parliamentary supplies, seizing large numbers of cattle and only attacking the enemy when they could be sure of success. The parliamentarians lost over sixty cavalrymen in a skirmish near Carlow, while a supply convoy bound for Colonel Venables in Ulster was wiped out as it passed through the Moyry Pass, near Newry in County Down. Another leading Tory, Colonel John Fitzpatrick, 'did much mischief' when he stormed the strategic outpost of Castlejordan in County Meath.[17]

In September 1651 the parliamentary commissioners informed the

Council of State in London that despite Ireton's success in the field
their work was 'not yet done in Ireland'. They urgently requested
further reinforcements and complained bitterly about the quality of
recruits hitherto sent from England. With the supply of regular
troops and volunteers long since dried up, parliament increasingly
relied on press gangs to provide replacements for service in Ireland.
The authorities in Dublin dismissed the new arrivals as a mere
rabble, 'a great part of them lame, blind, children, aged and fitter for
the hospital than the army, and all of them without clothes'.[18] Many
units suffered from large-scale desertions, and the parliamentary
commissioners issued an order in early 1652 to prevent these
runaways from returning to England.[19] In addition to manpower
shortages, they also suffered financial constraints, with contributions
'much decreased, and made impossible to be raised in many places,
by the great wasting the enemy hath made in all quarters of late'.[20]
There is of course an element of special pleading involved in these
reports, with the commissioners anxious to coax more resources
from an over-stretched English parliament, already dealing with
Charles Stuart and his Scottish forces invading from the north. The
greater the supposed threat from irregular units, the more likely that
MPs might pay attention to the war in Ireland, so the commissioners
warned, with some justification, of a possible 'universal rising in all
counties', with the Tories 'threatening excommunication, fire and
sword to all those that do not rise with them'.[21]

The surrender of Limerick on 27 October, however, seriously
demoralised the royalists and their supporters, depriving them of the
most suitable urban base from which to launch a major counteroffensive. In addition, the defeat of Charles Stuart by Cromwell at
Worcester the previous month not only destroyed all hope of a
royalist revival in England but also freed up parliamentary resources,
which could now be diverted to Ireland. With only Galway and a
handful of smaller garrisons still in royalist hands, the future looked
bleak for the marquis of Clanricarde and his regular forces.
Nonetheless, away from the Connacht campaign, the New Model
Army remained on the defensive, struggling to suppress partisan
activity in the other three provinces. Indeed as the winter

approached, the English feared an upsurge in Tory attacks, as 'the boggy places will be more advantage to them now than they are in the summer'.[22] Determined to fight on, despite the setbacks at Limerick and Worcester, Dongan and Scurlock assembled over 3,000 infantry and cavalry at Naas, just over 15 miles from Dublin, while Viscount Muskerry and Colonel Edmund O'Dwyer rallied similarly large numbers in Kerry and Tipperary respectively. Proof of Tory resolve came shortly afterwards when a parliamentary force attacked a stronghold of Colonel Fitzpatrick in County Tipperary. The place eventually fell after a hard fight, but one eyewitness reported that he had never seen 'the rogues more obstinately defend any place'.[23]

Although leading royalists such as Ormond believed the war in Ireland to be 'at an end to all intents but torying',[24] a detailed parliamentary report at the end of 1651 painted a very different picture of the military situation. According to this account, the English already maintained 350 garrisons in Ireland, but would need 100 more as further places capitulated, requiring at least 30,000 troops in total, at a cost of £20,000 per month in wages alone. Large tracts of the country remained under enemy control or produced no revenue, 'the inhabitants being universally enemies'. The list included five counties in Ulster (Cavan, Monaghan, Armagh, Tyrone and Fermanagh), five in Leinster (Wicklow, Longford, Queens, Kings, Westmeath), most of Connacht, and County Kerry in Munster. Along with the Wexford/Kilkenny/Carlow triangle, the principal Tory stronghold in the South East, these counties constituted almost two-thirds of the country. In fact, more than two years after Cromwell's arrival in Ireland, parliamentary authority essentially remained restricted to those areas controlled by royalists, parliamentarians or Scots during the 1640s, namely the Pale region around Dublin, the Cork enclave in the south, and north-east Ulster. The report estimated the enemy to be 30,000 strong, equal in number to the parliamentary army, but apart from garrisons in Galway, Sligo, Roscommon and Jamestown, the vast majority operated out of woods, bogs and 'other fastnesses'. Impossible to besiege, these natural strongholds worked better than walled towns as the Catholic Irish could 'draw all their strength out of them to act their designs, without hazarding the loss of the place'.[25]

The exploits of these guerrilla forces proved not only how bravely and tenaciously the Irish infantry could fight, but also how effective they could be under enterprising leadership. Properly coordinated with the conventional forces based west of the Shannon, they could have seriously undermined the parliamentary war effort by disrupting communications and harassing Ireton's army besieging Limerick. Neither Ormond nor Clanricarde, however, possessed the strategic vision or organisational ability to make use of the irregular troops in that fashion, so they never really threatened to overwhelm the invaders, although they did prolong the struggle. Despite exploiting Ireland's varied terrain to their own advantage, the Tories experienced a number of difficulties obtaining supplies. Facing a well-financed foe, based in hundreds of fortified garrisons, they had to live off the land. This placed an enormous burden on the civilian population, already heavily taxed by the English army. Moreover, in attacking parliamentary quarters, the Tories inevitably inflicted great hardship on their erstwhile supporters, 'there being no way left for them to escape ruin and destruction'.[26] Despite this, the irregular forces clearly enjoyed widespread popular support, and one parliamentarian remarked incredulously of the inhabitants, 'though a law were made to make it immediate death to relieve the enemy, yet would they undergo the danger and give them money'. As a result, he believed it would prove necessary in many parts 'to burn up the country, without which there can never be an end of the wars in that Nation'.[27] In contrast to the New Model Army, local guerrilla units received 'exact and constant intelligence from the natives ... whereas our forces seldom or never have any intelligence of their motions'.[28] An account published in a London news-sheet confirmed this assessment, explaining that the Irish enjoyed 'the advantage of intelligence, the country being so wholly theirs'.[29] This local knowledge gave the Tories a potentially decisive edge in their struggle against the New Model Army.

This lack of information proved deeply frustrating for the parliamentarians who fully understood the importance of good intelligence, both political and military. Writing in the 1650s,

Giovanni Sagredo, the Venetian Ambassador in London, argued that 'no government on earth discloses its own acts less and knows those of others more precisely than that of England'.[30] He identified the determination of the English authorities to restrict sensitive information to a mere handful of individuals, and the use of spies rather than ambassadors for intelligence-gathering, as the principal reasons for this success. Oliver Cromwell's secretary of state, John Thurloe, is usually credited with the growing professionalism of the English secret services, carrying on the pioneering work of Sir Francis Walsingham in the late sixteenth century. Thurloe, however, only assumed sole management of intelligence affairs in the summer of 1653, by which time the war in Ireland had reached its bloody conclusion. In fact, the real architect of the parliamentary intelligence machine was the MP and regicide, Thomas Scott, appointed in July 1649 'to manage the business of intelligence both home and abroad for the State'.[31] Holding the post until the dissolution of the Rump Parliament in April 1653, Scott's tenure of office coincided almost exactly with the duration of the Cromwellian War in Ireland.

Working on a budget, which he claimed never exceeded £2,500 per annum (including his own salary), Scott established a network of overseas correspondents throughout Europe, who by the mid-1650s resided in places as diverse as Danzig, Hamburg, Paris, Madrid, Genoa and Rome. On the domestic front, royalists claimed his informers swarmed 'over all England as Lice and Frogs did in Egypt', while others, even within the parliamentary camp, criticised the methods employed by these secret agents.[32] According to the radical army officer, Lieutenant Colonel John Lilburne, the spymaster and his associates believed that one 'must do evil that good may come of it'.[33] In a major intelligence coup, Scott obtained the services of Dr John Wallis, later professor of Geometry at Oxford, who specialised in breaking substitution codes. Wallis's skills enabled the parliamentarians to read intercepted royalist correspondence as well as diplomatic mail, and Scott later described the art of cryptography as 'a jewel for a prince's use'.[34] Although involved in handling sensitive information for much of the 1640s, Scott claimed that on assuming sole control of intelligence matters in 1649 he received no assistance or briefing from those previously responsible for secret affairs. It was a thankless, lonely task in many ways, and Scott's assistant, Captain George Bishop, recorded how the job brought him 'little advantage except the loss of my calling, the prejudice of my estate, the wearying of my body, breaking of my health, neglect of my family, and encountering temptations of all sorts, prejudices, censures, jealousies, envies, emulations, hatreds, malice, and abuses, which the faithful discharge of my duties has exposed me to, in no small measure, besides the mischiefs designed on me by the enemy.'[35]

Initially at least, Scott did not concern himself with Ireland, relying instead on Oliver Cromwell, commander-in-chief of the expeditionary army, to keep him informed on Irish affairs. Cromwell would have agreed with Henry Hexham's treatise on the art of war, published in 1642, that a general in the field 'should have good guides and spies about him, to get him intelligence of the state of an enemy, and ought to spare no money that way, for the breaking of an enemy's design, and for the advancing of his own'.[36] Throughout his nine-month campaign in Ireland, operating for the most part in hostile territory, Cromwell worked hard to ensure a good flow of intelligence, exploiting local knowledge, using spies where possible, and sending scouts out ahead of his main army. He appointed Captain Matthias Rowe, an experienced officer, as scoutmaster general of his forces. During the 1640s, the role of the scoutmaster involved gathering military intelligence for the army in the field, but gradually it expanded into more general espionage activities.

Rowe died in December 1649, and when Cromwell left Ireland for Scotland, Scott corresponded regularly with Rowe's successor, Henry Jones, Protestant bishop of Clogher and brother of Colonel Michael Jones, the hero of Rathmines. The bishop had gained valuable experience in intelligence matters during the early years of the Irish wars, when he headed the commission responsible for collecting witness statements from thousands of traumatised settlers fleeing the rebellion in Ulster. Indeed, for much of the 1640s, the English parliament relied on the local Protestant community to keep them informed on developments in Ireland. Large numbers of Protestants fled to England during this decade, including leading figures from the colonial administration in Dublin such as Sir Adam Loftus, Sir John Temple and Sir William Parsons. These men cultivated contacts with influential parliamentarians, advising them on Irish affairs. They advocated a hard line against Irish Catholics, through military conquest and a widespread confiscation of land. The majority of Protestants who remained in Ireland favoured these policies, and enthusiastically supported the English parliament where possible. Westminster maintained few English troops in Ireland during the 1640s, but local Protestant commanders such as Lord Inchiquin in Cork and Charles Coote in Derry acted as the eyes and ears of the parliamentary regime until the arrival of Oliver Cromwell.

Lord Inchiquin's decision in 1648–9 to back the king and subscribe to Ormond's peace treaty with the confederate regime outraged many Irish Protestants. Although shocked by the execution of Charles I, their hatred of Catholics ran deeper, and they still looked to England for salvation. Nonetheless, while the tide of war ran in favour of the royalists during the first half of 1649, both Ormond and Inchiquin managed to retain the loyalty of most of their co-religionists. In April 1649, Sir Hardress Waller, keenly aware of the undercurrent of Protestant discontent in Ireland, conferred with Cromwell about the possibility of sending a person to Munster. The following month, three agents, Lieutenant Colonel Pigott, Major Knight and a 'Mrs Foulkes' (presumably the wife of Major Francis Foulkes), departed for the southern province, 'to do some special service there' with every care taken 'that they might not be suspected'.[37] Cromwell maintained these secret contacts throughout the summer months as the parliamentary invasion force gathered in Milford Haven. In August, he dispatched Colonel Robert Phaire to negotiate with sympathisers in Cork, followed within a few months by the leading Protestant magnate in Munster, Roger Boyle, Lord Broghill, who played a key role in convincing the royalist garrisons of Youghal, Kinsale and Bandon to surrender, providing Cromwell's army with vital winter quarters.

Good intelligence alone, however, would not win the war for parliament, which desperately needed to maintain high levels of troops in Ireland. The switch of allegiance by Irish Protestants provided an opportunity for Cromwell to replenish his forces with local recruits. The first manifestation of this development actually occurred just before Cromwell's arrival in Ireland. Following Ormond's crushing defeat at Rathmines, the number of desertions from the royalist forces increased dramatically. Munster Protestants taken prisoner at that battle joined the parliamentary army *en masse*, and Inchiquin's subsequent decision to execute deserters failed to stem the flow. Cromwell eagerly welcomed these Irish Protestants into the ranks of the New Model Army. According to a contemporary correspondent, each local was worth six soldiers from England, while Ormond reckoned such men better able to cope with 'the hardness of war in this kingdom than any he [Cromwell] can have out of England'.[38] Accustomed to Irish weather conditions, and therefore less susceptible to diseases, the Munster Protestants also possessed valuable experience of fighting against their Catholic neighbours in difficult terrain.

While it might be expected that Irish Protestants would side with Westminster, the role of Irish Catholics in assisting English parliamentary forces is not so readily acknowledged. The issue of collusion, invariably a sensitive subject, has received little attention in the context of the Cromwellian Wars. Traditionally portrayed as a straightforward struggle between Catholic natives and Protestant invaders, this interpretation did not allow for any contact between the two sides other than on the field of battle. In the months prior to Cromwell's arrival, however, leaders of the native Irish of Ulster, Owen Roe O'Neill and the marquis of Antrim, tried to negotiate a deal with parliament, offering military support against the royalists in return for religious and political concessions. Initial talks in London, involving Abbot Crelly, collapsed with news of Cromwell's departure for Ireland. Crelly left England to petition the papacy for assistance, but he returned to London in the summer of 1650, and entered the service of Thomas Scott. Crelly, who resided in the residence of the Spanish ambassador, Don Alonso de Cárdenas, and used the pseudonyms Mr Haley and Captain Holland, exploited his clerical contacts across Europe to obtain intelligence relating to Irish affairs in France, Flanders, Spain, Austria and Rome. He also kept the English informed of the dealings between the Catholic Irish and the duke of Lorraine.[39]

In Ireland, Crelly's aristocratic benefactor entered parliamentary service in 1650 after almost two years of secret contacts. Motivated by an intense personal hatred of Ormond and an irrepressible streak of opportunism, Antrim believed the parliamentarians would win the war, and willingly provided them with military and political intelligence, including information about the king's alleged involvement with Irish Catholics in the months leading up to the outbreak of rebellion in October 1641. Ormond received a report that Antrim had taken a number of Ulster Irish regiments and some Highland Scots with him to fight for parliament. This unsubstantiated rumour is one of the first references to the possibility of Catholic Irish troops serving in the New Model Army. The lord lieutenant expressed scepticism, not doubting Antrim's capacity for treachery, 'but rather of his acceptance amongst them'.[40] For the next twelve months Antrim, with or without his own Irish and Scottish troops, concentrated on disrupting the royalist war effort in the MacDonnell/MacDonald heartland of northeast Ulster and western Scotland. Ireton valued his contribution, but the commissioners in Dublin distrusted this Catholic native who had switched sides so many times during the 1640s. In March 1651, they ordered the marquis to Dublin in order to keep a closer eye on his activities, and following Ireton's death in November, he disappears from official records for the remainder of the war.

Surviving evidence suggests that Antrim and Crelly should not simply be dismissed as maverick operators, unrepresentative of the wider Catholic community. Apart from the marquis, it is true that few prominent Irish Catholics openly sided with Oliver Cromwell, but lower down the social scale the picture becomes more complex, especially in relation to the composition of the New Model Army. The English army in Ireland, as already noted, suffered significant levels of wastage from diseases that killed far greater numbers of men than combat with the enemy. Between June 1649 and December 1651, the English shipped at least 43,000 troops to Ireland, where they joined somewhere in the region of 9,000 Protestant Irish soldiers already in the service of Michael Jones and Charles Coote, alongside thousands of deserters from the royalist side. Yet by the summer of 1652 only 35,000 soldiers remained in parliamentary service. The records indicate that no regiments returned home during this period, and even allowing for the disbandment of some local Protestant units, the overall attrition rate was therefore in the region of 30 to 40 per cent.[41] According to the parliamentary commissioners in Dublin, it was 'a sad thing to consider (and we are loathe to mention it) what vast numbers of men have perished in Ireland, by the hardship of service, cold (through want of clothes), and diseases of the country'. They estimated that at least one third of all the soldiers pressed into service and despatched from England during the course of 1651 died within the first twelve months, necessitating even more replacements, though they pleaded not to be sent 'aged, diseased persons and children'.[42] Neither England nor the relatively small Protestant population in Ireland could continue to supply the requisite manpower to maintain the field armies, as well as garrison all the newly occupied towns and cities.

Desperate for men, the military leaders in Ireland took the drastic decision to draft men from the local Catholic population into the ranks of the New Model Army. Given the bitter antagonism displayed by English Protestants towards Irish Catholics from the outbreak of the rebellion in 1641 such a development hardly seems credible. The problems associated with campaigning in hostile territory, however, required pragmatic rather than idealistic solutions. Local Protestant commanders, such as Ormond and Coote, had employed Catholics in their forces during the 1640s. In fact, Coote, a notorious bigot, highly recommended the Catholic Thomas Costello and his brother to Sir Philip Percivall in London. 'I confess they are Papists', he wrote, 'but such as never did any prejudice to the Protestants, but have constantly adhered to us and contribute much to our preservation'.[43] Similarly, royalists in Ulster accused the notoriously anti-Catholic Scottish covenanters of recruiting large numbers of Irish papists, even those active in the early days of the rebellion.[44] Arriving in Dublin towards the end of the campaign season in late August 1649, Cromwell needed a cooperative local population to provide food and other vital supplies to his forces. From the outset, he developed a sophisticated propaganda strategy. While Cromwell condemned those 'barbarous and bloodthirsty Irish' who had planned and led the rebellion, he publicly assured the lower social orders that he had no quarrel with them.[45] His policy of courting local support foundered following the massacres at Drogheda and Wexford. Yet, during the spring campaign in 1650, Cromwell adopted a more measured military approach while on campaign, offering generous terms of surrender, and sparing the common soldiers, if not the officers. His new tactics raised the possibility of recruiting local Catholic troops in significant numbers.

Writing after the war, an apologist for Ormond claimed that 'the Irish in all the quarters of which the enemy were possessed not only submitted and compounded, but very many of them entered into their service and marched with them in their armies'.[46] As early as March 1650, the garrison commanded by Donough Kelly, the Catholic governor of Ballyshannon in County Kildare, expressed the desire 'willingly to join' parliament's forces in return for a guarantee of religious toleration.[47] During that same month, the earl of Castlehaven complained to Ormond about increasing numbers of Catholic Irish agreeing terms with the enemy, providing them with provisions and manpower. The earl remarked incredulously how '[Cromwell's] army would soon be exhausted were it not daily supplied with the children and servants of contributors'. Castlehaven wanted the clergy to excommunicate all those who assist 'or serve' the rebels.[48] The archbishops of Dublin and Tuam acknowledged that some Catholics did in fact contribute both 'persons and substance' to the enemy, but no clerical censures ensued, as the royalist alliance began to fracture under the pressure of successive military defeats.[49] Ormond noted how the loss of numerous towns and garrisons, 'and the want of any visible power to protect them hath doubly induced many to contribute their subsistence and personal assistance to the rebels'.[50] Not all of this recruitment, however, was voluntary in nature. Following the fall of Wexford, Cromwell forced Irish prisoners to work in his army as 'Pioneers', while the marquis of Clanricarde later reported how the parliamentarians made peasants and even young boys 'march with them to make the greater show' of numbers.[51] More definitive proof of Catholic recruitment is provided by a Major Dongan, who reported to Ormond that after Carlow surrendered to the parliamentarians in July 1650 the majority of the garrison (exclusively Irish Catholics) took conditions 'to serve the rebels'.[52]

Not surprisingly, English sources for the period are almost completely silent on this issue, although the odd fragment of evidence has survived. Following the war, the parliamentarians forcibly transplanted those Catholic landowners who remained in the country to the province of Connacht. The commissioners entrusted with the task enquired whether to include 'Papists that first served in the rebel army, but then took service under the Commonwealth, if still on muster'.[53] The absence of any muster rolls for the New Model Army in Ireland, however, makes it impossible to estimate the numbers involved. Whatever the extent of the recruitment, parliamentary commanders would have experienced great difficulty in explaining why they accepted into their ranks those same bloodthirsty, murdering papists so effectively demonised by English propagandists. It may well be the case that officers in the field, desperate for manpower, simply chose not to inform their superiors, and that at least some of the new recruits conformed outwardly to the Protestant faith. A report in 1659 certainly suggests as much, with the authorities in Dublin anxious to identify former Catholics still in parliamentary service, who 'notwithstanding that they pretended to be Protestants', were nonetheless 'suspected to continue Papists'.[54]

After the restoration of the monarchy in 1660, neither Catholics nor Protestants in Ireland wished to be associated in any way with the Cromwellian regime, and subsequent accounts of the 1650s stressed the English nature of the invading army. Any Catholic complicity in the conquest appears to have been deliberately written out of history, or forgotten about over time, though Edmund Borlase, who wrote an account of the period, published in the 1680s, commented on how many of the Irish not only submitted to the parliamentarians but also 'entered into their service, and marched with them in their armies'.[55] During the war itself, royalist leaders remained acutely aware of the threat posed by Catholic recruitment into parliamentary forces. In September 1650 Ormond issued a proclamation condemning those who associated with the enemy, but the problem persisted. The following summer, Ormond's deputy, the marquis of Clanricarde, reported that the English were being 'assisted by very many of the Irish'.[56] In December 1651 an assembly of leading Munster Catholics denounced their co-religionists who fought for the parliamentarians. Assembly members, however, left the door open for a possible reconciliation, insisting that they did not intend 'to put any marks of incapacity upon any such of the natives as heretofore have been, or now are in arms and actual employment with the enemy and of their party'.[57] In May the following year, a meeting of Leinster clergymen pleaded with Irish Catholics not to take arms against those forces 'endeavouring to oppose' the English invaders.[58] In addition to these declarations, some military commanders resorted to more direct action. From early 1652, they attacked, maimed and in some instances killed Catholic Irish troops who made separate terms with the parliamentarians.[59] The frequency of complaints and condemnations between 1650 and 1652 suggests that Catholic recruitment into English forces continued until the conclusion of the war.

But what would induce an Irish Catholic to join the New Model Army, and assist the English parliament in completing the conquest of Ireland? The desire to support the winning side is one possible motive. As already mentioned, a number of Catholic leaders favoured an alliance with the victors in the English civil wars, in the mistaken belief that Cromwell, Ireton and their associates supported religious toleration, including Catholic worship. Many, such as the marquis of Antrim, despised the royalist leadership and as a consequence encouraged their supporters to ally with parliament. Economic factors also played a role, as Catholic troops frequently received little or no pay, forcing them to live off the land. The deprivations of these soldiers caused great hardship to the general population and drove large numbers to turn to the parliamentarians for protection. For others, the allure of secure employment in the English army simply proved too tempting, and the royalist, Sir Lewis Dyve, reported how many 'for want of livelihood, as having neither meat nor pay, flocked in unto the enemy'.[60] Whatever their motivations, these locally recruited Catholics provided the New Model Army with experienced troops and first-class intelligence, particularly as they continued to correspond with their friends in royalist-controlled areas.[61] As the war dragged on into 1652, the boundaries between the various antagonists became increasingly blurred. One report describes a prominent Catholic, Lieutenant Colonel James Barnwall, 'playing the ambo-dexter', switching from one side to the other as the situation dictated.[62] Similarly, soldiers oftentimes deserted from one army, only to re-enlist with their former opponents. As a consequence the parliamentarians specifically excluded from surrender terms those who had previously served in their forces. Some resourceful commanders exploited the confusion to their own advantage. In early 1651, Colonel Richard Bourke entered into talks with the English governor of Birr, 'simulating to become of his party'.[63] After re-supplying his troops for a few days at parliament's expense, Bourke revealed his true hand and promptly left the area.

Despite some conspicuous success in recruiting local forces, both Catholic and Protestant, the English parliamentarians continued to suffer from a military intelligence deficit. The authorities in Dublin introduced a number of measures to increase the flow of information to their forces, or at least to cut the links between the Tories and the local population. They offered bounties for private soldiers and officers, as well as named individuals such as Viscount Muskerry (£500) and Colonel Richard Grace (£300), while those bringing in prisoners received protection and pardon for life. Colonel Hewson, governor of Dublin, introduced the concept of collective responsibility, whereby an entire community would be punished for attacks by 'tories or rebels' within the territory controlled by parliament. For failing to warn the authorities of enemy raids, the colonel would fine the inhabitants of a barony £100 for every parliamentary officer killed, and £20 for all others, unless they handed over the murderers within 10 days of the attack.[64] In February 1651, in a move similar to British tactics during the Boer War, the parliamentarians established protected zones throughout the country, classifying entire counties such as Wicklow as hostile territory. They ordered all people residing among the enemy to move with their goods into designated areas. Anybody who failed to relocate was to be 'taken, slain and destroyed'.[65] The authorities sought to monitor the movement of the local population, and so all people over the age of ten received a pass, which contained detailed individual data, such as name, place of abode, family, qualities or callings, age, sex, stature and colour of hair. Those who failed to apply for this seventeenth-century equivalent of the ID card, or continued to live outside the parliamentary zones, would be 'deprived of the benefit of quarter'.[66] Colonel George Cooke, governor of Wexford, sometimes preferred to spare civilians in enemy territory, as they continued to consume scare supplies of food, thus causing widespread starvation. This he believed was 'the only way to make a speedy end of these wars'.[67]

Over the next twelve months, the authorities concentrated their military resources on certain problem districts, such as Wicklow, Wexford and Tipperary, destroying crops and killing livestock, in order to deprive the enemy of vital supplies. Allegedly, the authorities hanged at least five hundred 'poor labourers and women' throughout Tipperary, 'guilty of no other crime but being found within the imaginary lines drawn by the Governors of the several garrisons in the said county'.[68] The deliberately destructive parliamentary military campaign exacerbated famine conditions, which in turn facilitated the spread of diseases such as the plague, dysentery and typhus, which killed thousands 'to the deserting not only of houses and homes but cities and whole shires'.[69] It appears that few could escape the horrors of the conflict. The Catholic cleric, John Lynch, accused Colonel Cooke of the 'indiscriminate massacre' of as many as 4,000 men, women and children in Wexford.[70] In the confusion of warfare, such figures are impossible to verify, but news of Cooke's bloody campaign reached London, where Venetian sources recorded that the 'slaughter lasted four days running'.[71] Another account, published in March 1652, portrayed the scenes of devastation encountered on a journey through the Irish countryside. 'You may ride 20 miles', the author wrote, 'and scarce discern any thing or fix your eye upon any object, but dead men hanging on trees and gibbots: A sad spectacle but there's no remedy; so perfidious are the people, that we are enforced thereunto for the safeguard of our own lives'.[72] Unable to ignore the overwhelming evidence of parliamentary brutality, a few commentators addressed the issue of accountability. The influential Protestant settler, Vincent Gookin, admitted that those living under parliamentary protection suffered terrible injustices. He blamed rogue elements for the worst excesses, arguing that every army included 'some that swerved from the integrity of the rest'.[73] Writing during the Restoration, Roger Boyle, now earl of Orrery, agreed that private soldiers were 'apt to do amiss, when they have the power to do it, especially if not under the eye of their officers'.[74]

In July 1652 Charles Fleetwood received his commission to replace Cromwell as commander-in-chief in Ireland, with full power and authority to execute martial law against the enemy, 'and them to pursue, invade, resist, kill and destroy by all ways and means whatsoever'.[75] The civil commissioners in Dublin explained that this policy 'being done in the time of war and out of necessity, as affairs now stand shall not be any precedent or rule for future times'.[76] The temporary nature of these measures provided scant consolation to those suffering under the harsh parliamentary regime, and only when Henry Cromwell, son of the Lord Protector, assumed control of the Irish administration in 1655 did army officers cease to be 'civil justiciaries, and dispensers of fines and death at their discretion'.[77] It seems 'total war' demanded 'total victory', whatever the human cost. Faced with such brutal tactics, the Irish grew increasingly desperate, which greatly increased the flow of intelligence to the parliamentarians. For example, by 1652, the parliamentary commander in Ulster claimed he was 'promptly advised of all that is discussed in their [Catholic] provincial council' by those hoping to ingratiate themselves with the new regime.[78] In addition to such freely offered information, the Dublin authorities also employed numerous spies to sow dissent and undermine the last vestiges of resistance. The author of the 'Aphorismical Discovery' denounced these agents as 'scum and froth', men who would sell 'their proper souls for a paltry little gain and the lives of their best benefactors for nothing'.[79]

All sides in early modern conflict dealt harshly with those communicating with the enemy. The Swedish military manual, commissioned by King Gustavus Adolphus and used as a template all over Europe, stated simply that 'whosoever gives advice unto the enemy, any manner of way, shall die for it'.[80] Such strictures commonly applied to troops in service, but by early 1652, parliamentary commanders increasingly targeted civilians for maintaining contact with the regular Catholic forces, or Tory units. A unique record of the minutes of a military court in Dublin over a two-month period, between February and April 1652, reveals that the authorities in the city sentenced over twenty people to death for spying, including five women.[81] In mid-March, a council of war granted Colonel Hewson the authority to impose the death sentence on his own in order to speed up the prosecution process, while a Major Morgan received permission to dissect for the purposes of medical research the bodies of those executed, provided he agreed to bury the corpses afterwards at his own cost.[82] The figures from Dublin, if extended over a year, and applied across the country, suggest either a serious problem with civilian spies or wide scale, indiscriminate retaliation against the general population by the parliamentary authorities. Although the number of capital cases decreased dramatically as the war reached its conclusion, the execution of alleged spies continued into 1653. The sentence on women, however, was increasingly commuted from death to transportation to the sugar plantations in Barbados.

Spying, by its very nature, is a secretive business, which in combination with the patriarchal nature of early modern society, helped obscure the role of women in intelligence affairs. All sides in the conflict employed women as messengers, as well as major players in covert operations. As Cromwell moved against Drogheda in late August 1649, for example, the royalist commander, Sir Arthur Aston, complained to Ormond about 'these female spies that are here',

including a Lady Wilmot. The lord lieutenant replied sympathetically, remarking that women were indeed much inclined 'to
make little factions', and granted Aston the powers of 'martial law' to
deal with 'several ill-affected persons', particularly those giving
intelligence to the enemy. Although probably tempted to exact a
harsher sentence, Aston simply forced Lady Wilmot to leave
Drogheda and move to nearby Mellifont before Cromwell's arrival.[83]
Despite Ormond's disparaging remarks, the royalists also utilised
female spies of a high social standing. In September 1651, Frances and
Mary, two daughters of a leading Catholic landowner, Sir Nicholas
White, became involved in a plot to retake Athlone castle from the
parliamentarians. An informer warned the commander of the castle,
who foiled the scheme, killing fifty of the enemy in the process and
imprisoning the two ladies.[84] Some women suffered the ultimate
penalty, being executed for their espionage activities. On trial for his
life in December 1653, Viscount Muskerry vigorously defended his
decision to hang a number of spies, including a woman called Nora.
The parliamentarian judges accepted that such actions were justified
in times of war, and acquitted him on the charge of murder.[85]

Espionage and intelligence-gathering remained a high priority for
the parliamentarians throughout the 1650s, nowhere more so than in
Ireland. In all, during the Cromwellian Wars, they spent over £70,000
on intelligence matters in Ireland, or 2 per cent of the total military
budget for that country. In comparison, during the same four-year
period (1649–53), Thomas Scott claimed he received only £10,000 to
finance his domestic and Continental activities.[86] The figure for
Ireland reflects the greater resources available to military as distinct
from civil authorities, and also the scale of the intelligence problem
facing the parliamentarians in that country. As foreign invaders, they
relied heavily on local informers and recruits, both Protestant and
Catholic, all of which cost a lot of money. By 1652, however, the
parliamentarians were clearly losing the intelligence war, and as a
result, military commanders adopted increasingly crude methods to
disrupt the enemy's flow of information. Hangings, deportations and
imprisonment proved brutally effective in the short term, but while
such tactics may have broken enemy spy networks, and ground down

organised military resistance, success came at a heavy price. Despite Cromwell's declaration on landing in Dublin that he had no quarrel with the ordinary people of Ireland, by the end of the war the parliamentarians had not only totally alienated the local population, but also created a residue of bitterness that lasted for centuries.

While the New Model Army increasingly brutalised the local civilian population, the parliamentary authorities adopted a more flexible, conciliatory attitude towards Catholic soldiers, testimony to the increasing effectiveness of the Tories. In early 1651, the Commonwealth regime gave permission to Spain to recruit Catholics in Ireland, to help clear the country of potentially hostile troops, while the commissioners in Dublin, along with the commanders in the field, adopted a multi-faceted strategy to deal with those of the enemy inclined 'to come in and accept conditions'. Allegedly, by December 1651 'several of their considerable officers' had already made overtures, seeking licences to transport Catholic troops abroad into Spanish service. A meeting of commissioners and army officers in Dublin informed the Council of State in London that 'if some general tenders were made to the inhabitants', peace would quickly follow.[87] The parliamentary commissioners had already identified the lack of detailed settlement terms as a major obstacle to bringing the war to a conclusion, and explained to Westminster that nothing would facilitate peace more than 'an intimation of their pleasure towards this people'.[88] Despite persistent pleading, the authorities in London, preoccupied with the invasion of Charles Stuart from Scotland, remained silent on this issue.

These delays undoubtedly prolonged the war in Ireland, although the commissioners in Dublin did their best to speed up the settlement process. In January 1652 they recommended that the adventurers, who had loaned money to parliament back in 1642, be assigned lands, 'notwithstanding the war is not yet ended', to enable them to begin the process of plantation.[89] Not surprisingly, the adventurers proved reluctant to take possession of their lands while the fighting continued and an inconclusive debate over how best to proceed continued for a number of months, involving officials in Dublin and London. Anxious to bring the war to a conclusion, army commanders on the ground seized the initiative, as they had so often done in England during the 1640s, resuming the military offensive in the spring. The key breakthrough occurred early in February 1652, when frost-hardened bogs enabled Colonels Axtell, Sankey and Abbot to launch a surprise attack on the principal stronghold of Colonel John Fitzpatrick in County Tipperary. Although Fitzpatrick, whose father, Florence, had played a leading role in the initial rebellion, eluded the parliamentarians, they demolished his castle and put 500 of the defenders to the sword. The commissioners in Dublin wrote to the Council of State declaring confidently that as a result of this attack the enemy had been 'generally disabled from being so destructive to your quarters as formerly'. Not long afterwards, Fitzpatrick, 'the most considerable of their party', made overtures to submit, becoming the first major Catholic commander since the marquis of Antrim to break ranks, and sue independently for terms. Clanricarde and the Catholic clergy always insisted on a united approach, warning of the dangers associated with negotiating separately with parliament. Surprisingly, despite a litany of military disasters stretching back to August 1649, and serious internal tensions, the solidarity of Irish Catholic forces remained largely intact until Fitzpatrick's actions in 1652. In the absence of private papers it is difficult to be certain about the colonel's motives, though parliament clearly hoped that his example would encourage others into 'breaking their generally endeavoured union'.[90]

Negotiations took place in early March, as Fitzpatrick, chastened by his recent defeat in Tipperary, possibly decided to surrender while still in command of significant numbers of men, and in a position to dictate at least some of the terms. Moreover, with the city of Galway engaged in similar talks at this time, Catholic military prospects looked particularly bleak. On 6 March, Fitzpatrick delivered a set of proposals to the parliamentarians, primarily concerned with obtaining permission to transport his troops abroad into either French or Spanish service, but also including an act of indemnity for his father, liberty of religion 'though not affirmatively yet tacitly' and the retention of his personal estate.[91] The articles of agreement, signed the following day, granted a pardon to the colonel and all his men, except those responsible for the murder of settlers during the first year of the rebellion, or for any subsequent massacres committed on unarmed civilians. The second article guaranteed Fitzpatrick the liberty to transport his men, including those priests attached to his forces, within six months to any state not at war with England, while the remaining terms dealt with the technicalities of shipping the troops overseas. An additional article, which both the colonel and the parliamentarians understandably wanted to be kept secret, allowed him to retain possession of his estate 'or the value thereof'.[92] The agreement contained no provisions for his father, who died ignominiously in a ditch a few months later, while attempting to avoid capture. Moreover, the following year, the parliamentarians executed his mother for alleged atrocities committed during the first months of the rebellion. Much to the fury of the clergy, Fitzpatrick did not insist on any of the religious clauses, apart from the right of the priests assigned to his units to accompany him to the Continent. An assembly of Leinster Catholics called the agreement 'the first example and precedent of treason and perfidy', particularly at a time when Clanricarde was attempting unsuccessfully to negotiate a 'national treaty for the settlement of this realm'.[93] Catholic loyalists attacked and killed some of the colonel's troops as they awaited transportation abroad, while Fitzpatrick himself became the target of vitriolic abuse from contemporary commentators.

The parliamentary commissioners in Dublin, however, also felt obliged to justify agreeing terms with a notorious Catholic rebel, which crucially allowed him to retain his lands. Edmund Ludlow, commander of the English army, described Fitzpatrick's submission as 'a great blow' to the Irish, while the commissioners emphasised the scale of the threat posed by the colonel, claiming he commanded over 5,000 infantry and cavalry.[94] Despite repeated efforts, the English had failed to destroy Fitzpatrick's forces, and with the main army committed to the Connacht campaign, the colonel remained at large to attack parliamentary garrisons elsewhere. Moreover, those supporting the agreement hoped it would lead 'to the breaking of the Irish confederacy and to their insisting on national conditions'. They might even be brought 'to engage against each other'. On the sensitive issue of his estate, the commissioners argued that it was of little value, and would not set a precedent as the colonel wished to keep it concealed to maintain authority among his supporters. If somehow the details became public, the commissioners still believed that 'some few leading persons' might benefit in a similar manner, if only to further undermine enemy forces.[95] This detailed assessment proved uncannily accurate, and Fitzpatrick's agreement with the parliamentarians precipitated the surrender of Galway the following month. Increasingly, Clanricarde could do little to prevent individual groups in each of the four provinces from agreeing separate terms with parliament, thus destroying any prospect of a national settlement. This approach suited many Catholic commanders, and allowed them to depart to the Continent with their men, but left the majority of the population vulnerable to the unilateral imposition of harsh terms by the victorious parliamentarians.

For the moment, sporadic fighting continued throughout the country, as disparate groups of Tories either rejected a settlement outright, or created major disturbances in the hope of securing better conditions. Major Charles Kavanagh demolished the town of Enniscorthy in Wexford, while in the Wicklow Mountains the O'Byrnes inflicted heavy casualties on a parliamentary raiding party. A leading Tory commander, Colonel Richard Grace, burnt the town of Kildare, just 30 miles from the capital, and captured Birr in King's County the following month. In early April the parliamentarians also lost one of their most senior officers in Ireland, when an irregular unit ambushed and killed Colonel Cooke, governor of Wexford, on the road to Dublin. The bulk of the Catholic forces in Leinster, however, signed articles of surrender in May, while Viscount Muskerry did the same shortly afterwards for the Munster forces in County Kerry. Those who submitted received a pardon for life, enough income from their estates to maintain their families, and a pass overseas if they required one. Parliament only exempted those deemed guilty of the murder of civilians 'not in arms', or of soldiers after quarter had been given. Moreover, they reassured the Catholic Irish troops that they had no intention 'to force any to their worship and service contrary to their consciences'.[96] Although the terms sounded moderate, the vague terminology left them open to wide interpretation, a fact the parliamentarians subsequently exploited to their advantage. Two of the most active and successful Tories, Sir Walter Dongan and Thomas Scurlock, submitted under the Leinster articles, bringing over 800 troops with them. Clerical supporters, led by Colonel Richard Grace, bitterly condemned their actions. Grace went on the offensive in June, burning Portumna in County Galway, but the parliamentarians completely routed his forces at the end of the month, 'to the no small discouragement of the Catholic party in all Ireland'.[97] Around the same time the last major Catholic garrisons in Connacht, including Sligo and Ballymote, surrendered, while Clanricarde, despite one or two minor successes, including the capture of Ballyshannon in County Donegal, finally agreed terms. He received a safe conduct to travel overseas, and left for his estates in England before the end of the year.

Despite the rapid disintegration of organised resistance, thousands of Tories refused to surrender, 'being they are not pardoned for their murders', principal among them Hugh MacPhelim O'Byrne, who still commanded over 2,000 men in Wicklow.[98] The governor of Dublin, Colonel Hewson, determined to hunt him down, placed a £200 bounty on his head. Similarly, in Munster, Colonel Murrough O'Brien refused to come in with Viscount Muskerry, and remained at large in County Kerry. He went on the offensive with 1,500 troops, and in one engagement killed Captain Gibbons and thirty-four parliamentarians. His men also seized Dursey Island off west Cork before a lack of supplies forced them to disperse. By the end of the summer of 1652, parliamentary prisons overflowed with Tories, while increasing numbers of Catholic troops accepted terms and laid down their arms while awaiting transport abroad, including Lieutenant General Richard Farrell and the bulk of the Ulster forces. A report in early October claimed that a man could ride 60 miles anywhere in the country 'with a wand only in his hand', as the Catholic Irish no longer gathered 'in any formed troops or companies, unless in the bogs in Ulster'. Even in County Wicklow, a traditional stronghold of Catholic irregular forces, there was not 'ten men to be seen together'. The report concluded optimistically, and prematurely, that the Catholic Irish had at last been totally defeated. After eleven years of bloody warfare, tens of thousands of deaths and the widespread destruction of property, there was no longer any 'cause to fear them'.[99] In fact, the mopping-up operation went on for almost another twelve months, which meant that the disbandment of English forces in Ireland did not begin in earnest until August 1653, over three years after the departure of Oliver Cromwell. Only then could the parliamentarians set about claiming the spoils of victory.

9

Conclusion: Winners and Losers

Transport, transplant mo mheabhair ar Bhéarla
Shoot him, kill him, strip him, tear him
A tory, hack him, hang him, rebel
A rogue, a thief, a priest, a papist.
ÉAMONN AN DÚNA, *c.*1658[1]

In March 1653, Sir Phelim O'Neill stood before an English parliamentary court in Dublin on charges of murder. Since his heroic but ultimately unsuccessful defence of Charlemont in August 1650, O'Neill had remained at large in Ulster, fighting on against overwhelming odds until his capture in early 1653. Now the man whose actions on the night of 22 October 1641 had triggered the war in Ireland faced the death penalty. A London news-sheet reported that when this 'monster' first came to the bar, he was 'unable to stand for trembling or to speak for tears'.[2] After eleven years of bloody conflict, it seemed to many in England that justice at last would be served, and the massacre of Protestant settlers finally avenged, exposing the depraved and perfidious nature of the leaders of the revolt in the process. Contrary to published reports, however, Sir Phelim displayed tremendous personal courage during the final weeks of his life, refusing to implicate the executed sovereign Charles I in the rebellion of the Catholic Irish, despite the offer of a pardon. In a written statement, O'Neill identified his fellow conspirators during the summer of 1641, names long known to the parliamentarians, but insisted that he alone had forged the infamous commission from the king in support of the rebel actions. His inquisitors accused him of attempting to emulate the great traitor of the Nine Years War (1594–1603), his kinsman Hugh O'Neill, earl of Tyrone, but Sir Phelim denied ever having assumed 'that title or subscribed any of his writings as earl of Tyrone'.[3] With their prisoner refusing to cooperate, the interrogation did not last long, as the authorities believed they already possessed more than enough evidence to convict him.

The chief justice, Lord Gerard Lowther, opened the trial by denouncing O'Neill and all those involved in the initial insurrection. The judge spoke of innocent blood 'most wickedly and cruelly shed upon the land, against the laws of God and Man, of Nature and of Nations, the laws of the land, and the rights and rules of war, and the bonds of humanity and humane society'. According to Lowther, God would not allow 'such wickedness to pass without condign punishment'. He accused the Catholic Irish of killing 'some hundreds of thousands of these Protestants', a grossly inflated figure, but one widely accepted in parliamentary circles. The chief justice argued that traditional legal means were 'neither convenient nor possible' in these circumstances, and with the crime of murder grown so universal in Ireland 'the punishment must be extraordinary'. He admitted frankly that all sides in the conflict had committed atrocities but blamed the Catholic Irish alone, as 'they began this butchery and cruelty'.[4] With the outcome of this show trial never in any doubt, the court found O'Neill guilty and ordered his immediate execution in the typically brutal manner of the seventeenth century. A few days later, he was hanged until almost dead, then drawn and quartered, with various body parts subsequently impaled for public display in a number of towns, including Dublin and Drogheda.

Hundreds of similar trials took place from late 1652, following the establishment of High Courts of Justice in Dublin and other urban centres. The parliamentarians appointed over sixty commissioners 'to hear and determine all murders and massacres of any Protestants, English or other person or persons whatsoever', since October 1641. The judges included the top legal figures in the colonial administration, Chief Justice Lowther and Justice James Donnellan, the Irish Protestant leaders Charles Coote and Lord Broghill, and English parliamentary commanders such as Colonel Daniel Axtell, governor of Kilkenny, and Colonel Richard Lawrence, governor of Waterford. The surrender terms, however, agreed with the fragmented Catholic Irish forces during the course of 1652 severely restricted the remit of these courts in a number of important ways. Catholic rebels could only be tried for the killing of those 'not publicly entertained or maintained in arms as officers or private soldiers for and on the behalf of the English against the Irish'. Similarly, charges could not brought against those 'publicly entertained or maintained in arms as officers or private soldiers under the command and pay of the Irish against the English', except in cases of killing after quarter 'contrary to the rules of war'.[5] The parliamentarians had long since acknowledged that in order to end the war, they needed to offer the rebels some incentive to lay down their arms, and the limitations imposed on the courts protected those who fought in the regular confederate armies by recognising them as legitimate combatants.

In April 1653, a month after O'Neill's execution, his confederate colleague Colonel Philip MacHugh O'Reilly signed articles of surrender at Cloughoughter Castle very similar to the agreement between the parliamentarians and Colonel John Fitzpatrick just over a year earlier.[6] The capitulation of O'Reilly, who shortly afterwards transported his remaining troops into Spanish service, in many ways marked the end of the conflict, although significant bands of Tories continued to hold out, particularly in the south-west of the country. An enthusiastic participant in the rebellion from the very beginning, O'Reilly led the insurgents to their first major victory over government troops at Julianstown near Drogheda in November 1641. He loyally supported General Owen Roe O'Neill and the Catholic clergy throughout the 1640s, and subsequently fought bravely against the English parliamentarians, albeit at great personal cost, including the death of his son in a skirmish in 1652. On departing for the Continent, he left behind a country devastated by over a decade of bitter and bloody warfare. In the four years following Cromwell's invasion in 1649, Ireland suffered a 'demographic catastrophe', with mortality somewhere in the region of 20 per cent, due to a combination of fighting, famine and disease. This compares to an estimated 3 per cent population loss in England during the civil wars of the 1640s.[7] Many towns and villages lay in ruins, and in some cases totally deserted, while the systematic destruction of the agricultural system in areas of enemy activity meant that essential foodstuffs, including cattle, had now to be imported from overseas. Defeated, exhausted and defenceless, the Catholic Irish faced an uncertain future at the hands of an unforgiving and rapacious parliamentary regime.

The basic outline of the post-war settlement in the event of a parliamentary victory had not been in doubt since early 1642, when the Adventurers' Act detailed Westminster's plans to pay for the re-conquest of Ireland with land seized from Catholic rebels. The only question mark lay over the extent of the confiscations, and how best to divide the spoils among the victors. The length of the war had greatly expanded the cost of the conquest, thus increasing the pressure for a large-scale redistribution of property. The expropri-ation and transplantation of all Catholic landowners, regardless of guilt, guaranteed the maximum return of land. The imposition of such harsh conditions, however, leaving the confederates with little alternative but to fight to the bitter end, threatened to prolong the war indefinitely. Conversely, too lenient a settlement, allowing large numbers of Catholics to retain their estates, risked disappointing and alienating those seeking the repayment of long-standing debts. Since the early 1650s, this latter group included over 30,000 English soldiers serving in Ireland who, unlike the merchant adventurers in London, could not be easily ignored. As the conflict drew to a close, the military began to exert increasing pressure on parliament to make arrangements for the redistribution of confiscated lands. The challenge facing the English Commonwealth involved satisfying these demands, while at the same time providing some incentive for the Catholic Irish to lay down their arms. Ultimately the fiscal needs of parliament would determine the extent of the settlement but for much of 1651, faced with the more immediate threat posed by Charles Stuart and the Scots, the authorities prevaricated, either unwilling or unable to resolve the complexities of an Irish settlement.

As far back as April 1651, the English House of Commons had considered proposals from Henry Ireton and the parliamentary commissioners in Dublin for the exclusion of certain key groups and individuals from any future settlement. MPs quickly agreed to proscribe anybody involved in the first year of the rebellion, or who subsequently served on the confederate Supreme Council. They also requested that the English Council of State identify key individuals to be specifically named in a parliamentary bill. The Commons adjourned the following day, and did not debate the Irish question again until July, when members approved the final terms, though without the list promised by the Council of State.[8] The council's tardiness in this matter reflected growing tensions between the military and the civil government on a range of issues. Many MPs feared the growing power of the army, and supported moves towards a gradual demobilisation in England. On Ireland, however, all sides agreed on the need to complete the conquest, although they differed on the most suitable tactics needed to achieve this goal. Leading army officers, many of them religious radicals, advocated harsh measures against the entire Catholic population, based on the principle of collective guilt. This argument dovetailed neatly with the desire to secure the maximum return of confiscated land for English soldiers in lieu of pay. The civil commissioners in Dublin, no friends of the Catholic Irish, nonetheless adopted a more conciliatory position, in the hope of bringing the war to a speedy conclusion, thus facilitating a reduction in troop numbers.

The sudden death of Ireton after a short illness in November 1651, less than a month after the surrender of Limerick, temporarily enhanced the authority of the civil commissioners, particularly as the army remained without a supreme commander in the field until the appointment of Charles Fleetwood, another son-in-law of Oliver Cromwell, late the following summer. The commissioners made repeated requests to the Council of State in London to publicise terms for an Irish settlement, arguing that the Catholic leadership would lose support 'if some general tenders were made to the inhabitants'.[9] Facing a growing threat from Tories throughout the four provinces, they expressed a willingness to offer 'honourable terms' to the enemy, but the absence of precise directions from England seriously hampered their efforts at brokering a peace deal.[10] In March 1652, they tried to force the issue by signing articles with

Colonel John Fitzpatrick, which controversially guaranteed him possession of his personal estates. The following month Charles Coote reached a similar agreement with the citizens of Galway, allowing them to retain their property within the city. Appalled by the commissioners 'general aptness to lenity', Henry Jones, scout-master general of the army and one of the original commissioners appointed to take statements from Protestant refugees in 1641–2, intervened to prevent any further compromise deals with the Catholic Irish. In May 1652, he presented a selection of the 1641 depositions to the authorities in Dublin, which made an immediate and dramatic impact. Fearful of a backlash in England against their policy of appeasement, the commissioners expressed shock at the extent and nature of the crimes contained in Jones's report, claiming they could never 'sufficiently avenge the same'.[11] They dispatched this material, subsequently published under the title *An Abstract of some few of those barbarous, cruell massacres and murthers of the Protestants and English in some parts of Ireland, committed since the 23 of October 1641*, to Westminster. Stirred into action, the Council of State and House of Commons urgently began to address the issue of an Irish settlement. The 1641 depositions, therefore, once again played a key role in dictating English policy in Ireland, and in the words of the historian Walter Love, 'saved the [Cromwellian] settlement from moderation'.[12]

In a conversation with Edmund Ludlow, Cromwell had described Ireland as 'a clean paper', which following the victory of the New Model Army could be remodelled in the interests of England.[13] The Act of Settlement, passed in August 1652, finally outlined in detail the fate of the country and its inhabitants.[14] The preamble reassured the general population that the parliamentary regime did not intend 'to extirpate the whole nation', offering instead to extend mercy and pardon 'to all husbandmen, plowmen, labourers, artificers and others of the inferior sort', as long as they lived 'peaceably and obediently' under the colonial government. This statement, reminiscent of Cromwell's declaration on landing in Dublin three years earlier, sought to undermine popular support for the Tories, and drive a wedge between the community and its leadership. In contrast to the commoners, the Catholic elite, meaning those with estates valued at more than £10 annually, would be judged 'according to the respective demerits and considerations under which they fall'. The act contained a number of clauses specifically excluding a number of groups and named individuals from the general pardon. Predictably, the first clause condemned those guilty of the massacre of Protestant settlers, or of any involvement in the rebellion prior to 10 November 1642, 'being the time of the sitting of the first General Assembly at Kilkenny', and the date recognised by parliament as marking the official starting point of the war. The shocking events of 1641–2, grossly exaggerated in contemporary news-sheets and pamphlets, had largely defined English attitudes to the war in Ireland, and Oliver Cromwell, publicly at least, predicated his military intervention in 1649 on the need to exact revenge. While the November 1642 cut-off date conferred a degree of legitimacy on the confederate association, the parliamentarians defined 'involvement' in the broadest possible sense to include not only those actively 'bearing arms', but also any person who contributed 'men, arms, horse, plate, money, victual, or other furniture or habiliments of war' to the rebels during the first twelve months of the rebellion. Technically at least, this encompassed the vast bulk of the Catholic population living outside the few coastal enclaves controlled by government forces.

The second clause, equally broad in scope, excluded from pardon Catholic clergy who had 'contrived, advised, counselled, promoted, continued, countenanced, aided, assisted or abetted . . . the rebellion or war in Ireland'. From the beginning of the war the parliamentarians had invariably executed captured clerics, regardless of whether or not they bore arms. In 1649, Cromwell's troops killed all clergy they encountered at both Drogheda and Wexford, a policy enthusiastically endorsed by their commander-in-chief. High rank provided no protection, as a number of influential prelates subsequently discovered to their cost. The parliamentarians executed the bishop of Clogher two months after defeating the Ulster Irish at Scarrifhollis in June 1650, while Lord Broghill hanged the bishop of Ross that same summer. The bishop of Emly suffered a similar fate at the hands of Ireton following the fall of Limerick in 1651. In fact, for the period 1649 to 1653, the Vatican archives list 119 Irish martyrs recommended for beatification.¹⁵ The Act of Settlement, therefore, retrospectively bestowed a veneer of legitimacy on a long-established form of summary justice. The next clause specifically excluded over a hundred named individuals, starting with the royalist lord lieutenant, the marquis of Ormond, as well as a handful of his Irish Protestant supporters. Over 90 per cent of the list, however, consisted of prominent Catholic political and military leaders, men such as the marquis of Clanricarde, the earl of Castlehaven, Viscount Muskerry, Nicholas Plunkett, Philip MacHugh O'Reilly and, of course, Sir Phelim O'Neill. The roll call is far from comprehensive, reflecting perhaps the patchy nature of parliamentary intelligence in Ireland at the time. Some first names are missing, as in the case of '[   ] Fennell Doctor of Physick', while Sir Walter Dongan and Thomas Scurlock, two of the most successful Tory commanders of the early 1650s, do not feature at all. Nonetheless, the parliamentarians ensured that few of the major confederate/royalist landowners escaped proscription. Only a handful of these named individuals suffered the ultimate penalty. Many had already departed for the Continent, while others claimed the benefit of various surrender articles. All of them, however, forfeited their extensive estates.

In an effort to distinguish between regular soldiers and independent bands of Tories, the act condemned anybody who killed parliamentary troops when not 'publicly entertained and maintained in arms as officer or private soldier under the command and pay of the Irish against the English'. An additional clause, dealing with offences not punishable by death, ordered the banishment of all army officers and soldiers 'not being comprehended in any of the former qualifications', with the equivalent of one third of their estate to be assigned to them 'in such places in Ireland, as the parliament . . . shall think fit to appoint for that purpose'. Similarly, all those living in Ireland who did not manifest 'their constant and good affection to the interest of the Commonwealth of England' throughout the war would forfeit one third of their estates, with the value of the remainder transferred elsewhere. As the English parliament controlled little of Ireland for much of the 1640s, apart from a small enclave along the southern coast of Munster, few Catholics could possibly have avoided the confiscation of at least part of their lands. The act concluded with a guarantee that parliament would adhere to all articles of surrender already signed, although the authorities in Dublin reserved the right to move any individual to another part of the country if deemed necessary for reasons of 'public safety'.

The Act of Settlement, therefore, condemned all Catholic land-owners to full or partial confiscation of their estates, while thousands of civilians and soldiers faced possible execution for their activities as rebels during the initial insurrection, or subsequently as Tories. The savage nature of the conquest, however, combined with widespread deaths from disease and starvation, appears to have gradually sated the bloodlust of the parliamentarians. Executions by the High Court of Justice numbered in the hundreds not thousands, with few prominent leaders among them apart from Sir Phelim O'Neill, Miles Bourke, Viscount Mayo and Sir Walter Bagenal. The courts condemned Viscount Mayo for the massacre in 1642 of a group of Protestant settlers in an area technically under the control of his father, although neither man took any part in the killings. Bagenal, a major landowner in south Leinster and descendant of Sir Nicholas Bagenal, Knight Marshal in the army of Queen Elizabeth, admitted signing the death warrant of a government spy in May 1642, six months before the war officially began. Conscious of his high social status and illustrious lineage, the parliamentary commissioners in Dublin ordered the governor of Kilkenny, Colonel Daniel Axtell, a man with a notorious reputation for cruelty, to show Bagenal 'all civility', and allow the condemned man visitors, as long as conversations took place in the hearing of the gaolers, 'and that in English'.[16] A correspondent from Ireland subsequently reported that Bagenal 'had the honour of a beheading, a thing not usual in Ireland', but in all likelihood he suffered a soldier's fate of death by firing squad.[17] The records of the High Courts of Justice are fragmentary, but surviving evidence reveals a catalogue of executions from late 1652 through 1653, with at least eighteen sentenced to death in Kilkenny, thirty-two in Cork, twenty-three in Dublin, and another twenty-five in Carrickfergus.[18] The parliamentarians actually acquitted a handful of defendants, including remarkably, Donough MacCarthy, Viscount Muskerry, who courageously returned from Spain to face charges of murder. Prior to departing once again for the Continent, Muskerry publicly thanked the court, claiming to have met throughout the proceedings 'with justice, without any leaning to my prejudice'.[19]

As for the common soldiers and 'inferior sort', they provided a lucrative source of revenue to military entrepreneurs and merchants with shipping at their disposal. At the end of the Nine Years War in 1603, thousands of Irish swordsmen had fled into exile, finding service in the armies of France and Spain. Many of these men, or their descendants, returned home following the outbreak of the rebellion in 1641, to form the core of the regular confederate forces. As the war drew to a close, the process of migration turned full circle. Always short of seasoned troops, both France and Spain had tried to recruit Irish Catholics throughout the 1640s, but without any great success. In November 1650, however, Philip IV of Spain became the first major European monarch to recognise the English Commonwealth, gaining access to Irish manpower as a result. Shortly afterwards, the authorities in Dublin, anxious to rid the country of hostile soldiers, licensed military entrepreneurs to transport large numbers of Catholics into Spanish service. From 1652, articles of surrender invariably contained specific terms enabling Catholic commanders to depart for the Continent with their men. In March of that year, Colonel John Fitzpatrick received permission to transport 5,000 troops 'into any parts beyond the seas in amity with the Commonwealth of England'.[20] Three months later, Viscount Muskerry surrendered to parliament on condition that he could ship similar numbers abroad. With his keen eye for an economic opportunity, the exiled marquis of Ormond, believing the war in Ireland to be lost, tried unsuccessfully to negotiate with parliament to export soldiers to France.[21]

Between 1651 and 1654, as many as 40,000 Catholic Irishmen sailed for the Continent, often on English merchant ships. The vast majority entered Spanish service in Iberia and Flanders, while others enlisted into the French army, or those of the dukes of Lorraine and

Savoy. These exiles, widely admired for their professionalism and ability to endure tough conditions, gradually integrated into their adopted communities. Many dreamed of returning home, like Owen Roe O'Neill and Thomas Preston before them, to drive the English out of Ireland. The prospect of an invasion from abroad did concern the authorities in both London and Dublin, particularly after England declared war on Spain in 1655. Propagandists raised the spectre of an alliance between England's Continental enemies and papist exiles, thirsting for revenge, to justify the continued repression of Catholics in Ireland. The massacre in early 1655 of two hundred Protestants in northern Italy by the duke of Savoy's forces, including allegedly a number of Irish regiments, attracted particular attention. Predictably, pamphlets in London vastly exaggerated the numbers killed, and highlighted the presence of the Irish, who according to the reports acted 'through the instigation of the priests and Jesuits'.[22] The pamphleteers published graphic accounts of the slaughter alongside reprints of material relating to the 1641 massacres, drawing a close parallel between international and domestic events. Nonetheless, relatively few Irish exiles ever saw their native land again. Only a handful of individuals, such as Richard Talbot, the future duke of Tyrconnell, who as a young officer escaped the massacre at Drogheda in 1649, survived to take part in the last great conflict of seventeenth-century Ireland, the Jacobite Wars of the early 1690s.

Despite the departure abroad of so many soldiers, small Tory bands continued to pose a serious, if localised, military threat throughout the 1650s. The government in Dublin introduced a number of measures to restore some semblance of law and order, but the army struggled to contain the violence. Following a series of murders and robberies in late 1653, the authorities instructed all Catholics to surrender any arms and ammunition still in their possession, and shortly afterwards they began to gather the rural population into villages of at least thirty families, where they could be more easily monitored and controlled. Civilians who tried to live peacefully found themselves under pressure from both sides, for as one commentator explained if they failed to inform the authorities about Tory activities in their locality, 'the English hang them, if they do, the Irish kill them'.[23] The bounty system, introduced during the war, remained in operation, with forty shillings the normal price for information leading to the capture of a Tory, though this could rise to as much as £30 in the case of prominent individuals, such as 'Blind Donough' O'Derrick, whose band in the Kildare/Wicklow region targeted government officials attempting to survey confiscated estates.[24] Army officers frequently exacted revenge on the local population following a successful attack by the enemy. In 1656, for example, Colonel Robert Phaire, governor of Cork, executed a number of civilians and transplanted five whole villages for assisting Tories who had caused 'much mischief'.[25] Unable to suppress the disorder, the authorities took the drastic step of hiring ex-Tories to hunt down their former colleagues, in return for a pardon and cash reward. A handful of former confederate officers, such as Major Charles Kavanagh, willingly colluded with the army of occupation by accepting such employment.[26] The Tories, however, sustained by popular support, successfully exploited their knowledge of the local terrain to outwit and elude government forces. As late as October 1659, just a few months before the restoration of Charles II, the parliamentary commissioners in Dublin faced a security crisis in a number of counties.[27]

While the government encouraged enemy soldiers to leave for the Continent, a different fate awaited those civilians unsuitable for military service. From the beginning of the seventeenth century, England had acquired colonies in the Caribbean, and developed lucrative sugar plantations. African slaves provided most of the field labour, but a demand existed for indentured servants of European stock, who worked for a fixed period of time, 'under a yoke harsher even than that of the Turks', before eventually obtaining their freedom.[28] The first shipment from Ireland occurred in late 1649, when Oliver Cromwell ordered the few surviving members of the Drogheda garrison to be sent to Barbados.[29] Over the next ten years, unscrupulous merchants shipped thousands of Catholic women and children, many of them destitute and homeless as a result of the wars, across the Atlantic. The authorities in Dublin, concerned by the 'great multitudes of poor swarming in all parts of this nation' welcomed this trade in human cargo as a means of clearing the country of vagrants.[30] They also periodically emptied the jails by sending shiploads of convicts to the colonies, a practice which continued until the late nineteenth century, with Australia replacing the West Indies as the principal destination. In 1656, as part of the war against Spain, an English fleet captured the island of Jamaica. Shortly afterwards, the government in Ireland arranged for over 2,000 Catholics to be transported there, as indentured servants.[31] The destruction of so many records from this period makes it difficult to verify exact numbers, but estimates suggest that by the 1660s as many as 12,000 Irish resided in the Caribbean, compared with 50,000 African slaves.[32]

Surprisingly, despite the official sanction given by the Act of Settlement to the summary execution of Catholic clergy, the authorities gradually adopted a more conciliatory approach as the war drew to a close. Exile to the Continent replaced execution as the normal fate of those clerics who fell into the hands of parliamentary forces. Indeed, Vatican archives list only a handful of Irish martyrs for the period from 1653 until the restoration of the Stuart monarchy seven years later. In January 1653, the commissioners in Dublin ordered all clerics to leave the country within twenty days, and prescribed stiff penalties for those guilty of sheltering them. At the same time, however, they confirmed Cromwell's earlier promise not to 'meddle' with any man's conscience by enforcing compulsory attendance at Protestant services.[33] Many priests accompanied those regiments transported into service abroad, but some stayed in the country, while a handful of the sick and elderly actually received licences to remain as long as they made no attempt to minister to the community. The authorities offered a £5 reward for information leading to the arrest of unlicensed clergy, and many priest hunters, in the words of one incredulous commentator, were in fact 'disgraceful bastard children of the Catholic religion'.[34] Although from 1656 the Aran Islands off the coast of Galway acted as a temporary prison for those awaiting deportation, the government operated a policy of de facto toleration during the final years of the Interregnum, and a significant number of clerics quietly returned from exile. The need to maintain good relations with the major powers on the Continent possibly moderated the conduct of the English, but continued indiscriminate targeting of clergy also threatened to stir up the local population unnecessarily, and increase support for the Tories.

With Catholic soldiers, clergy and vagrants all exiled to the Continent or the Caribbean, the authorities could turn their attention to the principal target of the post-war settlement, the Catholic landowners. The Act of Settlement condemned the majority to lose their entire estates, but failed to specify the fate of those who only forfeited part of their holdings. Would they continue to reside in their own homes, or as the act suggested, be transported to lands elsewhere in the country? The ongoing power struggle between the military and civil government in England prevented the parliamentary commissioners in Dublin from making any significant progress in the redistribution of land. A dispute over proposed parliamentary elections triggered a major crisis in April 1653. Serious disagreements on Ireland, including arguments over whether the merchant adventurers should get priority over army claimants, also contributed to Oliver Cromwell's decision to banish members from the House of Commons that same month, and establish military rule.[35] Conscious of the need for the support of his military colleagues, Cromwell always sided with the army when under severe political pressure. He accepted the post of Lord Protector in December, and despite summoning a nominated or elected assembly on a number of occasions over the next five years, Cromwell ruled England, Ireland and Scotland virtually as a military dictator until his death in 1658.

Much had happened in Ireland between Cromwell's departure from Youghal in May 1650 and his seizure of power three years later. During this period, he did not play a major role in the affairs of the country. Focusing primarily on the threat from Scotland, he left Ireton and then Fleetwood to command the army in his absence. Although he continued to sit on the English Council of State, the civil commissioners in Dublin, Edmund Ludlow, Miles Corbet, John Jones and John Weaver, answered directly to parliament. The military coup in April 1653, however, enabled him to move centre stage once more. He allowed the civil commissioners to remain in office, but between the end of April and early July 1653, when a new parliament met at Westminster, Cromwell dominated governmental proceedings, and policy initiatives during this two-month period may be attributed directly to him. In late June, the Council of State declared the rebellion in Ireland 'appeased and ended', and commanded the authorities there to survey all forfeited lands, 'in order to the satisfying of Adventurers for Ireland, and arrears of officers and soldiers'.[36] Further instructions a few days later outlined the fate of those Catholic proprietors entitled to retain a portion of their estates. They had until 1 May 1654 to 'remove and transplant themselves into the province of Connacht, and the county of Clare, or one of them, there to inhabit and abide'. As soon as they crossed the river Shannon, they would receive lands worth either a third or two-thirds of their original estates, as dictated by the terms of the Act of Settlement. Landowners refusing to move, and found residing in the provinces of Ulster, Leinster or Munster after 1 May, would be 'reputed as spies and enemies', liable to the death penalty. Finally, those few Protestants with lands in Connacht could exchange them for property elsewhere in the country.[37] On 26 September, a parliament consisting of members nominated by the ruling military junta passed the Act of Satisfaction, confirming the council's instructions. For security reasons, the act prohibited Catholics from living in, or even entering, any port, town or garrison in Connacht and Clare, effectively sealing them off from the outside world. With Catholic landowners corralled in a ghetto west of the Shannon, the authorities turned their attention towards the wider population.

On 1 August 1653, shortly after receiving their instructions from London, the commissioners in Dublin established a standing committee to advise them on the transplantation process. The committee, reflecting the dominance of the military in government circles, consisted of the hard-line Munster planters Lord Broghill and Sir Hardress Waller, alongside two representatives of the army, Colonels Hierome Sankey and Richard Lawrence. In addition to examining means of propagating the Protestant faith, they also

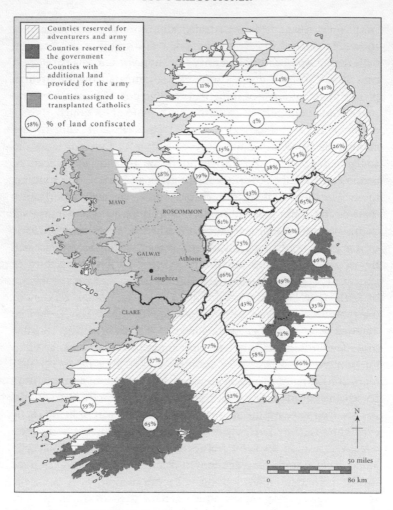

Map 9 Cromwellian Land Confiscation

considered 'whether it be advisable that all Irish papists be removed [to Connacht]', or only out of some counties, such as Kerry, Wexford and Waterford, where the Tories continued to pose a serious threat.[38] In the meantime, a declaration on 14 October ordered Catholic landowners who qualified for transplantation to submit the names and descriptions of all family members and dependants travelling with them, along with the quantity of livestock and tillage in their possession 'to the end that certificates might be forthwith given to them and lands set out unto them'.[39] The following January, five commissioners travelled to Loughrea in County Galway, former residence of the marquis of Clanricarde, to oversee the distribution of land in Connacht. They provisionally allocated estates to the applicants, based on the information contained in the certificates, taking care to disperse landowners from the same county, as well as those belonging to 'the several septs, clans, or families of one name'.[40] A separate committee in Athlone subsequently examined each individual case, using information from the 1641 depositions, the confederate books of government and examinations by the commissioners of the High Court of Justice to expose the guilty. They then permanently assigned estates to those Catholic landowners who qualified under the terms of the Act of Settlement based on a recently commissioned land survey.

By 1 May 1654, the commissioners at Loughrea had received certificates of transplantation containing 44,000 names of those intending to cross over the Shannon into Connacht. This figure represented about 5 per cent of the total population, although it is impossible to know how many actually undertook the journey.[41] A few surviving examples of the certificates illustrate the extent to which the great Catholic landowners, the dominant social class in many rural and urban communities for hundreds of years, had fallen on hard times. James Butler, Lord Dunboyne of Tipperary, a member of the Irish House of Lords and relative of the marquis of Ormond, listed twenty-one dependants, but in terms of possessions, he only brought four cows, ten carthorses and two pigs. The certificate of Sir Nicholas Comyn, former mayor of Limerick, described him as 'numb at one side of the body of a dead palsy, accompanied only by his Lady, Catherine Comyn, aged 35 years, flaxen-haired, middle stature, and one servant, Honor ny McNamara, aged twenty years, brown hair, middle stature, having no substance, but expecting the benefit of his qualification'.[42] Another great Munster lord, Viscount Maurice

Roche of Fermoy, who sat on the confederate Supreme Council and commanded troops in the southern province throughout the Cromwellian Wars, suffered great personal tragedy in the midst of this countrywide upheaval. In late 1652, the High Court of Justice ordered the execution of his wife for allegedly shooting a soldier during a siege of the family residence. Widowed and dispossessed of his estates, Roche brought his four young daughters with him to Connacht, but failed to obtain new lands. He spent the remainder of the decade homeless, and living on charity.[43] According to one clerical commentator, 'the entire island rang with the desperate cries of Catholics, lamenting the loss of their goods, the death of their dearest ones, chains, imprisonment and various exiles and transportations of the rest'.[44]

Meanwhile, the process of redistribution began in earnest, when in January 1654 representatives of the adventurers and soldiers drew lots at Grocers' Hall in London, to determine the division of the ten counties set aside to satisfy their claims – Meath, Westmeath, Kings and Queens in Leinster; Waterford, Tipperary and Limerick in Munster; Armagh, Down and Antrim in Ulster. Few adventurers travelled immediately to Ireland, but clashes soon occurred between soldiers, determined to take possession of their allotted lands, and existing owners/tenants, unwilling to be driven destitute onto the road. Struggling to meet the May deadline to transplant into Connacht, many families applied for an extension. In response to a flood of petitions, the commissioners in Loughrea, anxious to avoid serious social unrest, authorised family members, especially women and children, to stay behind over the summer to collect the harvest, with the new proprietors receiving a proportion of the crop in compensation.[45] As late as April 1655, John Talbot of Malahide, who lost his estate on the outskirts of Dublin to the parliamentary commissioner, Miles Corbet, received a pass to return from Connacht to dispose of his corn and other goods.[46] The commissioners also granted temporary dispensations to individuals on grounds of sickness and age, and exempted informers, or those giving evidence in the High Courts of Justice, from moving at all, in recognition of the fact that they could not be expected to live safely among the Catholic Irish. Even Colonel Richard Lawrence, governor of Waterford, a man not hitherto noted for his compassion, felt compelled to respond to the human tragedy unfolding around him. In October 1654, he appealed on behalf of the widow Elinor Butler to the authorities in Dublin, who ruled that 'she be permitted to bring back her cattle from Connacht towards the maintenance of herself and [her] children'.[47] In addition to the growing number of dispensations, the commissioners in Loughrea proved predictably susceptible to bribery. For a price, they willingly allocated estates to Catholics specifically excluded by the terms of the Act of Settlement.

Corruption, exemptions and continued Tory activity all seriously disrupted the transplantation scheme. Rather than move to Connacht, some landowners and their dependants had 'out of their desperate and malicious designs, taken occasion to run out again into the bogs, woods and other fast and desert places of the land to commit murders, rapine and spoil upon the well affected'. Others crossed the Shannon but quickly returned to their former estates, where they committed 'great stealths' against the new arrivals.[48] In addition to these problems, the inadequacy of the initial land survey also created major difficulties as it quickly became clear that the original ten counties set aside for soldiers and adventurers did not contain sufficient land to satisfy all the claimants. Moreover, the expected influx of Protestant settlers from England failed to materialise, and many soldiers in particular sold their prospective holdings in return for some desperately needed cash, allowing major Protestant landowners to consolidate their estates. New proprietors, finding themselves heavily reliant on Catholic tenants and labourers, felt particularly isolated and vulnerable. In July 1654, therefore, the commissioners in Dublin attempted to revive a plan proposed during the war, to create an exclusively English plantation between the river Boyne and the river Barrow, by removing the entire Catholic population from much of Carlow, Wexford, Wicklow, Dublin and Kildare.[49] Shortly afterwards, Charles Fleetwood assumed total control of the Irish administration with the title of Lord Deputy, assisted by a council of advisers from England, who replaced the commissioners. This move reflected the growing dominance of the army in Ireland and presaged the introduction of tougher policies towards Irish Catholics. In October, Fleetwood appointed yet another committee, consisting of supporters of the army such as Sir Hardress Waller and Colonel Richard Lawrence, 'for the effectual and real prosecution of the work of transplanting the Irish into Connacht and Clare'.[50] On 30 November, the authorities ordered that all those who qualified under the terms of the Act of Settlement move west of the Shannon by the following March, regardless of any previously granted dispensations or extensions.[51]

Irish Protestants, however, frustrated at their exclusion from the corridors of power in Dublin, grew increasingly disillusioned with Lord Deputy Fleetwood and the narrow clique of army radicals who controlled the government. Although they fully supported the policy of transplanting Catholic landowners into Connacht, plans for a larger forced migration appalled them, for practical as much as humanitarian reasons. Deprived of any income from their estates for much of the war, these Old Protestants (as they were now known) understood the importance of utilising local manpower, knowledge and skills, as well as the need to minimise further disruptions to the local economy. The Munster planter, Vincent Gookin, emerged as an effective spokesman for this group in early 1655. Raised on the family estate in County Cork, Gookin had returned to England with his family prior to the outbreak of the civil war. He supported parliament against the king, and, during the Cromwellian invasion in 1649, played a key role in convincing the southern ports to abandon the royalist cause. He enjoyed the patronage of Richard Boyle, second earl of Cork, one of the leading landowners in Ireland, and was similarly well connected in England. In early 1655, Gookin anonymously published a tract entitled *The great case of transplantation in Ireland discussed*, an uncompromising attack on the army interest in Ireland.[52] Originally written to lobby MPs at Westminster against proposals for a universal transplantation of the Catholic population, it triggered a bitter pamphlet war between the competing Protestant factions in Ireland.

In his tract, Gookin did not deny the general engagement of the Irish nation in the rebellion, but claimed that the majority had acted largely through ignorance or 'infirmity, partly fearing their priests' threats, partly their landlords' frowns'. Courageously, albeit anonymously, Gookin also blamed the excesses of the Protestant/English forces 'who at the beginning reckoned an Irish man and a rebel tantamount, and on that score forced many into war who desired peace'. Moreover, the constant recourse to military law ensured that more families had been 'destroyed under the protection of Protestants than in opposition against them'. He complained of the 'violence and oppression' inflicted by some soldiers, crimes which went 'daily unpunished'. Gookin believed that the harsh policies of the regime in Dublin made the common people 'so completely miserable' that necessity forced them 'turn thieves and Tories, and then they are persecuted with fire and sword for being so'. Gookin pleaded with the English to show compassion to the Irish as 'the bloody persons (known) are all dead by sword, famine, pestilence, the hand of civil justice, or remain still liable to it', and warned that 'the fair virtue of justice (overdone) degenerates into the stinking weed of tyranny'.[53]

On the specifics of the land question, Gookin believed the transplantation of the entire Catholic population to be 'an impossible work' and that the English should 'leave undone that which they are not able to do'. He accepted the need to punish guilty landowners, but criticised the sweeping terms of the Act of Settlement, arguing that 'not one hundred of them in 10,000' could escape the penalty of losing life and estate as a result. With 40,000 'of the most spirited active men' departing into Spanish service, only 'poor, laborious, useful, simple creatures' remained in the country, more to be pitied than feared. This resource needed to be properly exploited, particularly as English soldiers and adventurers lacked any knowledge of the husbandry 'proper to that country', while the local women 'possessed skills 'in dressing hemp and flax, and making of linen and woollen cloth', vital for the development of industry. Moreover, through the promotion of non-segregated communities in Ireland, Gookin believed it should rather 'be expected that the Irish will turn English'. This conversion of the Irish nation to English customs, manners and religion would be 'a more pious work than their eradication'. He called on parliament to reconsider the entire project, and urged MPs to listen to the more moderate voice of the long-established Protestant community in Ireland. Gookin concluded with an observation that while the unsettling of a nation was 'an easy work, the settling is not'. After years of warfare, 'prudence and mercy' would, in his opinion, prove far more effective than brute force.[54]

Predictably, the authorities in Dublin responded with fury to this savage public attack on their policies. Fleetwood complained about Gookin's 'strange scandalous book', and the governor of Waterford, Colonel Richard Lawrence, replied directly in print, with a pamphlet entitled *The interest of England in the Irish transplantation stated*.[55] Lawrence criticised Gookin for 'misrepresenting' the situation, and for the many 'mistakes, absurdities and impertinencies' contained in his treatise. The colonel saw the transplantation scheme 'as essential to the future peace and safety of the English interest there, as the stopping the leak of a ship is, to keep it from sinking'. Lawrence denied the existence of plans for a universal transplantation of the Catholic Irish, though without ruling out the possibility sometime in the future. He opposed any form of compromise, or 'the exercise of too much lenity and tenderness towards a people that are likely to ill requite it, and to take advantage thereby'. Lawrence did not distinguish between the Catholic 'nobility, gentry, clergy and commonalty', who together, and without provocation, 'engaged as one nation in this quarrel to root out and wholly extirpate all English Protestants from amongst them'. He argued passionately that in order to protect themselves 'the English inhabiting in that Nation should live together in distinct plantations or colonies, separated from the Irish', with the number of native servants and tenants restricted to one-fifth of the population. In this way, the three provinces of Ulster, Leinster and Munster would become 'wholly British, and thereby enable the English interest in Ireland to support itself'. As for the Catholic elite, in the policy of transplantation 'lay the axe to root out the tree of their [future] hopes of recovering their lost ground'.[56]

Despite Lawrence's assurances, influential figures continued to advocate a policy of 'total and universal transplantation'.[57] In early 1655 a petition of army officers from Dublin, Carlow, Kilkenny and Wexford declared that any proposal 'for transplanting only the proprietors and such as have been in arms will neither answer the end of safety nor what else is aimed at thereby'.[58] Lord Deputy Fleetwood and his council adopted increasingly harsh measures against recalcitrant Catholic landowners. In March, they instructed the army to apprehend those proprietors who refused to move, and 'to proceed to their trial, condemnation and execution, according to the laws of war in [the] case of spies'.[59] Two weeks later, a court martial in Dublin sentenced Edward Hetherington to death for disobeying 'several declarations', and subsequently hanged him with placards bearing the words 'for not transplanting', while Peter Bath and many others narrowly avoided a similar fate, when the authorities ordered their transportation to Barbados instead.[60] In April, an increasingly desperate administration forbade 'inferior officers and others' from issuing passes out of Connacht to Catholics, 'under penalty of being cashiered [from] the army', and in June they revoked all former dispensations granted to English proprietors enabling them to keep Irish tenants on their estates.[61] The following month, in blatant contravention of the treaty of surrender signed by the citizens of Galway with Charles Coote in 1652, Fleetwood commanded that all Catholics leave the city. The inhabitants of Waterford, Limerick, Kilkenny and many other towns and cities suffered a similar fate, paying the price for their spirited resistance to the Cromwellian invasion. Despite all these initiatives, however, it was patently clear that few outside a handful of radical army officers and officials in Dublin supported the idea of extending the transplantation scheme to the wider Catholic community.

As the dispute between the Old Protestant settler community and the regime in Dublin continued to escalate, Oliver Cromwell intervened decisively to restore some semblance of stability. He sent his son, Henry, to Ireland in July 1655 as commander-in-chief of the army, and invited the ineffectual Fleetwood to return to England. The young Cromwell, who replaced Fleetwood as Lord Deputy in November 1657, adopted a far more pragmatic approach than his predecessor, actively seeking the support of the old Protestant community. The transplantation of Catholic proprietors continued, but the idea of moving the entire population no longer found favour in official circles. A more accurate survey of Irish lands, commissioned by the government from William Petty, physician general of the army, facilitated the process of redistribution, but the scheme remained incomplete at the time of Cromwell's death on 3 September 1658, the anniversary of two of his greatest triumphs at Dunbar and Worcester. Cromwell's health had never fully recovered from the serious fever which almost killed him in Ireland during the winter of 1649, and the long years of campaigning, combined with the pressures of high office, undoubtedly contributed to his relatively rapid decline in 1658. Despite all his military victories, political success ultimately eluded the Lord Protector, as he failed to establish a system of government robust enough to survive his passing. His eldest son Richard assumed the title of Protector but lacking both charisma and political skills he could not sustain the family dynasty. Within a few months, Richard's opponents in England forced him to step down and recalled the rump parliament dissolved by his father back in 1653. The political instability presented the exiled Charles Stuart with his first real opportunity in almost a decade to restore the monarchy, and overthrow the experiment in republican government.

The collapse of the Cromwellian Protectorate also resulted in Henry Cromwell relinquishing control of the administration in Ireland in 1659. The former parliamentary commissioners resumed their posts after a five-year absence, but their triumph proved short-lived. In December, leading Irish Protestants, including the ubiquitous Charles Coote and Lord Broghill, seized control of Dublin in a carefully orchestrated coup, and anxiously awaited developments in England. Few Protestants in Ireland, of whatever political persuasion, had not collaborated with the Cromwellian regime to some degree, and the return of Charles Stuart threatened to undermine the entire post-war land settlement. Many leading Irish Catholics had joined him on the Continent, sharing the hardships of exile, and they expected to be suitably rewarded for their loyalty, recovering forfeited estates. Moreover, with the marquis of Ormond firmly established as one of the king's closest advisers, they hoped to revive the treaty he signed with the confederates in 1649, which included a number of significant concessions to Irish Catholics. Irish Protestants, therefore, faced a serious dilemma, anxious for a return of traditional monarchical government, but terrified of losing their newly acquired estates in the process. Similarly, the Cromwellian adventurers and soldiers urgently needed to develop a strategy to help secure their estates in the event of a regime change. In early 1660, a Protestant convention in Dublin, consisting of old and new Protestants, soldiers and civilians, worked together to preserve their respective interests, regardless of past differences, and presented the king with a powerful, united front he simply could not ignore.

Charles Stuart returned in triumph to London in May 1660, after almost ten years of exile, amid scenes of wild celebration, determined to avenge his father. The public expressions of joy, however, masked his political weakness, and his reliance on many stalwarts of the Cromwellian regime, particularly leading figures in the army. They only agreed to support the restoration of the monarchy after receiving assurances that it would not result in widespread acts of recrimination. This arrangement suited Irish Protestants, and the Dublin convention sent a delegation to England to press their claims, and counter the arguments of the Irish Catholic representative, Nicholas Plunkett, formerly chairman of the confederate Supreme Council and agent to the duke of Lorraine. Intense negotiations followed, before Charles, painfully aware of the hostility felt by the majority of Englishmen towards Irish Catholics, predictably sided with his Protestant subjects. An act of pardon and indemnity in August 1660 specifically excluded those involved 'in the plotting, contriving, or designing the great and heinous rebellion of Ireland', or who had subsequently assisted the rebels in any way.[62] The king retained the right, however, to pardon individual Catholics, regardless of their actions during the 1640s, for loyal service to the crown, especially during the years of exile. The act also denied a pardon to named individuals who had taken part in the trial and execution of Charles I, including many of the leading players in Irish affairs from 1649. Three of the parliamentary commissioners, John Jones, Miles Corbet and Edmund Ludlow, were among the indicted, along with the spymaster, Thomas Scott, and military figures such as Colonel Daniel Axtell and Colonel John Hewson. Ludlow and Hewson escaped to the Continent, but the others all died on the scaffold, while the king ordered the bodies of Oliver Cromwell and Henry Ireton to be disinterred, put through the ritual of execution and dumped in an unmarked grave. A sympathiser managed to retrieve Cromwell's skull, which is now interred beneath the floor of his alma mater, Sidney Sussex College in Cambridge. Few in Ireland would have mourned this ignominious fate and a satirical epitaph composed at the time claimed that 'into his life he fitted about sixty years' worth of age, but a millennium's worth of evil', before concluding 'so damn his dead ashes to Hell, traveller, and then be on your way'.[63]

At the end of November 1660, Charles II published a 'Gracious Declaration', outlining in detail his plans for Ireland. The king acknowledged the 'many difficulties, in the providing for, and complying with the several interests and pretences there', but highlighted the debt he owed to Protestant leaders for facilitating the restoration of the monarchy. Charles accepted the validity of the peace treaty signed by the marquis of Ormond with the confederates in 1649, but expressed himself 'miserably disappointed . . . by an unhappy part of them which foolishly forfeited all the grace which they might have expected from us', a clear reference to Ormond's Catholic opponents in 1650. Crucially, the declaration confirmed all the adventurers and soldiers in their estates, with the exception of those named in the act of pardon for taking part in the execution of Charles I.[64] Not surprisingly, Ormond (soon to become a duke) recovered his entire estate, as did Murrough O'Brien, Lord Inchiquin, and all leading Protestant royalists. Adventurers or soldiers who lost lands as a result were to be compensated with holdings of equal value elsewhere in the kingdom. Similarly, Charles ordered the restoration of the handful of Catholic landowners who had not colluded in any way with the confederate regime, with the exception of those living in towns and cities. This latter group, 'including the popish inhabitants of Cork, Youghal and Kinsale' would instead receive lands 'near the said corporations', leaving the Protestants in control of the major urban centres. As for those Catholics entitled to benefit from the terms of the Ormond peace, Charles distinguished between supporters who had followed him into exile, and those who subsequently accepted lands as part of the transplantation scheme. He restored the former to their original estates, but insisted that the transplanted landowners 'stand bound' by the terms of the Cromwellian settlement and remain in Connacht, in effect penalising them for not abandoning their families. The declaration went on to name thirty-eight individuals, mostly nobles such as the marquis of Clanricarde (recently deceased), the earl of Clancarthy (formerly Viscount Muskerry) and Viscount Taaffe, to be fully restored to their former estates 'without being put to any further proofs', while the king deemed a further 200 Catholic officers who had served overseas to be worthy of royal grace and favour. Only after settling the 'jarring interests' relating to land did Charles intend to pass a general act of pardon in Ireland, except of course for those 'notorious murderers' involved in the initial rebellion.

The king's 'Gracious Declaration', therefore, established the year 1659, not 1641, as the benchmark for all future land claims, consolidating the Cromwellian land settlement in the process, and dashing the hopes of Irish Catholics. Thousands of families never recovered their estates, and only in the province of Connacht did a significant Catholic landowning elite survive. Moreover, Protestants now dominated the corporate towns, traditional bastions of the Old English Catholic interest in Ireland. An embittered cleric reflected how all the 'towns, cities, free-towns and market towns, in which the Catholic faith had sat as if upon a royal throne, became sewers, sinks and dung-pits of English heresies'.[65] The Irish parliament, now an exclusively Protestant assembly, apart from a handful of Catholic nobles in the House of Lords, subsequently passed the Act of Settlement (1662) and the Act of Explanation (1665) enabling hundreds of Catholics, particularly those connected to the new lord lieutenant, the duke of Ormond, to plead their innocence before the courts. Years of litigation followed, as Cromwellian proprietors for the most part refused to relinquish their holdings, and as many as 500 adventurers, along with 7,500 soldiers, successfully retained their estates. The mass plantation envisaged by Lawrence and others during the 1650s may not have occurred, but Protestants nonetheless emerged as the clear victors from the wars of the mid-seventeenth century, with Catholics left in possession of only one fifth of the land total, a huge reduction from the 60 per cent they owned prior to the 1641 rebellion.[66] This represented the largest single shift in land ownership anywhere in Europe during the early modern period, and proved to be Cromwell's lasting legacy in Ireland.

That legacy was briefly threatened by the accession of a Catholic monarch, James II, in 1685. His appointment of a Catholic lord lieutenant, Richard Talbot, duke of Tyrconnell, briefly raised hopes of reversing the Cromwellian transfer of land and power. Driven from England by his son-in-law, William of Orange, James fled to Ireland via France, and in 1689 presided over a parliament in Dublin. This Jacobite assembly, composed almost entirely of Catholics, many of them direct descendants of the confederates, seized the opportunity to overthrow the Cromwellian land settlement, and proscribed thousands of Protestant landowners in the process. The subsequent military defeats of the Jacobites, however, at the Boyne in 1690, and Aughrim the following year, confirmed English Protestant supremacy, and the ascendancy class which emerged dominated the political and social life of the country until Catholic emancipation and major land reforms transformed the landscape of nineteenth-century Ireland. In contributing to the destruction of the Catholic landowning elite, Cromwell also inadvertently played a key role in the development of modern Irish nationalism. Although the confederate association had brought Old English and native Irish Catholics closer than at any time over the previous 400 years, Cromwell's refusal to distinguish between them completed the process. Together they shared the disasters of the 1650s, the 1690s and beyond, striving to preserve their customs and beliefs in the face of official persecution, and repeated military setbacks, before eventually rediscovering their political voice during the course of the nineteenth century. Oliver Cromwell, therefore, helped shape Irish nationalist identity to an extent few other individuals could rival.

So how then does Cromwell deserve to be remembered in the annals of Irish history? For the great English historian A. J. P. Taylor, writing on the 300th anniversary of Cromwell's death, Ireland was the 'one great blot' on the great man's reputation, and his actions there 'beyond all excuse or explanation'. In fact, Taylor believed that the 'curse of Cromwell' would still be remembered when all his other achievements had been forgotten.[67] In Ireland itself, the Protestants of Ulster, uncomfortable perhaps with his reputation as a regicide, choose to commemorate William of Orange instead, while for many Catholics he remains a figure of hate, guilty of crimes against humanity. Few would attempt to justify his record during the nine-month military campaign in 1649–50, or the inequities of the subsequent land settlement. Despite possessing many exceptional qualities, Cromwell's dealings with Catholic Ireland mark him out as a man of his times. He shared the racial, cultural and religious prejudices of his fellow Englishmen. His contempt for Irish Catholics 'rationalised a desire to exploit', and he found little difficulty in excusing shockingly brutal acts, such as the massacres at Drogheda and Wexford.[68] Ireland brought out the worst in Cromwell, and provided little outlet for his undoubted talents as an inspirational leader and radical reformer. He subscribed unhesitatingly to the doctrine that 'error has no rights', and treated the Catholic Irish accordingly.

In the mid-seventeenth century, a lethal combination of racial superiority and religious bigotry, reinforced by a genuine sense of outrage at events during the initial months of the Ulster rebellion, created the ideal conditions for Cromwell's campaign of terror against Irish Catholics. His conduct shocked contemporary opinion, not only in Ireland, but also on the Continent, and almost certainly prolonged the war by a number of years. This conflict resulted in a catastrophic loss of life, both soldiers and civilians, alongside the destruction of much of the country's economy and infrastructure. As commander-in-chief of the army, the responsibilities for the excesses of the military must be laid firmly at his door, while the harsh nature of the post-war settlement also bears his personal imprint. Cromwell was no monster, but he did commit monstrous acts. A warrior of Christ, somewhat like the crusaders of medieval Europe, he acted as God's executioner, exacting revenge and crushing all opposition, convinced throughout of the legitimacy of his cause, and striving to build a better world for the chosen few. In many ways, therefore, he remains a remarkably modern figure, relevant to our understanding of both the past and the present, somebody to be closely studied and understood, rather than revered or reviled.

Notes

ABBREVIATIONS USED IN THE NOTES

BL   British Library
Bodl Bodleian Library Oxford
CSP   Calendar of State Papers
HMC   Historical Manuscripts Commission
TCD   Trinity College Dublin
TNA   The National Archives, Kew

CHAPTER 1   INTRODUCTION

1 Lynch, John, *Cambrensis Eversus*, 3 vols (Dublin, 1848–52 edn, translated by Matthew Kelly), vol. 1, p. 7.
2 The *Independent* newspaper, 7 July 2006, p. 12.
3 Marcus Tanner, *Ireland's Holy Wars: the struggle for a nation's soul, 1500–2000* (New Haven, 2001), p. 145.
4 Seán Ó Conaill, 'Tuireamh na hÉireann', in Cecile O'Rahilly (ed.), *Five Seventeenth-century Political Poems* (Dublin, 1977), p. 75.
5 Thomas Carlyle (ed.), *The Letters and Speeches of Oliver Cromwell*, 3 vols (London, 1904 edn), vol. 1, pp. 10–16.
6 J. P. Prendergast, *The Cromwellian Settlement of Ireland* (London, 1996 edn), p. xi.
7 Denis Murphy, *Cromwell in Ireland: a history of Cromwell's Irish campaign* (Dublin, 1883).
8 Blair Worden, *Roundhead Reputations: the English Civil Wars and the passions of posterity* (London, 2001), pp. 311–12.
9 There is a very brief discussion of the most recent material on Cromwell and Ireland in the bibliography section of the book.

10 S. R. Gardiner, *Cromwell's Place in History* (London, 1897), p. 57.
11 Speech to parliament, 12 September 1654, quoted in Christopher Hill, *God's Englishman: Oliver Cromwell and the English Revolution* (Middlesex, 1983), p. 33.
12 A. J. P. Taylor, *Essays in English History* (London, 1976), pp. 23–6.
13 Ibid.
14 Gerard Boate, *Ireland's Natural History* (London, 1652).
15 'History' by Richard Bellings, although written in the 1670s, was not published until the late nineteenth century. See J. T. Gilbert (ed.), *History of the Irish Confederation and the War in Ireland*, 7 vols (Dublin, 1882–91), vol. 1, pp. 2–3.
16 Sir John Temple, *The Irish Rebellion* (London, 1646), p. 16.
17 W. C Abbott (ed.), *The Writings and Speeches of Oliver Cromwell*, 4 vols (Cambridge, 1937–47), vol. 2, p. 198.
18 For a discussion on codes of conduct throughout the 1640s–50s see Micheál Ó Siochrú, 'Atrocity, codes of conduct and the Irish in the British civil wars, 1641–1653', *Past and Present*, no. 195 (May 2007), pp. 55–86.
19 Vincent Carey, 'John Derricke's *Image of Ireland*, Sir Henry Sidney and the massacre at Mullaghmast, 1578', *Irish Historical Studies*, vol. 31 (1999), p. 327.
20 Thomas Churchyard, *A Generall Rehearsall of Warres* (London, 1579), Sig.Q. i–iii.
21 L. Boynton, 'Martial Law and the Petition of Right', *English Historical Review*, vol. 74 (1964), p. 280.

CHAPTER 2   IRELAND INDEPENDENT

1 'Remonstrance of the Catholics of Ireland, Dec 1641', in J. T. Gilbert (ed.), *A Contemporary History of Affairs in Ireland from 1641 to 1652*, 3 vols (Dublin, 1879–80), vol. 1, pp. 360–1.
2 The papal nuncio, Rinuccini, made this comment, in a different context, after his return to Rome from Ireland in 1649. See G. Aiazza (ed.), *The Embassy in Ireland of Monsignor G. B. Rinuccini, Archbishop of Fermo, in the Years 1645–49*, translated by Annie Hutton (Dublin, 1873), p. 499.
3 'Journal of Henry McTully O'Neill', in John Lodge (ed.), *Desiderata Curiosa Hibernica*, 2 vols (London, 1772), vol. 2, p. 485.
4 James Tuchet, *The Earl of Castlehaven's Review or his Memoirs* (London, 1684), pp. 28–9.
5 Edmund Borlase, *The History of the Execrable Irish Rebellion* (London, 1680), pp. 57–8.

6 *A Great Conspiracy by the Papists in the Kingdome of Ireland Discovered by the Lords Justices and Counsell at Dublin and Proclaimed there Octob. 23, 1641* (London, 1641), p. 1.

7 'The humble petition of the Lords, knights, gentlemen, and others, inhabitants of the English Pale of Ireland', in J. T. Gilbert (ed.), *History of the Irish Confederation and the War in Ireland*, 7 vols (Dublin, 1882–91), vol. 1, p. 238.

8 Thomas Fitzpatrick (ed.), *The Bloody Bridge and Other Papers Relating to the Insurrection of 1641* (London, 1970 edn), p. 158.

9 See Sir John Temple, *The Irish Rebellion* (London, 1646), section 2, p. 36, and 'History' by Richard Bellings, in Gilbert (ed.), *History of Irish Confederation*, vol. 1, p. 64.

10 Temple, *Irish Rebellion*, p. 1.

11 *Mr Pym, his Speech in Parliament . . . for the Present Pressing of 15,000 Men to be Immediately Transported to Ireland* (London, 1642), p. 4.

12 Joad Raymond, *Making the News: an anthology of the newsbooks of revolutionary England, 1641–1660* (Gloucester, 1993), p. 19.

13 *A Declaration of the Commons Assembled in Parliament; concerning the rise and progress of the grand rebellion in Ireland* (London, 1643). Thanks to Aidan Clarke for bringing this reference to my attention.

14 James Cranford, *The Teares of Ireland* (London, 1642), p. 3.

15 [Adam Meredith], *Ormond's Curtain Drawn: in a short discourse concerning Ireland* (London, 1646), pp. 3, 6, 16.

16 See Karl Bottigheimer, *English Money and Irish Land: the 'Adventurers' in the Cromwellian settlement of Ireland* (Oxford, 1971), p. 70; *Calendar of State Papers relating to Ireland, Adventurers, 1642–1659* (London, 1903), pp. 319–20; 'Register of Adventurers, 1658', Marsh's Library, Dublin, MS Z2.1.5, f. 27.

17 14 January 1642, 'Declaration by the Lords Justices and Council', in Robert Steele (ed.), *Tudor and Stuart Proclamations*, 2 vols (Oxford, 1910), vol. 2, p. 43.

18 Toirdealbhach Ó Meallán, 'Cín Lae Uí Mhealláin', *Louth Archaeological Journal*, vol. 6 (1925), p. 34.

19 Lords Justices and Council to His Majesty's Commissioners for the Affairs of Ireland, 7 June 1642, in *HMC, Ormonde MSS*, new series, vol. 2, pp. 130–1.

20 Colonel Thomas Pigott to Sir Philip Percival, 1 Oct 1647, in *HMC, Egmont MSS*, vol. 1, p. 473.

21 Lords Justices and others to the King, 16 March 1643, in *HMC, Ormonde MSS*, new series, vol. 2, p. 252.

22 'Acts of the Ecclesiastical Congregation, 10–13 May 1642' in BL Stowe MS 82, ff. 271–4.

23 'Acts of General Assembly of Confederation, October 1642', in Gilbert (ed.), *History of the Irish Confederation*, vol. 2, pp. 73–84.

24 'Confederate explanation of propositions', ibid., vol. 3, pp. 298–305.

25 John Elliott, 'Revolution and continuity', in Geoffrey Parker and L. M. Smith, *The General Crisis of the Seventeenth Century* (London, 1978), pp. 110–33.

26 Bellings, 'History', in Gilbert (ed.), *History of Irish the Confederation*, vol. 1, p. 37.

27 Pádraig Lenihan, *Confederate Catholics at War, 1641–49* (Cork, 2001), p. 5.

28 18 January 1643, Preston to Clanricarde, in Thomas Carte, *The Life of James, Duke of Ormond,* 6 vols (Oxford, 1851), vol. 5, pp. 383–5; 'Journal of Colonel Henry McTully O'Neill' in Lodge (ed.), *Desiderata Curiosa Hibernica*, vol. 2, p. 497.

29 'Journal of Captain William Tucker, 1642–3', in Gilbert (ed.), *History of the Irish Confederation*, vol. 2, p. 199.

30 Lords Justices and others to the King, 16 March 1643, in *HMC, Ormonde MSS*, new series, vol. 2, pp. 251–2.

31 [Adam Meredith], *Ormond's Curtain Drawn: in a short discourse concerning Ireland* (London, 1646), pp. 13, 29.

32 Otto von Guericke quoted in Geoff Mortimer, *Eyewitness Accounts of the Thirty Years' War, 1618–48* (Basingstoke, 2002), pp. 69–70.

33 Jerrold Casway, *Owen Roe O'Neill and the Struggle for Catholic Ireland* (Philadelphia, 1984), p. 65.

34 Sir James Turner, *Memoirs of his Own Life and Times, 1632–1670* (Edinburgh, 1829), p. 26.

35 Robert Monro, *The Scotch Military Discipline Learned from the Valiant Swede* (London, 1644).

36 Turner, *Memoirs*, p. 20.

37 Ibid., pp. 20, 25.

38 Quoted in Charles Carlton, *Going to the Wars: the experience of the British civil wars, 1638–51* (London, 1994), p. 257.

39 *A Letter from the Right Honourable Lord Inchiquin and Other Commanders in Munster to his Majestie* (London, 1644), p. 2.

40 John Rushworth (ed.), *Historical Collections of Private Passages of State, Weighty Matters of Law, Remarkable Proceedings in Five Parliaments,* 7 vols (London, 1680–1701), vol. 5, pp. 953–71.

41 Thomas Emitie, *A New Remonstrance from Ireland: declaring the barbarous cruelty and inhumanity of the Irish rebels against the Protestants there* (London, 1642), p. 5.

42 Mark Stoyle, *Soldiers and Strangers: an ethnic history of the English Civil War* (New Haven, 2005), pp. 209–10; Ian Gentles, *The English Revolution*

and the Wars of the Three Kingdoms, 1638–1652 (Harlow, 2007), p. 203.

43 Keith Lindley and David Scott (eds), *The Journal of Thomas Juxon, 1644–1647*, Camden Fifth Series, vol. 13 (Cambridge, 1999), p. 56.

44 *Two Ordinances of the Lords and Commons Assembled in Parliament, 24 Oct. 1644* (London, 1644).

45 *A Letter from the Earl of Essex to His Highness Prince Rupert . . . with His Highnesse Answer Thereunto* (Bristol, 1645).

46 Will Coster, 'Massacre and codes of conduct in the English Civil War', in Mark Levene and Penny Roberts (eds), *The Massacre in History* (New York and Oxford, 1999), p. 100.

47 Patrick Gordon, *A Short Abridgement of Britane's Distemper, 1639–49* (Aberdeen, 1844), pp. 160–1.

48 Geoffrey Smith and Margaret Toynbee, *Leaders of the Civil Wars, 1642–1648* (Kineton, 1977), p. 131.

49 Quoted in Carlton, *Going to the Wars*, pp. 262–3.

50 'Ormond's report to the king at Hampton Court', BL Egerton MS 2541, ff. 377–81.

51 'Cín Lae Uí Mhealláin', *Louth Archaeological Journal*, vol. 6 (1925), pp. 36–7.

52 *An Exact and Full Relation of the Great Victory Obtained Against the Rebels at Dungans-Hill* (London, 1647), p. 10.

53 Fairfax is quoted in Barbara Donagan, 'Codes and conduct in the English civil war', *Past and Present*, no. 118 (1988), p. 80.

54 *A Collection of Some of the Murthers and Massacres Committed on the Irish in Ireland, Since the 23rd of October 1641* (London, 1662), p. 13.

55 Lenihan, *Confederate Catholics at war*, pp. 209–14.

56 'John Byron's account of the siege of Chester, 1645–6', *Cheshire Sheaf*, vol. 6 (1971), p. 23.

57 *Lawes and Ordinances of Warre, Established for the Good Conduct of the Army, by Colonell Michael Jones* (Dublin, 1647).

CHAPTER 3   PRELUDE TO INVASION

1 *Mercurius Elencticus*, no. 22 (17–24 September 1649), p. 169.

2 *The Marquesse of Ormonds Proclamation Concerning the Peace Concluded with the Irish Rebells . . . with a speech delivered by Sir Richard Blake, Speaker of the Assembly at Kilkenny. Also a speech by the marquesse of Ormond in answer to the same.* (London, 1649).

3 John Milton, *Articles of Peace Made and Concluded with the Irish Rebels . . . Upon all which are added observations* (London, 1649), p. 54.

4 10 February 1649, Bellings to [Lane], Bodl. Carte MS 23, f. 452.

5 14 February 1649 Daniel O'Neill to George Lane, ibid., f. 483.
6 4 April 1649, Bishop French to Ormond, Bodl. Carte MS 24, f. 368; 6 March 1649, Ormond to Inchiquin, Bodl. Carte MS 199, f. 24v.
7 The full list of commissioners is as follows: Alexander MacDonnell, Turlough O'Neill and Myles O'Reilly (Ulster); Lord Dillon, Nicholas Plunkett, Richard Barnewall (Leinster); Geoffrey Browne, Lord Athenry, Lucas Dillon (Connacht); Viscount Muskerry, Donough O'Callaghan, Gerald Fennell (Munster).
8 'Aphorismical Discovery', in J. T. Gilbert (ed.), *A Contemporary History of Affairs in Ireland from 1641 to 1652*, 3 vols (Dublin, 1879–80), vol. 2, p. 44.
9 21 January 1649 Ormond to Lord Hatton, Bodl. Carte MS 23, f. 291.
10 22 January 1649 Ormond to Lord Digby, ibid., f. 303.
11 14 February 1649 Ormond to Henry Jones, ibid., ff. 480–2.
12 16 March 1649, Ormond to Coote, Bodl. Carte MS 24, f. 142.
13 14 March 1649, Michael Jones to Ormond, ibid., f. 129.
14 27 March 1649 Ormond to Michael Jones, ibid., ff. 290–1.
15 31 March 1649, Michael Jones to Ormond, in Gilbert (ed.), *Contemporary History*, vol. 2, pp. 16–17.
16 9 March 1649, William Hyde to [Edgeman], Bodl. Clarendon MS 37, f. 40.
17 'An Account of the war and rebellion in Ireland since the year 1641', National Library of Ireland, MS 345, f. 1006.
18 Richard O'Ferrall and Robert O'Connell, *Commentarius Rinuccinianus, de Sedis Apostolicae Legatione ad Foederatos Hiberniae Catholicos per Annos 1645–9*, 6 vols (Dublin, 1932–49), vol. 4, pp. 300–1.
19 Milton, *Articles of Peace Made and Concluded with the Irish Rebels*, p. 46.
20 4 December 1645, Waller to Sir Philip Percivalle, in *HMC, Egmont MSS*, vol. 1, pp. 264–5.
21 'Cromwell's speech to the General Council of the army at Whitehall, 23 March 1649', in W. C. Abbott (ed.), *The Writings and Speeches of Oliver Cromwell*, 4 vols (Cambridge, 1937–47), vol. 2, pp. 36–9.
22 Quoted in R. A. Stradling, *Europe and the Decline of Spain* (London, 1981), p. 107.
23 'Cromwell's speech to the General Council', in Abbott (ed.), *Writings of Oliver Cromwell*, vol. 2, pp. 36–9.
24 Ireton's words are quoted in Edmund Ludlow, *Memoirs of Edmund Ludlow Esq.*, 2 vols (Vivay, 1698), vol. 1, p. 375.
25 9 May 1649, Council of State, *Calendar of State Papers, Domestic (1649–50)*, p. 132.
26 Thomas Waring, *A Brief Narration of the Plotting, Beginning & Carrying on of that Execrable Rebellion and Butcherie in Ireland* (London, 1650), pp. 41–2, 64.

27 16 November 1650, William Hickman to Oliver Cromwell, in John Nickolls (ed.), *Original Letters and Papers of State Addressed to Oliver Cromwell* (London, 1743), p. 29; Milton, *Articles of Peace Made and Concluded with the Irish Rebels*, pp. 46–9.

28 3 April 1649, Council of State to Colonel Tothill, TNA, SP 25/94, f. 65.

29 28 February 1649, Ormond to Clanricarde, Bodl. Carte MS 23, f. 586.

30 22 January 1649, Ormond to Prince Charles, Bodl. Clarendon MS 34, f. 77.

31 20/30 March 1649, Prince Charles to Ormond, Bodl. Carte MS 24, f. 181.

32 31 March, Hyde to Jermyn, *Clarendon State Papers*, 3 vols (Oxford, 1767–86), vol. 2, pp. 473–4.

33 2/12 April 1649, Lord Byron to Ormond, Bodl. Carte MS 24, f. 416.

34 12 April 1649, Hyde to Berkeley, *Clarendon State Papers*, vol. 2, pp. 476–8.

35 Two copies of this paper exist, one dated 29 March, the other 29 May. See 'Paper delivered by Charles to the States General', Bodl. Clarendon MS 37, ff. 43 and 145.

36 23 March 1649, Ormond to Prince Rupert, Bodl. Carte MS 24, f. 228.

37 27 [March] 1649, Inchiquin to Ormond, ibid., f. 259; 'Report from Cork', 25 March 1649, ibid., ff. 248–9.

38 29 March/8 April 1649, Nicholas to Ormond, ibid., f. 388.

39 23 April 1649, Ormond to Colonel William Legg, ibid., f. 556.

40 29 April 1649, Ormond to Rupert, ibid., ff. 541–2.

41 27 March 1649, Richard Fanshawe to George Lane, ibid., f. 265.

42 5 March 1649, Council of State to the Commissioners of the Navy, TNA, SP 25/94, f. 22.

43 17 April 1649, Council of State to Colonel Horton, ibid., ff. 100–1.

44 1 May 1649, Council of State proceedings, ibid., ff. 126–7.

45 7 May 1649, Council of State to the Generals at Sea, ibid., f. 150.

46 22 May 1649, Legg to Ormond, Bodl. Carte MS 24, ff. 765–6.

47 16 May 1649, Castlehaven to Ormond, Bodl. Carte MS 24, ff. 717, 719.

48 16 May 1649 Darcy to Ormond, ibid., ff. 714–5.

49 23 May 1649, Ormond to Queen Henrietta Maria, ibid., f. 770.

50 29 May 1649, Ormond to Nicholas, ibid., ff. 795–6.

51 28 June 1649, Ormond to Prince Charles, Bodl. Carte MS 25, ff. 19–22.

52 29 May 1649, Ormond to Nicholas, Bodl. Carte MS 24, ff. 795–6.

53 'Aphorismical discovery' in Gilbert (ed.), *Contemporary History*, vol. 2, p. 35.

54 8 August 1649, Ormond to Clanricarde, Bodl. Carte MS 25, f. 193.

55 Aphorismical discovery' in Gilbert (ed.), *Contemporary History*, vol. 2, p. 46.

56 Edmund Borlase, *History of the Execrable Irish Rebellion* (London, 1680),

with manuscript additions, BL Stowe MS 82, f. 241.

57 3 August 1649, Commissioners of Trust to Ormond, Bodl. Carte MS 25, f. 133.

58 3 August 1649, Commissioners of Trust to various corporations, ibid., f. 137.

59 8 August 1649, Ormond to Prince Charles, ibid., f. 195; 27 September 1649, Ormond to the king, ibid., ff. 596–8.

60 8 August 1649, Ormond to Clanricarde, ibid., f. 193.

61 13 August 1649, Ormond to Clanricarde, ibid., f. 252.

CHAPTER 4   CROMWELL AT DROGHEDA AND WEXFORD

1 Thomas Cobbe, 'A poeme uppon Cromwell and his Archtrayterous Rabble of Rebellious Racailles, and English Jaolebirdes', in Andrew Carpenter (ed.), *Verse in English from Tudor and Stuart Ireland* (Cork, 2003), p. 301.

2 *Cromwelliana: A chronological detail of events in which Oliver Cromwell was engaged from the year 1642 to his death 1658* (London, 1810), p. 62.

3 Ormond to Clanricarde, 22 August 1649, Bodl. Carte MS 25, f. 321.

4 13 August 1649, Cromwell to Richard Mayor, in W. C. Abbott (ed.), *The Writings and Speeches of Oliver Cromwell*, 4 vols (Cambridge, 1937–47), vol. 2, p. 103.

5 Quoted ibid., p. 102.

6 16 August 1649, Hugh Peters to the Council of State, in *A Perfect Diurnall of Some Passages in Parliament,* no. 318 (27 August–3 September 1649), p. 2,736.

7 Cromwell's speech of 15 August was published ibid. no. 317 (20–27 August 1649), [p. 2,688].

8 *A Declaration by the Lord Lieutenant of Ireland Concerning his Resolutions for the Peace and Safety of Ireland* (London, 1649) p. 2.

9 Butler also noted that Cromwell hanged troopers for stealing three herrings. The letters of Butler and Castlehaven are in P. H. Hore, *History of the Town and County of Wexford*, 6 vols (London, 1906), vol. 5, pp. 278–80.

10 *A Letter from Sir Lewis Dyve to the Lord Marquis of Newcastle* (The Hague, 1650), p. 28.

11 *The Loyall Declaration of His Excellency the Right Honourable, James, Marquesse of Ormond* (London, 1649), p. 5.

12 23 August 1649, Council of War at Drogheda, Bodl. Carte MS 25, f. 341.

13 Quoted in Charles Carlton, *Going to the Wars: the experience of the British civil wars, 1638–51* (London, 1992) p. 256.

14 10 September 1649, Cromwell to Aston, in J. T. Gilbert (ed.), *A Contemporary History of Affairs in Ireland from 1641 to 1652*, 3 vols (Dublin, 1879–80), vol. 2, p. 260.

15 9 September 1649, Sir Edmund Verney to Ormond, Bodl. Carte MS 25, f. 501.

16 Hewson's letter, written on 22 September, was published in a London news-sheet shortly afterwards. See *Perfect Occurrences of Every Daie Journal of the Parliaments Armies Proceedings* no. 144 (28 September–4 October, 1649), pp. 1275–6.

17 16 September 1649, Cromwell to Bradshaw, in Abbott (ed.), *Writings of Oliver Cromwell*, vol. 2, pp. 124–5.

18 17 September 1649, Cromwell to Lenthall, ibid., pp. 125–8.

19 17 September 1649, Cromwell to Lenthall, ibid.

20 17 September 1649, Cromwell to Lenthall, ibid.

21 Quoted in Geoffrey Parker, *Empire, war and faith in early modern Europe* (London, 2002), p. 155.

22 16 September 1649, Cromwell to Bradshaw, in Abbott (ed.), *Writings of Oliver Cromwell*, vol. 2, pp. 124–5.

23 17 September 1649, Cromwell to Lenthall, ibid., pp. 125–8.

24 17 September 1649, Cromwell to Lenthall, ibid.

25 *A Perfect Diurnall of Some Passages in Parliament . . . 1–8 October* (London, 1649), [p. 2,695].

26 15 September 1649, Inchiquin to Ormond, Bodl. Clarendon MS 38, f. 24.

27 *Severall Proceedings in Parliament* no. 97, (31 July–7 Aug 1651), pp. 1486–90.

28 15 September 1649, Inchiquin to Ormond, Bodl. Clarendon MS 38, f. 24.

29 Sir James Turner, *Memoirs of his Own Life and Times, 1632–1670* (Edinburgh, 1829), p. 47.

30 'Petition of Captain Teague Connor', Bodl. Carte MS 156, f. 272. Dillon's escape is recorded in a 'Narrative of military operations during 1649', Bodl. Carte MS 26, ff. 440–6.

31 Nicholas Bernard, 'The farewell sermons of comfort and concord preached at Drogheda in Ireland', published in his book *The Penitent Death of a Woeful Sinner* (London, 1651, 3rd imp.), pp. 259, 311–13.

32 T. Gogarty (ed.), *Council Book of the Corporation of Drogheda* (Louth, 1988), pp. 24–5.

33 Bernard, 'The farewell sermons of comfort and concord', pp. 320–1. See also *A Brief Relation of that Bloody Storm at Drogheda in Ireland and the Doctors Sufferings by Oliver Cromwell in it, and after it, with his Preservation*, published in Tom Reilly, *Cromwell: an honourable enemy* (Dingle, 1999), pp. 282–4.

34 Ibid.

35 Geraldine Talon (ed.), *Court of claims: Submissions and evidence* (Dublin, 2006), pp. 81, 97, 282, 317.

36 *Letters from Ireland . . . together with a list of the chief commanders, and the number of officers and soldiers slain at Drogheda* (2 October, London, 1649).

37 Thomas Carlyle (ed.), *The letters and speeches of Oliver Cromwell*, 3 vols (London, 1904 edn, with an introduction by C. H. Firth), vol. 1, pp. 474–6.

38 2 October 1649, 'Order in Parliament', TNA, SP 25/87, f. 89.

39 17 October 1649, 'Warrant book of the Committee of Irish Affairs', TNA, SP 21/29, f. 146; 2 October 1649, 'Proceedings of the Council of State', *Calendar of State Papers Domestic, 1649–50* (London, 1875), pp. 327–8.

40 Bulstrode Whitelocke, *Memorials of the English affairs or an historical account* (London, 1682), pp. 411–12.

41 Anthony Wood, *The life of Anthony à Wood from the year 1632 to 1672 written by himself* (Oxford, 1772), pp. 68–9.

42 *Calendar of State Papers, Venetian*, vol. 28 (London, 1927), p. 121; E. S. De Beer (ed.), *The diary of John Evelyn* (London, 1959), p. 281.

43 16/26 October 1649, Secretary Nicholas to Ormond, Bodl. Carte MS 25, ff. 747–8.

44 18 November 1649, James Buck to Sir Ralph Verney, in *HMC, Report 7, appendix* (1879), p. 457.

45 *The moderate messenger* no. 22 (17–24 September 1649), p. 152. The news from the Dublin vessel was published in *A modest narrative of intelligence* no. 25 (15–22 September 1649) pp. 197–200.

46 *Mercurius Elencticus* no. 22 (17–24 September 1649), p. 169.

47 *Mercurius Pragmaticus* no. 24 (25 September–2 October 1649), pp. 7–8. Peters's arrival in Dublin is noted in *Two letters one from Dublin in Ireland, and the other from Liverpoole or a bloody fight in Ireland, at the taking of Drogheda by the Lord Lieutenant Cromwell* (London, 1649), p. 6.

48 *Mercurius Elencticus* no. 21 (10–17 September 1649), p. 167.

49 *The Man in the Moon* no. 24 (26 September–10 October 1649), p. 202.

50 *The Kingdomes Weekly Intelligencer* no. 331 (25 September–2 October 1649), pp. 1518–19, and *Perfect Occurrences of Every Daie Journal of the Parliaments Armies Proceedings* no. 144 (28 September–4 October, 1649), p. 1273, included the phrase, while *The Perfect Weekly Account* (26 September–3 October 1649), p. 622, *Severall Proceedings in Parliament* no. 1 (25 September–9 October 1649), p. 3, and *A Perfect Diurnall of Some Passages in Parliament* no. 323, (1–8 October 1649), p. 2,815, did not.

51 *A Brief Relation of Some Affaires and Transactions, Civil and Military, both forraigne and domestique* no. 1 (2 October 1649), p. 8.

52 *The Moderate Intelligencer* (27 September–4 October 1649), pp. 2,296–7.
53 *Mercurius Elencticus* no. 24 (8–15 October 1649), p. 187.
54 *The Man in the Moon* no. 26 (17–24 October 1649), p. 213.
55 'Aphorismical Discovery' and [September] 1649 Ormond to Charles II, both in Gilbert (ed.), *Contemporary History*, vol. 2, pp. 50, 270.
56 18 September 1649, Ormond to Prince Rupert, Bodl. Carte MS vol. 25, f. 553.
57 27 September 1649, Ormond to Prince Charles, ibid., ff. 596–8.
58 29 September 1649 Ormond to Lord Byron, ibid., ff. 628–30.
59 Richard O'Ferrall and Robert O'Connell, *Commentarius Rinuccinianus, de Sedis Apostolicae Legatione ad Foederatos Hiberniae Catholicos per Annos 1645–9*, 6 vols (Dublin, 1932–49), vol. 4, p. 295.
60 *The Irish Monthly Mercury* no. 1 (Cork, 1649), p. 3
61 The letter from the commander of Wexford, Col. Sinnott, is in Gilbert (ed.), *Contemporary History*, vol. 2, p. 282.
62 3 October 1649, Cromwell to Sinnott, in Abbott (ed.), *Writings of Oliver Cromwell*, vol. 2, p. 136.
63 'Aphorismical Discovery' in Gilbert (ed.), *Contemporary History*, vol. 2, p. 54.
64 14 October 1649, Cromwell to Lenthall, in Abbott (ed.), *Writings of Oliver Cromwell*, vol. 2, pp. 140–3.
65 O'Ferrall and O'Connell, *Commentarius Rinuccinianus*, vol. 4, pp. 296–7; 'Petition of the surviving inhabitants of Wexford', National Library of Ireland, MS 9696, ff. 30–3.
66 *A Perfect and Particular Relation of the Several Marches and Proceedings of the Armies of Ireland from the taking of Drogheda to this Present* (London, 1649), p. 8.
67 17 October 1649, Commissioners of Trust to Ormond, Bodl. Carte MS 25, f. 762.
68 [25 October] 1649, Thomas Roche to Cromwell, BL Add MS 4769B, f. 4; Copies of letters relating to Ireland, 1649–50, with narrative, ibid., f. 8v.
69 27 August 1649, Clanricarde to Ormond, Bodl. Carte MS 25, f. 362.
70 19 September 1649, O'Neill to Ormond, in Gilbert (ed.), *Contemporary History*, vol. 2, p. 276
71 16 October 1649, Daniel O'Neill to Ormond, ibid., pp. 297–8.
72 October 1649, 'Official Account of the proceedings of the English army in Ireland', ibid., pp. 309–10.
73 17 October 1649, Cromwell to Taaffe, in Carlyle (ed.), *The Letters and Speeches of Oliver Cromwell*, vol. 1, p. 490.
74 18 October 1649, Ormond to Commissioners of Trust, Bodl. Carte MS 25, f. 778.

75 19 October 1649, Cromwell to Sir Lucas Taaffe, in Abbott (ed.), *Writings of Oliver Cromwell*, vol. 2, p. 146. See also Gilbert (ed.), *Contemporary History*, vol. 2, pp. 306–7.

76 The Remonstrance and Resolutions of the Protestant Army of Munster now in Corcke, (Cork 1649).

77 23 January 1650, Sir Richard Fanshawe to George Lane, Bodl. Clarendon MS 39, ff. 40–2.

78 'Aphorismical Discovery', in Gilbert (ed.), *Contemporary History*, vol. 2, p. 55.

79 26 August 1649, Taaffe to Ormond, Bodl. Carte MS 25, f. 360.

80 25 September 1649, Daniel O'Neill to the President of Munster, and 1 November 1649, Owen Roe to Ormond, both in Gilbert (ed.), *Contemporary History*, vol. 2, pp. 277–8, 314–5.

81 'Aphorismical Discovery' in Gilbert (ed.), *Contemporary History*, vol. 2, p. 61.

82 October 1649, 'Major Benson's considerations on the bridge at Ross', Bodl. Carte MS 26, f. 70; 4 November 1649, Inchiquin to Ormond, Bodl. Clarendon MS 38, f. 109.

83 11 November 1649, Castlehaven to Ormond and 12 November 1649, Castlehaven to Ormond, Bodl. Carte MS 26, ff. 172, 188.

84 17 November 1649, Castlehaven to Ormond and 22 November 1649, Castlehaven to Ormond, ibid., ff. 223, 254–5.

85 21 November 1649, Mayor of Waterford to Ormond, ibid., f. 247.

86 19 December 1649, Cromwell to Lenthall, in Abbott (ed.), *Writings of Oliver Cromwell*, vol. 2, pp. 176–9.

87 5 December 1649, Ormond to Clanricarde, Bodl. Carte MS 26, f. 326.

88 31 December 1649, Cromwell to John Sadler, in Abbott (ed.), *Writings of Oliver Cromwell*, vol. 2, pp. 186–7.

CHAPTER 5   CROMWELL'S ADVANCE

1 19 December 1649, Inchiquin to Ormond, *Clarendon State Papers*, 3 vols (Oxford, 1767–86), vol. 2, pp. 503–4.

2 6 November 1649, Fanshawe to Ormond, Bodl. Carte MS 26, ff. 118–19.

3 29 November 1649, Ormond to Lord Byron, ibid., f. 276.

4 20 November 1649, Dean Boyle to Ormond, ibid., f. 241.

5 13 November 1649, Bishop of Derry to Lane, and 16 November 1649, Bishop of Derry to Ormond, ibid., ff. 208, 217.

6 *Certain Acts and Declarations Made by the Ecclesiastical Congregation at Clonmacnoise* (Kilkenny, 1649) was one of only a handful of items produced by the Kilkenny press in 1649.

7 *Mercurius Elencticus* no. 24 (8–15 October 1649), pp. 186–7.

8 27 October 1649, Muskerry to Ormond, Bodl. Carte MS 26, ff. 45–6.

9 25 October 1649, Barry to Ormond, ibid., f. 25.

10 16 November 1649, John Walsh to Ormond, ibid., f. 219.

11 Castlehaven related how rumours abounded that Ormond had made a deal with parliament and betrayed Ireland. See 17 November 1649, Castlehaven to Ormond, ibid., f. 223.

12 27 October 1649, Muskerry to Ormond, ibid., ff. 45–6.

13 26 December 1649, Clanricarde to Ormond, ibid., f. 415.

14 22 October 1649, Ormond to Castlehaven, ibid., f. 15.

15 1 November 1649, Castlehaven to the Commissioners of Trust, ibid., ff. 78–9.

16 30 October 1649, Ormond to Muskerry, ibid., f. 55.

17 [September] 1649, Ormond to Prince Charles, in J. T. Gilbert (ed.), *A Contemporary History of Affairs in Ireland from 1641 to 1652*, 3 vols (Dublin, 1879–80), vol. 2, p. 270; 29 September 1649, Ormond to Lord Byron, Bodl. Carte MS 25, ff. 628–30.

18 13 October 1649, Ormond to Owen Roe O'Neill, in Gilbert (ed.), *Contemporary History*, vol. 2, p. 297.

19 30 November 1649, Ormond to Prince Charles, ibid. pp. 329–30.

20 26 June 1650, Ormond to Prince Charles, Bodl. Carte MS 28, [f. 54].

21 4 November 1649, Sir Robert Stewart to Prince Charles, Bodl. Carte MS 130, f. 94.

22 *A Letter from Sir Lewis Dyve to the Lord Marquis of Newcastle from the Hague* (The Hague, 1650), pp. 24, 34–6.

23 26 December 1649, Clanricarde to Ormond, Bodl. Carte MS 26, f. 415.

24 10 November 1649, John Walsh to Ormond, ibid., f. 167.

25 17 November 1649, Castlehaven to Ormond, ibid., f. 223.

26 [Dec, 1649], 'Narrative of military operations during 1649', ibid., f. 446v.

27 1 October 1649, Castlehaven to Rochford, and 5 Oct 1649, Rochford to Ormond, both in Bodl. Carte MS 25, ff. 644, 672.

28 'History' by Richard Bellings in J. T. Gilbert (ed.), *History of the Irish Confederation and the War in Ireland*, 7 vols (Dublin, 1891), vol. 7, p. 7.

29 21 November 1649, Mayor of Waterford to Ormond, Bodl. Carte MS 26, f. 247.

30 30 November 1649, Ormond to Lord Jermyn, ibid., f. 292.

31 17 December 1649, Clanricarde to Ormond, ibid., f. 388.

32 15 December 1649, Ormond to Prince Charles, ibid., ff. 381–3.

33 *A Declaration of the Lord Lieutenant of Ireland, for the Undeceiving of Deluded and Seduced People*, in W. C. Abbott (ed.), *The Writings and Speeches of Oliver Cromwell*, 4 vols (Cambridge, 1937–47), vol. 2, pp. 196–205.

34 Ibid.

35 17 September 1649, Cromwell to Lenthall, in Abbott (ed.), *Writings of Oliver Cromwell*, vol. 2, pp. 125–8.

36 James Scott Wheeler, *Cromwell in Ireland* (Dublin, 1999), p. 119.

37 16 February 1650, Ormond to Clanricarde, Bodl. Carte MS 26, f. 696.

38 27 February 1650, Clanricarde – intelligence out of King's County, Bodl. Carte MS 27, f. 39; 21 March 1650, George Lane to Lord Dillon, ibid., f. 157.

39 18 February 1650, Ormond to Castlehaven, Bodl. Carte MS 142, f. 131.

40 25 March 1650, Castlehaven to Ormond, Bodl. Carte MS 27, ff. 198–9; 23 March 1650, Lord Dillon to George Lane, in Gilbert (ed.), *Contemporary History*, vol. 2, pp. 373–4.

41 25 March 1650, Castlehaven to George Lane, and 25 March 1650, Castlehaven to Ormond, both in Bodl. Carte MS 27, ff. 196, 198–9.

42 2 April 1650, Cromwell to Lenthall, in Abbott (ed.), *Writings of Oliver Cromwell*, vol. 2, pp. 231–5.

43 4 April 1650, Inchiquin to Ormond, Bodl. Carte MS 27, f. 244.

44 3 April 1650, Butler to Ormond, ibid., f. 240; Richard O'Ferrall and Robert O'Connell, *Commentarius Rinuccinianus, de Sedis Apostolicae Legatione ad Foederatos Hiberniae Catholicos per Annos 1645–9*, 6 vols (Dublin, 1932–49), vol. 4, pp. 387–90.

45 3 April 1650, Butler to Ormond, Bodl. Carte MS 27, f. 240.

46 2 April 1650, Cromwell to Richard Mayor, Abbott (ed.), *Writings of Oliver Cromwell*, vol. 2, p. 235.

47 8 November 1649, Ormond to John Walsh, Bodl. Carte MS 26, f. 141.

48 3 March 1650, Ormond to O'Neill and 27 April 1650, O'Neill & mayor of Clonmel to Ormond, both in Gilbert (ed.), *Contemporary History*, vol. 2, pp. 368, 398.

49 Edmund Hogan (ed.), *The History of the Warr of Ireland from 1641 to 1653 by a British Officer of the Regiment of Sir John Clotworthy* (Dublin, 1873), p. 111.

50 P. O'Connell and W. Darmody (eds.), *Siege of Clonmel Commemoration: tercentenary souvenir record* (Clonmel, 1950), pp 26–7. See also May 1650, S. Dillingham to Sancroft, in Charles McNeill (ed.), *The Tanner Letters* (Dublin, 1943), p. 329.

51 *A Perfect Diurnall . . . of the Armies in England and Ireland* no. 25 (27 May–3 June, 1650), p. 277.

52 Hogan (ed.), *History of the Warr of Ireland*, p. 109.

53 *A Perfect Diurnall . . . of the Armies in England and Ireland* no. 26 (3–10 June, 1650), p. 284; ibid., no. 25 (27 May–3 June, 1650), pp. 278–80.

54 The translation of Milton's work is in F. A. Patterson (ed.), *The Works of*

John Milton, 18 vols (New York, 1931–8), vol. 8, p. 219; for Marvell see Nigel Smith (ed.), *The Poems of Andrew Marvell* (Harlow, 2007 edn), pp. 273–9.

55 16 March 1650, Ormond to Commissioners of Trust, Bodl. Carte MS 27, f. 124; 22 March, Commissioners of Trust to Ormond, ibid., f. 164.

56 17 May 1650, Ormond to Cromwell, ibid., f. 519; 30 April 1650, Axtell to Preston, ibid., f. 396.

57 18 April 1650, Sir George Monro to Ormond, ibid., f. 333.

58 17 April 1650, Inchiquin to Commissioners of Trust, ibid., f. 311.

59 15 Feb 1650, Ormond to Prince Charles, Bodl. Carte MS 26, f. 682.

60 5 March 1650, Clanricarde to the bishops gathered at Limerick, Bodl. Carte MS 27, ff. 33–4.

61 5 March 1650, Clanricarde to Ormond, ibid., f. 37.

62 8 March 1650, Demands of the clergy and Commissioners of Trust at Limerick, Royal Irish Academy, MS H.VI.I (Collection of papers relating to Ireland), ff. 51v–57.

63 27 March 1650, Inchiquin to Ormond, Bodl. Carte MS 27, f. 207.

64 9 April 1650, Ormond to Inchiquin, ibid., f. 273.

65 7 April 1650, Gerald Fennell to Ormond, ibid., f. 253.

66 8 April 1650, John Walsh to Ormond, ibid., f. 270.

67 [10 April] 1650, Ormond to Walsh, ibid., f. 264.

68 9 April 1650, Ormond to Darcy, ibid., f. 278.

69 10 April 1650, Ormond to the bishop of Derry, ibid., f. 285.

70 14 April 1650, Richard Everard & Gerald Fennell to Ormond, ibid., f. 303.

71 24 April 1650, Daniel O'Neill to Ormond, ibid., f. 346.

72 Correspondence between the Assembly at Loughrea and Ormond, Royal Irish Academy, MS H.VI.I, ff. 65–73.

73 14 May 1650, John Creagh to Ormond, Bodl. Carte MS 27, f. 511.

CHAPTER 6   ROYALIST COLLAPSE

1 Richard O'Ferrall and Robert O'Connell, *Commentarius Rinuccinianus, de Sedis Apostolicae Legatione ad Foederatos Hiberniae Catholicos per Annos 1645–9*, 6 vols (Dublin, 1932–49), vol. 4, pp. 360–2.

2 'Aphorismical Discovery', in Gilbert, (ed.), *A Contemporary History of Affairs in Ireland from 1641 to 1652*, 3 vols (Dublin, 1879–80), vol. 2, p. 70.

3 Ibid., p. 84; Edmund Hogan (ed.), *The History of the Warr of Ireland from 1641 to 1653 by a British Officer of the Regiment of Sir John Clotworthy* (Dublin, 1873), p. 115.

4 16 February 1650, Ormond to Clanricarde, Bodl. Carte MS 26, f. 696.

5 7 May 1650, Westmeath to [Ormond], Bodl. Carte 27, f. 467.

6 26 December 1649, Clanricarde to Ormond, Bodl. Carte MS 26, f. 415

7 14 May 1650, Clanricarde to Ormond, Bodl. Carte MS 27, f. 505.

8 1 June 1650, Clogher to Ormond, and 30 May 1650, Clogher to Beresford, both in Gilbert (ed.), *Contemporary History*, vol. 2, pp. 421, 423.

9 *Severall Proceedings in Parliament* no. 41 (1–8 July 1650), p. 578.

10 'Aphorismical Discovery', in Gilbert (ed.), *Contemporary History*, vol. 2, p. 88.

11 18 August 1650, Ulster bishops and others to Ormond, ibid., vol. 3, p. 173.

12 The evidence that Ormond reneged on his promises comes from an admittedly hostile, if contemporary, source. See 'Aphorismical discovery' in Gilbert (ed.), *Contemporary History*, vol. 2, p. 70.

13 3 June 1650, Ormond to Clanricarde, Bodl. Carte MS 27, f. 611.

14 4 June 1650, Clanricarde to Ormond, ibid., f. 618.

15 8 June 1650, Ormond to Clanricarde, ibid., f. 633.

16 23 June Clanricarde to Ormond, Bodl. Carte MS 28, f. 18.

17 23 June 1650, Clanricarde to Ormond, ibid., f. 18.

18 26 June 1650, Clanricarde to Ormond, and 28 June 1650, Clanricarde to Ormond, both ibid., ff. 50, 79.

19 1 July 1650, Ormond to Clanricarde, ibid., f. 107.

20 3 April 1650, Preston to Ormond, and 29 April 1650 Preston to Ormond, both in Bodl. Carte MS 27, ff. 243, 389, 391–2.

21 17 April 1650, Proceedings against John Leonard, ibid., ff. 404–5.

22 8 May 1650, Ormond to Preston, ibid., f. 478.

23 5 June 1650, Address from the mayor, council and citizens of Waterford to Preston, ibid., ff. 627–8.

24 10 June 1650, Preston to Ormond, ibid., ff. 641–2.

25 19 June 1650, Ormond to Taaffe, ibid., f. 726.

26 2 July 1650, Preston to Ormond, Bodl. Carte MS 28, ff. 110–11.

27 13 July 1650, Ormond to Preston, ibid., f. 172.

28 10 August 1650, Preston to Ormond, ibid., ff. 292–3.

29 14 June 1650, Ormond to Clanricarde, Bodl. Carte MS 27, f. 680

30 30 May 1650, Stackpoole and Comyn, report from Limerick, ibid., ff. 577–8.

31 5 June 1650, Colonel Walsh to Ormond, ibid., f. 623.

32 11 June 1650, Clanricarde to Ormond, ibid., f. 655.

33 14 June 1650, Ormond to mayor of Limerick, ibid., f. 678.

34 6 July 1650, Clanricarde to the Father Provincial of the Dominican Order, Bodl. Carte MS 28, f. 140.

35 15 June 1650, Colonel Walsh to Ormond, Bodl. Carte MS 27, f. 682.

36 16 June 1650, Ormond to Taaffe, ibid., f. 729.

37 26 June 1650, Ormond to Prince Charles; 26 June 1650, Ormond to Lord

Byron, and 27 June 1650, Ormond to Lord Jermyn, all in Bodl. Carte MS 28, ff. [54], [55], 66–7.

38 29 June 1650, Ormond to the mayor of Limerick, and 30 June 1650, Ormond to Clanricarde, both ibid., ff. 78, 89.

39 5 July 1650, Ormond to Clanricarde, ibid., ff. 137–8.

40 10 July 1650, Ormond to Clanricarde, ibid., f. 156.

41 12 July 1650, Ormond to John Walsh, ibid., f. 167.

42 20 July 1650, Ormond to Clanricarde; 19 July 1650, Ormond to Clanricarde; 19 July 1650, Declaration by the mayor and corporation of Galway, all ibid., ff. 152, 213–14.

43 14 July 1650, Ormond to Muskerry, ibid., f. 178.

44 18 July 1650, Ormond to Secretary Long, ibid., ff. 205–6.

45 16 August 1650, 'Declaration by Charles II', Bodl. Clarendon MS 40, ff. 160v–161.

46 *A Perfect Diurnall . . . of the Armies in England and Ireland* no. 42 (23/30 September 1650), [p. 553].

47 'Aphorismical discovery' in Gilbert (ed.), *Contemporary History*, vol. 2, p. 126.

48 24 July 1650, bishops to Ormond, Bodl. Carte MS 28, f. 228.

49 2 August 1650, Ormond to the bishops, ibid., ff. 259–60.

50 12 August 1650, Declaration by the bishops at Jamestown against the continuance of Ormond's government, ibid., ff. 300–2.

51 13 August 1650, Bishop Dromore and Dr Kelly to Ormond, ibid., f. 303.

52 Ibid. (with Ormond's reply), ff. 303, 305.

53 'Regarding alleged breaches of the treaty', Royal Irish Academy, MS H.VI.I (Collection of papers relating to Ireland), ff. 92v–145.

54 20 August 1650, Ormond to Clanricarde, both in Bodl. Carte MS 28, f. 355.

55 31 August 1650, Ormond's reply to the bishops, ibid., ff. 408–9.

56 2 September 1650, Ormond to Secretary Long, and 2 September 1650, Ormond to Prince Charles, both ibid., ff. 413–14, 421.

57 9 September 1650, Waller to the Commander in Chief of Limerick, ibid., f. 433.

58 13 September 1650, Catholic bishops to the bishop of Clonfert and Dr Kelly, ibid., f. 448.

59 21 September 1650, bishops to commanders of Leinster forces, ibid., f. 488.

60 16 September 1650, Ormond to Viscount Dillon, ibid., f. 465.

61 17 September 1650, Stackpoole to Ormond, ibid., f. 467.

62 18 September 1650 O'Neill to Ormond, Bodl. Carte MS 30, f. 353; 19 September 1650, Inchiquin to Ormond, Bodl. Carte MS 28, f. 479.

63 11 October 1650, Muskerry to Ormond, Bodl. Carte MS 28, f. 554.

64 6 October 1650, 'Protest against declarations of the bishops', ibid., f. 529.

65 14 October 1650, Mayor of Limerick to Ormond, ibid., f. 563.

66 2 November 1650, Clanricarde to Ormond, ibid., f. 614.

67 23 October 1650, The bishop of Limerick to John Walsh, ibid., f. 591.

68 15 October 1650, Relation by Dean King to Ormond, ibid., ff. 567–8.

69 October 1650, Commissioners of Trust to Ormond, Royal Irish Academy, MS H.VI.I, ff. 148v–151v.

70 29 October 1650, Commissioners of Trust to Committee of Congregation [at Galway], with answers, ibid., ff. 152–71.

71 2 November 1650, Clanricarde to Ormond, Bodl. Carte MS 28, f. 614; 14 November 1650, Ormond to Castlehaven, ibid., f. 634.

72 30 November 1650, 'Address by Blake on behalf of the Assembly', ibid., f. 681.

73 6 December 1650, Ormond to Clanricarde, and 9 December 1650, Ormond to Clanricarde, both in Bodl. Carte MS 29, ff. 4, 14.

74 *A Perfect Diurnall . . . of the Armies in England and Ireland* no. 48 (4–11 November 1650), p. 615.

CHAPTER 7   FOREIGN INTERVENTION

1 'Aphorismical discovery', in J. T. Gilbert (ed.), *A Contemporary History of Affairs in Ireland from 1641 to 1652,* 3 vols (Dublin, 1879–80), vol. 3, p. 49. A version of this chapter appeared in *The Historical Journal,* 48, 4 (2005), pp. 905–32.

2 Fritz Redlich, *The German Military Enterpriser and his Work Force,* 2 vols (Wiesbaden, 1964–5), vol. 1, pp. 370–1; vol. 2, pp. 5–7.

3 3 October 1627, Marc Antonio Padavin, Venetian ambassador in Savoy, to the Doge and Senate, in *Calendar of State Papers [CSP], Venetian, 1626–8,* p. 405.

4 *The Lord Digby's Cabinet and Dr Goff's Negotiations* (London, 1646), p. 8.

5 Richard O'Ferrall and Robert O'Connell, *Commentarius Rinuccinianus, de Sedis Apostolicae Legatione ad Foederatos Hiberniae Catholicos per Annos 1645–9,* 6 vols (Dublin, 1932–49), vol. 4, pp. 409–13.

6 28 June 1649, Ormond to Prince Charles, Bodl. Carte MS 25, ff. 19–22; 29 May 1649, Ormond to Nicholas, Bodl. Carte MS 24, ff. 795–6.

7 *The Marquesse of Ormond's Letter to His Majestie King Charles II* (London, 1649); *Joyfull Newes from the Marquesse of Ormond and the Princes army in Ireland* (London, 1649).

8 O'Ferrall and O'Connell, *Commentarius Rinuccinianus,* vol. 4, pp 369–74.

9 21 April 1648, Giovanni Battista Nani, Venetian ambassador in France, to the Doge and Senate, in *CSP, Venetian, 1647–52,* pp. 54–5.

10 2/12 March 1650, Long to Ormond, Bodl. Carte MS 27, ff. 82–3; 16 January 1650, Charles to Ormond, Bodl. Carte MS 26, f. 512.

11 11 February 1650, Nicholas to Ormond, ibid., ff. 652–3.

12 20/30 March 1650, Long to Ormond, Bodl. Carte MS 27, f. 144.

13 1 April 1650, Prince Charles to Ormond, and 'Instructions', both ibid., ff. 221, 232.

14 18 July 1650, Ormond to Secretary Long, Bodl. Carte MS 28, ff. 205–6; 1 April 1650, Long to Ormond, Bodl. Carte MS 27, ff. 230–1.

15 8 April 1650, de Vic to Ormond, and 10 April 1650, de Vic to Ormond, both Bodl. Carte MS 27, ff. 268–9, 281.

16 22 May 1650, Rochford to Ormond, ibid., f. 544.

17 5 June 1650, Ormond to Clanricarde, ibid., f. 625.

18 19 June 1650, Ormond to Taaffe, and 10 June 1650, Instructions from Ormond to Taaffe for Prince Charles, both ibid., ff. 637–8, 726

19 25 June 1650, Instructions from Ormond for Taaffe, Athenry, Browne in treaty with Synott, Bodl. Carte MS 28, f. 46.

20 30 June 1650, Browne to Ormond, ibid., f. 88.

21 1 July 1650, Clanricarde to Ormond, ibid., f. 98. See also 1 July 1650, Synott to Ormond, in Gilbert (ed.), *Contemporary History*, vol. 2, p. 432.

22 18 July 1650, Ormond to Long, Bodl. Carte MS 28, ff. 205–6.

23 3 December 1650, Taaffe to Lady Ormond, and 3 Jan 1651, Taaffe to Ormond, both in Bodl. Carte MS 29, ff. 5, 152–3.

24 *A Perfect Diurnall . . . of the Armies in England and Ireland* no. 44 (30 September–7 October 1650), [p. 477].

25 3 January 1651, Taaffe to Ormond, Bodl. Carte MS 29, ff. 152–3; 1 Jan 1651, Lorraine to the Lords of the Kingdom, in Ulick Bourke, *Clanricarde Memoirs* (Dublin, 1744), pp. 145–6.

26 29 April 1651, Taaffe to Ormond, Bodl. Carte MS 29, ff. 427–8.

27 3 January 1651, Taaffe to Ormond, ibid., ff. 152–3.

28 5 January 1651, Taaffe to Ormond, ibid., f. 154.

29 18 February 1651, Clanricarde to Ormond, ibid., ff. 246–7.

30 18 February 1651, Clanricarde to Ormond, ibid., ff. 246–7. See also O'Ferrall and O'Connell, *Commentarius Rinuccinianus*, vol. 4, pp. 539–44, 565–7.

31 16 March 1651, George Lane to Ormond, Bodl. Carte MS 29, ff. 320–2.

32 Bourke, *Clanricarde Memoirs*, pp. 14–17.

33 10 April 1650, Bellings to Ormond, in J. T. Gilbert (ed.), *History of the Irish Confederation and the War in Ireland*, 7 vols (Dublin, 1891), vol. 7, pp. 367–71.

34 Bourke, *Clanricarde Memoirs*, pp. 45–7.

35 James Tuchet, *The Earl of Castlehaven's Review or his Memoirs* (London,

1684), p. 171; 12 April 1651, Clanricarde to Ormond, in Bourke, *Clanricarde Memoirs*, pp. 63–7.

36 12 April 1650, Clanricarde to Taaffe, Bodl. Carte MS 29, ff. 384v–85.

37 12 April 1650, Instructions for Taaffe, Plunkett and Browne, in Bourke, *Clanricarde memoirs*, pp. 53–6.

38 *Severall Proceedings in Parliament* no. 81 (10–17 April 1651), pp. 1240–1.

39 [April] 1651, Parliamentary commissioners for the affairs of Ireland, in Henry Cary (ed.), *Memorials of the Great Civil War in England from 1646 to 1652*, 2 vols (London, 1842), vol. 2, pp. 253–7; 8 May 1651, Council of State to Ireton, in *CSP, Domestic, 1651*, p. 186.

40 *Severall Proceedings in Parliament* no. 87 (22–29 May 1651), p. 1331.

41 *Faithful Scout* no. 17 (11–18 April 1651), p. 135; 5 September 1651, Council of State, *CSP, Domestic, 1651*, p. 410.

42 *A Perfect Diurnall . . . of the Armies in England and Ireland* no. 76 (19–26 May 1651), [p. 1058].

43 *Faithful Scout* no. 22 (16–23 May 1650), p. 171.

44 Edmund Ludlow, *Memoirs of Edmund Ludlow Esq.*, 2 vols (Vivay, 1698), vol. 1, p. 348.

45 James Scott Wheeler, *Cromwell in Ireland* (Dublin, 1999), p. 195.

46 'Aphorismical Discovery', in Gilbert (ed.), *Contemporary History*, vol. 2, pp. 161–2.

47 *A Perfect Diurnall . . . of the Armies in England and Ireland* no. 71 (14–21 April 1651), p. 968.

48 29 April 1651, Taaffe to Ormond, Bodl. Carte MS 29, ff. 427–8.

49 29 May 1651, Ormond to Digby; 4 June 1651, Digby to Ormond, all ibid., ff. 492, 507.

50 8 June 1651, Ormond to Inchiquin, ibid., f. 519.

51 24 June 1651, Browne to Ormond, ibid, ff. 565–6.

52 3 August 1651, Ormond to Nicholas, BL, Egerton MS 2534 (Nicholas Papers), f. 103; 30 June 1651, Ormond to Hyde, Bodl. Carte MS 29, f. 576.

53 21 July 1651, Hyde to Ormond, ibid., f. 624.

54 July 1651, Bishop French to Viscount Taaffe, Geoffrey Browne and Sir Nicholas Plunkett, 'Aphorismical Discovery' in Gilbert (ed.), *Contemporary History*, vol. 2, p. 152.

55 1 August 1651, 'Ulster congregation at Cloughoughter', ibid., pp. 182–3.

56 24 September 1651, 'Ecclesiastical Congregation at Belladrohide in Leinster', ibid., vol. 3, pp. 12–13.

57 22 July 1651, 'Articles of agreement', in *HMC, Ormonde MSS* (new series), vol. 1, pp. 173–6.

58 31 July/10 August 1651, Taaffe to Ormond, ibid., pp. 182–3.

59 20 September 1651, Lorraine to Clanricarde, in Burke, *Clanricarde*

Memoirs, pp. 83–4.

60 [April] 1652, Statement by agent of Lorraine, and 14 April 1652, Lorraine to the Irish commissioners, both in Bodl. Clarendon MS 43, ff. 66–7, 71.

61 The views of a French traveller in 1644 are quoted in Jane Ohlmeyer (ed.), *Ireland from Independence to Occupation, 1641–1660* (Cambridge, 1995), pp. 80–1.

62 20 October 1651, Clanricarde to Lorraine, and 20 October 1651, Clanricarde to Plunkett & Browne, both in Bourke, *Clanricarde Memoirs*, pp. 85–7, 88–92.

63 15 October 1651, Mayor & council of Galway to Lorraine, ibid., pp. 98–9; 19 November 1651, Colonel Jones to Thomas Scott, in Joseph Mayer (ed.), 'Inedited letters of Cromwell, Col. Jones, Bradshaw and other regicides', *Transactions of the Historic Society of Lancashire and Cheshire* (ns), vol. 1 (1860–1), p. 195.

64 18 October 1651, Mayor of Galway to Clanricarde, in Bourke, *Clanricarde Memoirs*, pp. 101–2; 13 November 1651, Clanricarde's instructions to John Lambert, Bodl. Clarendon MS 42, ff. 246–7.

65 *A Perfect Diurnall . . . of the Armies in England and Ireland* no. 103 (24 November–1 December 1651), [pp. 1500–1].

66 *Severall Proceedings* no. 114 (27 November–4 December 1651), pp. 1762–7.

67 Ibid.

68 Quoted in article on Geoffrey Barron by Father Athanasius in *The Commemoration of the Siege of Limerick* (Limerick, 1951), pp. 52–60.

69 'Aphorismical discovery' in Gilbert (ed.), *Contemporary History*, vol. 3, p. 21; Ludlow, *Memoirs*, vol. 1, pp. 374–5.

70 20/30 September 1651, Taaffe to Ormond, in *HMC, Ormonde MSS* (new series), vol. 1, pp. 212–3.

71 7 December 1651, Instructions for Patrick Archer, ibid., pp. 250–3.

72 17/27 March 1652, Ormond to Clanricarde, and 'Considerations on the articles with Lorraine', both in Bourke, *Clanricarde Memoirs*, pp. 127–31, 134–44.

73 5 January 1651, Taaffe to Ormond, Bodl. Carte MS 29, f. 154; 23 March 1652, Prince Charles to Clanricarde, in Bourke, *Clanricarde Memoirs*, pp. 119–21.

74 29 November 1651, Propositions of Clanricarde for Galway and 10 December 1651 Clanricarde to mayor and council of Galway, both in *HMC, Ormonde MSS* (new series), vol. 1, pp. 238–40, 243–4.

75 12 February 1652, Blake to Clanricarde, Clarendon MS 42, f. 387.

76 24 February 1652, Ludlow to Clanricarde, Clarendon MS 43, f. 13.

77 9 March 1652, Blake to Ludlow, ibid., f. 34.

78 12 April 1652, Clanricarde to Philip MacHugh O'Reilly, in Gilbert (ed.)

Contemporary History, vol. 3, p. 76.

79 4 October 1652, Hyde to Nicholas, in *Clarendon State Papers*, 3 vols (Oxford, 1767–86), vol. 3, pp. 103–5.

80 15 January 1653, Parliamentary Commissioners to Sir Hardress Waller, in Robert Dunlop (ed.), *Ireland under the Commonwealth*, 2 vols (Manchester, 1913), vol. 2, p. 311.

81 28 July 1653, 'Report from J. Peterson in Holland', in Thomas Birch (ed.), *A Collection of the State Papers of John Thurloe,* 7 vols (London, 1742), vol. 1, p. 384. See also 28 March 1653, Hyde to Rochester, Bodl. Clarendon MS 44, f. 192.

82 14 April 1652, Duke of Lorraine to the Irish Commissioners, Bodl. Clarendon MS 43, f. 71.

CHAPTER 8 GUERRILLA WAR

1 [1652], 'Some particulars in order to break the enemy's strength' in Robert Dunlop (ed.), *Ireland under the Commonwealth*, 2 vols (Manchester, 1913), vol. 1, pp. 119-20.

2 7 October 1651, Commissioners in Ireland to the Council of State, ibid., pp. 61–2.

3 18 September 1651, Commissioners in Ireland to parliament, and 23 September 1651, Commissioners in Ireland to the Council of State, both ibid., pp. 49–50, 57.

4 Nicholas Canny, *Making Ireland British, 1580–1650* (Oxford, 2001), p. 570.

5 Clanricarde quoted in Mary O'Dowd, *Power, Politics and Land: early modern Sligo, 1568–1688* (Belfast, 1991), pp. 128–9.

6 *Severall Proceedings in Parliament* no. 53 (26 September–3 October 1650), p. 780.

7 *A Perfect Diurnall . . . of the Armies in England and Ireland* no. 64 (24 February–3 March 1651), pp. 866–7.

8 *Faithful Scout* no. 15 (28 March–4 April 1651), p. 119.

9 *Faithful Scout* no. 47 (5–12 December 1651), p. 368; 8 October 1651, Commissioners to Parliament, in Dunlop (ed.), *Commonwealth*, vol.1, p. 64.

10 *Severall Proceedings in Parliament* no. 84 (1–8 May 1651), pp. 1278, 1282.

11 *Faithful Scout* no. 28 (20–27 June 1651), p. 213.

12 23 September 1651, Commissioners to Council of State, in Dunlop (ed.), *Commonwealth*, vol. 1, p. 57.

13 1 July 1651, Commissioners to Council of State, and 21 August 1651, Commissioners to Council of State, both ibid., pp. 6–9, 27–8.

14 1 July 1651, Commissioners to Parliament, ibid., pp. 5–6.

15 2 September 1651, 'Order by Parliamentary Commissioners', ibid., p. 32.

16 *A Perfect Diurnall . . . of the Armies in England and Ireland* no. 97 (13–20 October 1651), [p. 1385].

17 'Aphorismical discovery', in J. T. Gilbert (ed.), *A contemporary history of affairs in Ireland from 1641 to 1652,* 3 vols (Dublin, 1879–80), vol. 3, p. 1.

18 18 September 1651, Commissioners to Parliament, in Dunlop (ed.), *Commonwealth,* vol. 1, pp. 49–50.

19 25 March 1652, 'Order by the parliamentary commissioners', ibid., p. 162.

20 *Severall Proceedings in Parliament* no. 105 (25 September–2 October 1651), p. 1628.

21 7 October 1651, Commissioners to Council of State, in Dunlop (ed.), *Commonwealth,* vol. 1, pp. 61–2.

22 *Perfect Passages of Every Daies Intelligence from the Parliaments Army* no. 46 (5–12 December 1651), pp. 327–8.

23 *Faithful Scout* no. 47 (5–12 December 1651), p. 366.

24 24 July/3 August 1651, Ormond to Inchiquin, in *HMC, Ormonde MSS* (new series), vol. 1, p. 178.

25 'Some particulars offered in order to the breaking of the enemy's strength', and 'Counties in Ireland yielding as yet on contribution of profit', both in Dunlop (ed.), *Commonwealth,* vol. 1, pp. 118–20, 140.

26 *A Perfect Diurnall . . . of Armies in England and Ireland* no. 44 (7–14 October 1650), [p. 479].

27 Ibid. no. 42(?) (23–30 September 1650), [p. 536].

28 'Some particulars offered in order to the breaking of the enemy's strength', in Dunlop (ed.), *Commonwealth,* vol. 1, pp. 118–20.

29 *A Perfect Diurnall . . . of the Armies in England and Ireland* no. 103 (24 November–1 December 1651), p. 1475.

30 26 November 1655, Giovanni Sagredo, Venetian ambassador in England to the Doge and Senate, in *CSP, Venetian, 1655–6,* pp. 142–3.

31 4 July 1649, Council of State, 'Day's proceedings', in *CSP, Domestic, 1649–50,* p. 221.

32 Clement Walker is quoted in David Underdown, *Royalist Conspiracy in England, 1649–1660* (Hew Haven, 1960), p. 20.

33 *A Defensive Declaration of Lieut. Col. John Lilburn* (London, 1653), p. 6.

34 C. H. Firth (ed.), 'Thomas Scot's account of his actions as Intelligencer during the Commonwealth', *English Historical Review,* vol. 12 (1897), p. 121. See also Philip Aubrey, *Mr Secretary Thurloe: Cromwell's Secretary of State, 1652–1660* (London, 1990), pp. 28, 43.

35 6 September 1653, Captain George Bishop to the Council of State, *CSP, Domestic, 1653–4,* pp. 133–4.

36 Henry Hexham, *The second part of the principles of the art military,*

practised in the warres of the United Provinces (London, 1642), p. 13.

37 2 May 1649, Letter Book of the Council of State, TNA, SP 25/94, f. 129. 10 April and 2 May 1649, Council of State, day's proceedings, *CSP, Domestic, 1649–50*, pp. 77, 121.

38 23 January 1650, Sir Richard Fanshawe to George Lane, Bodl. Clarendon MS 39, ff. 40–2; 20 December 1649, Ormond to Clanricarde, Bodl. Carte MS 26, ff. 390–1.

39 Crelly's relationship with Scott is described in Firth (ed.), 'Thomas Scot's account', pp. 119–21.

40 11 May 1650, Ormond to Clanricarde, Bodl. Carte MS 27, f. 491.

41 These figures are taken from James Scott Wheeler, *Cromwell in Ireland* (Dublin, 1999), pp. 193–4.

42 5 February 1652, Commissioners to Council of State, in Dunlop (ed.), *Commonwealth*, vol. 1, pp. 132–4.

43 4 June 1647, Coote to Percivall, in *HMC, Egmont MSS*, vol. 1, pp. 412–3.

44 TCD MS 838 (Antrim Depositions), ff. 9, 11, 13.

45 Cromwell's speech of 15 August in *A Perfect Diurnall of Some Passages in Parliament, 20–27 Aug* (London, 1649) [p. 2,688]; *A Declaration by the Lord Lieutenant of Ireland Concerning his Resolutions for the Peace and Safety of Ireland* (London, 1649) pp. 1–2.

46 'A short view of the state and condition of the kingdom of Ireland from the year 1640 to this time', Bodl. Clarendon MS 121, f. 73v.

47 3 March 1650, John Hewson to Speaker Lenthall, in Gilbert (ed.), *Contemporary History*, vol. 2, pp. 370–2.

48 Castlehaven vowed to 'destroy all contributors with fire and sword'. See 28 March 1650, Castlehaven to Ormond, Bodl. Carte MS 27, ff. 217–8.

49 24 July 1650, Dublin and Tuam to Ormond, Royal Irish Academy, MS H.VI.I (Collection of papers relating to Ireland), ff. 78–9.

50 2 August 1650, Ormond to Archbishops of Tuam and Dublin, Bodl. Carte MS 28, ff. 259–60.

51 19 August 1650, Clanricarde to Ormond, ibid., f. 349; *A Perfect and Particular Relation of the Several Marches and Proceedings of the Armies of Ireland from the Taking of Drogheda to this Present* (London, 1649), p. 8.

52 3 August 1650, Ormond to Clanricarde, Bodl. Carte MS 28, f. 263.

53 Quoted in J. P. Prendergast, *The Cromwellian Settlement of Ireland* (London, 1996 edn), p. 46.

54 9 September 1659, 'Order for inquiry', in Dunlop (ed.), *Commonwealth*, vol. 2, pp. 711–12.

55 Edmund Borlase, *The History of the Execrable Irish Rebellion* (London, 1680), with manuscript additions, BL, Stowe MS 82, f. 215.

56 27 August 1651, Clanricarde to Richard Fanshawe, in *HMC, Ormonde*

MSS (new series), vol. 1, p. 195; 10 September 1650, 'Proclamation by Ormond', Bodl. Carte MS 162, f. 331.

57 12 December 1651, 'Assembly at Ross', in Gilbert (ed.), *Contemporary History*, vol. 3, p. 27.

58 25 May 1652, 'Leinster Congregation', ibid., pp. 111–12

59 6 May 1652, Commissioners in Dublin to Council of State, in Charles McNeill (ed.), *The Tanner Letters* (Dublin, 1943), pp. 360–3; 'The Aphorismical Discovery' in Gilbert (ed.), *Contemporary History*, vol. 3, p. 69.

60 *A letter from Sir Lewis Dyve to the Lord Marquis of Newcastle . . . Sept 1648–July 1650* (The Hague, 1650), p. 41.

61 'A short view of the state and condition of the kingdom of Ireland', Bodl. Clarendon MS 121, f. 76v.

62 'Aphorismical Discovery' in Gilbert (ed.), *Contemporary History*, vol. 2, p. 136.

63 'Aphorismical Discovery' ibid., p. 131.

64 25 February 1650[1], 'Proclamation published by Colonel Hewson', King's Inns, Prendergast Papers, vol. 1, ff. 719–23.

65 'Orders of State: Commissioners of Parliament for the Affairs of Ireland, 27 Feb. 1650', BL, Egerton MS 1761, ff. 6v–9v. Similarly, in September 1649, Ormond ordered all inhabitants within a 15-mile radius of the parliamentary–held city of Dublin to withdraw or be treated as enemies. See *Mercurius Elencticus* no. 23 (24 September–1 October 1649), pp. 181–2.

66 29 April 1652, 'Order by the Commissioners of Parliament', in Dunlop (ed.), *Commonwealth*, vol. 1, p. 178. See also 29 April 1652, Orders of State (1650–4), BL, Egerton MS 1761, ff. 93–100. An order for 40,000 of these tickets of protection was issued on 5 May 1652. See King's Inns, Dublin, Prendergast Papers, vol. 1, f. 8; Edmund Ludlow, *The Memoirs of Edmund Ludlow esq.*, 2 vols (Vivay, 1698), vol. 1, p. 391.

67 17 March 1651[2], Colonel Cooke to the commissioners of Parliament, in Henry Cary (ed.), *Memorials of the Great Civil War in England from 1646–1652*, 2 vols (London, 1842), vol. 2, pp. 419–23.

68 *A Collection of Some of the Murthers and Massacres Committed on the Irish in Ireland Since the 23rd of October 1641* (London, 1662), p. 21.

69 'Aphorismical Discovery' in Gilbert (ed.), *Contemporary History*, vol. 2, p. 98.

70 John Lynch, *Cambrensis Eversus*, 3 vols (Dublin, 1848–52), vol. 3, p. 193.

71 18 April 1652, 'Advices from London', in *CSP, Venetian, 1647–1652* (London, 1927), p. 224.

72 *A Bloody Fight in Ireland between the Parliaments Forces . . . and the Kings Forces* (London, 1652), p. 8.

73 Vincent Gookin, *The Author and Case of Transplanting the Irish into Connaught Vindicated from the Unjust Aspersions of Colonel Richard Laurence* (London, 1655), p. 16.

74 Roger Boyle, earl of Orrery, *A Treatise of the Art of War* (London, 1677), p. 65.

75 10 July 1652, Cromwell to Fleetwood, in W. C. Abbott (ed.), *The Writings and Speeches of Oliver Cromwell*, 4 vols (Cambridge 1937–47) vol. 2, p. 563.

76 'Orders of State: Commissioners of Parliament for the Affairs of Ireland, 29 April 1652', BL, Egerton MS 1761, ff. 93–100.

77 Until then, according to the Munster settler Vincent Gookin, 'all went as they [army officers] would have it'. See 22 November 1656, Gookin to Cromwell, in Thomas Birch (ed.), *A Collection of the State Papers of John Thurloe*, 7 vols (London, 1742), vol. 5, p. 647.

78 11 April 1652, 'Advices from London', in *CSP, Venetian, 1647–52*, p. 223.

79 'Aphorismical Discovery' in Gilbert (ed.), *Contemporary History*, vol. 3, pp. 125–6.

80 [Wm. Watt], *The Swedish Discipline, Religious, Civil and Military* (London, 1632), p. 54.

81 'Minutes of Court Martials held in Dublin, 1651/2', Marsh's Library, MS Z3.2.17[2].

82 December 1652, 'Order regarding major Morgan', King's Inns, Prendergast Papers, vol. 1, f. 41.

83 27 August 1649, Aston to Ormond; 28 August 1649, Ormond to Aston; 1 September 1649, Aston to Ormond, all in Gilbert (ed.), *Contemporary History*, vol. 2, pp. 236, 238, 246–7, 452. Ormond granted Aston powers for the summary punishment of those communicating with the enemy. See Bodl. Carte MS 162, ff. 46–8.

84 18 September 1651, Commissioners in Dublin to the Council of State, in Dunlop (ed.), *Commonwealth*, vol. 1, pp. 53–4.

85 For an account of Muskerry's trial, see Mary Hickson, *Ireland in the Seventeenth Century or the Irish Massacres of 1641–2*, 2 vols (London, 1884), vol. 2, p. 200–4

86 'An abstract of all moneys received and paid for the public service in Ireland, July 1649–November 1656', Trinity College, Dublin, MS 650/7.

87 26 December 1651, Commissioners and Army Officers to Council of State, in Dunlop (ed.), *Commonwealth*, vol. 1, pp. 113–4.

88 1 July 1651, Commissioners to Council of State, ibid., pp. 6–9.

89 8 January 1652, 'Proposals of the Commissioners of Parliament', in *HMC, Portland MSS*, vol. 1 (London, 1891), pp. 622–5.

90 22 March 1652, Commissioners to Council of State, in Dunlop (ed.), *Commonwealth*, vol. 1, pp. 147–9.

91 6/7 March 1652, 'Articles of agreement', ibid., pp. 149–50.

92 7 March 1652, 'Articles of agreement', ibid., pp. 151–3.

93 'Declaration by the Leinster Assembly', ibid., pp. 187–8.

94 Ludlow, *Memoirs*, vol. 1, p. 403; 'Considerations for a conclusion with Colonel Fitzpatrick', in Dunlop (ed.), *Commonwealth*, vol. 1, pp. 154–7.

95 'Considerations for a conclusion with Colonel Fitzpatrick', ibid., pp. 154–7.

96 22 June 1652, 'Articles of surrender at Ross', ibid., pp. 227–8.

97 Aphorismical Discovery' in Gilbert (ed.), *Contemporary History*, vol. 3, p. 118.

98 *A Perfect Diurnall . . . of the Armies in England and Ireland* no. 135 (28 June–5 July 1652), p. 1998.

99 Ibid. no. 148 (4–11 October 1652), p. 2,222.

CHAPTER 9   CONCLUSION: WINNERS AND LOSERS

1 This poem by Éamonn an Dúna, '*Mo lá leóin go deo go n-éagad*', was published in Cecile O'Rahilly (ed.), *Five Seventeenth-century Political Poems* (Dublin, 1977), p. 90. The term *mo mheabhair ar Bhéarla* translates as 'my understanding of English'.

2 *Mercurius Politicus* no. 144 (10–17 March 1653), p. 2,308.

3 23 February 1653, 'The examination of Sir Phelim O'Neill', Trinity College, Dublin, MS 836, ff. 167–8; 28 February 1682, 'Reflections of John Kerr, dean of Ardagh, on the trial of Sir Phelim O'Neill', King's Inns, Dublin, Prendergast Papers, vol. 3, ff. 609–13.

4 'Lord Lowther's speech at the trial of Sir Phelim O'Neill', in 'Edmund Borlase's papers relating to the Irish rebellion', BL, Stowe MS 82, ff. 236–40.

5 'Establishment of the High Court in Kilkenny', Marsh's Library, Dublin, MS Z2.1.7, f. 51.

6 27 April 1653, 'Cloughoughter Articles', Royal Irish Academy, MS 24.H.24, ff. 93–7.

7 Pádraig Lenihan, 'War and population', *Irish Economic and Social History*, vol. 24 (1997), pp. 18–21. For the English figures see Charles Carlton, 'The impact of the fighting', in John Morrill (ed.), *The Impact of the English Civil War* (London, 1991), p. 20.

8 *Journals of the House of Commons*, vol. 6 (1648–51), pp. 566–7, 607, 609, 621.

9 26 December 1651, Commissioners and officers of the army to the Council of State, in Robert Dunlop (ed.), *Ireland under the Commonwealth*, 2 vols (Manchester, 1913), vol. 1, pp. 113–4.

10 5 February 1652, Commissioners to Council of State, ibid., pp. 132–4.

11 5 May 1652, Commissioners to Parliament, ibid., pp. 178–80.

12 Walter Love, 'Civil war in Ireland: Appearances in three centuries of historical writing', *Emory University Quarterly*, vol. 22 (1966), p. 68.

13 Edmund Ludlow, *Memoirs of Edmund Ludlow Esq.*, 2 vols (Vivay, 1698), vol. 1, p. 319.

14 *An act for the setling of Ireland* (London, 1652).

15 Austin Woolrych, *Britain in Revolution, 1625–1660* (Oxford, 2002), p. 676.

16 11 September 1652, Parliamentary Commissioners to Colonel Axtell, King's Inns, Prendergast Papers, vol. 2, f. 253.

17 The letters relating to Bagenal's execution are in King's Inns, Prendergast Papers, vol. 2, f. 253; vol. 3, ff. 591, 597. According to the 'Aphorismical Discovery', Bagenal was shot 'like a soldier'. See Gilbert, *Contemporary History*, vol. 3, p. 135.

18 The figures come from lists in King's Inns, Prendergast Papers, vol. 3, ff. 615–35.

19 Mary Hickson (ed.), *Ireland in the Seventeenth Century, or the Irish Massacres of 1641–2*, 2 vols (London, 1884), vol. 2, p. 204.

20 7 March 1652, 'Articles of agreement', in Dunlop (ed.), *Commonwealth*, vol. 1, p. 151.

21 [25 Oct 1651], Ormond to Muskerry, Bodl. Carte MS 69, ff. 101–4; 22 June 1652, 'Articles of surrender at Ross', in Dunlop (ed.), *Commonwealth*, vol. 1, pp. 224–7n.

22 *The Barbarous and Inhumane Proceedings Against the Professors of the Reformed Religion within the Dominion of the Duke of Savoy, April 27 1655* (London, 1655), p. 3.

23 Vincent Gookin, *The Great Case of Transplantation in Ireland Discussed or Certain Considerations Wherein the Many Great Inconveniences in the Transplanting the Natives of Ireland Generally out of the Three Provinces of Leinster, Ulster and Munster into the Province of Connacht are Shown* (London, 1655), p. 13.

24 3 October 1655, 'Bounty for Tories', in Dunlop (ed.), *Commonwealth*, vol. 2, p. 542n.

25 10 December 1655, Council to Colonel Phaire, ibid., pp. 556–7.

26 J. P. Prendergast, *The Cromwellian Settlement of Ireland* (London, 1996 edn), p. 173.

27 14 October 1659, 'Order for suppressing Tories', in Dunlop (ed.), *Commonwealth*, vol. 2, pp. 713–14.

28 Richard O'Ferrall and Robert O'Connell, *Commentarius Rinuccinianus, de Sedis Apostolicae Legatione ad Foederatos Hiberniae Catholicos per Annos 1645–9*, 6 vols (Dublin, 1932–49), vol. 5, pp. 174–7.

29 17 September 1649, Cromwell to Lenthall, in W. C. Abbott (ed.), *The Writings and Speeches of Oliver Cromwell*, 4 vols (Cambridge, 1937–47), vol. 2, pp. 125–8.

30 12 May 1653, 'Declaration printed by the Council', in Prendergast, *Cromwellian Settlement*, p. 149n.

31 Prendergast, *Cromwellian Settlement*, pp. 239–40.

32 P. J. Corish, 'The Cromwellian regime, 1650–1660', in T. W. Moody, F. X. Martin and F. J. Byrne (eds), *A New History of Ireland*, vol. 3, *Early Modern Ireland, 1534–1691* (Oxford, 1991), p. 364.

33 6 January 1653, 'Order for banishing all priests', and order of 19 February 1653, both in King's Inns, Prendergast Papers, vol. 2, ff. 65–6, 99–100.

34 O'Ferrall and O'Connell, *Commentarius Rinuccinianus*, vol. 5, pp. 158–63.

35 Sarah Barber, 'Irish undercurrents to the politics of April 1653', *Historical Research*, vol. 65 (1992), pp. 315–35.

36 29 June 1653, 'Instructions to Charles Fleetwood esq., Lieutenant General of the army in Ireland, Edmund Ludlow esq., Lieutenant General of the Horse, Miles Corbet esq., John Jones esq.', in *An Act for the Speedy and Effectual Satisfaction of the Adventurers for Lands in Ireland: and of the arrears due to the soldiery there* (London, 1653), pp. 101–3.

37 2 July 1653, 'Further instructions' ibid., pp. 123–9.

38 1 August 1653, 'matters referred to the standing committee at Cork House', in Dunlop (ed.), *Commonwealth*, vol. 2, pp. 369–70.

39 14 October 1653, 'Declaration', ibid., pp. 474–5. In January 1655 the commissioners complained that many had still not done so.

40 6 January 1654, 'Instructions for Wm Edwards, Edward Doyley, Charles Holcroft, James Shane and Henry Greenaway', ibid., pp. 387–9.

41 Karl Bottigheimer, *English Money and Irish Land: the 'Adventurers in the Cromwellian settlement of Ireland* (Oxford, 1971), p. 140.

42 Prendergast, *Cromwellian Settlement*, pp. 32–3.

43 Ibid., pp. 74–5.

44 O'Ferrall and O'Connell, *Commentarius Rinuccinianus*, vol. 5, pp. 174–7.

45 Prendergast, *Cromwellian Settlement*, pp. 34–6.

46 Ibid.

47 16 Oct 1654, 'Order of the Lord Deputy and Council', ibid., p. 39.

48 October 1658, John Perceval in *HMC, Egmont MSS*, vol. 1, p. 600; 27 August 1656, Council in Dublin, in Dunlop (ed.), *Commonwealth*, vol. 2, p. 619.

49 Prendergast, *Cromwellian Settlement*, pp. 133–4.

50 26 October 1654, 'Appointment of a committee', in Dunlop (ed.), *Commonwealth*, vol. 2, p. 454.

51 S. R. Gardiner, 'The transplantation to Connacht', *English Historical*

Review, vol. 14 (1899), p. 722.

52 Vincent Gookin, *The Great Case of Transplantation in Ireland . . .*,
    pp. 1–29

53 Ibid.

54 Ibid.

55 Richard Lawrence, *The Interest of England in the Irish Transplantation
    Stated . . . as an Answer to a Scandalous, Seditious Pamphlet Entitled 'The
    Great Case of Transplantation in Ireland Discussed'* (London, 1655).
    Fleetwood is quoted in Toby Barnard, 'Crises of identity among Irish
    Protestants, 1641–1685', *Past and Present*, no. 127 (1990), p. 62.

56 Richard Lawrence, *The Interest of England in the Irish Transplantation*,
    pp. 3–32.

57 Lawrence used the phrase, but only to deny the existence of any such
    scheme, ibid., p. 17.

58 'The humble petition of the officers within the precincts of Dublin,
    Catherlough, Wexford and Kilkenny', in Prendergast, *Cromwellian
    Settlement*, p. 61.

59 'Order of 19 March 1655', in Dunlop (ed.), *Commonwealth*, vol. 2,
    pp. 488–90.

60 Prendergast, *Cromwellian Settlement*, pp. 53–4; 31 July 1654, 'Order
    concerning Peter Bath', in Dunlop (ed.), *Commonwealth*, vol. 2, p. 437.

61 'Order 5 April, 1655', in Dunlop (ed.), *Commonwealth*, vol. 2, pp. 497–8.

62 *An Act of Free and General Pardon, Indemnity and Oblivion* (London,
    1660), p. 15.

63 O'Ferrall and O'Connell, *Commentarius Rinuccinianus*, vol. 5, pp. 317–9.

64 *His Majesties Gracious Declaration for the Settlement of his Kingdom of
    Ireland* (London, 1660), pp. 1–3, 6–8.

65 O'Ferrall and O'Connell, *Commentarius Rinuccinianus*, vol. 5, pp. 174–6.

66 J. G. Simms, 'The restoration, 1660–85', in Moody, Martin and Byrne
    (eds) *New History of Ireland*, vol. 3, p. 428.

67 A. J. P. Taylor, *Essays in English History* (London, 1976), p. 26.

68 Christopher Hill, *God's Englishman: Oliver Cromwell and the English
    Revolution* (Middlesex, 1983), p. 133.

Bibliography

The following bibliography lists some of the primary and secondary sources I have consulted over the past few years. Despite the destruction of the bulk of confederate and Cromwellian records, much still survives in archives scattered throughout Europe. This study has focused for the most part on the English-language material in London, Oxford and Dublin, and more systematic research is required of the enormous manuscript collections in Brussels, Paris, Salamanca and Rome. Scholars such as Tadhg Ó hAnnracháin, Tom O'Connor, Éamonn Ó Ciosáin and others have begun this process, uncovering material vital to our overall understanding of events in Ireland and of the wider European context. Irish language sources are restricted for the most part to bardic poetry, but this has provided a rich seam for historical research, and Breandán Ó Buachalla's *Aisling Ghéar: na Stíobhartaigh agus an t-aos léinn, 1603–1788* will remain the definitive work in this area for years to come.

Although I reflected in the introduction on the relative scarcity of secondary material relating to Cromwell and Ireland, a number of important studies has appeared in the last forty years. In the 1970s, Patrick Corish's survey chapters in the *New History of Ireland* series, alongside the definitive works of Toby Barnard and Karl Bottigheimer, provided the key building-blocks for studying this period. Barnard's *Cromwellian Ireland: English government and reform in Ireland, 1649–1660* concentrated on the mechanics of Cromwellian government in Ireland during the 1650s, while Bottigheimer's *English Money and Irish Land: the 'Adventurers' in the Cromwellian settlement of Ireland* examined the evolution of the land settlement. On the military side, in the early 1990s, Ian Gentles' authoritative study of the English military machine, *The New Model Army in England, Ireland and Scotland, 1645–53*, contained an important chapter on the war in Ireland, and in 1999 James Scott Wheeler produced a long overdue book-length survey of the conflict. Both Martyn Bennett and Charles Carlton have explored the experience of warfare throughout the three Stuart kingdoms, but much work remains to be done on the impact of the Cromwellian conquest in the localities. Two key biographies by Jane Ohlmeyer (Randal MacDonnell, marquis of Antrim) and Patrick Little (Roger Boyle, Lord Broghill) illustrate the need for further studies of the leading players in mid-seventeenth-century Irish politics. Aidan Clarke's masterful dissection of the collapse of the English parliamentary regime, *Prelude to Restoration in Ireland: the end of the Commonwealth, 1659–1660* filled an important gap in the story, while in the last few years John Morrill, Pádraig Lenihan and others have focused productively on various aspects of Cromwellian Ireland.

Recent books by Pádraig Lenihan and Raymond Gillespie have synthesised much of this latest research and provide an excellent introduction to Ireland in the seventeenth century, while Ian Gentles has done the same for the wars of the three kingdoms. One book relating specifically to the topic of Cromwell and Ireland, Tom Reilly's *Cromwell: an honourable enemy*, has proved particularly controversial. As the title suggests, Reilly approached the topic from the premise that Cromwell's brutal reputation in Ireland was entirely unjustified, the result, he argues, of a deliberate distortion of the facts by nationalist historians. In his eagerness to prove this thesis, however, Reilly simply dismissed or ignored any contrary evidence. As C. H. Firth said of Thomas Carlyle's approach to Cromwell, 'like too many other historians he found in the past just what he went to the past to find'.*

Footnotes have for the most part been restricted to direct quotes from contemporary sources, but I would like to acknowledge fully the contribution of all those listed above and many others in assisting my endeavours. Cromwell's legacy in Ireland will, of course, be subject to further analysis and reinterpretation over the coming years, particularly in light of new research in the Continental archives, and I hope that this book contributes in some way to this process.

* Thomas Carlyle (ed.), *The Letters and Speeches of Oliver Cromwell,* 3 vols (London, 1904 edn), vol. 1, p. xlviii.

Manuscript Sources
Bodleian Library, Oxford
    Carte MSS
        2–29 (1649–52)
        63–5, 67, 69, 103, 118, 130, 142, 155–7, 162, 167, 176, 199, 207, 215,
        Official reports, petitions, miscellaneous letters and documents
    Clarendon MSS
        34, 37–45, December 1648–June 1653
        121 'A short view of the state and condicion of the kingdome
            of Irelande from . . . 1640 to the this tyme'
        137 Journal of the embassy into Spain (1649–54) by Wm. Edgeman
    Tanner MS
        54–6 (1649–52)

British Library
    Add. MSS
        4769B Copies of letters relating to Ireland, 1649–50
        4819 Collectanea de Rebus Hibernicis
        6491 Miscellaneous papers
        15856 Copies of official documents, 1634–58
        25287 Lord Broghill's letter book
        32093 Malet collection (state papers, etc.)
        46932–4 Egmont papers
    Egerton MSS
        212 Extracts from the Irish Council Books, 1650–2
        1048 Collection of historical and parliamentary papers, 1620–60
        1761 Orders of State: Commissioners of parliament for the affairs of
            Ireland, vol. 1
        2533–4 Nicholas papers
        2618 Historical letters and papers, 1556–1753
        2620 Letters of Oliver Cromwell, 1648–54
    Sloane MSS
        1008 Borlase papers relating to the Irish Rebellion
        3838 'A short view of the state and condition of Ireland . . .'
    Stowe MS 82
        Borlase 'History of the Execrable Irish Rebellion' (manuscript additions)

Dublin City Library
    Gilbert Collection
        MS 101 A collection of some of the murders and massacres committed
            on the Irish in Ireland since the 23rd October 1641

MS 219 A collection of the proceedings of the commissioners, from the convention in Ireland (1660)

King's Inns Library, Dublin
Prendergast Papers, vols 1–14

Marsh's Library, Dublin
MS Z2.1.5 Register of Adventurers
MS Z2.1.7 ff 50–1 Miscellaneous Commonwealth documents
MS Z3.1.1. ff 68, 70–1 Miscellaneous Commonwealth documents
MS Z3.2.17 [2] Minutes of court martials held in Dublin, 1651/2–3

National Library of Ireland
D.16181–8 Petition of George Peppard
MS 345 Account of the war and rebellion in Ireland since the year 1641
MSS 476–7 A light to the blind
MSS 2315–7 Ormonde Manuscripts
MS 2701 Annesley Manuscripts (photocopies)
MS 5065 Lane Papers
MS 9696 Original documents about Wexford, etc.
MS 15,773 [1] Miscellaneous manuscripts

The National Archives (London)
State Papers Commonwealth
SP 21/29 Committee on Irish affairs [Warrant book]
SP 25/62–3 Order-book of the Council of State, 1649–50
SP 25/87–9 Parliamentary order-book
SP 25/94–7 Letter-book of the Council of State, 1649–52
SP 25/118 The charge to the Commonwealth of the war in Ireland
SP 28/125 Muster rolls for Ireland, 1649–51
State Papers Ireland
SP 63/282 – Ireland 1649–52
SP 63/304 – Ireland (Charles II) September–November 1660
SP 63/307 – Ireland (Charles II) April 1661
State Papers Foreign
SP 77/31 – Flanders (1641–57)
SP 78/86–113 – France (1630–52)
SP 80/10 – Holy Roman Empire (1636–59)
SP 84/159 – Holland (1649–53)
SP 94/43 – Spain (1649–59)

Royal Irish Academy
   MS 24 H.24 Articles of surrender 1647–53
   MS H.VI.I Collection of papers relating to Ireland

Trinity College Dublin
   MS 650/7 An abstract of all the moneys received and paid for the public
      service in Ireland (1649–56)
   MSS 809–41 Depositions, 1640s–50s
   MS 836 The examination of Sir Phelim O'Neill
   MS 844 Miscellaneous Documents

Printed Sources

Abbott, W. C. (ed.), *The Writings and Speeches of Oliver Cromwell,* 4 vols
   (Cambridge, 1937–47).
Adair, Patrick, *A True Narrative of the Rise and Progress of the Presbyterian
   Church in Ireland, 1623–1670* (Belfast, 1866).
Aiazza, G. (ed.), *The Embassy in Ireland of Monsignor G. B. Rinuccini,
   Archbishop of Fermo, in the Years 1645–49,* trs Annie Hutton (Dublin,
   1873).
Barry, Garrett, *A Discourse of Military Discipline Divided into Three Books*
   (Brussels, 1634).
Bernard, Nicholas, *The penitent Death of a Woeful Sinner . . .* (London, 1651,
   3rd imp.)
Bergin, O. J. (ed.), 'Pairlement Chloinne Tomáis', *Gadelica,* 1 (1912–3), pp.
   35–50, 127–31, 137–50, 220–36.
Binden, S. H. (ed.), *The Historical Works of the Right Reverend Nicholas
   French, Bishop of Ferns,* 2 vols (Dublin, 1846).
Birch, Thomas (ed.), *A Collection of the State Papers of John Thurloe,* 7 vols
   (London, 1742).
Boate, Gerard, *Ireland's Natural History* (London, 1652).
Borlase, Edmund, *The History of the Execrable Irish Rebellion* (London,
   1680).
Bourke, Ulick, *Clanricarde Memoirs* (Dublin, 1744).
Boyle, Roger, Earl of Orrery, *A Treatise of the Art of War* (London, 1677).
Calendar of State Papers Relating to Ireland, Adventurers 1642–1659 (London,
   1903).
Calendar of State Papers, Domestic Series, 1649–53 (London, 1875–8).
Calendar of State Papers, Ireland, 1647–60 (London, 1903).
Calendar of State Papers, Venetian, 1626–54, vols 20–9 (London, 1914–29).
Carlyle, Thomas (ed.), *The Letters and Speeches of Oliver Cromwell,* 3 vols
   (London, 1904).

Carpenter, Andrew (ed.), *Verse in English from Tudor and Stuart* Ireland (Cork, 2003).

Carte, Thomas, *The Life of James, Duke of Ormond*, 6 vols (Oxford, 1851).

Cary, Henry (ed.), *Memorials of the Great Civil War in England from 1646 to 1652*, vol. 2 (London, 1842).

Churchyard, Thomas, *A Generall Rehearsall of Warres* (London, 1579)

Clarendon, Edward Hyde, earl of, *The History of the Rebellion and Civil Wars in England*, 6 vols (Oxford, 1888 edn).

— *The History of the Rebellion and Civil War in Ireland* (Oxford, 1816).

Clarendon State Papers, 3 vols (Oxford, 1767–86).

Crist, T. (ed.), *Charles II to Lord Taaffe: letters in exile* (Cambridge, 1974).

Cromwelliana: a chronological detail of events in which Oliver Cromwell was engaged from the year 1642 to his death 1658 (London, 1810).

De Beer, E. S., *The Diary of John Evelyn* (London, 1959).

Dunlop, Robert, *Ireland Under the Commonwealth*, 2 vols (Manchester, 1913).

Firth, C. H. (ed.), *The Memoirs of Edmund Ludlow*, 2 vols (Oxford, 1894).

— *Scotland and the Commonwealth: letters and papers relating to the military government of Scotland from August 1651 to December 1653* (Edinburgh, 1895).

Gardiner, S.R. (ed.), *The Constitutional Documents of the Puritan Revolution, 1625–1660* (Oxford, 1968 edn).

Gilbert, J. T. (ed.), *A Contemporary History of Affairs in Ireland from 1641 to 1652*, 3 vols (Dublin, 1879–80).

— *History of the Irish Confederation and the war in Ireland*, 7 vols (Dublin, 1882–91).

Gogarty, T. (ed.), *Council Book of the Corporation of Drogheda* (Louth, 1988).

Gordon, Patrick, of Ruthven, *A Short Abridgement of Britane's Distemper, 1639–49* (Aberdeen, 1844).

Green, M. A. E. (ed.), *Letters of Queen Henrietta Maria* (London, 1857).

Hartnett, Michael (ed.), *Haicéad* (Meath, 1993).

— *Ó Bruadair* (Dublin, 1985).

Henry Hexham, *The Second Part of the Principles of the Art Military, Practised in the Warres of the United Provinces* (London, 1642)

Hickson, Mary, *Ireland in the Seventeenth Century or the Irish Massacres of 1641–2*, 2 vols (London, 1884).

Historical Manuscripts Commission

  Egmont MSS, vol. 1 (London, 1905)

  Finch MSS, vol. 2 (London, 1922)

  Ormonde MSS, vols 1–2 (London, 1895–9)

  Ormond MSS [ns], vol. 1 (London, 1902)

  Portland MSS, vol. 1 (London, 1891)

Report 7, Appendix (London, 1879)

Report 8, Appendix, Part 1 (London, 1881)

Report 10, Appendix 4 (London, 1885)

Report 13, Appendix, Part 1 (London, 1891)

Hogan, Edmund (ed.), *The History of the Warr of Ireland from 1641 to 1653 by a British Officer of the Regiment of Sir John Clotworthy* (Dublin, 1873).

Jennings, Brendan (ed.), *Wild Geese in Spanish Flanders* (Dublin, 1964).

Jones, J. G., G. W. Owen and R. T. Jones (eds), *Gweithiau Morgan Llwyd O Wynedd* (Caerdydd, 1994).

Journals of the House of Commons, 1547–1714, vols 5–7 (1646–60).

Keating, Geoffrey, *The History of Ireland*, 4 vols (London, 1902–14).

Lindley, Keith and David Scott (eds), *The Journal of Thomas Juxon, 1644–1647*, Camden Fifth Series, vol. 13 (Cambridge, 1999),

Lodge, John (ed.), *Desiderata Curiosa Hibernica*, 2 vols (London, 1772).

Ludlow, Edmund, *Memoirs of Edmund Ludlow Esq.*, 2 vols (Vivay, 1698).

Lynch, John, *Cambrensis Eversus* (1662, translated by Matthew Kelly, Dublin, 1848–52).

MacLysaght, E. (ed.), 'Commonwealth state accounts, 1650–1656', *Analecta Hibernica*, 15 (1944), pp. 229–321.

McNeill, Charles (ed.), *The Tanner Letters* (Dublin, 1943).

Mayer, Joseph (ed.), 'Inedited letters of Cromwell, Col. Jones, Bradshaw and other regicides' in *Transactions of the Historic Society of Lancashire and Cheshire* [ns] vol. 1 (1860–1), pp. 177–300.

[Meredith, Adam], *Ormond's Curtain Drawn: in a short discourse concerning Ireland* (London, 1646).

Monro, Robert, *The Scotch Military Discipline Learned from the Valiant Swede* (London, 1644).

Moran, P. F. (ed.), *Spicilegium Ossoriense: being a collection of original letters and papers illustrative of the history of the Irish Church from the Reformation to the year 1800*, 3 vols (Dublin, 1874–84).

Morrice, Thomas (ed.), *A Collection of the State Letters of Roger Boyle, First Earl of Orrery*, 2 vols (Dublin, 1743).

Nickolls, J. (ed.), *Original Letters and Papers of State Addressed to Oliver Cromwell* (London, 1743).

O'Ferrall, Richard and Robert O'Connell, *Commentarius Rinuccinianus, de Sedis Apostolicae Legatione ad Foederatos Hiberniae Catholicos per Annos 1645–9*, 6 vols (Dublin, 1932–49).

O'Meagher, J. C. (ed.), 'Diary of Dr Jones, scout-master general to the army of the Commonwealth', *Journal of the Royal Society of Antiquaries of Ireland*, 5th series, 3 (1893), pp. 44–54.

Ó Meallán, Toirdealbhach, 'Cín Lae Uí Mhealláin', published in stages (with an English translation) in the Louth Archaeological Journal, 1923–30.

O'Rahilly, Cecile (ed.), *Five Seventeenth-century Political Poems* (Dublin, 1977).

Ó Tuama, Seán and Thomas Kinsella, *An Dunaire, 1600–1900: Poems of the dispossessed* (Portlaoise, 1985).

Petty, William, *The Political Anatomy of Ireland* (London, 1691).

Roberts, Edmond and Robert des, 'Documents inédits sur la captivité de Charles IV à Tolède, 1654–1659', *Mémoires de la sociéte d'archéologie Lorraine*, 4th series, 60, (1910), pp. 333–420.

Roots, Ivan (ed.), *The Speeches of Oliver Cromwell* (London, 1989).

Rushworth, John (ed.), *Historical Collections of Private Passages of State, Weighty Matters of Law, Remarkable Proceedings in Five Parliaments*, 7 vols (London, 1680–1701).

Steele, Robert (ed.), *Tudor and Stuart Proclamations*, vol. 2 (Oxford, 1910).

Talon, Geraldine (ed.), *Court of Claims: submissions and evidence* (Dublin, 2006).

Temple, Sir John, *The Irish Rebellion* (London, 1646).

Tuchet, James, *The Earl of Castlehaven's Review or his Memoirs* (London, 1684).

Turner, Sir James, *Memoirs of his Own Life and Times, 1632–1670* (Edinburgh, 1829).

Warner, G. F. (ed.), *The Nicholas Papers*, 2 vols (London, 1886–92).

[Watt, Wm.], *The Swedish Discipline, Religious, Civil and Military* (London, 1632).

Whitelocke, Bulstrode, *Memorials of the English Affairs or an Historical Account* (London, 1682).

Wood, Anthony, *The Life of Anthony à Wood from the Year 1632 to 1672 Written by Himself* (London, 1772).

Worden, Blair (ed.), 'A voice from the watch tower, part five: 1660–1662', Camden 4th series, vol. 21 (London, 1978).

Young, R. M. (ed.), 'A diary of the proceedings of the Leinster army, under governor Jones', *Ulster Journal of Archaeology*, 2nd series, 3 (1893), pp. 153–61.

Weekly News-Sheets
A Brief Relation of Some Affaires and Transactions, Civil and Military, both forraigne and domestique
Every Daies Intelligence from the Parliaments Army
The Faithful Scout
The Impartial Intelligencer
The Irish Monthly Journal
The Kingdoms Faithful and Impartial Scout

The Kingdoms Weekly Intelligencer
The Man in the Moon
Mercurius Aulicus
Mercurius Elencticus
Mercurius Pragmaticus
The Moderate Intelligencer
The Moderate Messenger
A Modest Narrative of Intelligence
A Perfect Diurnall of Some Passages in Parliament
A Perfect Diurnall of some Passages and Proceedings of, and in Relation to, the Armies in England and Ireland
Perfect Occurrences of Every Daie Journall of Parliaments Armies Proceedings
Perfect Passages of Every Daies Intelligence from the Parliaments Army
A Perfect Summary of Exact Passages of Parliament
The Perfect Weekly Account
Several Proceedings in Parliament

Pamphlet Literature

The Thomason Collection in the British Library contains hundreds of published items relating to Ireland in the years 1649 to 1653, almost all of which are now available on Early English Books Online. The following is a very brief list, arranged chronologically, of those pamphlets directly referenced in the text (including a handful from before 1649 and after 1653).

A Great Conspiracy by the Papists in the Kingdome of Ireland Discovered by the Lords Justices and Counsell at Dublin and Proclaimed there October. 23, 1641 (London, 1641)

The Teares of Ireland, by James Cranford (London, 1642).

Thomas Emitie, *A New Remonstrance from Ireland: declaring the barbarous cruelty and inhumanity of the Irish rebels against the Protestants there* (London, 1642).

Mr Pym, his Speech in Parliament . . . for the Present Pressing of 15,000 Men to be Immediately Transported to Ireland (London, 1642)

A Declaration of the Commons Assembled in Parliament; concerning the rise and progresse of the grand rebellion in Ireland (London, 1643)

A Letter from the Right Honourable Lord Inchiquin and Other Commanders in Munster to his Majestie (London, 1644).

Two Ordinances of the Lords and Commons Assembled in Parliament, 24 Oct. 1644 (London, 1644).

A Letter from the Earl of Essex to His Highness Prince Rupert . . . with His Highnesse Answer Thereunto (Bristol, 1645).

The Lord Digby's Cabinet and Dr Goff's Negotiations . . . and Other Letters Taken at the Battle at Sherborn in Yorkshire about the 15th of October Last (London, 1646).

Lawes and Ordinances of Warre, Established for the Good Conduct of the Army, by Colonell Michael Jones (Dublin, 1647).

The Marquesse of Ormond's Proclamation Concerning the Peace Concluded with the Irish Rebels ... with a Speech Delivered by Sir Richard Blake ... also a Speech Delivered by the Marquesse of Ormond (London, 1649).

John Milton, *Articles of Peace Made and Concluded with the Irish rebels . . . Upon all which are Added Observations* (London, 1649), p. 54.

Letters from Ireland, Relating the Several Great Successes it hath Pleased God to Give unto the Parliaments Forces there, in the Taking of Drogheda, Trym, Dundalk, Carlingford, and the Nury (London, 1649).

A Letter from Ireland Read in the House of Commons on Friday September 28 1649. From Mr. Hugh Peters, Minister of Gods Word, and Chaplain to the Lord Lieutenant Cromwell. Of the taking of Tredagh in Ireland, (London, 1649).

[R. L.] *The Taking of Wexford*, (London, 1649).

The Marquesse of Ormond's Declaration, Proclaiming Charles the Second, King of England, Scotland, France, and Ireland (London, 1649).

A Declaration by the Lord Lieutenant of Ireland Concerning his Resolutions for the Peace and Safety of Ireland (London, 1649)

Two Letters One from Dublin in Ireland, and the Other from Liverpoole or a Bloody Fight in Ireland, at the Taking of Drogheda by the Lord Lieutenant Cromwell (London, 1649).

William Basil *A Letter from the Atturney of Ireland Concerning the Taking of the Towne of Wexford by Storme, on the 11 of October Last* (London, 1649).

The Loyall Declaration of His Excellency, the Right Honourable, James, Marquesse of Ormond, Earle of Ormond, and Ossary, &c. Lord Lieu. Generall, and Generall Governour of the Kingdome of Ireland. August the 11. 1649 (London, 1649).

Joyfull Newes from the Marquesse of Ormond and the Princes Army in Ireland (London, 1649).

A Letter from the Lord Lieutenant of Ireland, to the Honorable William Lenthal Esq; Speaker of the Parliament of England (London, 1649).

Letters from Ireland . . . Together with a List of the Chief Commanders, and the Number of Officers and Soldiers Slain at Drogheda (London, 1649).

John Canne *The Improvement of Mercy: or a short treatise, shewing how, and in what manner, our rulers and all well-affected to the present government should make a right and profitable use of the late great victory in Ireland* (London, 1649).

The Marquesse of Ormonds Proclamation Concerning the Peace Concluded with the Irish Rebells, by the Kings Command, at the Generall Assembly at Kilkenny (London, 1649).

The Remonstrance and Resolutions of the Protestant Army of Munster now in Corcke (Cork, 1649).

A Very Full and Particular Relation of the Great Progresse and Happy Proceedings of the Army of the Commonwealth of England Towards the Reducing of Ireland (London, 1649).

A Perfect and Particular Relation of the Several Marches and Proceedings of the Armies of Ireland from the Taking of Drogheda to this Present (London, 1649).

Certain Acts and Declarations made by the Ecclesiastical Congregation at Clonmacnoise (Kilkenny, 1649)

Thomas Waring, *A Brief Narration of the Plotting, Beginning & Carrying on of that Execrable Rebellion and Butcherie in Ireland* (London, 1650).

A Letter from Sir Lewis Dyve to the Lord Marquis of Newcastle (The Hague, 1650).

A Declaration by the Kings Majesty, to his Subjects of the Kingdomes of Scotland, England, and Ireland (Edinburgh, 1650).

Sad Newes from Ireland (London, 1651).

Propositions Approved of and Granted by the Deputy-General of Ireland to Colonel Richard Laurence, for the Raising in England and Transporting into Ireland, a Regiment of Twelve Hundred Footmen, for the Planting and Guarding the City of Waterford, and Towns of Ross and Carwick, with Other Places Adjacent (London, 1651).

An Act for the Impresting of Soldiers for the Service of the Commonwealth in Ireland (London, 1651).

An Act for the Setling of Ireland (London, 1652).

A Great and Bloody fight in Ireland. The killing of Collonel Cook, and many other commission officers and souldiers to the Parliament of England, by a party of Irish Tories commanded by Generall Owen Oneale (London, 1652).

An Act for the Speedy and Effectual Satisfaction of the Adventurers for Lands in Ireland (London, 1653).

A Defensive Declaration of Lieut. Col. John Lilburn (London, 1653).

The Barbarous and Inhumane Proceedings against the Professors of the Reformed Religion within the Dominion of the Duke of Savoy, April 27 1655 (London, 1655).

A Collection of Narrative sent to His Highness the Lord Protector of the Commonwealth of England, Scotland and Ireland Concerning the Bloody and Barbarous Massacres, Murthers and other Cruelties Committed on Many Thousands of Reformed or Protestants Dwelling in the Vallies of

Piedmont, by the Duke of Savoy's Forces, Joined Therein with the French Army, and Several Irish regiments (London, 1655).

[Vincent Gookin], *The Great Case of Transplantation in Ireland Discussed* (London, 1655).

Richard Lawrence, *The Interest of England in the Irish Transplantation Stated* (London, 1655).

Vincent Gookin, *The Author and Case of Transplanting the Irish into Connaught Vindicated from the Unjust Aspersions of Colonel Richard Laurence, by Vincent Gookin* (London, 1655).

An Act of Free and General Pardon, Indemnity and Oblivion (London, 1660).

His Majesties Gracious Declaration for the Settlement of his Kingdom of Ireland (London, 1660).

[R.S.], *A collection of some of the murthers and massacres committed on the Irish in Ireland since the 23rd of October 1641* (London, 1662).

Secondary Sources

Armstrong, Robert, *Protestant War: the British of Ireland and the wars of the three kingdoms* (Manchester, 2005).

Andrews, K. R., Nicholas Canny and P. E. Hair (eds), *The Westward Enterprise: English activities in Ireland, the Atlantic and America, 1480–1650* (Liverpool, 1978).

Ashley, Maurice, *Cromwell's Generals* (London, 1954).

Aubrey, Philip, *Mr Secretary Thurloe: Cromwell's Secretary of State, 1652–1660* (London, 1990)

Baker, D. J., *Between Nations: Shakespeare, Spenser, Marvell and the question of Britain* (Stanford, 1997).

Barber, Sarah, 'Irish undercurrents to the politics of April 1653', *Historical Research*, 65 (1992), pp. 315–35.

— 'Nothing but the first chaos: making sense of Ireland', *Seventeenth Century*, 14 (1999), pp. 24–42.

— 'Settlement, transplantation and expulsion: a comparative study of the placement of peoples', in Ciaran Brady and Jane Ohlmeyer (eds), *British Interventions in Early Modern Ireland* (Cambridge, 2005), pp. 280–98.

Barnard, Toby, 'Planters and policies in Cromwellian Ireland', *Past and Present*, 61 (1973), pp. 31–69.

— 'Crises of identity among Irish Protestants, 1641–1685', *Past and Present*, 127 (1990), pp. 39–83.

— 'Irish images of Cromwell', in R. C. Richardson (ed.), *Images of Oliver Cromwell* (Manchester, 1993), pp. 180–206.

— 'The protestant interest, 1641–1660', in Jane Ohlmeyer (ed.), *Ireland from Independence to Occupation, 1641–1660* (Cambridge, 1995), pp. 218–40.

— 'Settling and unsettling Ireland: the Cromwellian and Williamite revolutions', in Jane Ohlmeyer (ed.), *Ireland from Independence to Occupation, 1641–1660* (Cambridge, 1995), pp. 265–91.

— *Cromwellian Ireland: English government and reform in Ireland, 1649–1660* (Oxford, 2000 edn).

Bennett, Martyn *The Civil Wars Experienced: Britain and Ireland, 1638–1661* (London, 2000).

Bigby, D. A., *Anglo-French Relations, 1641–9* (London, 1933).

Blake, J. W., 'Transportation from Ireland to America, 1653–60', *Irish Historical Studies*, 3 (1943), pp. 267–81.

Bottigheimer, Karl, *English Money and Irish Land: the 'Adventurers' in the Cromwellian settlement of Ireland* (Oxford, 1971).

— 'Kingdom and colony: Ireland in the westward enterprise, 1536–1660', in K. R. Andrews, Nicholas Canny and P. E. Hair (eds), *The Westward Enterprise: English activities in Ireland, the Atlantic and America, 1480–1650* (Liverpool, 1978), pp. 45–64.

Boynton, Lindsay, 'Martial Law and the Petition of Right', *English Historical Review*, 74 (1964), pp. 255–84.

Breslow, M. A., *A Mirror of England: English Puritan views of foreign nations, 1618–1640* (Cambridge, Mass., 1970).

Bumas, E. Shaskan, 'The cannibal butcher shop: Protestant uses of Las Casas's *Brevísima relación* in Europe and the American colonies', *Early American Literature*, 35 (2000) pp. 107–36.

Burke, James, 'Siege warfare in seventeenth-century Ireland', in Pádraig Lenihan (ed.), *Conquest and Resistance: war in seventeenth-century Ireland* (Leiden, 2001), pp. 257–91.

Canny, Nicholas, (ed.), *The Oxford History of the British Empire*, vol. 1, *The Origins of Empire* (Oxford, 1998).

— *Making Ireland British, 1580–1650* (Oxford, 2001).

Capp, Bernard, 'George Wharton, *Bellum Hybernicale*, and the cause of Irish freedom', *English Historical Review*, 112 (1997), pp. 671–7.

Capua, J. V., 'The early history of Martial Law in England from the fourteenth century to the Petition of Right', *Cambridge Law Journal*, 36 (1977), pp. 152–73.

Carey, Vincent, 'John Derricke's *Image of Ireland*, Sir Henry Sidney and the massacre at Mullaghmast, 1578', *Irish Historical Studies*, vol. 31 (1999), p. 327

Carlin, Norah, 'Ireland and Natural Man in 1649', in Francis Barker (ed.), *Europe and its Others* (Colchester, 1985), pp. 91–111.

— 'The Levellers and the conquest of Ireland', *Historical Journal*, 30 (1987) pp. 269–88.

— 'Extreme or mainstream? The English Independents and the reconquest of

Ireland', in Brendan Bradshaw, A. Hadfield and W. Maley (eds), *Representing Ireland: literature and the origins of conflict, 1534–1660*, (Cambridge, 1993) pp. 209–26.

Carlton, Charles, *Going to the Wars: the experience of the British civil wars, 1638–51* (London, 1992).

— 'Civilians', in John Kenyon and Jane Ohlmeyer (eds), *The Civil Wars: a military history of England, Scotland and Ireland, 1638–1660* (Oxford, 1998), pp. 272–305.

Casway, Jerrold, *Owen Roe O'Neill and the Struggle for Catholic Ireland* (Philadelphia, 1984).

— 'The Belturbet Council and election of March 1650', *Clogher Record*, 22 (1986), pp. 159–70.

— 'Gaelic Maccabeanism: the politics of reconciliation', in Jane Ohlmeyer (ed.), *Political Thought in Seventeenth-century Ireland* (Cambridge, 2000), pp. 176–88.

Clarke, Aidan, 'The 1641 Depositions', in Peter Fox (ed.), *Treasures of the Library Trinity College Dublin* (Dublin, 1986), pp. 111–22.

— 'Colonial constitutional attitudes in Ireland, 1640–1660', *Proceedings of the Royal Irish Academy*, section C, 90 (1990), pp. 357–75.

— *Prelude to Restoration in Ireland: the end of the Commonwealth, 1659–1660* (Cambridge, 1999).

— 'Patrick Darcy and the constitutional relationship between Ireland and Britain', in Jane Ohlmeyer (ed.), *Political Thought in Seventeenth-century Ireland* (Cambridge, 2000), pp. 35–55.

— *The Old English in Ireland, 1625–42* (Dublin, 2002 edn)

Clifton, Robin, 'The popular fear of catholics during the English Revolution', *Past and Present*, 52 (August 1971), pp. 23–55.

— '*An indiscriminate blackness*? Massacre, counter-massacre and ethnic cleansing in Ireland, 1640–1660', in Mark Levene and Penny Roberts (eds), *The Massacre in History* (NY/Oxford, 1999), pp. 107–26.

Commemoration of the Siege of Limerick (Limerick, 1951).

Corish, P. J., 'The Cromwellian conquest, 1649–53', in T. W. Moody, F. X. Martin and F. J. Byrne (eds), *A new history of Ireland*, vol. 3, *Early modern Ireland, 1534–1691* (Oxford, 1991), pp. 336–52.

— 'The Cromwellian regime, 1650–1660', in T. W. Moody, F. X. Martin and F. J. Byrne (eds), *A new history of Ireland*, 3, *Early modern Ireland, 1534–1691* (Oxford, 1991), pp. 353–86.

Coster, Will, 'Massacre and codes of conduct in the English civil war', in Mark Levene and Penny Roberts (eds), *The Massacre in History* (NY/Oxford, 1999), pp. 89–105.

Coward, Barry, *Cromwell: profiles in power* (Essex, 1991).

Cregan, Dónal, 'An Irish Cavalier: Daniel O'Neill in the Civil Wars, 1642–51', *Studia Hibernica*, 5 (1965), pp. 104–33.

Cunningham, Bernadette, 'Representations of king, parliament and the Irish people in Geoffrey Keating's *Foras Feasa ar Éirinn* and John Lynch's *Cambrensis Eversus* (1662)' in Jane Ohlmeyer (ed.), *Political Thought in Seventeenth-century Ireland* (Cambridge, 2000), pp. 131–54.

Cust, Richard and Ann Hughes (eds), *The English Civil War* (London, 1997).

D'Alton, John, *History of Drogheda*, vol. 2 (Dublin, 1863).

Davis, J. C., *Oliver Cromwell* (London, 2001).

Donagan, Barbara, 'Codes and conduct in the English civil war', *Past and Present*, 118 (1988), pp. 65–95.

— 'Atrocity, war crime and treason in the English Civil War', *American Historical Review*, 99 (1994) pp. 1137–66.

Dow, Frances, *Cromwellian Scotland, 1651–1660* (Edinburgh, 1979).

Durston, Chris, '*Let Ireland be Quiet*: opposition in England to the Cromwellian conquest of Ireland', *History Workshop Journal*, 21 (1986), pp. 105–12.

Edwards, David, 'Beyond Reform: martial law and the Tudor reconquest of Ireland', *History Ireland*, 5 (1997), pp. 16–21.

Esson, D. M. R., *The Curse of Cromwell: a history of the Ironside conquest of Ireland, 1649–1653* (New Jersey, 1971).

Farr, David, *Henry Ireton and the English Revolution* (Woodbridge, 2006).

Ferguson, Kenneth, 'Contemporary accounts of the battle of Rathmines, 1649', *Irish Sword*, 21, (1986), pp. 363–86.

Firth, C. H. (ed.), 'Thomas Scot's account of his actions as Intelligencer during the Commonwealth', *English Historical Review*, vol. 12 (1897) pp. 116–26.

— and Godfrey Davies, *The Regimental History of Cromwell's army*, 2 vols (Oxford, 1940).

Fissel, Mark Charles (ed.), *War and Government in Britain, 1598–1650* (Manchester, 1991).

Fitzpatrick, Thomas, *Waterford During the Civil War, 1641–53*, (Waterford, 1912).

— (ed.), *The bloody bridge and other papers relating to the insurrection of 1641* (London, 1970 edn)

Flatman, R. M., 'Some inhabitants of the baronies of Newcastle and Uppercross, Co. Dublin c. 1650', *Irish genealogist*, 7 (1986–9), pp. 496–504; vol. 8 (1990–3), pp. 3–14, 162–74, 322–32, 498–529.

Gardiner, S. R., *Cromwell's Place in History* (London, 1897).

— 'The transplantation to Connaught', *English Historical Review*, 14 (1899), pp. 700–34.

— *History of the Commonwealth and Protectorate, 1649–1656*, 4 vols (New York, 1965 edn).

Gaunt, Peter, *Oliver Cromwell* (Oxford, 1997).

Gentles, Ian, *The New Model Army in England, Ireland and Scotland, 1645–53* (Oxford, 1992).

— *The English Revolution and the Wars of the Three Kingdoms, 1638–1652* (Harlow, 2007).

Geyl, Pieter, *Orange and Stuart, 1641–72* (London, 1969, trs A. Pomerans)

Grainger, J. D., *Cromwell Against the Scots: the last Anglo-Scottish war, 1650–1652* (East Lothian, 1997).

Grell, Ole Peter, 'Godly charity or political aid? Irish Protestants and international Calvinism, 1641–5', *Historical Journal*, 39 (1996), pp. 743–53.

Gouhier, Pierre, 'Mercenaires Irlandais au service de la France (1635–1664)', *Irish Sword*, 7 (1965), pp. 58–75.

Hill, Christopher, *God's Englishman: Oliver Cromwell and the English Revolution* (Middlesex, 1983).

— 'Seventeenth-century English radicals and Ireland', in Christopher Hill, *A nation of change and novelty: radical politics, religion and literature in seventeenth-century England* (London, 1990), pp. 133–51.

Hore, P. H., *History of the Town and County of Wexford*, vol. 5 (London, 1906).

Howard, Michael, '*Temperamenta Belli*: can war be controlled?' in Howard, Michael (ed.), *Restraints on war* (Oxford, 1979), pp. 1–15.

Howell, Roger Jr, 'Images of Oliver Cromwell', in R. C. Richardson (ed.), *Images of Oliver Cromwell* (Manchester, 1993), pp. 20–32.

Hutton, Ronald, *Charles the Second: King of England, Scotland and Ireland* (Oxford, 1989).

— *Debates in Stuart History* (Basingstoke, 2004).

Johnson, J. T., *Ideology, Reason and the Limitations of war: religious and secular concepts, 1200–1740* (Princeton, 1975).

Keane, Ronan, 'The will of the general: martial law in Ireland, 1535–1924', *Irish Jurist*, 25–27 (1990–2), pp. 150–80.

Kelsey, Sean, *Inventing a Republic: the political culture of the English Commonwealth, 1649–1653* (Stanford, 1997).

Kenyon, John and Jane Ohlmeyer (eds), *The Civil Wars: a military history of England, Scotland and Ireland, 1638–1660* (Oxford, 1998).

Kerr, A.W., *An Ironside in Ireland* (London, 1923).

Kidd, Colin, *British Identities before Nationalism: ethnicity and nationhood in the Atlantic World, 1600–1800* (Cambridge, 1999).

Kitson, Frank, *Old Ironsides: the military biography of Oliver Cromwell* (London 2004).

Knachel, P. A., *England and the Fronde: the impact of the English Civil War and Revolution on France* (New York, 1967).

Knoppers, Laura, *Constructing Cromwell: ceremony, portrait and print 1645–1661* (Cambridge, 2000).

Korr, Charles, *Cromwell and the New Model Foreign Policy: England's policy towards France, 1649–58* (Berkeley, 1975).

Lake, Peter, 'Anti-popery: the structure of a prejudice', in Richard Cust and Ann Hughes (eds), *The English Civil War* (London, 1997), pp. 181–210.

Leerssen, Joep, *Mere Irish and Fíor-Ghael* (Cork, 1996).

Lenihan, Pádraig, 'War and population', *Irish Economic and Social History*, 24 (1997), pp. 1–21.

— *Confederate Catholics at War, 1641–49* (Cork, 2001).

— (ed.), *Conquest and Resistance: war in seventeenth-century Ireland* (Leiden, 2001).

Lenman, Bruce, *England's Colonial Wars, 1550–1688* (Essex, 2001).

Lindley, Keith, 'The impact of the 1641 rebellion upon England and Wales, 1641–5', *Irish Historical Studies*, 18 (1972), pp. 143–76.

Little, Patrick, 'The English parliament and the Irish constitution, 1641–9', in Micheál Ó Siochrú (ed.), *Kingdoms in crisis; Ireland in the 1640s* (Dublin, 2001), pp. 106–21.

— 'The Irish "Independents" and Viscount Lisle's Lieutenancy of Ireland', *Historical Journal*, 44 (2001), pp. 941–61.

— *Lord Broghill and the Cromwellian Union of Ireland and Scotland* (Suffolk, 2004).

— 'The Irish and Scottish Councils and the dislocation of the Protectoral Union', in Patrick Little (ed.), *The Cromwellian Protectorate* (Woodbridge, 2007).

Litton, Helen, *Oliver Cromwell: an illustrated history* (Dublin, 2000).

Love, Walter 'Civil war in Ireland: Appearances in three centuries of historical writing', *Emory University Quarterly*, vol. 22 (1966)

MacCormack, J. R., 'The Irish Adventurers and the English civil war', *Irish Historical Studies*, 10 (1956–7), pp. 21–58.

Macinnes, A. I., *Clanship, Commerce and the House of Stuart, 1603–1788* (East Lothian, 1996).

— 'Slaughter under trust: clan massacres and British state formation', in Mark Levene and Penny Roberts (eds), *The Massacre in History* (NY/Oxford, 1999), pp. 127–48.

— 'Covenanting ideology in seventeenth-century Scotland', in Jane Ohlmeyer (ed.), *Political thought in seventeenth-century Ireland* (Cambridge, 2000), pp. 191–220.

Marshall, Alan, *Intelligence and Espionage in the Reign of Charles II, 1660–1685* (Cambridge, 1994).

— *Oliver Cromwell Soldier: the military life of a revolutionary at war* (London, 2004).

Marx, Karl and Fredrich Engels, *Ireland and the Irish Question* (Moscow, 1986).

McCarthy, William, 'The royalist collapse in Munster, 1650–1652', *Irish Sword*, 6, no. 24 (1964), pp. 171–9.

McCormack, Timothy (ed.), *The Law of War Crimes: national and international approaches* (The Hague, 1997).

McElligott, Jason, *Cromwell: our chief of enemies* (Dundalk, 1994).

McKenny, Kevin, *The Laggan Army in Ireland, 1640–1685: the landed interests, political ideologies and military campaigns of the North-West Ulster settlers* (Dublin, 2005).

Meron, Theodor, *War Crimes Law Comes of Age* (Oxford, 1998).

Merriman, R. B., *Six Contemporaneous Revolutions* (London, 1963).

Mitchell. N. J., *Agents of Atrocity: leaders, followers, and the violation of human rights in civil war* (New York, 2004).

Moody, T. W., F. X. Martin and F. J. Byrne, (eds), *A New History of Ireland*, vol. 3, *Early Modern Ireland, 1534–1691* (Oxford, 1991).

Morrill, John, (ed.), *Reactions to the English Civil War, 1642–1649* (London, 1982).

— (ed.), *Oliver Cromwell and the English Revolution* (London, 1990).

— (ed.), *The Impact of the English Civil War* (London, 1991).

— 'The religious context of the English Civil War', in Richard Cust and Ann Hughes (eds), *The English Civil War* (London, 1997), pp. 159–81.

— 'The English, the Scots and the dilemma of union, 1638–1654', in T. C. Smout (ed.), *Anglo-Scottish Relations from 1603–1900* (Oxford, 2005), pp. 57–74.Mortimer, Geoff, *Eyewitness Accounts of the Thirty Years' War, 1618–48* (Basingstoke, 2002).

Mortimer, Geoff, *Eyewitness accounts of the Thirty Years' War 1618–48* (Basingstoke, 2002).

Murdoch, Steve, 'The search for northern allies: Stuart and Cromwellian propagandists and protagonists in Scandinavia, 1649–60', in B. Taithe and T. Thornton (eds), *Propaganda, Political Rhetoric and Identity, 1300–2000* (Gloucester, 1999), pp. 79–96.

Murphy, Andrew, *But the Irish Sea Betwixt us: Ireland, colonialism and renaissance literature* (Kentucky, 1999).

Murphy, Denis, *Cromwell in Ireland: a history of Cromwell's Irish campaign* (Dublin, 1883).

Murphy, J. A., 'The sack of Cashel, 1647', *Journal of the Cork Historical and Archaeological Society*, 70 (1965), pp. 55–62.

— 'The politics of the Munster Protestants, 1641–1649', *Journal of the Cork Historical and Archaeological Society*, 76 (1971), pp. 1–20.

Murray, R. H., 'Cromwell at Drogheda: A reply to Mr J. B. Williams', *The Nineteenth Century and after*, 72 (1912), pp. 1220–41.

Noonan, Kathleen, '*The cruell pressure of an enraged, barbarous people*: Irish and English identity in seventeenth-century policy and propaganda', *The Historical Journal*, 41 (1998), pp. 151–77.

Ó hAnnracháin, Tadhg, '*Though hereticks and politicians should misinterpret their goode zeal*: Political ideology and catholicism in early modern Ireland', in Jane Ohlmeyer (ed.), *Political Thought in Seventeenth-century Ireland* (Cambridge, 2000), pp. 155–75.

— *Catholic Reformation in Ireland: the mission of Rinuccini, 1645–1649* (Oxford, 2002).

Ó Buachalla, Breandán, *Aisling Ghéar: Na Stíobhartaigh agus an t-aos léinn, 1603–1788* (Baile Átha Cliath, 1996).

Ó Ciardha, Éamonn, "Tories and moss troopers in Scotland and Ireland during the Interregnum: a political dimension', in John Young (ed.), *Celtic Dimensions of the British Civil Wars* (Edinburgh, 1997), pp. 141–63.

O'Connell, P. and W. Darmody, *Siege of Clonmel Commemoration: tercentenary souvenir record* (Clonmel, 1950).

O'Dowd, Mary, *Power, Politics and Land: early modern Sligo, 1568–1688* (Belfast, 1991).

O'Hara, David, *English Newsbooks and the Irish rebellion, 1641–1649*, (Dublin, 2006).

Ohlmeyer, Jane, (ed.), *Ireland from Independence to Occupation, 1641–1660* (Cambridge, 1995).

— '*Civilizinge of Those Rude Partes*: colonization within Britain and Ireland, 1580s–1640s', in Nicholas Canny (ed.), *The Oxford History of the British Empire*, vol. 1, *The Origins of Empire* (Oxford, 1998), pp. 124–47.

— (ed.), *Political Thought in Seventeenth-century Ireland* (Cambridge, 2000).

— *Civil War and Restoration in the Three Stuart kingdoms: The career of Randal MacDonnell, Marquis of Antrim* (Dublin, 2001 edn).

— 'A laboratory for empire? Early modern Ireland and English imperialism', in Kevin Kenny (ed.), *Ireland and the British Empire* (Oxford, 2004), pp. 26–60.

Ó hÓgáin, Dáithí, 'Nótaí ar Chromail i mbéaloideas na hÉireann', *Sinsear*, 2 (1980), pp. 73–83.

Ó Siochrú, Micheál, *Confederate Ireland, 1642–1649: a constitutional and political analysis* (Dublin, 1999).

— (ed.), *Kingdoms in Crisis: Ireland in the seventeenth century* (Dublin, 2001).

— 'Catholic confederates and the constitutional relationship between Ireland and England, 1641–1649, in Ciaran Brady and Jane Ohlmeyer (eds), *British Interventions in Early Modern Ireland* (Cambridge, 2005), pp. 207–29.

— 'The duke of Lorraine and the international struggle for Ireland, 1649–1653', *The Historical Journal*, 48, 4 (2005), pp. 905–932.

— 'Atrocity, codes of conduct and the Irish in the British civil wars 1641–1653,

Past and Present, 195 (May 2007), pp. 55–86.

— 'Propaganda, rumour and myth: Oliver Cromwell and the massacre at Drogheda', in David Edwards, Pádraig Lenihan and Clodagh Tait (eds), *Age of Atrocity: violence and political conflict in early modern Ireland* (Dublin, 2007), pp. 266–82.

O'Sullivan, Harold, 'Military operations in County Louth in the run-up to Cromwell's storming of Drogheda', *Journal of the County Louth Archaeological and Historical Society*, 22 (1990), pp. 187–208.

Parker, Geoffrey, *The Army of Flanders and the Spanish Road 1557–1659: the logistics of Spanish victory and defeat in the Low Countries' wars* (Cambridge, 1972).

— (ed.), *The Thirty Years' War* (London, 1987)

— 'The etiquette of atrocity: The laws of war in early modern Europe', in Geoffrey Parker, *Empire, War and Faith in Early Modern Europe* (London, 2002), pp. 143–68.

— and L. M. Smith, *The General Crisis of the Seventeenth Century* (London, 1978).

Patterson, F. A. (ed.), *The Works of John Milton*, 18 vols (New York, 1931–8)

Peacy, Jason, 'The hunting of the Leveller: the sophistication of parliamentarian propaganda, 1647–53', *Historical Research*, 78 (2005), pp. 15–42.

Pincus, Steven, *Protestantism and Patriotism: ideologies and the making of English foreign policy, 1650–1668* (Cambridge, 1996).

Prendergast, J. P., *The Cromwellian Settlement of Ireland* (London, 1996 edn).

Rankin, Deana, *Between Spenser and Swift: English writing in seventeenth-century Ireland* (Cambridge, 2005).

Raymond, Joad *Making the News: an anthology of the newsbooks of revolutionary England, 1641–1660* (Gloucester, 1993)

— *The Invention of the Newspaper: English newsbooks, 1641–1649* (Oxford, 1996).

Redlich, Fritz, *The German Military Enterpriser and his Work Force*, 2 vols (Wiesbaden, 1964–5)

Reid, James Morgan, 'Atrocity, propaganda and the Irish rebellion', *Public Opinion Quarterly*, 2 (1938), pp. 229–44.

Reilly, Tom, *Cromwell: an honourable enemy* (Dingle, 1999).

Rice, Gerard, 'The five martyrs of Drogheda', *Ríocht na Midhe*, 9 (1997), pp. 102–27.

— 'Four wills of the Old English merchants of Drogheda, 1654–1717', *Journal of the County Louth Archaeological and Historical Society*, 20 (1982), pp. 96–105.

Richardson, R. C. (ed.), *Images of Oliver Cromwell* (Manchester, 1993).

Robert, Ferdinand des, *Charles IV et Mazarin, 1643–1661* (Paris, 1899).

Rodier, Paul, *Charles IV, duc de Lorraine et de Bar* (Épinal, 1904).

Roosevelt, Theodore, *Oliver Cromwell* (London, 1900).

Scally, John, 'The rise and fall of the covenanter parliaments, 1639–51', in Keith Brown and Alastair Mann (eds), *The History of the Scottish Parliament*, vol. 2, *Parliament and Politics in Scotland, 1567–1707* (Edinburgh, 2005), pp. 138–62.

Schama, Simon, *A History of Britain: the British wars, 1603–1776* (London, 2001).

Seymour, John, 'The storming of the Rock of Cashel by Lord Inchiquin in 1647', *English Historical Review*, 32 (1917), pp. 373–81.

Shagan, Ethan, 'Constructing discord: Ideology, propaganda and English responses to the Irish rebellion of 1641', *Journal of British Studies*, vol. 36 (1997), pp. 4–34.

Simms, J. G. 'The restoration, 1660–85', in *New history of Ireland*, vol. 3

Smith, Geoffrey and Margaret Toynbee, *Leaders of the Civil Wars, 1642–1648* (Kineton, 1977).

Smith, Nigel (ed.), *The poems of Andrew Marvell* (Harlow, 2007 edn)

Sproxton, Judy, *Violence and Religion: attitudes towards militancy in the French civil wars and the English Revolution* (London, 1995).

Stevenson, David, *Scottish Covenanters and Irish Confederates* (Belfast, 1981).

— *Revolution and Counter-Revolution in Scotland, 1644–51* (London, 1977).

— 'Cromwell, Scotland and Ireland', in John Morrill (ed.), *Oliver Cromwell and the English Revolution* (London, 1990), pp. 149–80.

Stoyle, Mark, 'English nationalism, Celtic particularsim, and the English Civil War', *Historical Journal*, 3 (2000), pp. 1113–28.

— *Soldiers and Strangers: an ethnic history of the English Civil War* (New Haven, 2005).

Stradling, R. A., *Europe and the Decline of Spain* (London, 1981).

— *The Spanish Monarchy and Irish Mercenaries: the Wild Geese in Spain, 1618–68* (Dublin, 1994).

Tanner, Marcus, *Ireland's Holy Wars: the struggle for a nation's soul, 1500–2000* (New Haven, 2001).

Taylor, A. J. P., *Essays in English History* (London, 1976).

Theibault, John, 'The rhetoric of death and destruction in the Thirty Years' War', *Social History*, vol. 27 (1993), pp. 271–90.

— *German Villages in Crisis: rural life in Hesse-Kassel and the Thirty Years' War, 1580–1720* (Boston, 1995).

Underdown, David *Royalist conspiracy in England, 1649–1660* (Hew Haven, 1960).

Venning, Timothy, *Cromwellian Foreign Policy* (London, 1996).

Wheeler, James Scott, 'Logistics and supply in Cromwell's conquest of Ireland', in M. C. Fissel (ed.), *War and Government in Britain, 1598–1650*

(Manchester, 1991), pp. 38–56.

— *Cromwell in Ireland* (Dublin, 1999).

— *The Irish and British Wars, 1637–54: triumph, tragedy and failure* (London, 2002).

Williams, J. B., 'Fresh light on Cromwell at Drogheda', *The Nineteenth Century and after*, 72 (1912), pp. 471–90.

Woolrych, Austin, *Britain in Revolution, 1625–1660* (Oxford, 2002).

— *Commonwealth to Protectorate* (London, 2002 edn).

Worden, Blair, *The Rump Parliament, 1648–1653* (Cambridge, 1974).

— *Roundhead Reputations: the English civil wars and the passions of posterity* (London, 2001).

Young, J. R. (ed.), *Celtic Dimensions of the British Civil Wars* (Edinburgh, 1997).

— 'Invasions: Scotland and Ireland, 1641–1691', in Pádraig Lenihan (ed.), *Conquest and Resistance: War in seventeenth-century Ireland* (Leiden, 2001), pp. 53–86.

Unpublished theses

Donovan, Iain, 'Bloody news from Ireland': The pamphlet literature of the Irish massacres of the 1640s (M. Litt., Trinity College Dublin, 1995).

Duffy, E. P., 'The marquis of Clanricarde as Irish Lord Deputy-General, 1650–1652' (MA, University College Galway, 1965).

Menarry, David, 'The Irish and Scottish landed elites from Regicide to Restoration (PhD, University of Aberdeen, 2001).

Reynolds, Neil, 'The Stuart court and courtiers in exile, 1644–54' (PhD, University of Cambridge, 1996).

Index

303

attributed to 15; influenced by
Temple's portrayal of rebellion 19
initial contact with Irish affairs 30–1,
62; brutal tactics in Irish wars 49, 85;
command of victorious army at
Preston 50, 54, 167; Ormond's
denunciation of 59, 94–5; rapid rise
in military affairs of state 61–2;
offered command of expedition to
Ireland 62; speech accepting
command of expedition to Ireland
62 31 actions to restore order in
discontented army 64; financial
terms demanded for army
command 65; gathering of army and
tactics for invading Dublin 72; effect
of Rathmines rout on campaign
73–4, 74, 204; arrival and speech in
Dublin 76, 79, 168, 215; preparations
for Irish campaign 77–8;
conciliatory policy towards Dublin
inhabitants 79–80, 207; siege of
Drogheda 81–2, 82–6, 87, 88, 90, 93,
213; growing reputation for cruelty
and savagery 82, 93, 98; likely to have
troubled conscience about atrocities
85, 87, 117; taking of other towns
after Drogheda victory 91; reports of
barbarity at Drogheda by royalist
press 93; approach south towards
Wexford 95–6; negotiations at
Wexford 96–7; siege of Wexford and
massacre of inhabitants 97–8;
options after Wexford 98; and
surrender of Ross 100, 192; story of
his comment on Ormond's portrait
101; attempted capture of Waterford
103–4; assessment of autumn
campaign 104–5; lifting of siege of
Waterford 104, 116; reply to bishops'
declaration at Clonmacnoise 116–17;
resumption of military campaign in
January 1650 117–18, 118–19; recalled
to England due to impending war
with Scotland 118, 133, 202; in battle
of Kilkenny 120, 121–2, 194; assault

on Clonmel 124–5; return to
England 125–6; campaign in
response to Charles's arrival in
Scotland 126; agreement with
Protestant royalists in Cashel 127–8;
departure from Youghal 132–3, 234;
campaign's effect of creating
partisan activity 193; assessment of
Ireland following England's victory
226; role in policy intiatives
regarding settlement 235;
intervention in dispute between Old
Protestant settlers and Fleetwood
243–4; decline in health and death
244–6; lasting legacy to Ireland
248–50; role in development of
modern Irish nationalism 248–9;
Cromwell, Richard (Cromwell's
son) 6, 244
Cromwell, Robert (Cromwell's father)
5

de Propaganda Fide (Rome) 176, 183
Deane, Admiral Richard 69, 96
Depositions (1641) 226, 237
Derry 14, 35; Coote's enclave 54, 71, 203;
as exception to Ormond's
government 56; O'Neill's temporary
alliance with Coote 61, 99; English
navy's help for parliamentary
enclave 69, 70
Devereux, Robert see Essex, Robert
Devereux, 3rd Earl of
Dillon, James see under Roscommon
Dillon, Viscount 121, 149, 154, 155, 180
Donegal (county) 99, 219
Dongan, Sir Walter 192, 195, 197, 199,
208, 219, 228
Drogheda 11, 27, 54; massacres by New
Model Army (1649) 2, 5, 82–3, 91–2,
98, 105, 207, 231, 249; rebels' failure
to capture 31; seized by Inchiquin 71,
76; Cromwell's plan to take 79;
royalist preparations to defend 80–1;
Cromwell's campaign 81–3, 83–6, 87,
88, 90; controversial issue of civilian

INDEX

Galway *contd*
159, 160; as possible platform for
renewed royalist offensive 161, 172,
189; and negotiations for treaty with
Lorraine 176, 178, 184, 186; as last city
under royalist control 187, 189, 198,
199; Catholic assembly urging
negotiations 189–90; Coote's offer of
terms for surrender 190, 226, 242
Germany 38, 163, 174, 181
Gookin, Vincent, tract on the transplantation of Catholics 212, 240–2
Grace, Colonel Richard 210, 218, 219
Gustavus Adolphus, King of Sweden
17, 28, 213

Henin, Abbot Stephen de 174, 176, 177,
178
Henrietta Maria, Queen of England
47–8, 148, 166, 167, 173, 175, 182–3, 185
Hewson, Col. John 121, 140, 180, 194,
196–7, 197, 219, 246; account of siege
of Drogheda 83, 84; issue of
punishments for collusion with
enemy 210–11, 213
High Courts of Justice, Dublin 222,
229, 238
Hyde, Edward 66, 67, 81, 168, 183, 190

Inchiquin, Murrough O'Brien, Lord 12,
43, 47, 70, 78, 82, 101, 103; declaration
for parliament 41, 53; brutal battle
tactics 49, 110; change of sides to
royalists and truce with Kilkenny 50,
53, 55, 56, 107, 165, 183, 203; Munster
Protestants' unease under 53–4, 59,
72; seizure of Drogheda 71, 76; and
splitting of royalists as Cromwell
advanced 72, 75; letters to Ormond
86–7, 155; as problematic military
leader 110; rumours of treachery 114;
and Cashel agreement with
Cromwell 127, 128; depleted number
of royalist troops under 127; concern
over Catholic bishops' intentions
130, 131; noting of Cromwell's

departure 132–3; as intelligence
gatherer for parliamentary regime
203; refusal to surrender 219;
recovery of entire estate 246
intelligence (military)
parliamentarian activities 178, 201–3,
214–15, 228, 233; Irish advantage of
local knowledge 200, 232;
parliamentarians' frustration at lack
of 200–1, 210; English government's
use of spies 201; Abbot Crelly's
activities 204–5; increased flow from
Irish 212–13; role of women 213–14
Ireton, Henry 6, 63, 178, 192, 205
push north towards Kilkenny 12, 103,
119; command of invasion flotilla
initially heading south 72, 78–9;
continuation of Cromwell's Irish
campaign 87, 125, 126, 132, 161, 180,
234; arrival at Waterford 144;
advance on Connacht 149, 154, 155,
157, 179–80, 181, 194, 195; at siege of
Limerick 185, 200, 227; death in
aftermath of Limerick victory 187;
proposals for exclusions from post-
war settlement 224–5; disinterment
of body and ritual of execution 246
Irish parliament 17, 22, 23, 247
Irish rebellion (October 1641) 7, 12, 15,
167, 206, 221, 230, 247; as turning
point 18–19; planning of 22–3;
mobilisation of forces 23–4;
massacres and reprisals 25–6;
reaction in England 27–30, 42, 63,
227; Depositions 29–30, 226, 237;
revenge for 51, 53, 55, 79, 84, 117, 222;
alleged involvement of Charles I
205; links with Savoy 231

Lawrence, Col. Richard 222, 235, 239,
240, 242
Leinster (province) 9, 11, 13, 14, 26, 132,
173; unrest after attack on Dublin 24;
Cromwell's besieging of towns 73, 79,
113, 119; O'Neill's decision to
intervene 99; new Model Army's